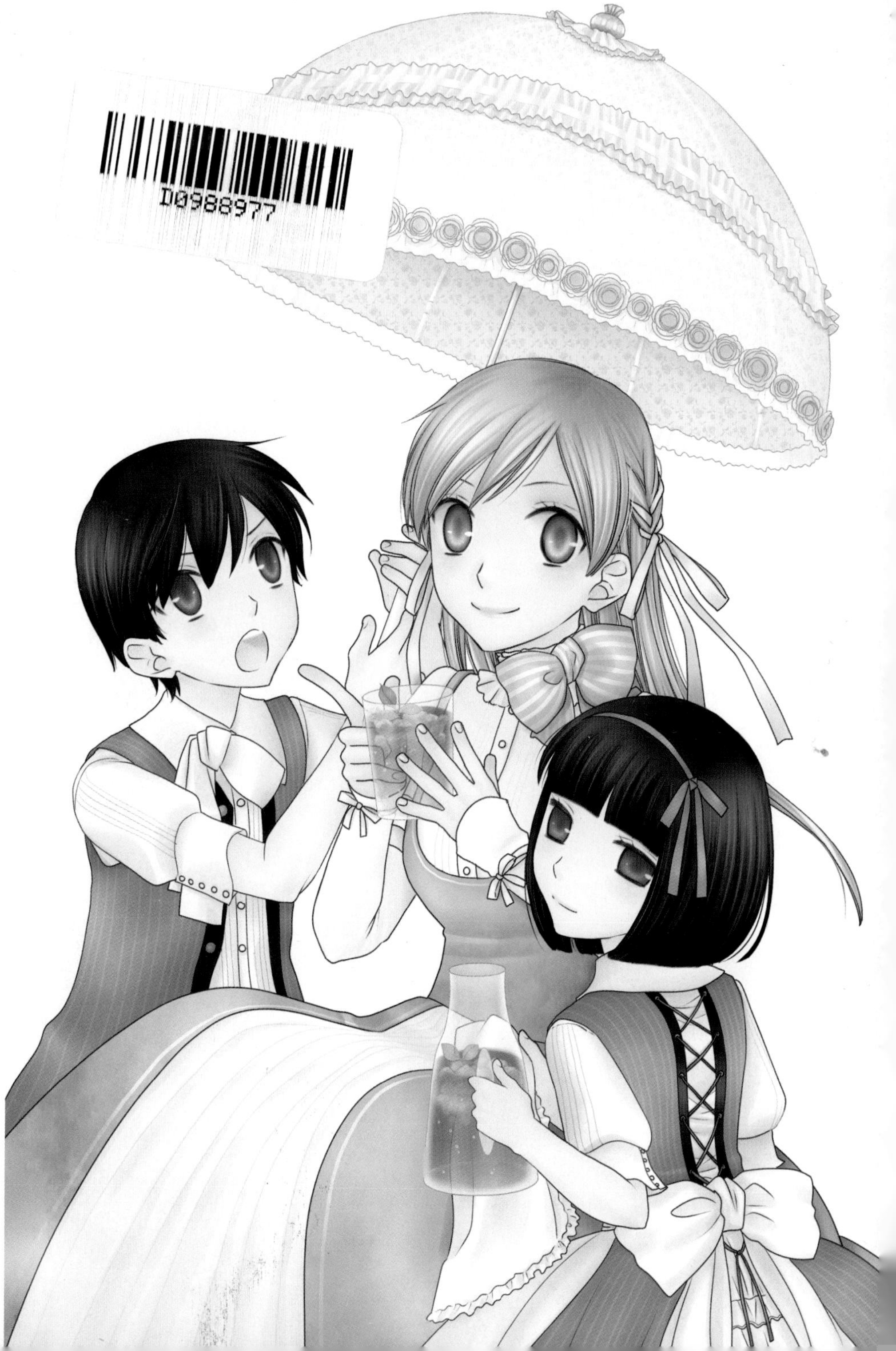

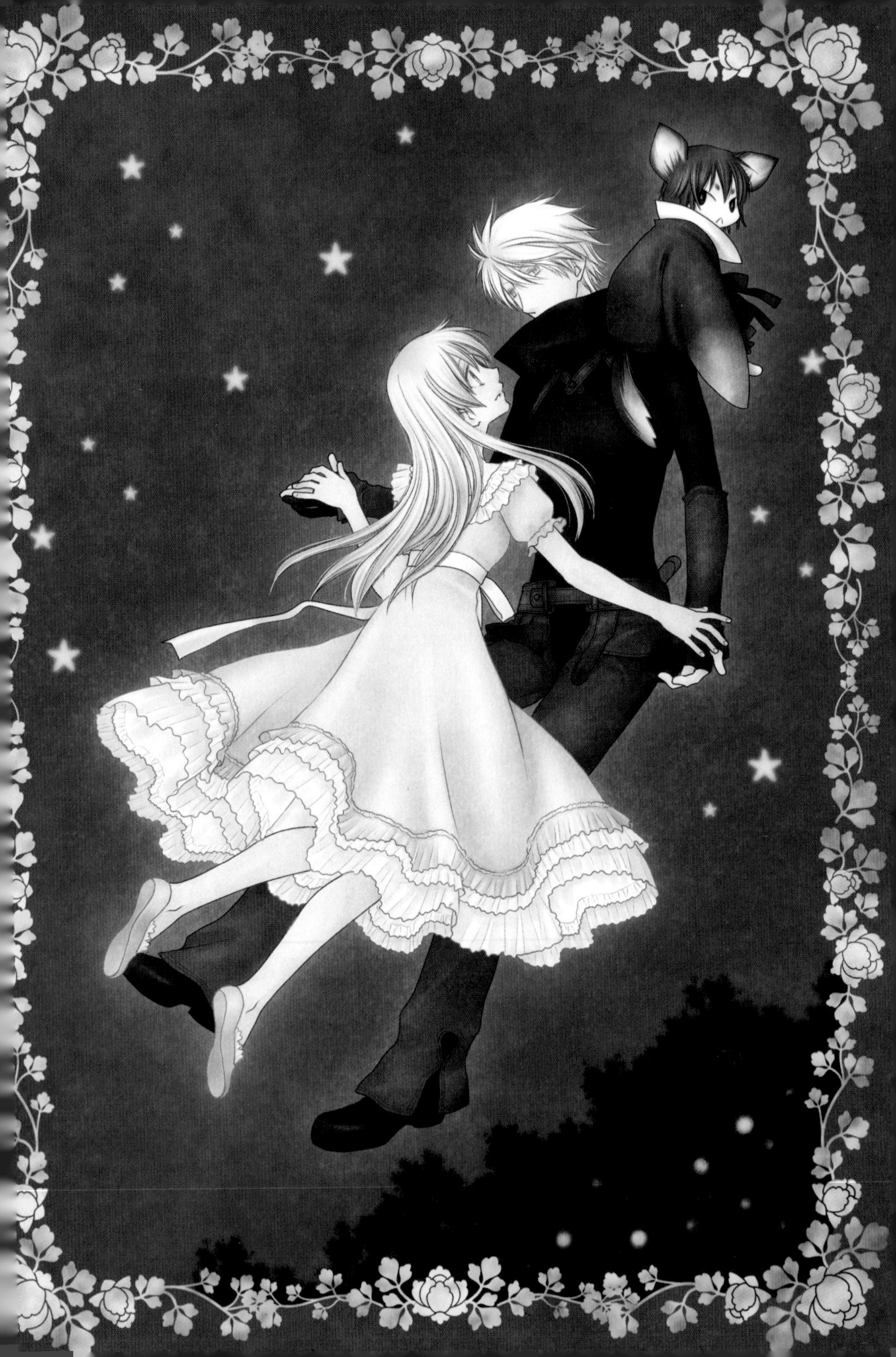

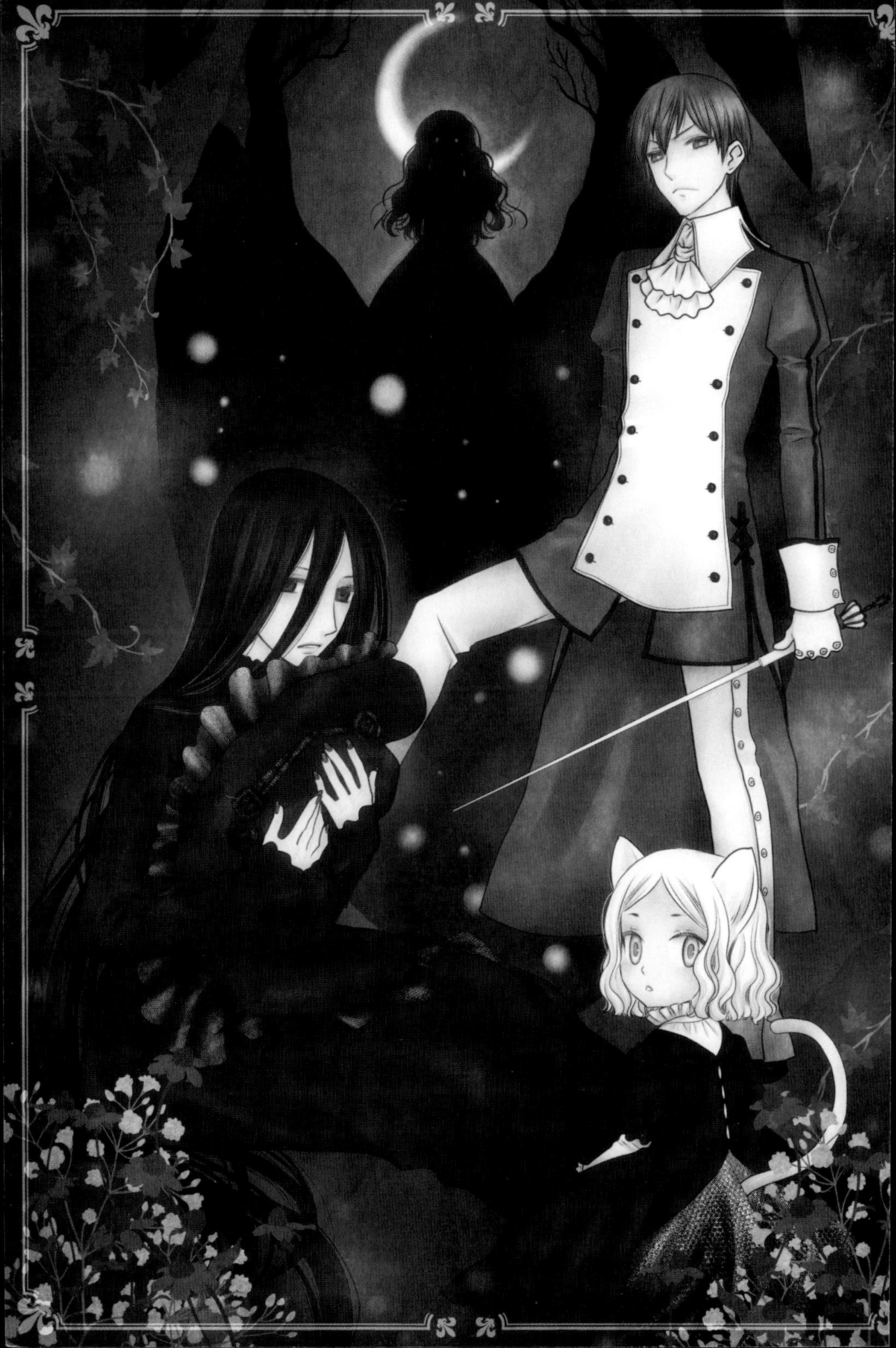

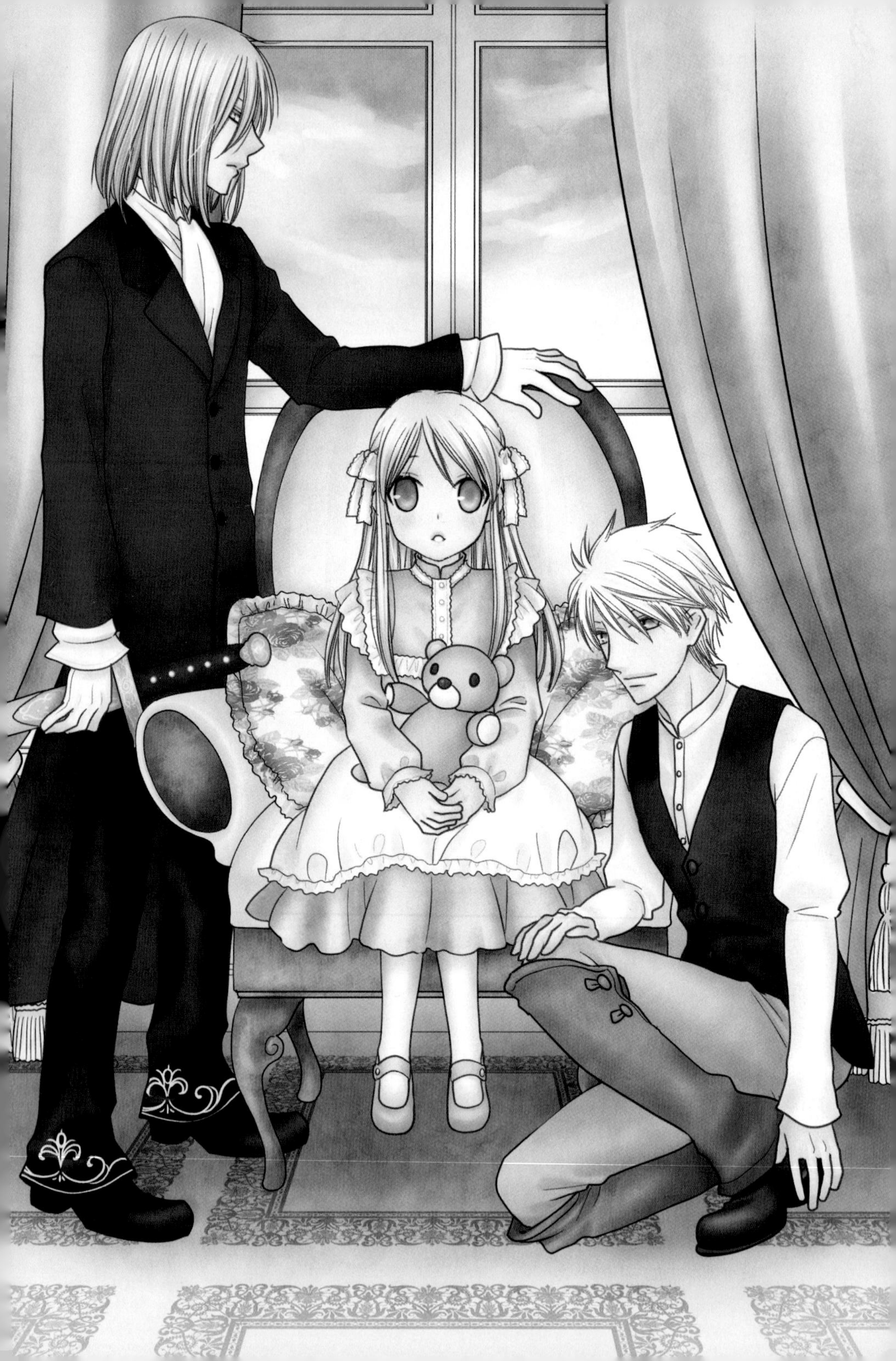

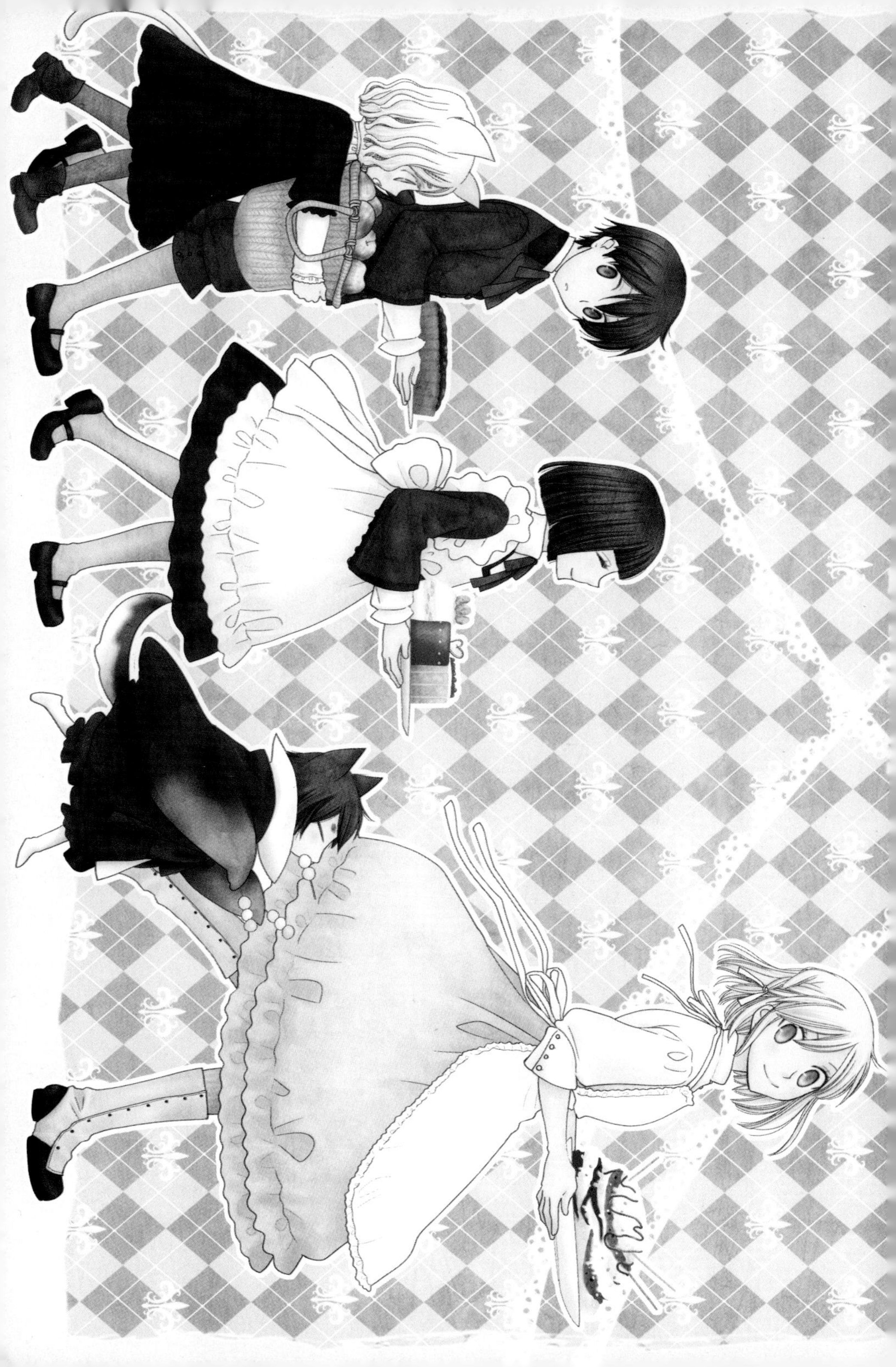

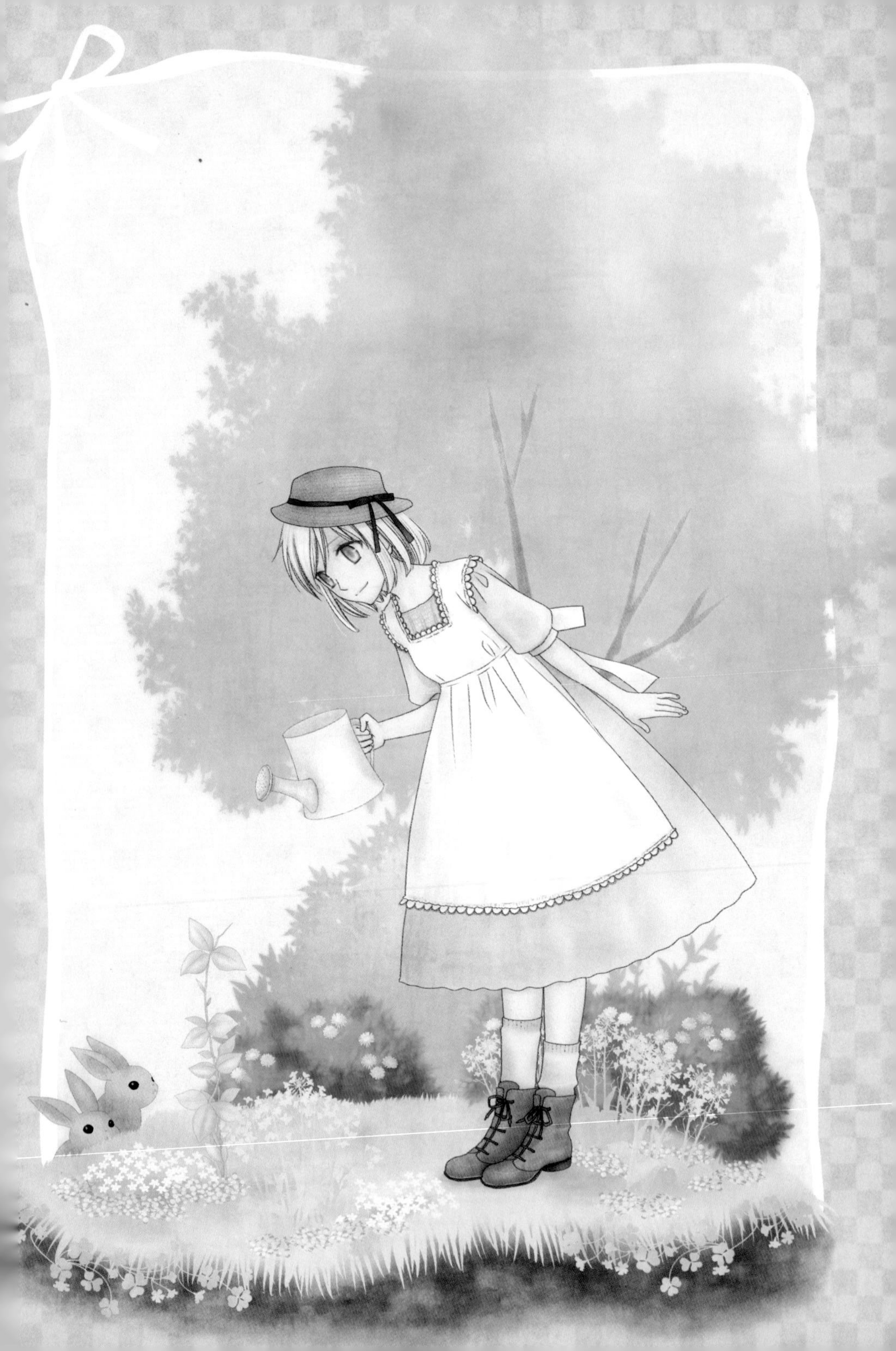

Liselotte & Witch's Forest

3

NATSUKI TAKAYA

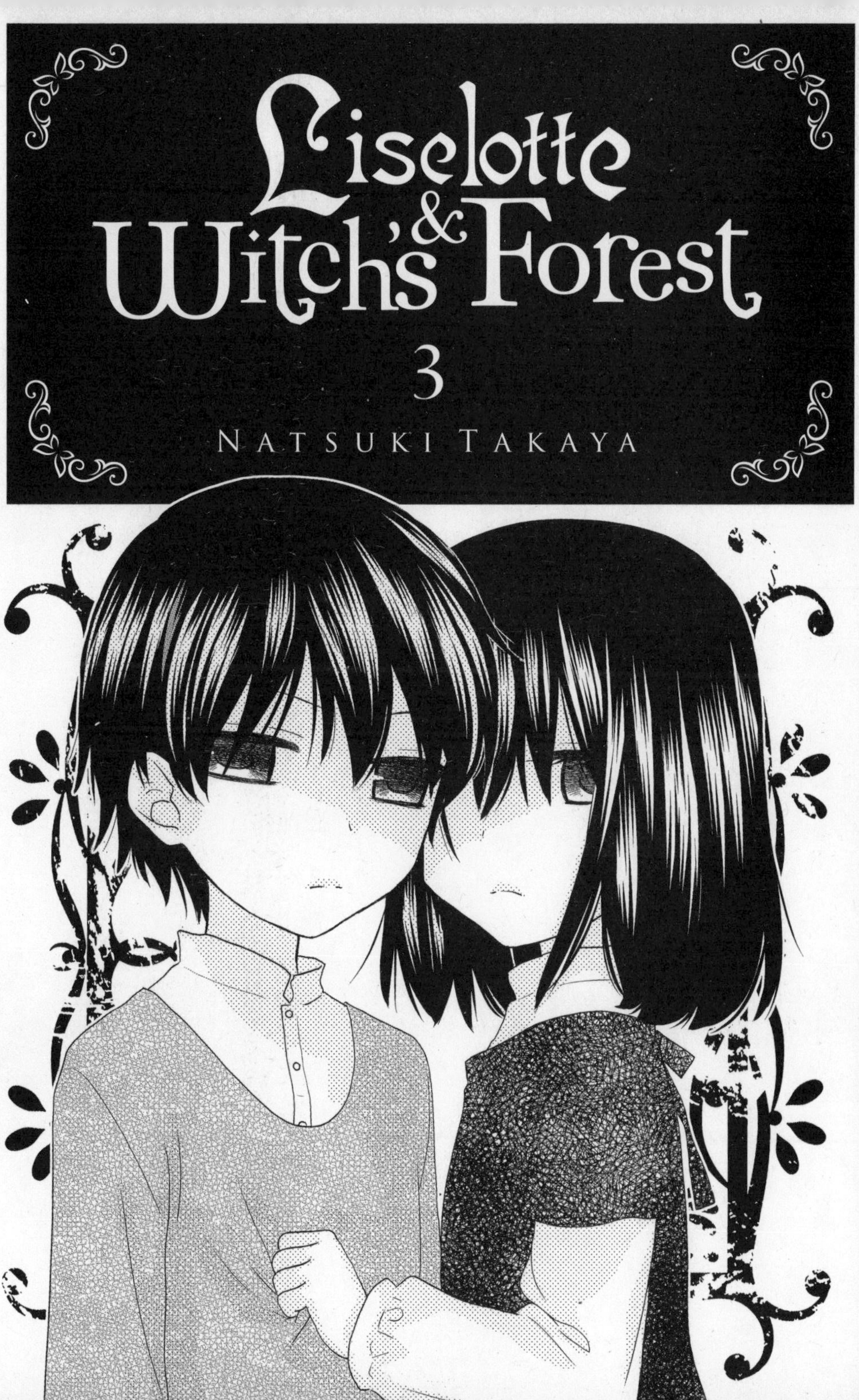

Liselotte & Witch's Forest by Natsuki Takaya

SUMMARY

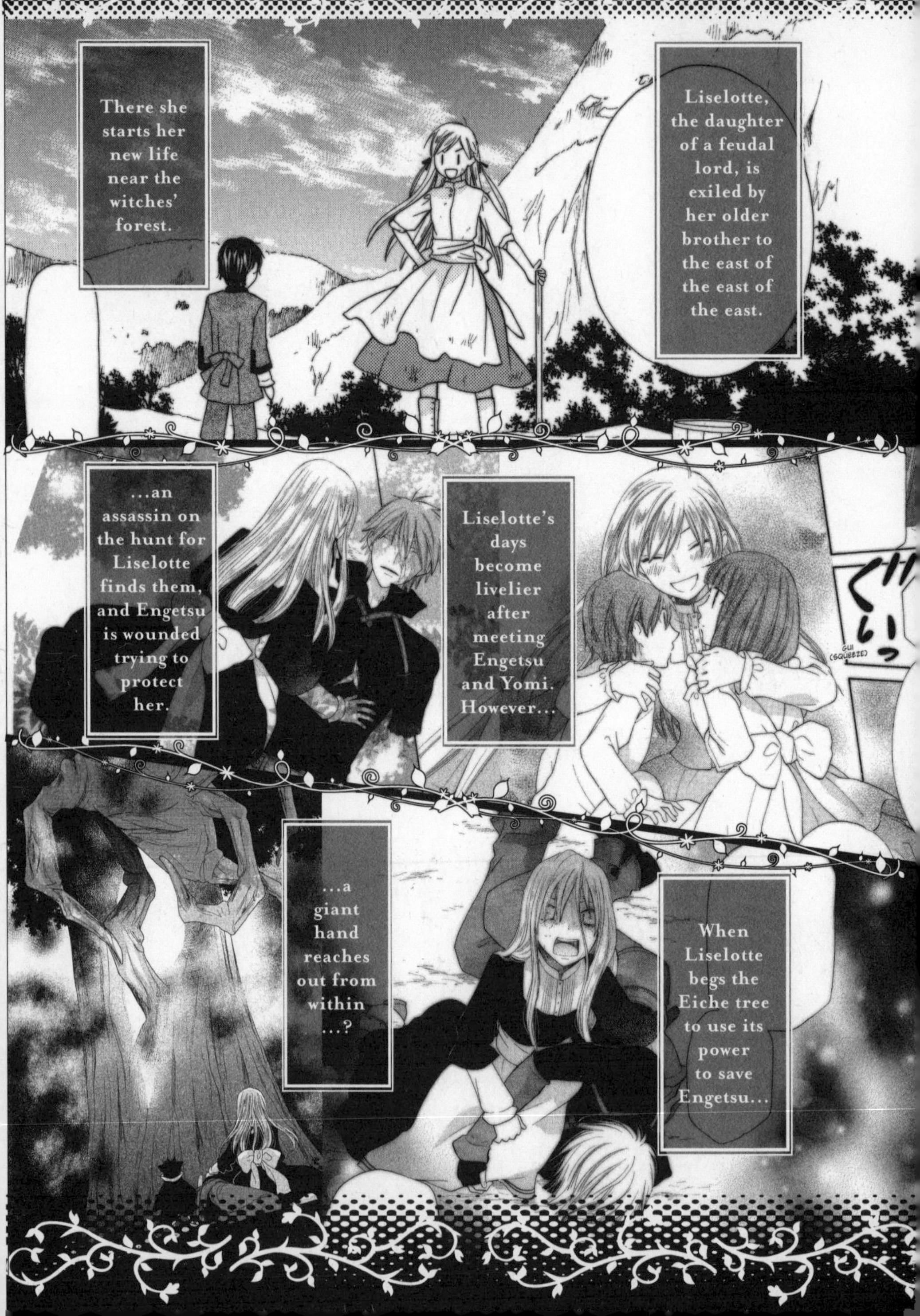
Liselotte, the daughter of a feudal lord, is exiled by her older brother to the east of the east of the east.
There she starts her new life near the witches' forest.
GUI (SQUEEZE)
Liselotte's days become livelier after meeting Engetsu and Yomi. However...
...an assassin on the hunt for Liselotte finds them, and Engetsu is wounded trying to protect her.
When Liselotte begs the Eiche tree to use its power to save Engetsu...
...a giant hand reaches out from within ...?

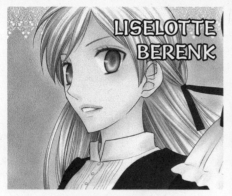

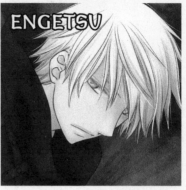

ENGETSU

Lise-sama's childhood friend, Enrich. Brought back to life as a puppet and returned to her.

LISELOTTE BERENK

A young woman from a high-class family. Currently learning how to cook and work the land.

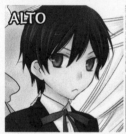

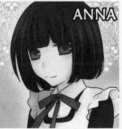

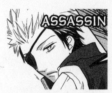

ASSASSIN

Came to murder Lise-sama but was captured by Engetsu, who was wounded in the process.

ANNA

Lise-sama's servant. The younger twin.

ALTO

Lise-sama's servant. The elder twin.

YOMI

The witch Vartelinde's familiar.

WITCHES WHO LIVE IN THE FOREST
VERGUE
HILDE
MYRTE

Rumors say they live on their own deep in the forest, but occasionally they emerge to use their power on humans—sometimes to help, sometimes to harm.

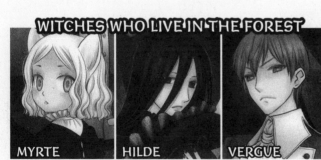

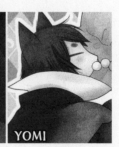

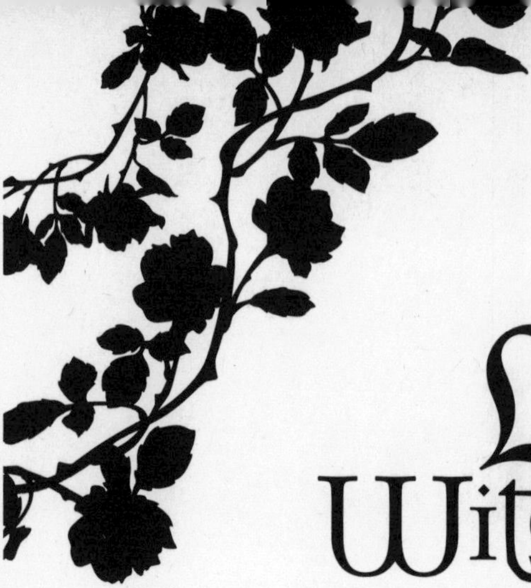

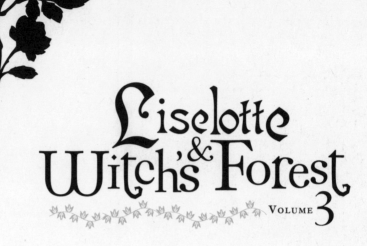

Liselotte & Witch's Forest

Volume 3

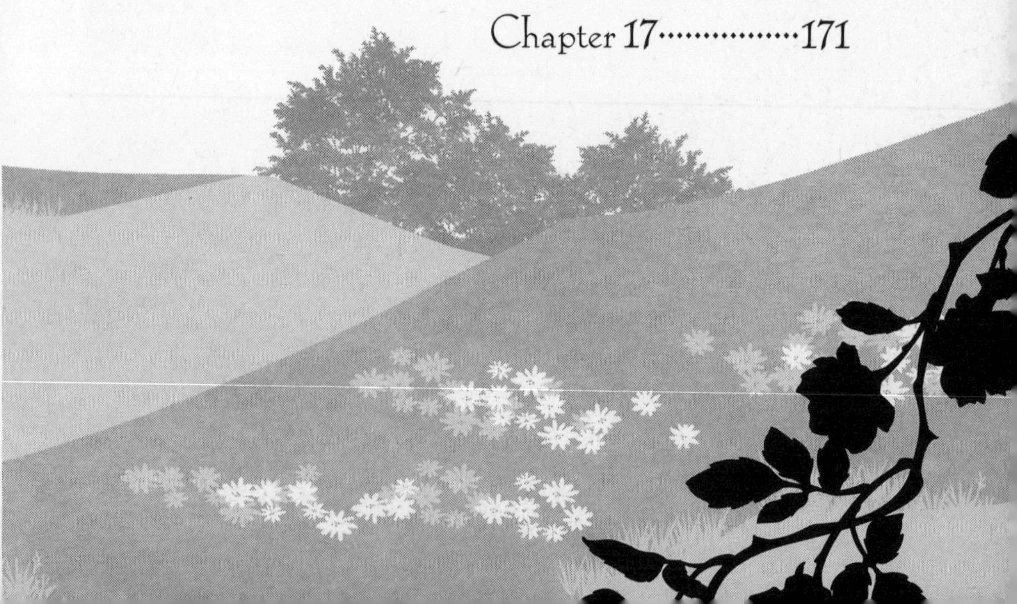

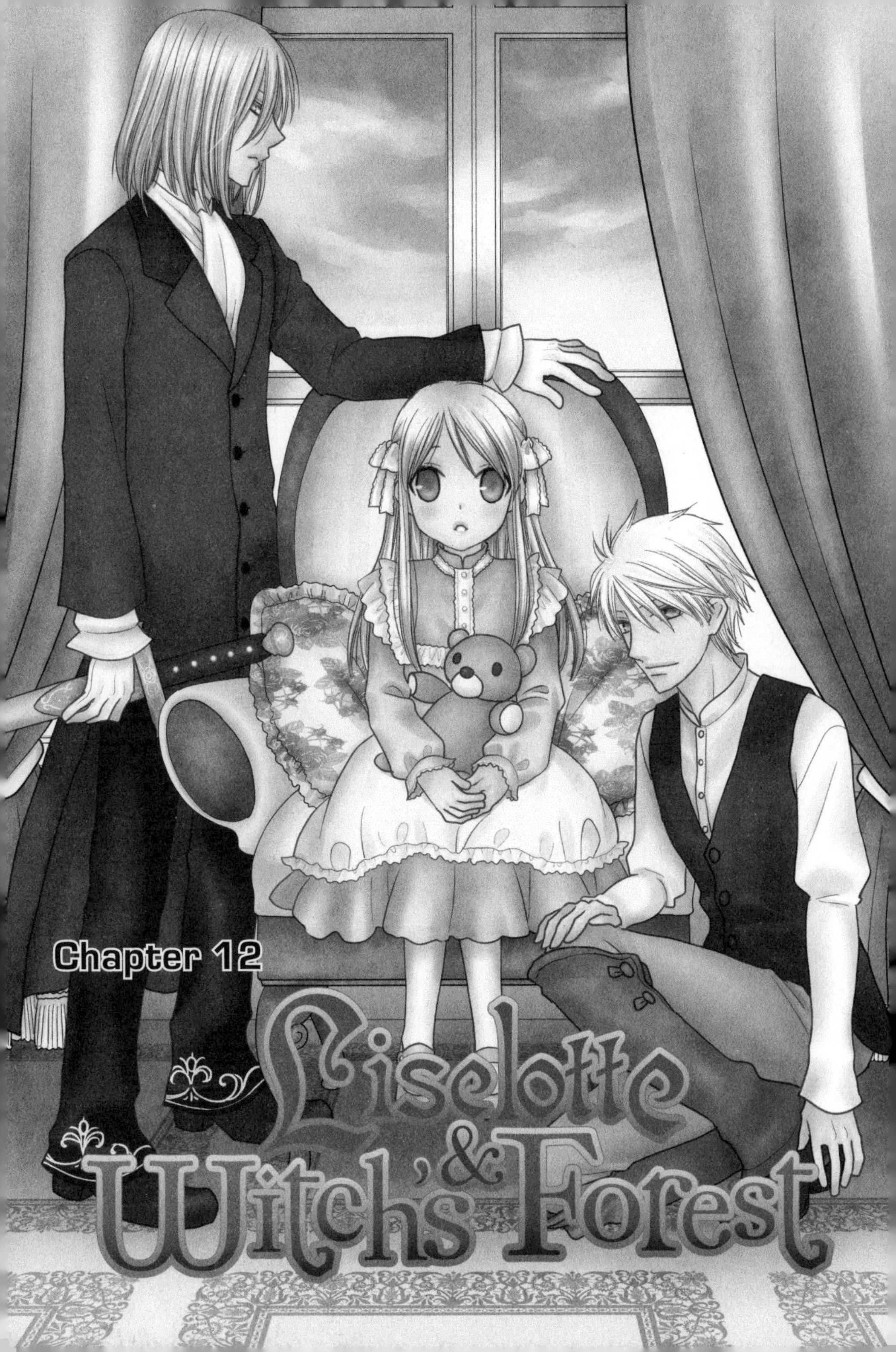
Chapter 12
Liselotte & Witch's Forest

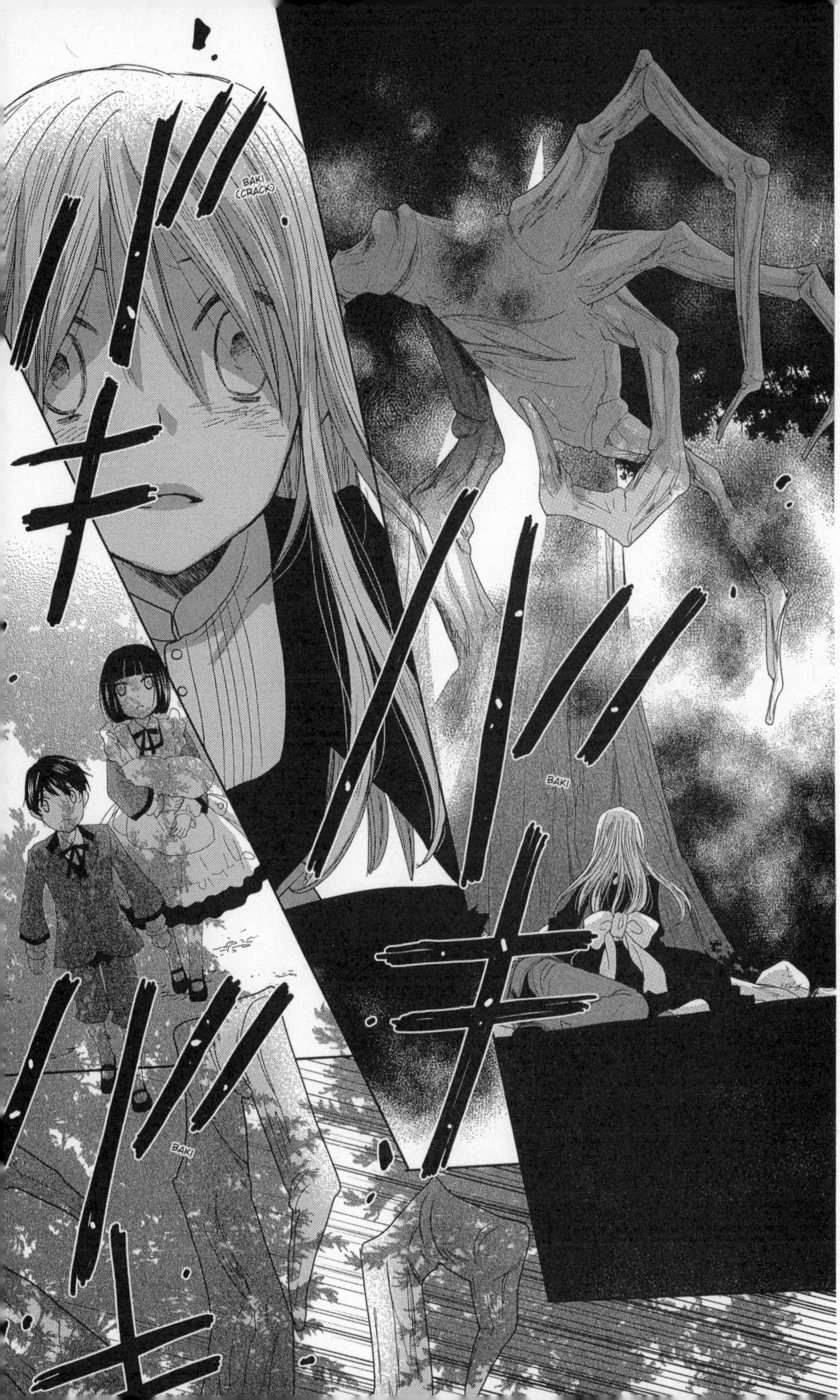
BAKI
(CRACK)
BAKI
BAKI

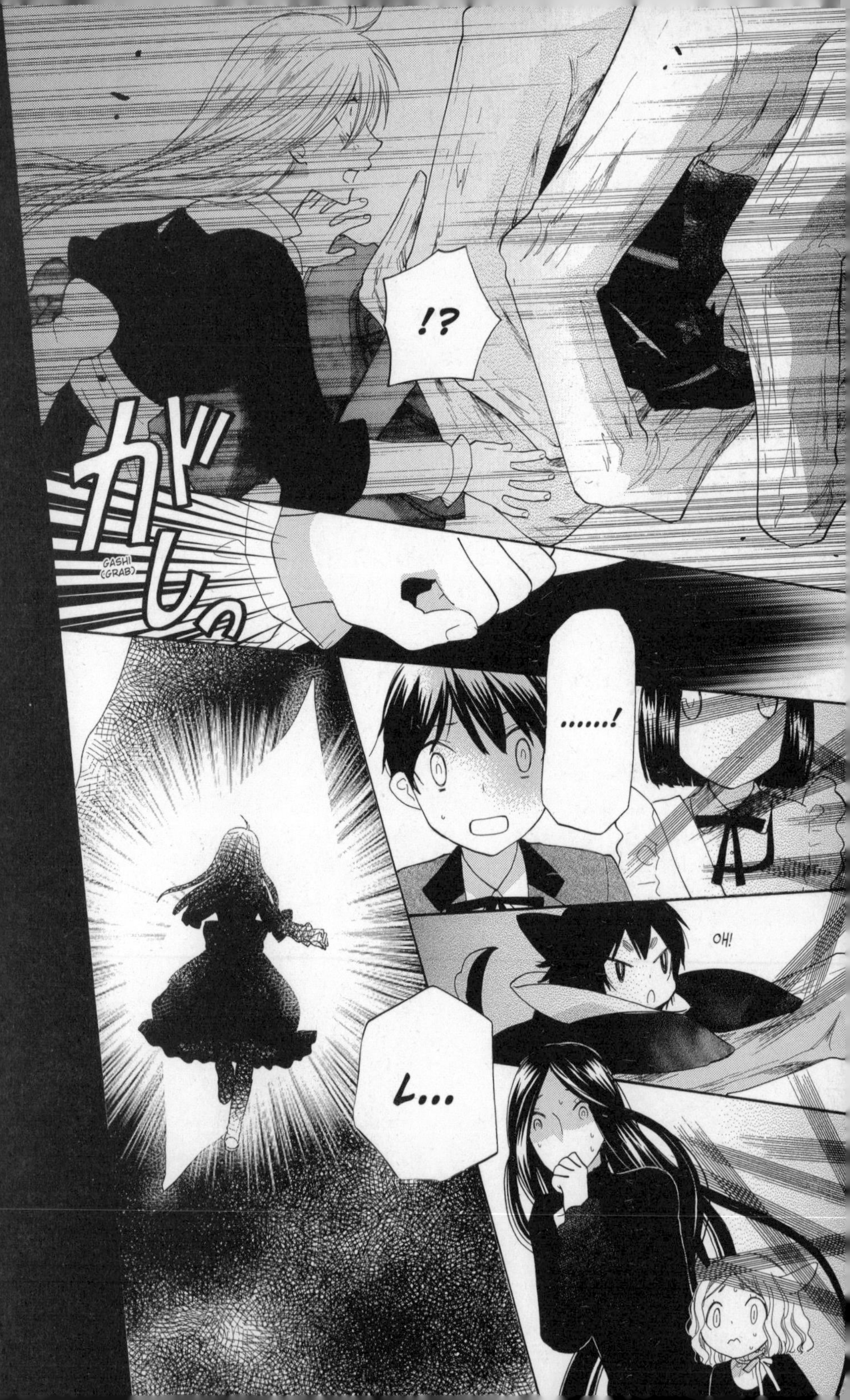
!?
がしっ
GASHI (GRAB)
......!
OH!
L...

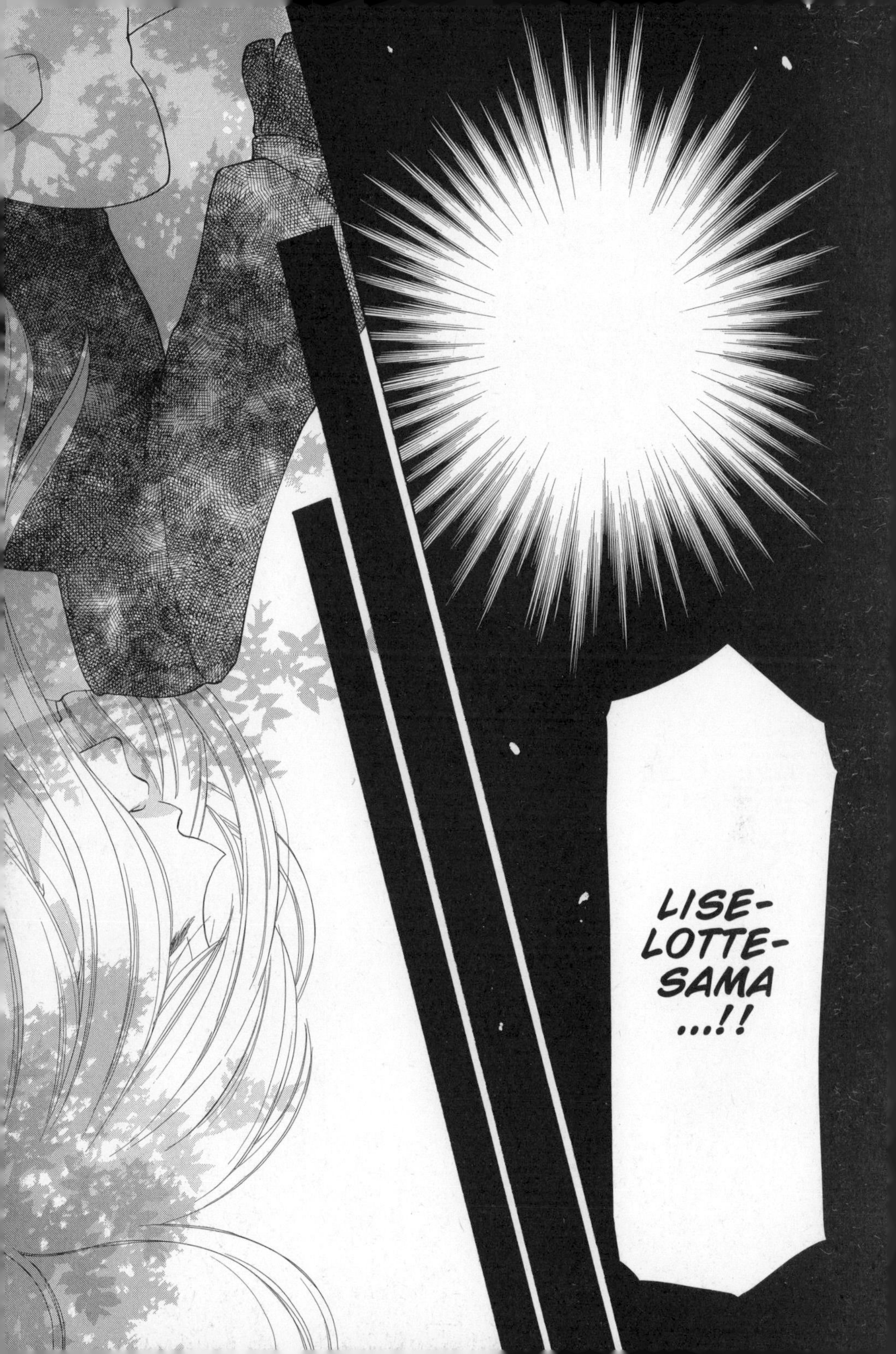
LISE-
LOTTE-
SAMA
...!!

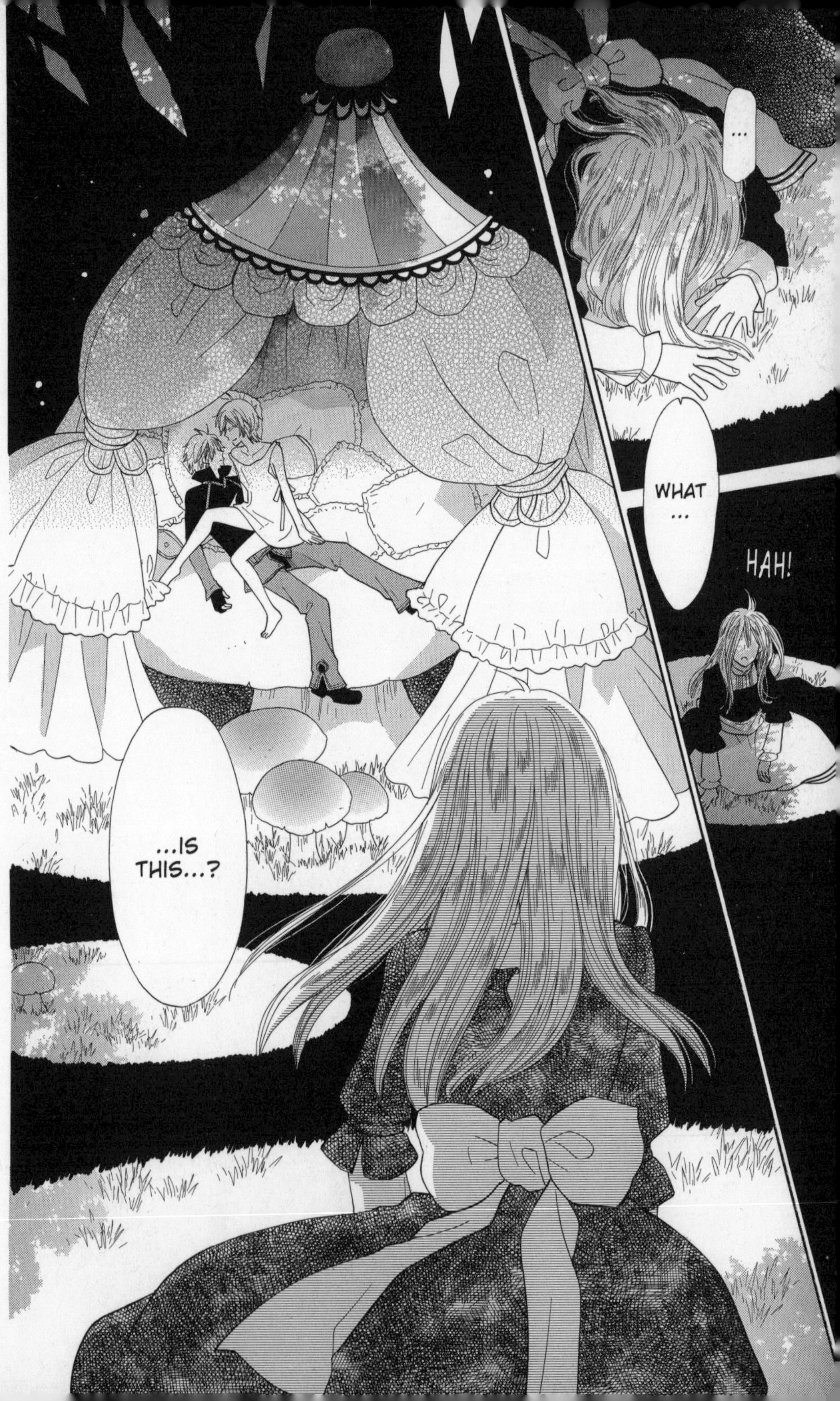
...
WHAT ...
HAH!
...IS THIS...?

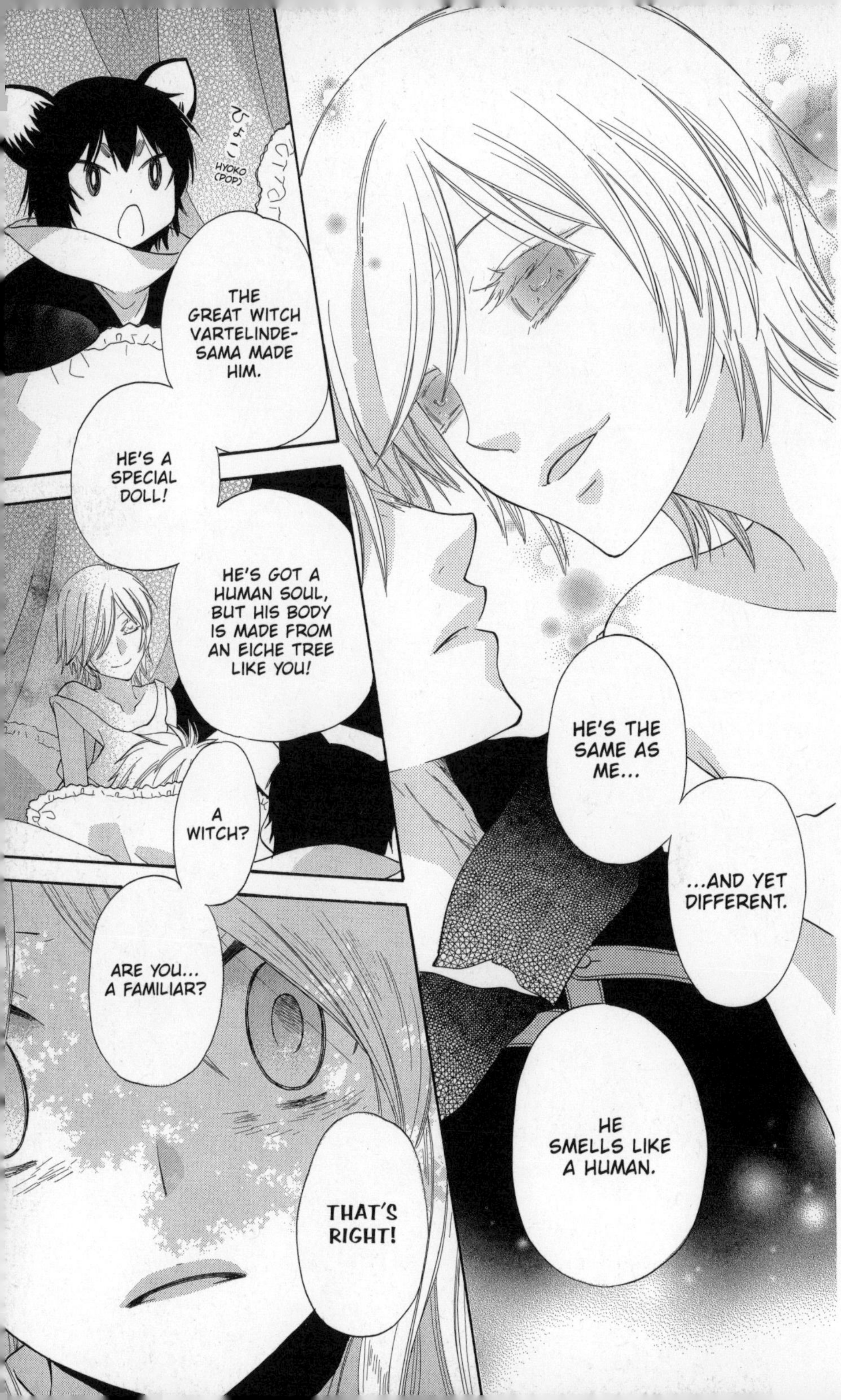
HE'S THE SAME AS ME...
...AND YET DIFFERENT.
HE SMELLS LIKE A HUMAN.
ぴょこ
HYOKO (POP)
THE GREAT WITCH VARTELINDE-SAMA MADE HIM.
HE'S A SPECIAL DOLL!
HE'S GOT A HUMAN SOUL, BUT HIS BODY IS MADE FROM AN EICHE TREE LIKE YOU!
A WITCH?
ARE YOU... A FAMILIAR?
THAT'S RIGHT!

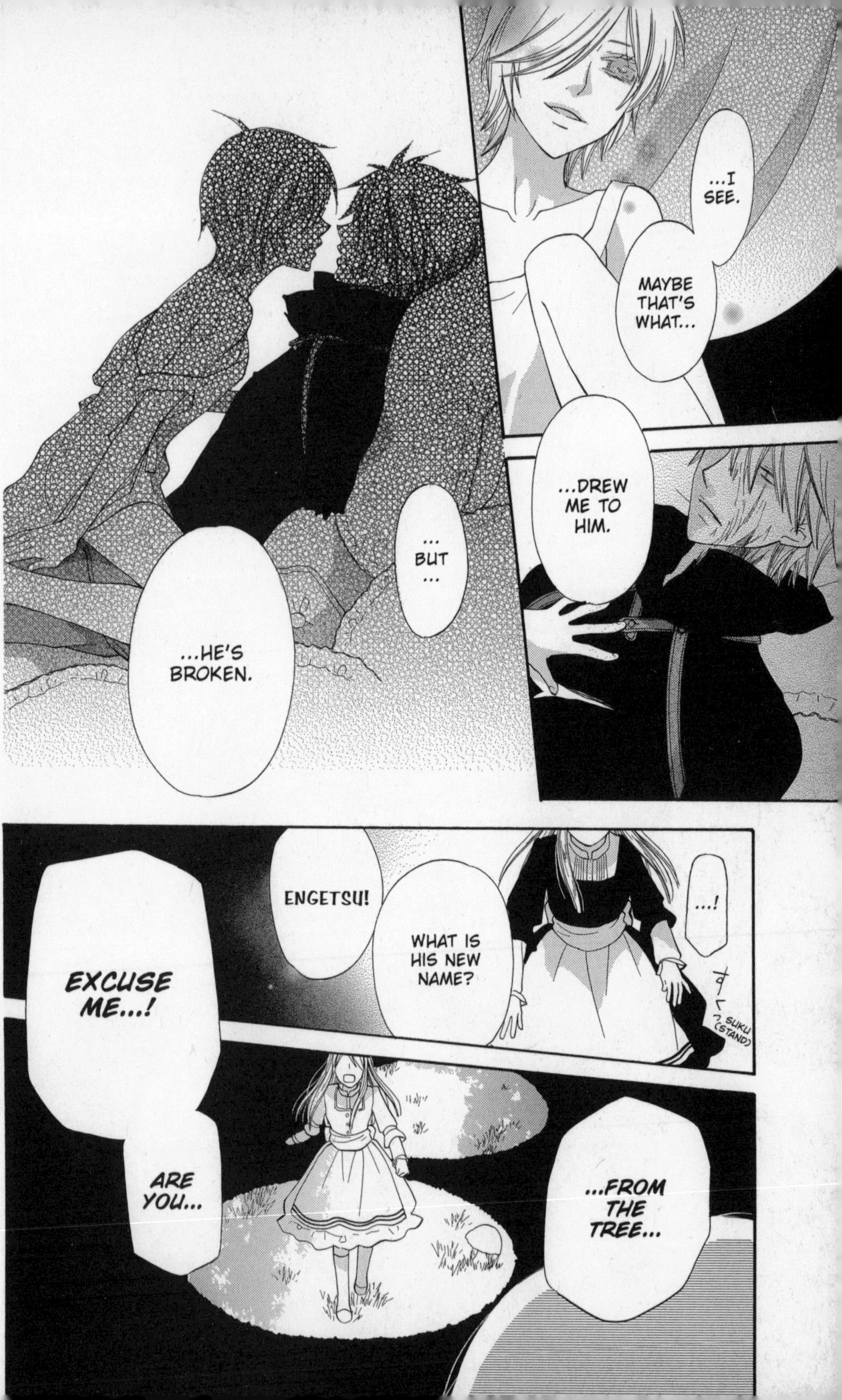
...I SEE.
MAYBE THAT'S WHAT...
...DREW ME TO HIM.
...BUT...
...HE'S BROKEN.
...!
すくっ SUKU (STAND)
ENGETSU!
WHAT IS HIS NEW NAME?
EXCUSE ME...!
ARE YOU...
...FROM THE TREE...

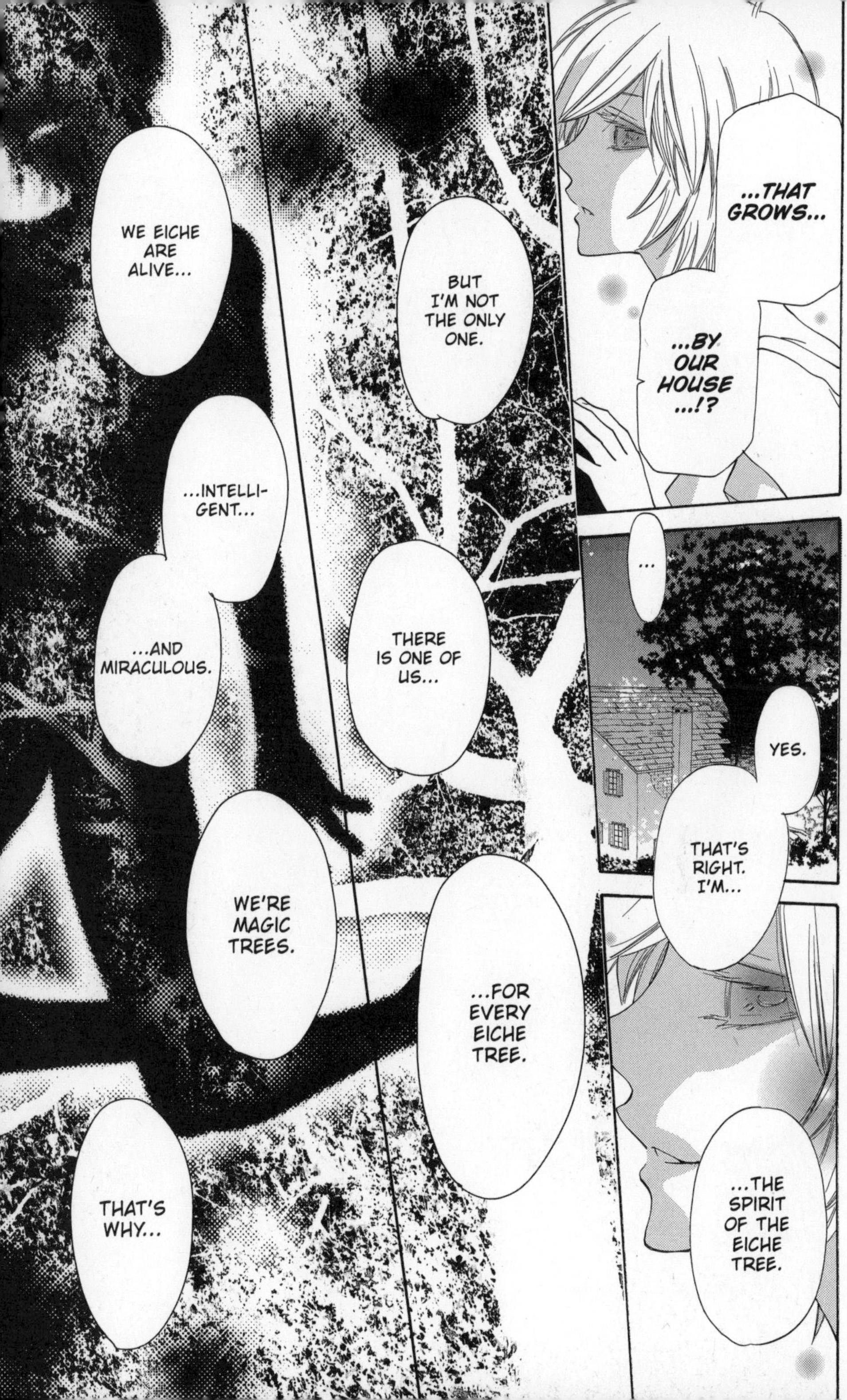
...THAT GROWS...
...BY OUR HOUSE ...!?
...
YES.
THAT'S RIGHT. I'M...
...THE SPIRIT OF THE EICHE TREE.
BUT I'M NOT THE ONLY ONE.
THERE IS ONE OF US...
...FOR EVERY EICHE TREE.
WE EICHE ARE ALIVE...
...INTELLI-GENT...
...AND MIRACULOUS.
WE'RE MAGIC TREES.
THAT'S WHY...

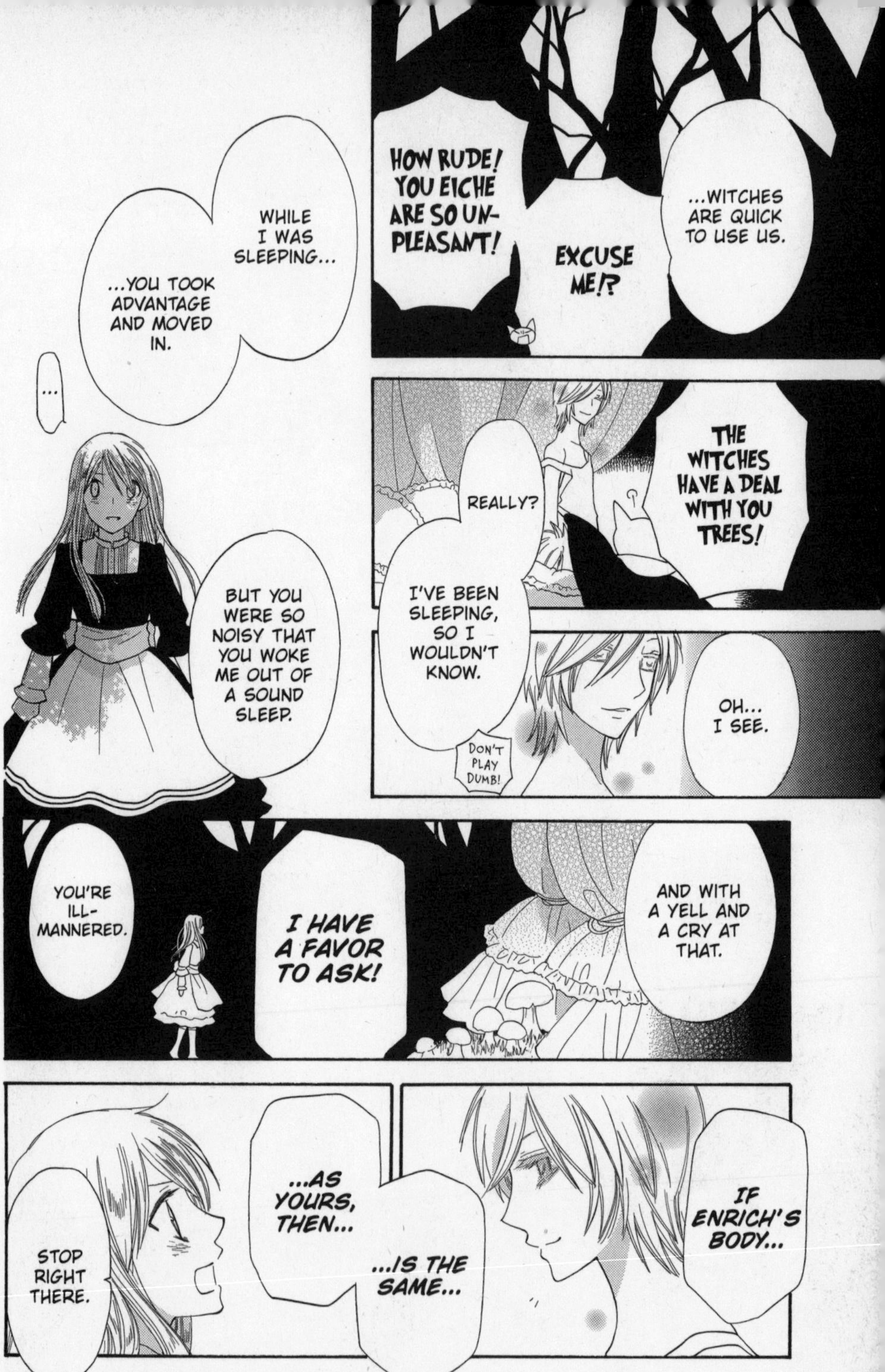
...WITCHES ARE QUICK TO USE US.
EXCUSE ME!?
HOW RUDE! YOU EICHE ARE SO UN-PLEASANT!
THE WITCHES HAVE A DEAL WITH YOU TREES!
REALLY?
I'VE BEEN SLEEPING, SO I WOULDN'T KNOW.
OH... I SEE.
DON'T PLAY DUMB!
WHILE I WAS SLEEPING...
...YOU TOOK ADVANTAGE AND MOVED IN.
...
BUT YOU WERE SO NOISY THAT YOU WOKE ME OUT OF A SOUND SLEEP.
AND WITH A YELL AND A CRY AT THAT.
I HAVE A FAVOR TO ASK!
YOU'RE ILL-MANNERED.
IF ENRICH'S BODY...
...IS THE SAME...
...AS YOURS, THEN...
STOP RIGHT THERE.

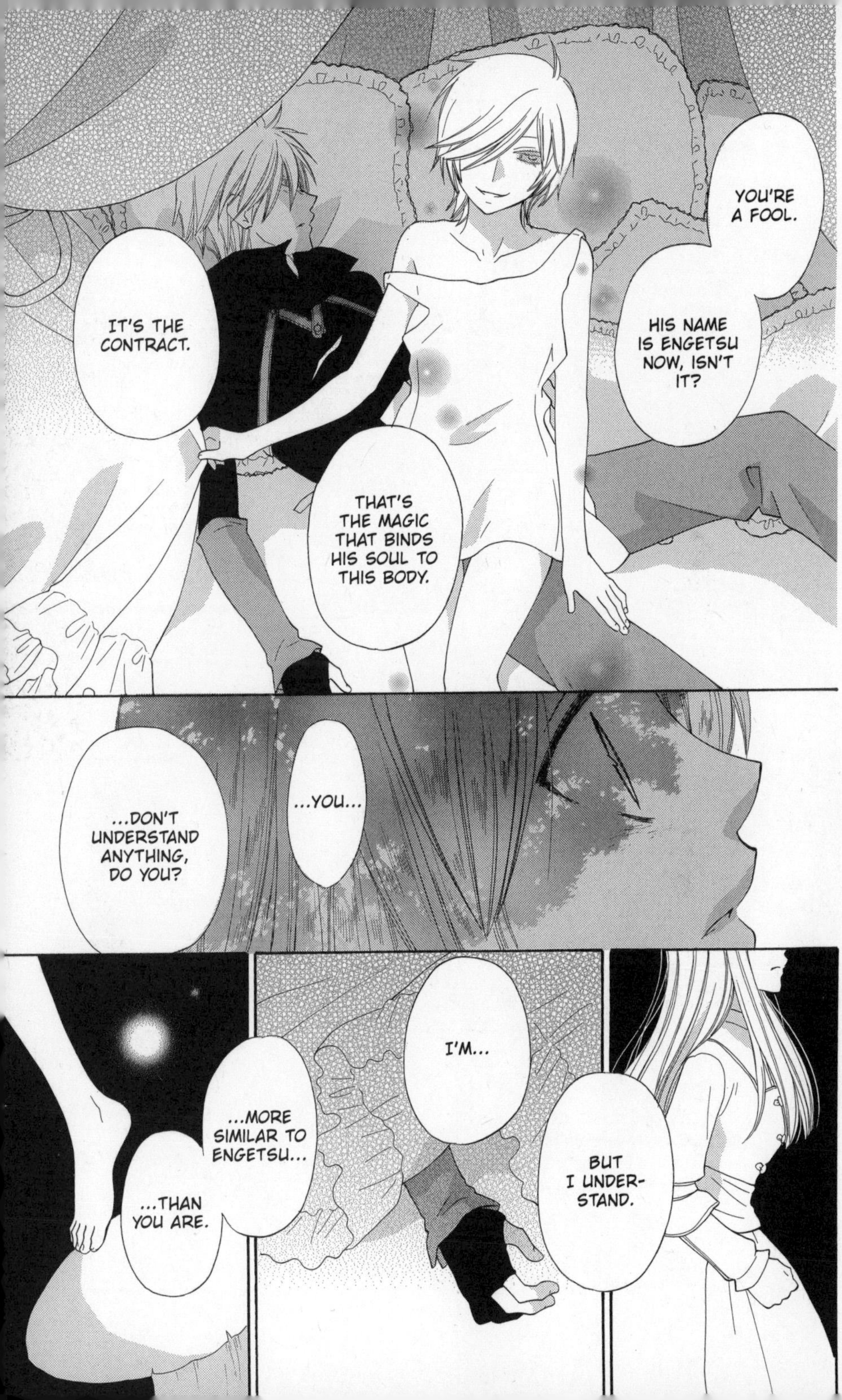
YOU'RE A FOOL.
HIS NAME IS ENGETSU NOW, ISN'T IT?
IT'S THE CONTRACT.
THAT'S THE MAGIC THAT BINDS HIS SOUL TO THIS BODY.
...YOU...
...DON'T UNDERSTAND ANYTHING, DO YOU?
BUT I UNDER-STAND.
I'M...
...MORE SIMILAR TO ENGETSU...
...THAN YOU ARE.

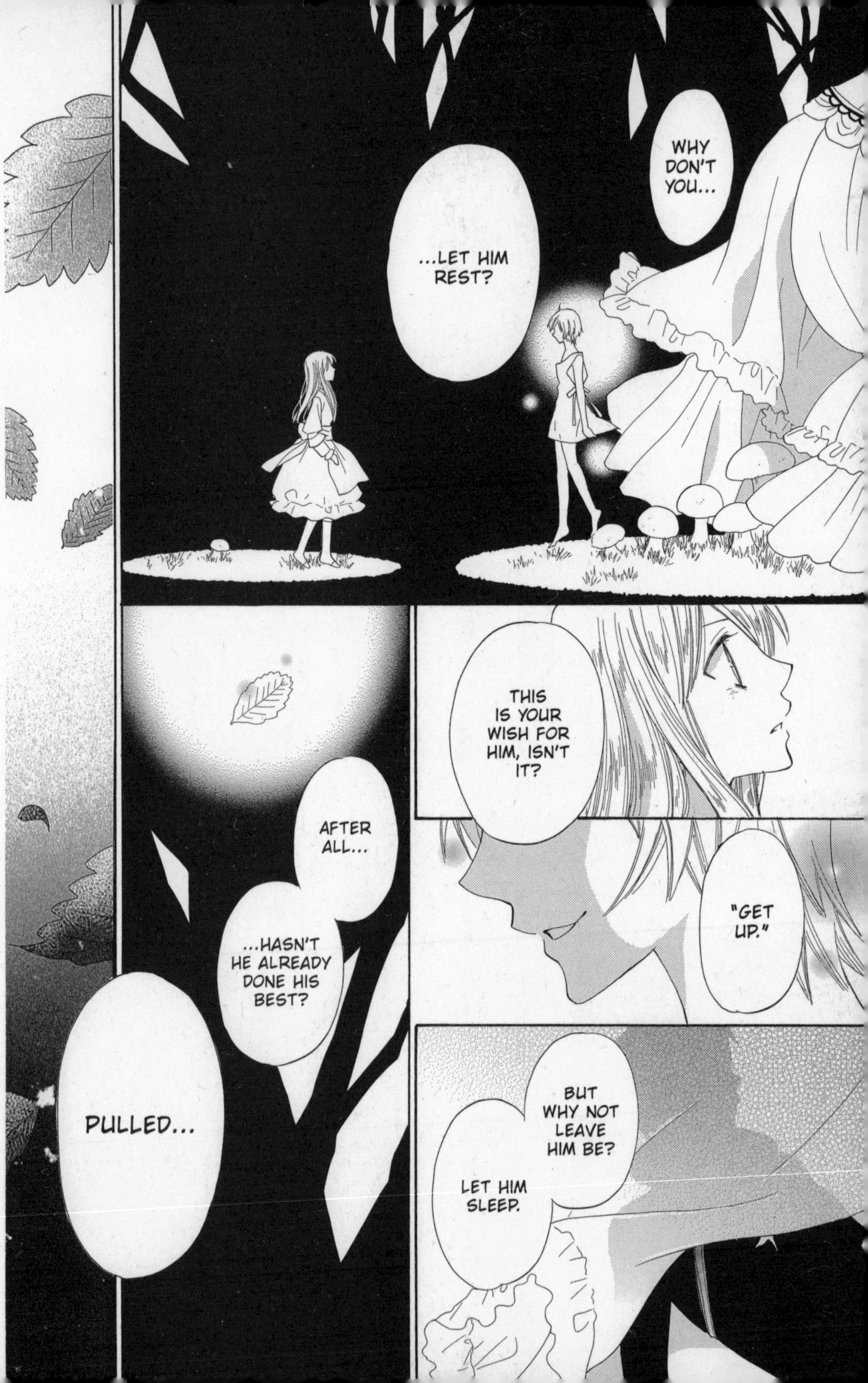
WHY DON'T YOU...
...LET HIM REST?
THIS IS YOUR WISH FOR HIM, ISN'T IT?
"GET UP."
BUT WHY NOT LEAVE HIM BE?
LET HIM SLEEP.
AFTER ALL...
...HASN'T HE ALREADY DONE HIS BEST?
PULLED...

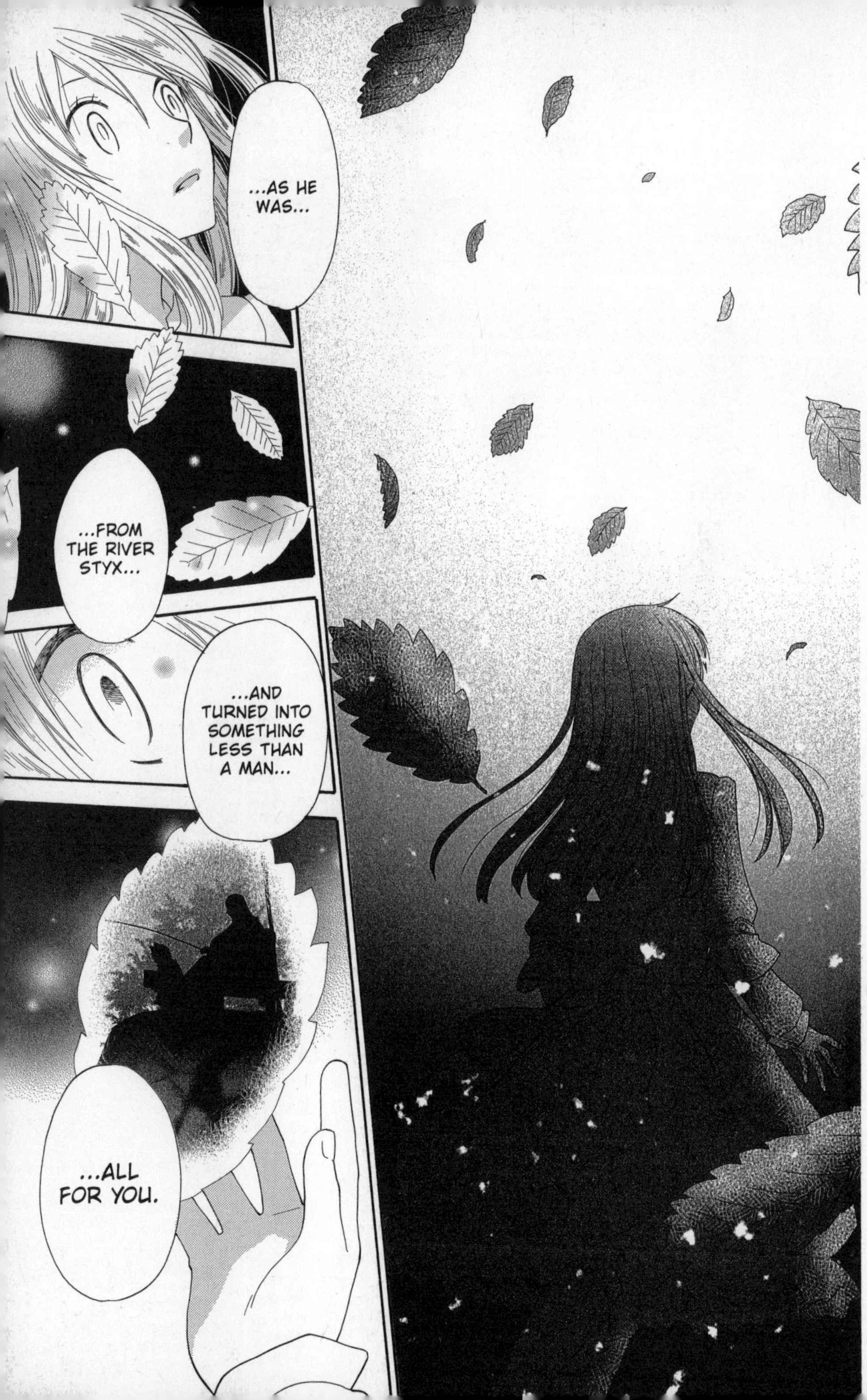
...AS HE WAS...
...FROM THE RIVER STYX...
...AND TURNED INTO SOMETHING LESS THAN A MAN...
...ALL FOR YOU.

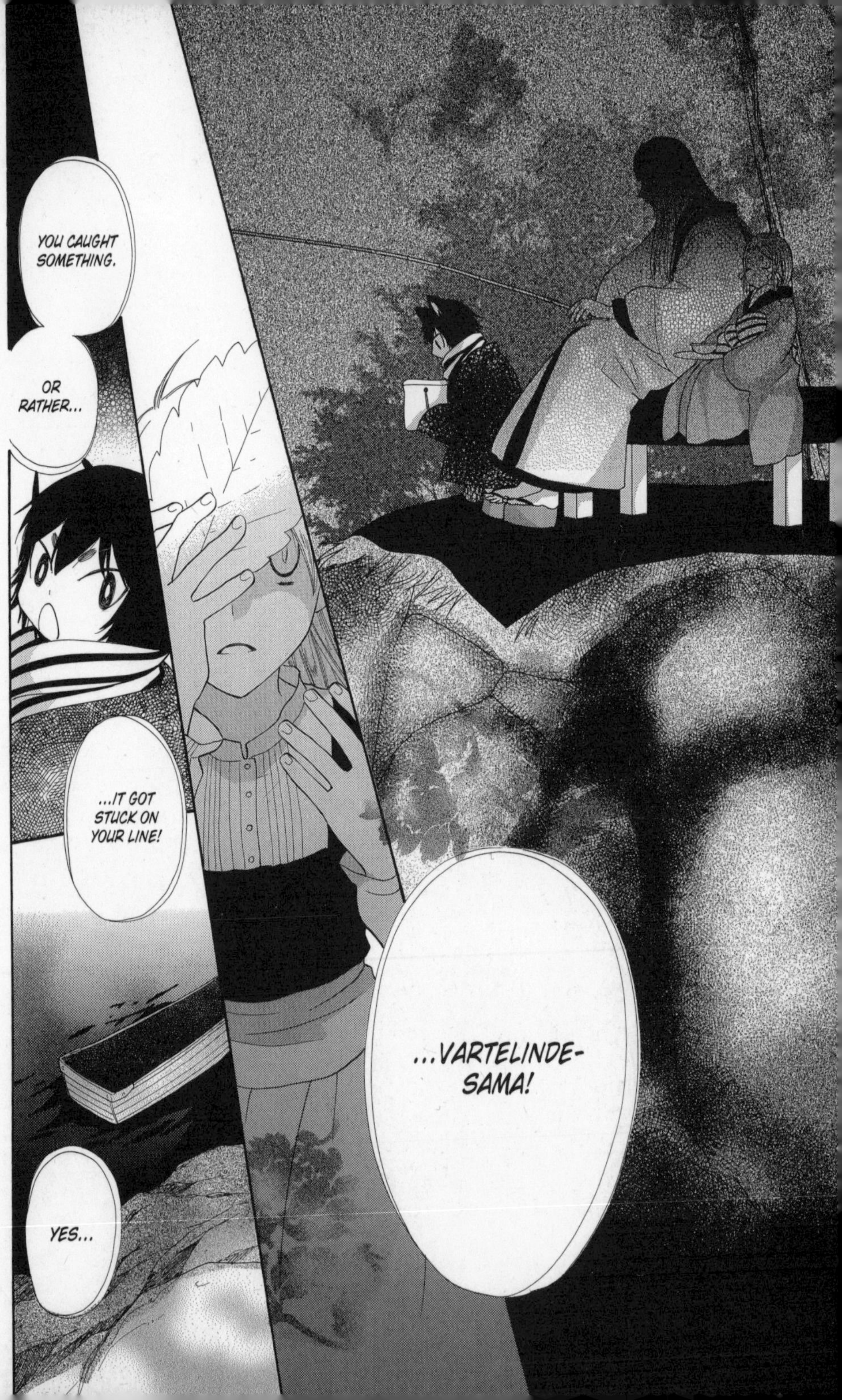
...VARTELINDE-SAMA!
YOU CAUGHT SOMETHING.
OR RATHER...
...IT GOT STUCK ON YOUR LINE!
YES...

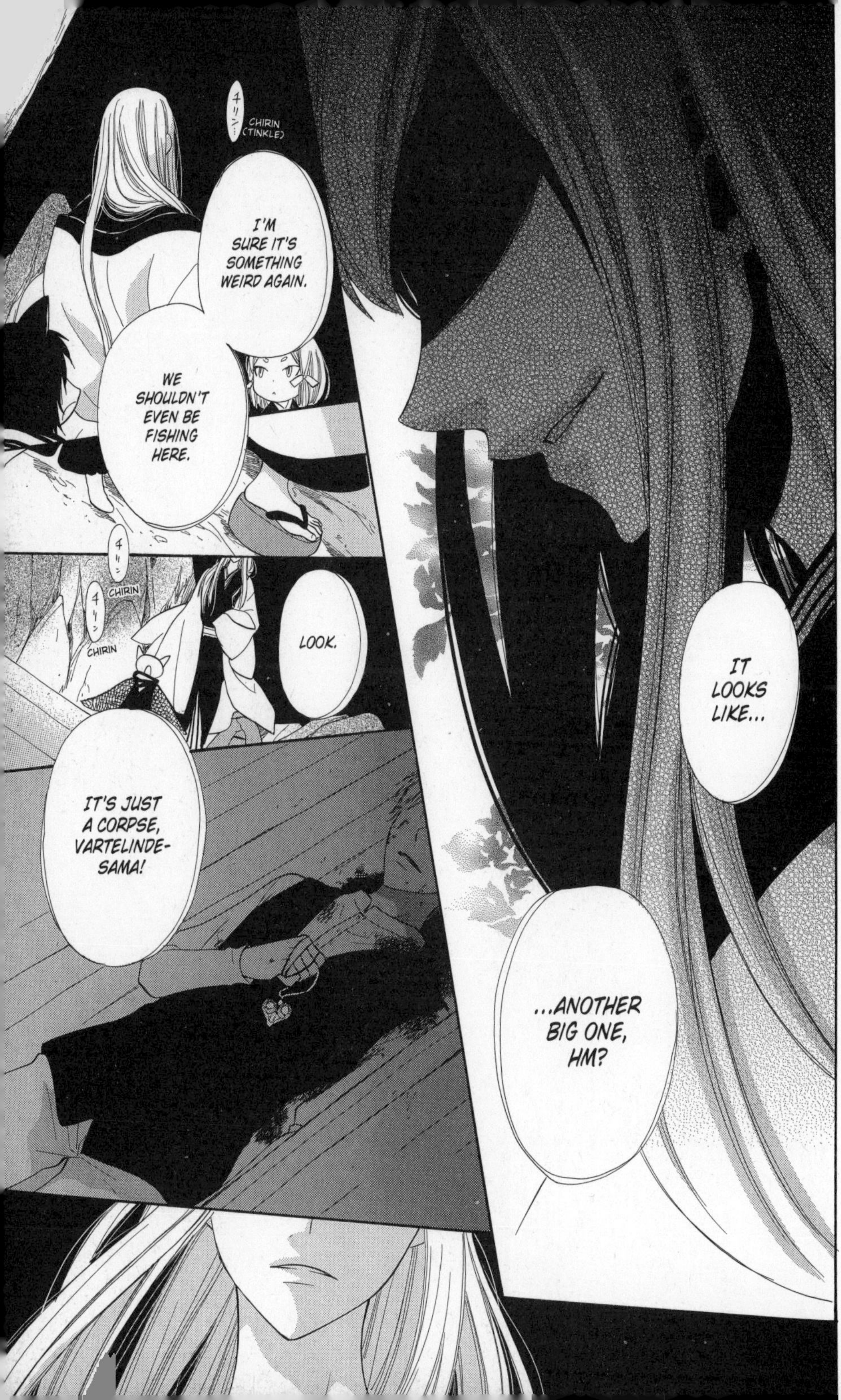
IT LOOKS LIKE...
...ANOTHER BIG ONE, HM?
チリン…
CHIRIN (TINKLE)
I'M SURE IT'S SOMETHING WEIRD AGAIN.
WE SHOULDN'T EVEN BE FISHING HERE.
チリン
CHIRIN
チリン
CHIRIN
LOOK.
IT'S JUST A CORPSE, VARTELINDE-SAMA!

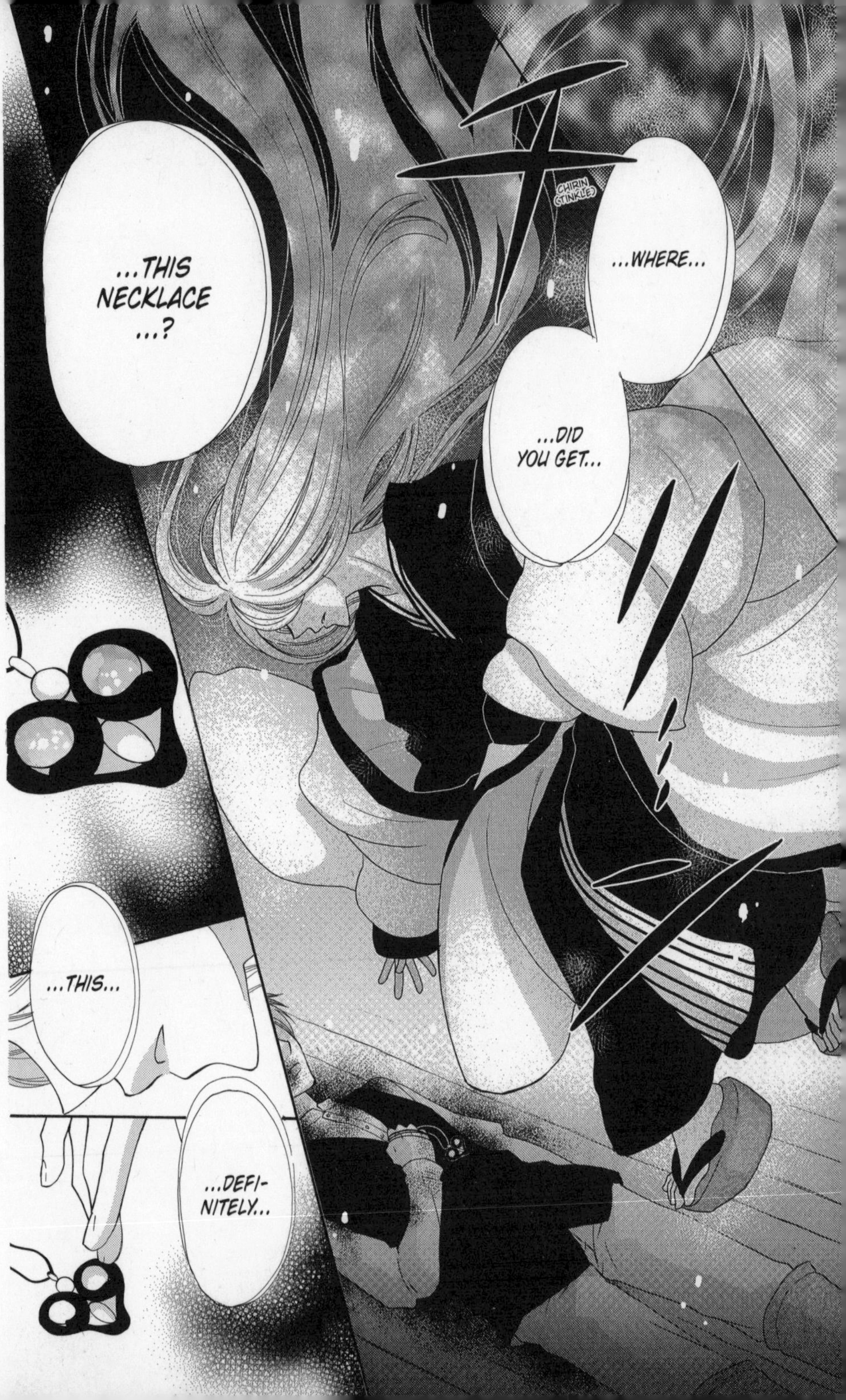
CHIRIN (TINKLE)
...WHERE...
...DID YOU GET...
...THIS NECKLACE ...?
...THIS...
...DEFI-NITELY...

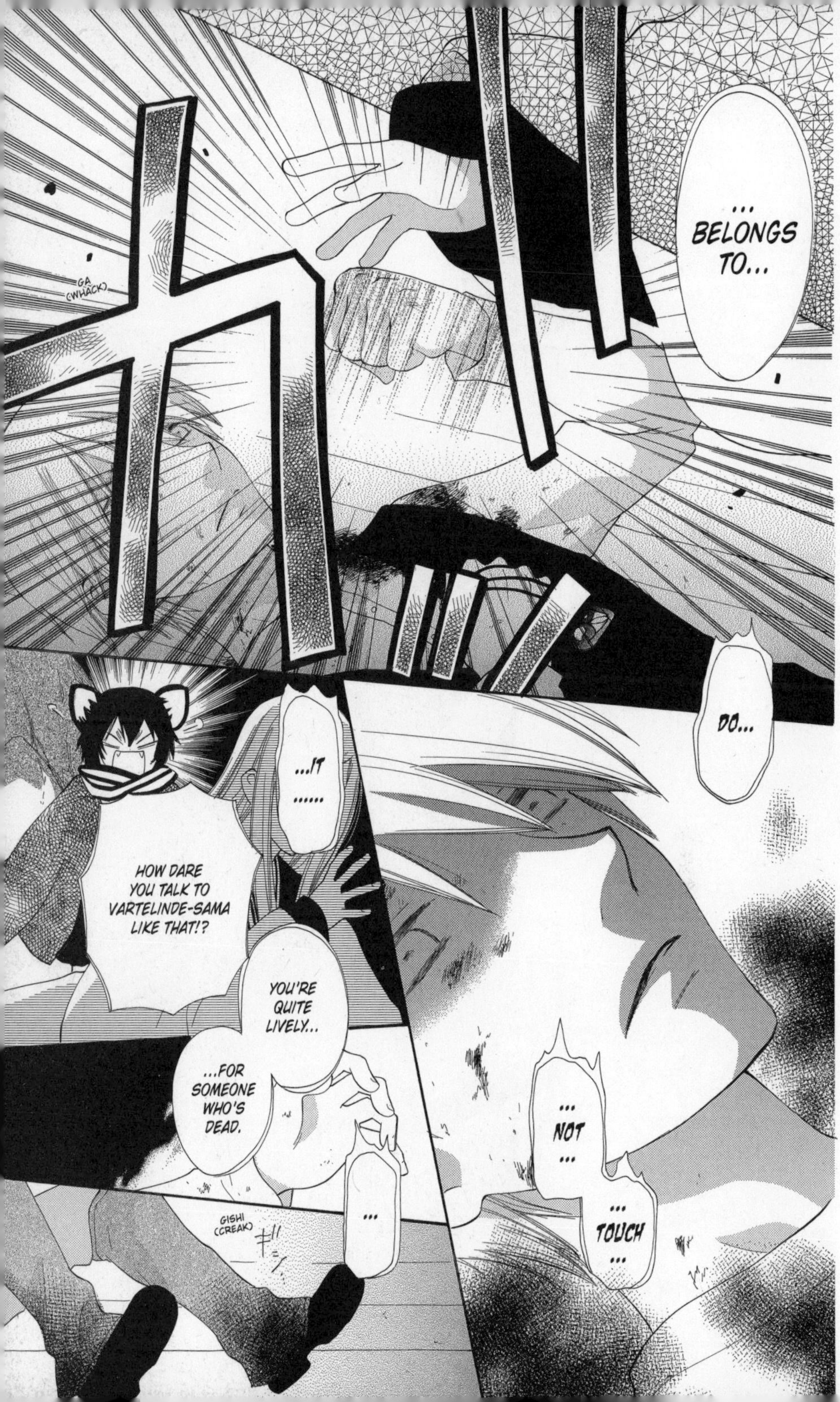
... BELONGS TO...
GA (WHACK)
DO...
... NOT ...
... TOUCH ...
...IT ......
HOW DARE YOU TALK TO VARTELINDE-SAMA LIKE THAT!?
YOU'RE QUITE LIVELY...
...FOR SOMEONE WHO'S DEAD.
...
GISHI (CREAK)

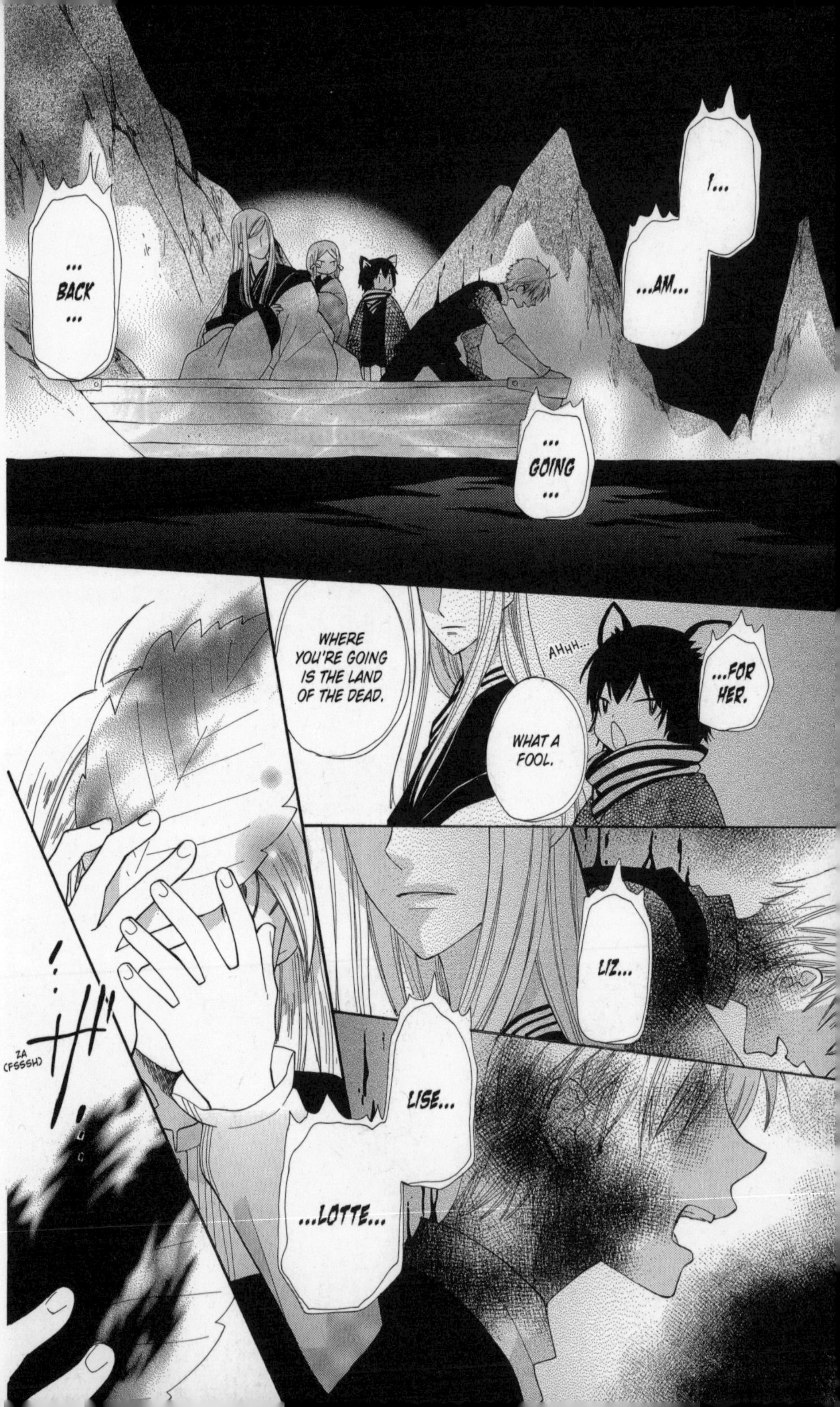
I...
...AM...
...GOING...
...BACK...
...FOR HER.
AHHH...
WHERE YOU'RE GOING IS THE LAND OF THE DEAD.
WHAT A FOOL.
LIZ...
LISE...
...LOTTE...
ZA (FSSSH)

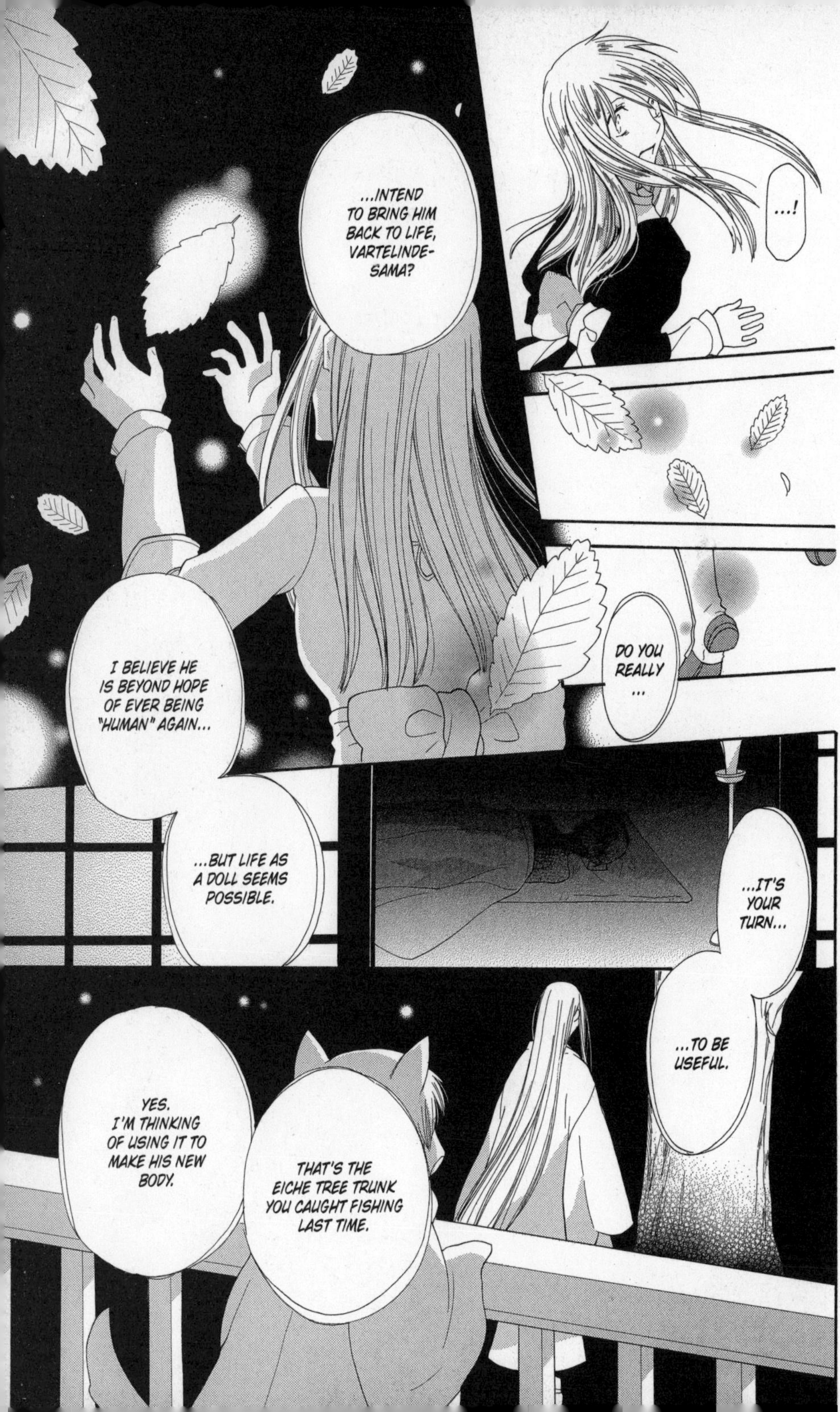
...!
DO YOU REALLY ...
...INTEND TO BRING HIM BACK TO LIFE, VARTELINDE-SAMA?
I BELIEVE HE IS BEYOND HOPE OF EVER BEING "HUMAN" AGAIN...
...BUT LIFE AS A DOLL SEEMS POSSIBLE.
...IT'S YOUR TURN...
...TO BE USEFUL.
THAT'S THE EICHE TREE TRUNK YOU CAUGHT FISHING LAST TIME.
YES. I'M THINKING OF USING IT TO MAKE HIS NEW BODY.

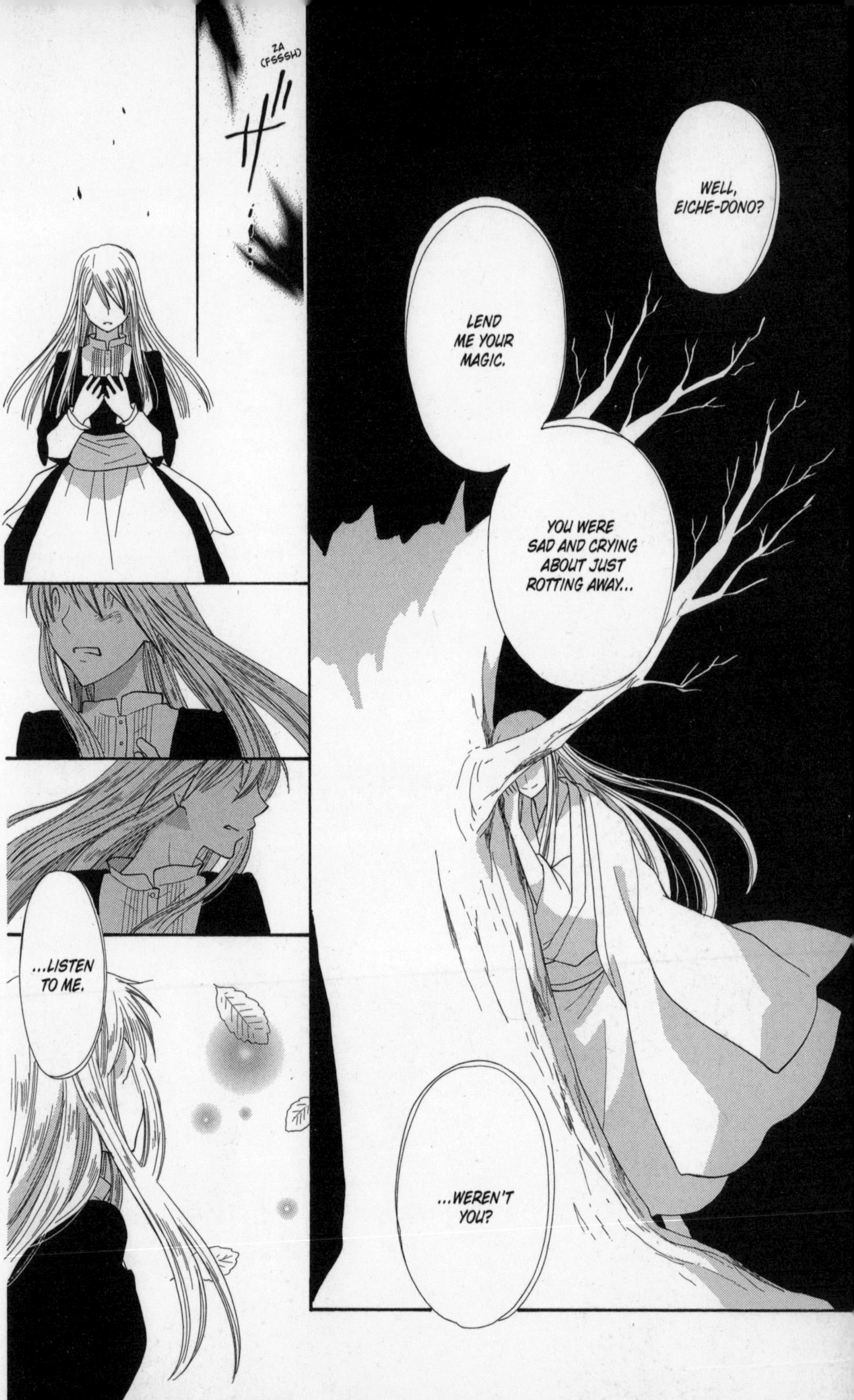
WELL, EICHE-DONO?
LEND ME YOUR MAGIC.
YOU WERE SAD AND CRYING ABOUT JUST ROTTING AWAY...
...WEREN'T YOU?
ZA (FSSSH)
...LISTEN TO ME.

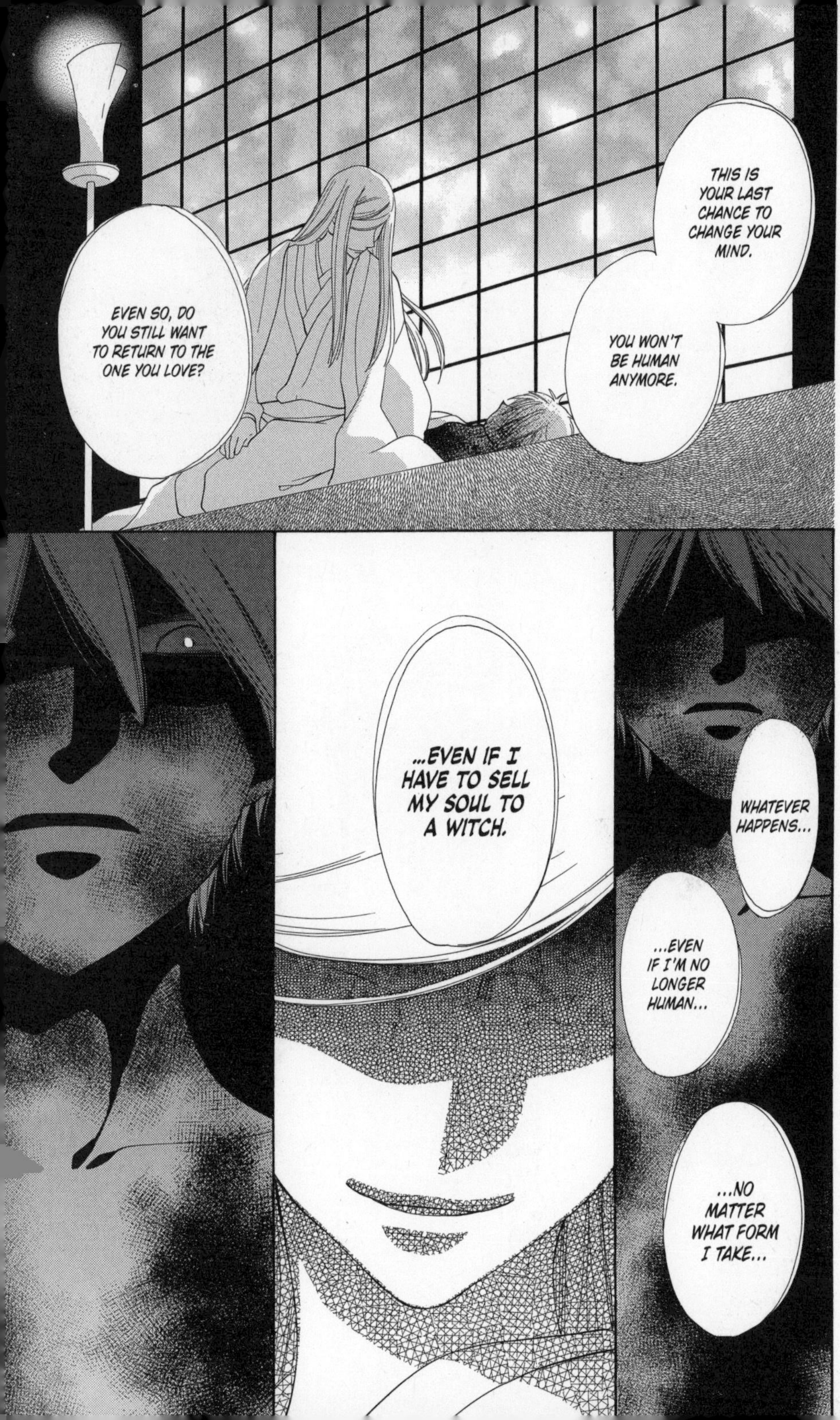
THIS IS YOUR LAST CHANCE TO CHANGE YOUR MIND.
YOU WON'T BE HUMAN ANYMORE.
EVEN SO, DO YOU STILL WANT TO RETURN TO THE ONE YOU LOVE?
WHATEVER HAPPENS...
...EVEN IF I'M NO LONGER HUMAN...
...NO MATTER WHAT FORM I TAKE...
...EVEN IF I HAVE TO SELL MY SOUL TO A WITCH.

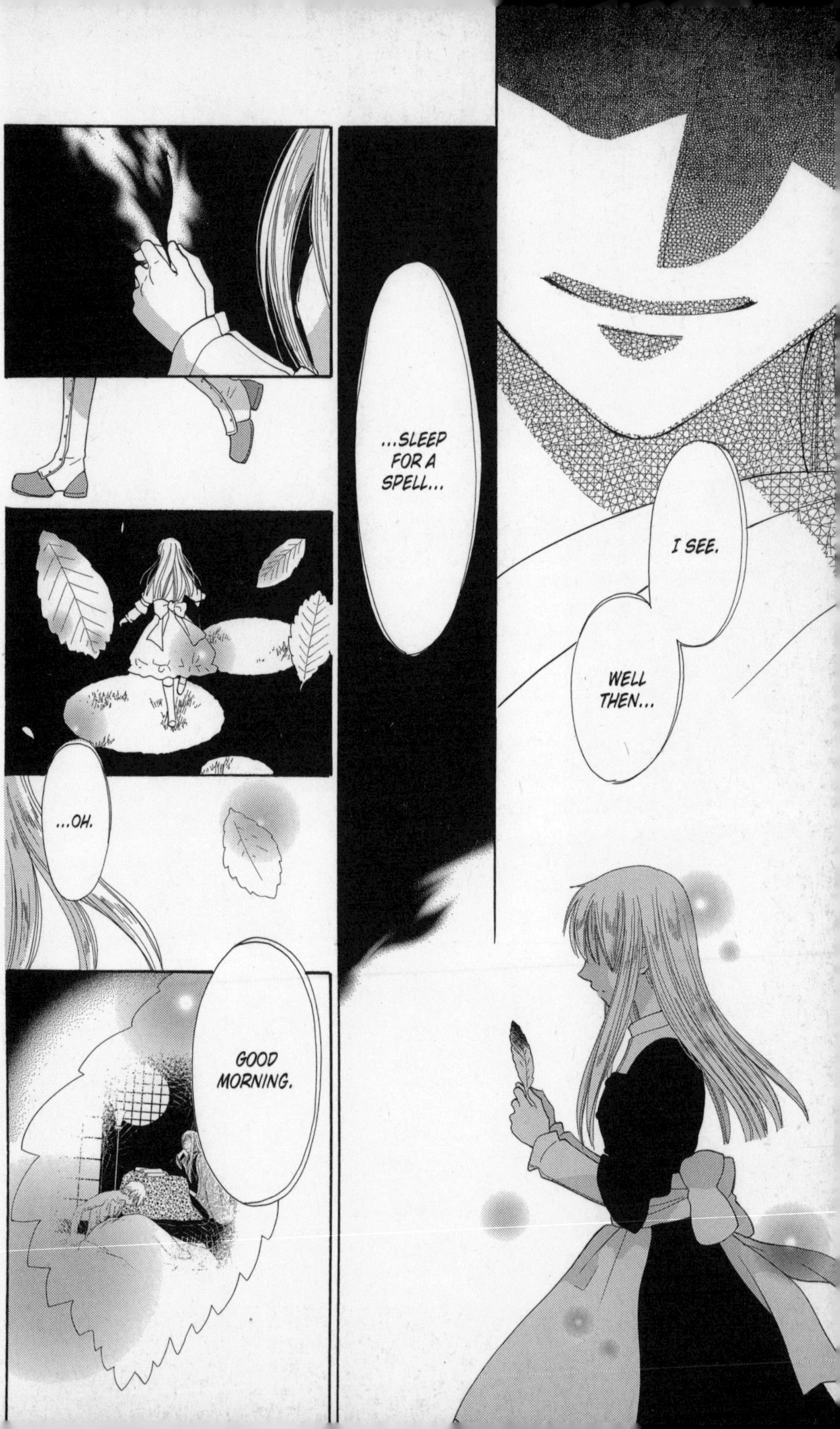
I SEE.
WELL THEN...
...SLEEP FOR A SPELL...
...OH.
GOOD MORNING.

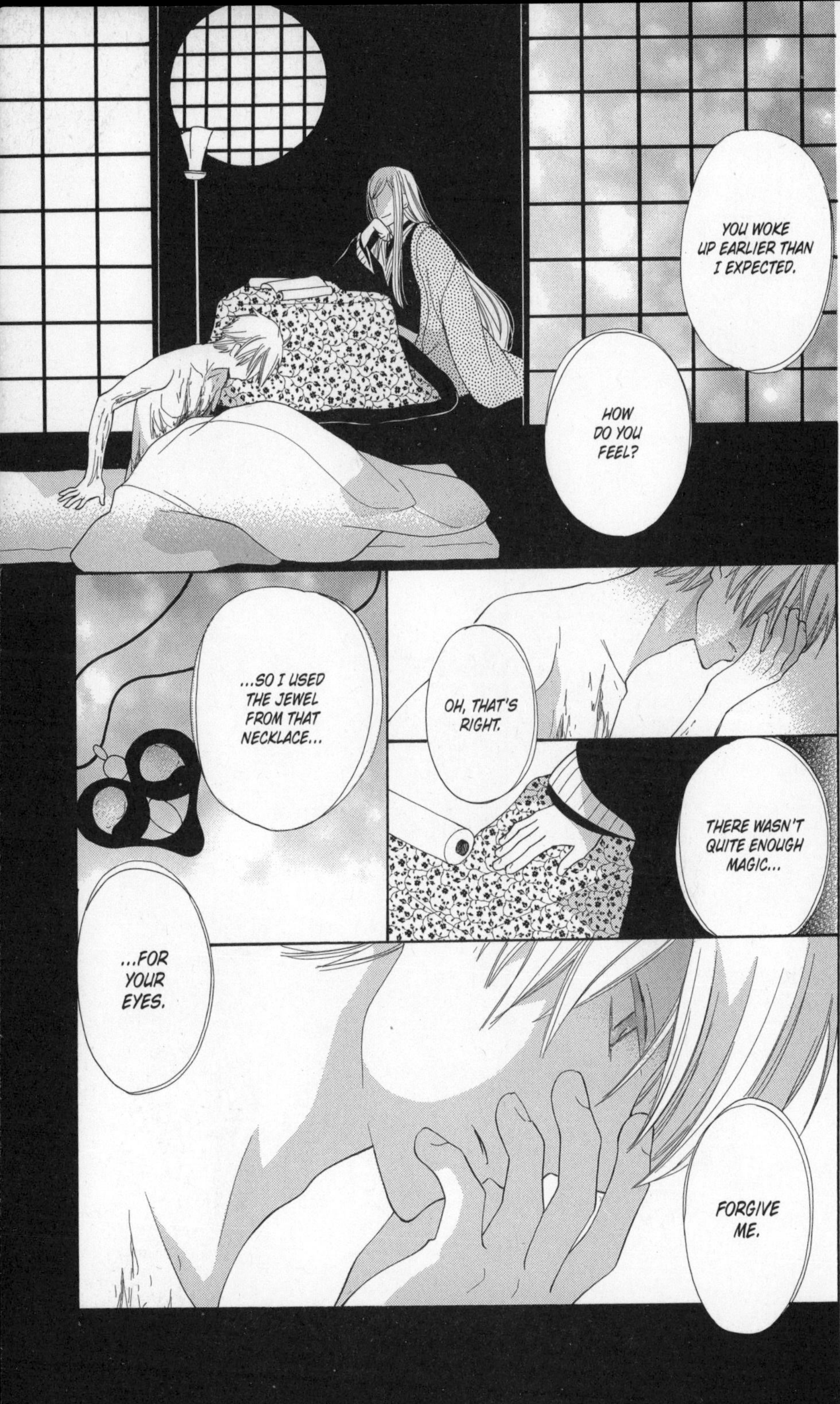
YOU WOKE UP EARLIER THAN I EXPECTED.
HOW DO YOU FEEL?
OH, THAT'S RIGHT.
THERE WASN'T QUITE ENOUGH MAGIC...
...SO I USED THE JEWEL FROM THAT NECKLACE...
...FOR YOUR EYES.
FORGIVE ME.

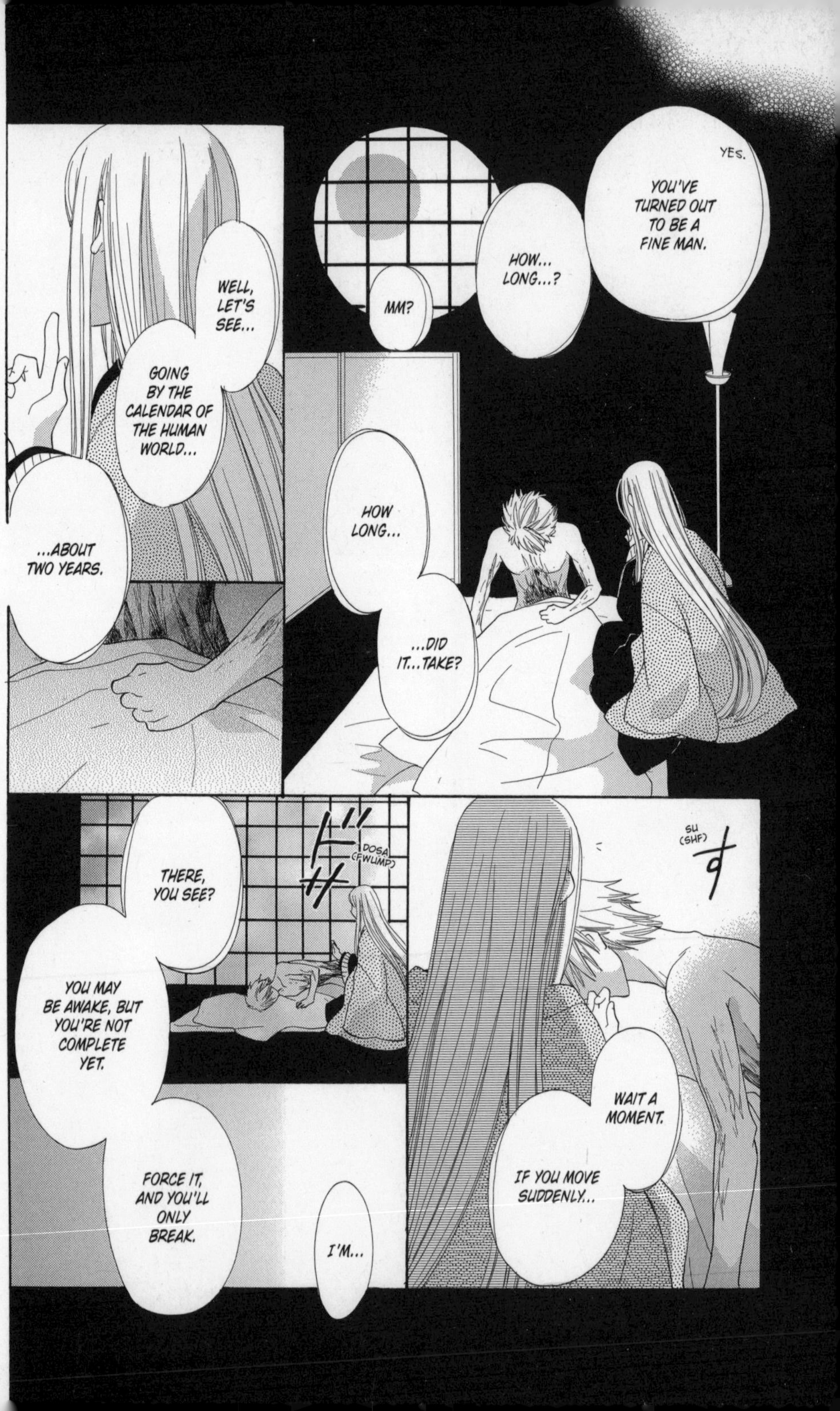
YES.
YOU'VE TURNED OUT TO BE A FINE MAN.
HOW... LONG...?
MM?
HOW LONG...
...DID IT...TAKE?
WELL, LET'S SEE...
GOING BY THE CALENDAR OF THE HUMAN WORLD...
...ABOUT TWO YEARS.
SU (SHF)
WAIT A MOMENT.
IF YOU MOVE SUDDENLY...
I'M...
DOSA (FWUMP)
THERE, YOU SEE?
YOU MAY BE AWAKE, BUT YOU'RE NOT COMPLETE YET.
FORCE IT, AND YOU'LL ONLY BREAK.

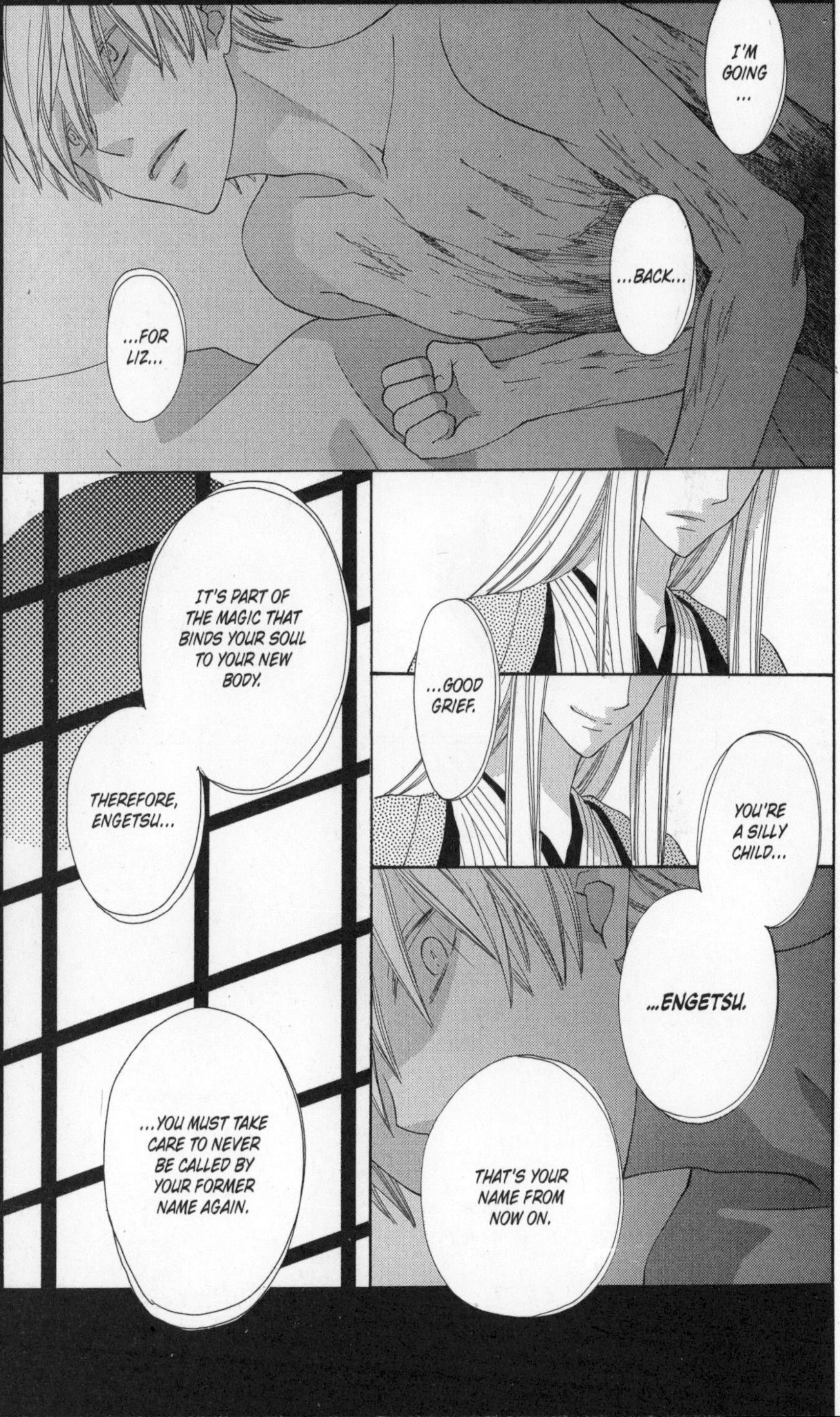
I'M GOING ...
...BACK...
...FOR LIZ...
...GOOD GRIEF.
YOU'RE A SILLY CHILD...
...ENGETSU.
THAT'S YOUR NAME FROM NOW ON.
IT'S PART OF THE MAGIC THAT BINDS YOUR SOUL TO YOUR NEW BODY.
THEREFORE, ENGETSU...
...YOU MUST TAKE CARE TO NEVER BE CALLED BY YOUR FORMER NAME AGAIN.

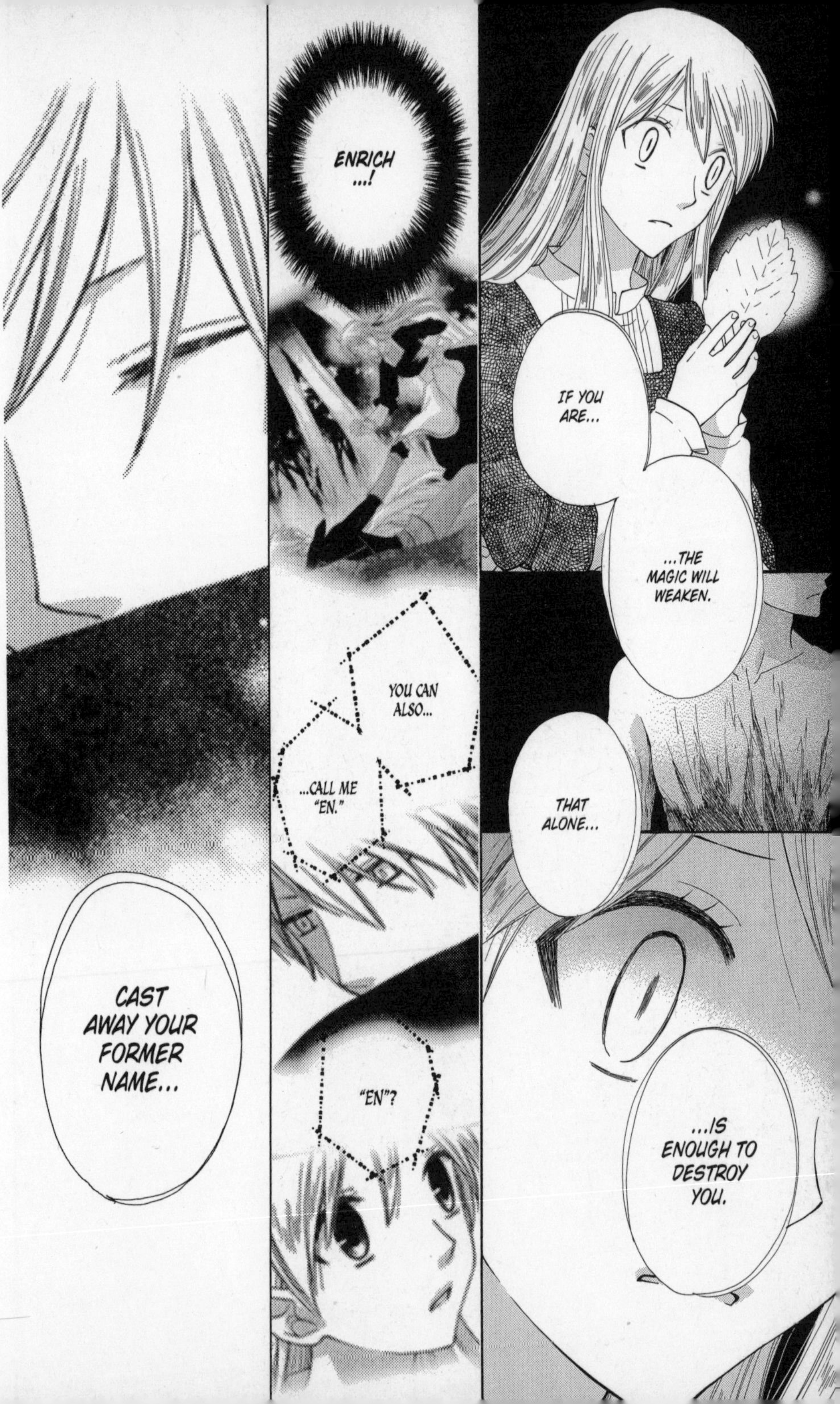
IF YOU ARE...
...THE MAGIC WILL WEAKEN.
THAT ALONE...
...IS ENOUGH TO DESTROY YOU.
ENRICH ...!
YOU CAN ALSO...
...CALL ME "EN."
"EN"?
CAST AWAY YOUR FORMER NAME...

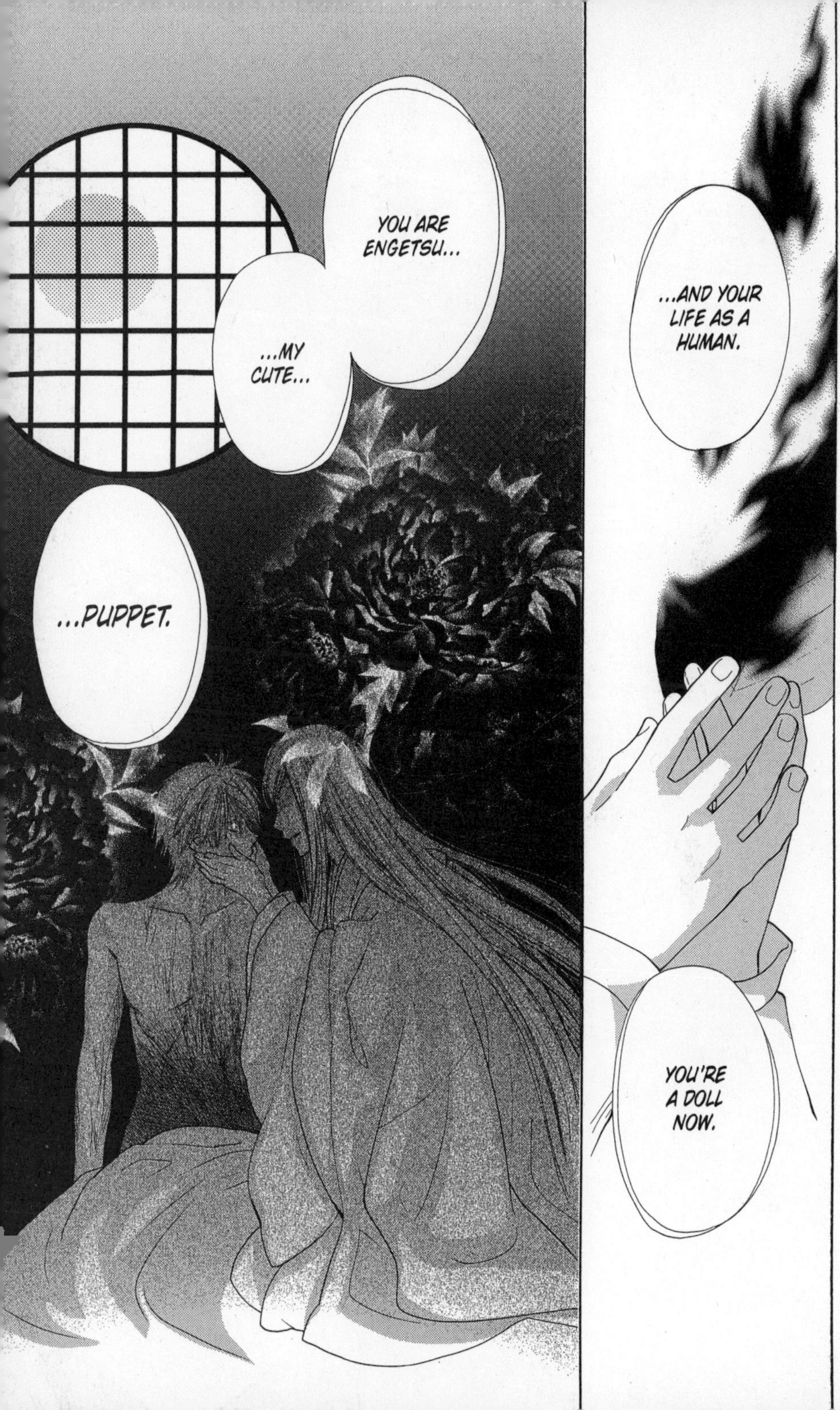
...AND YOUR LIFE AS A HUMAN.
YOU'RE A DOLL NOW.
YOU ARE ENGETSU...
...MY CUTE...
...PUPPET.

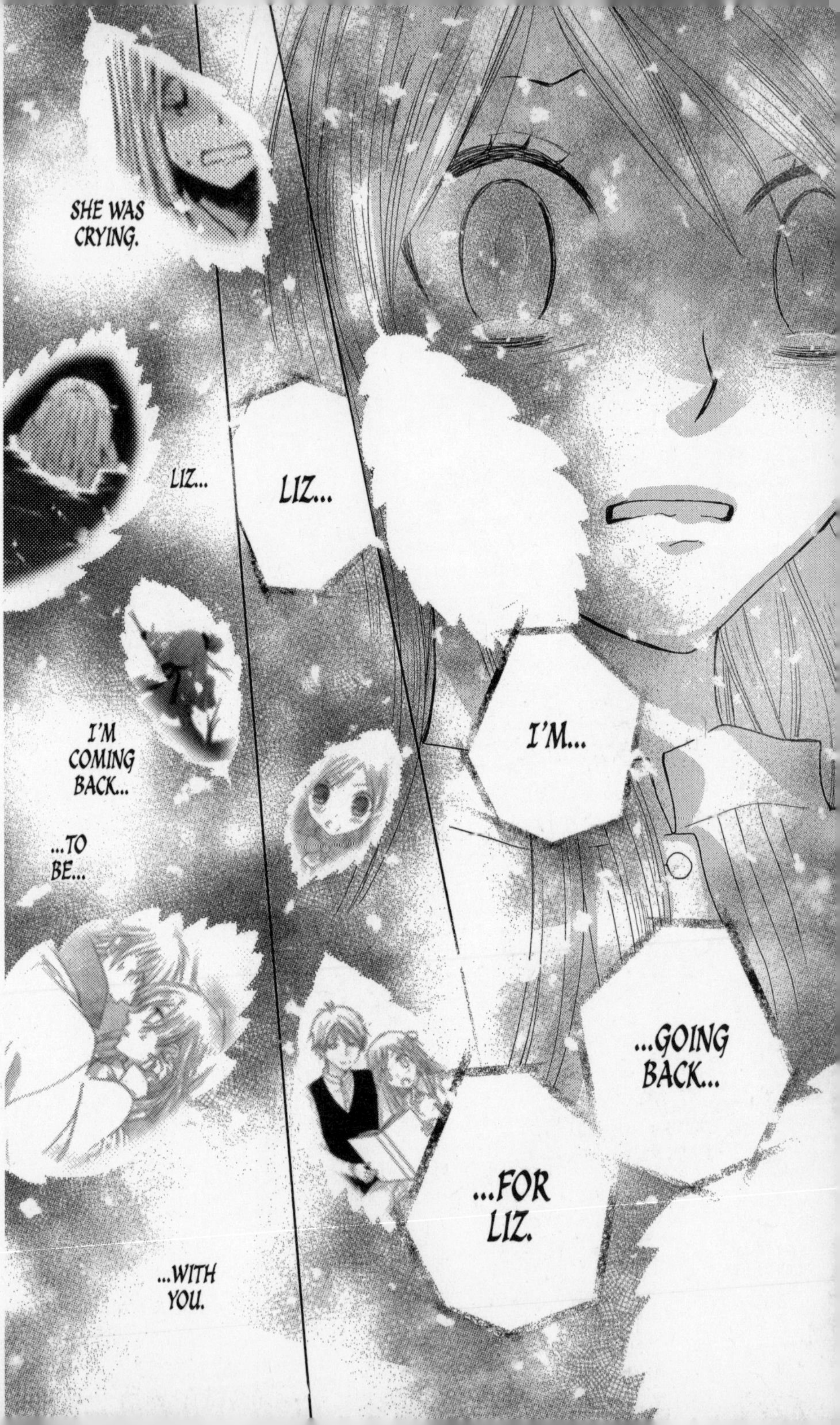
I'M...
...GOING BACK...
...FOR LIZ.
LIZ...
SHE WAS CRYING.
LIZ...
I'M COMING BACK...
...TO BE...
...WITH YOU.

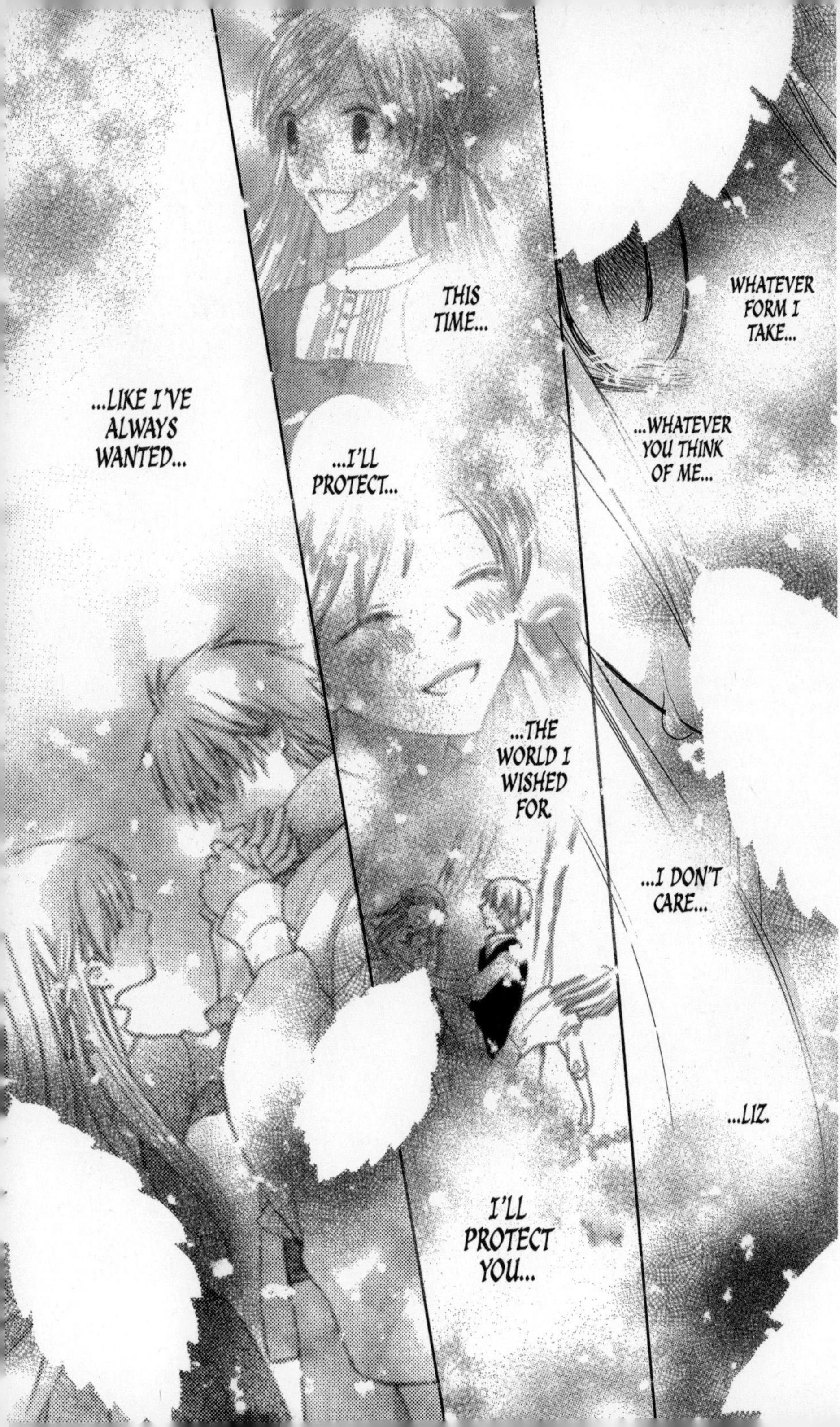
WHATEVER FORM I TAKE...
...WHATEVER YOU THINK OF ME...
...I DON'T CARE...
...LIZ.
THIS TIME...
...I'LL PROTECT...
...THE WORLD I WISHED FOR.
I'LL PROTECT YOU...
...LIKE I'VE ALWAYS WANTED...

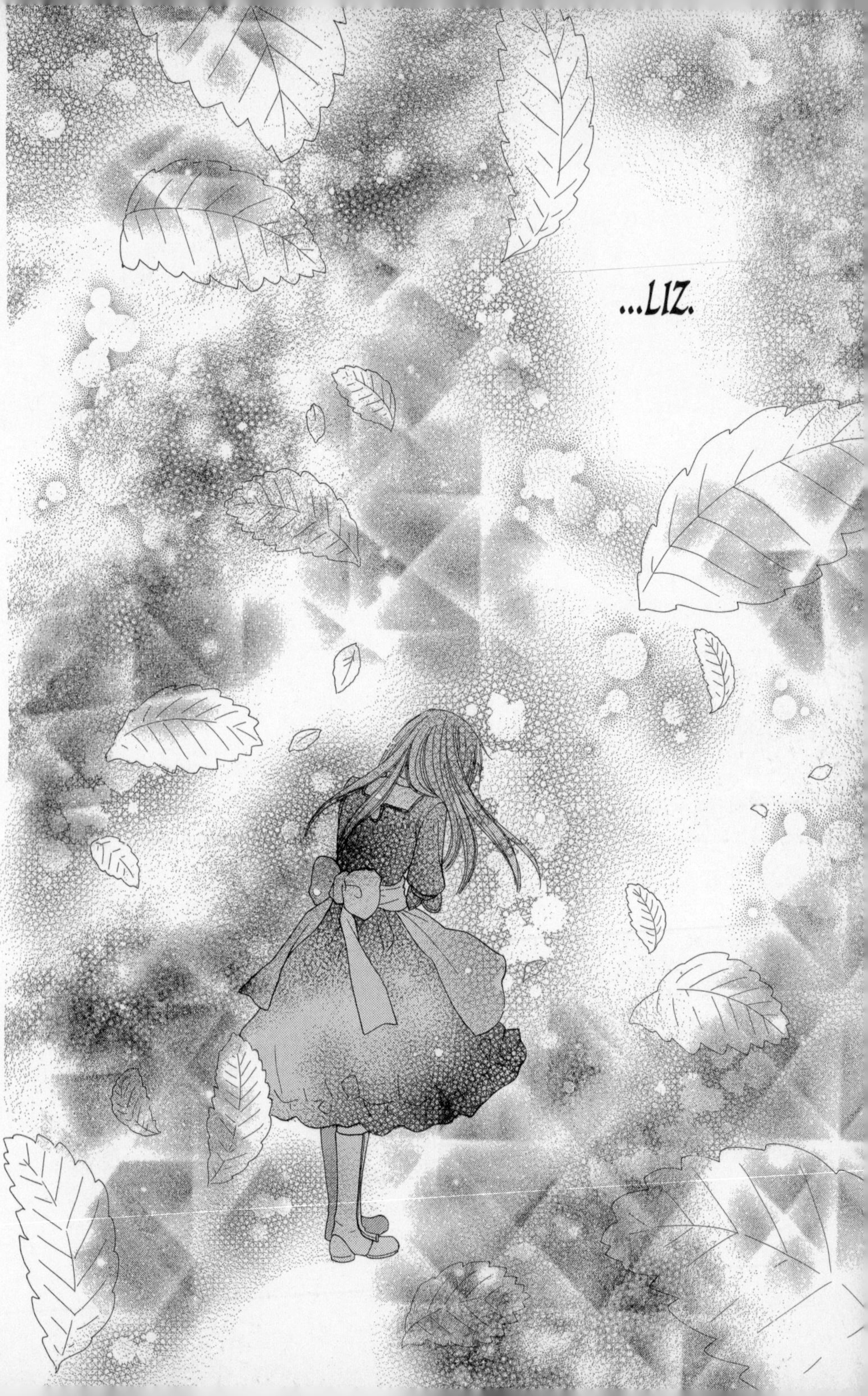
...LIZ.

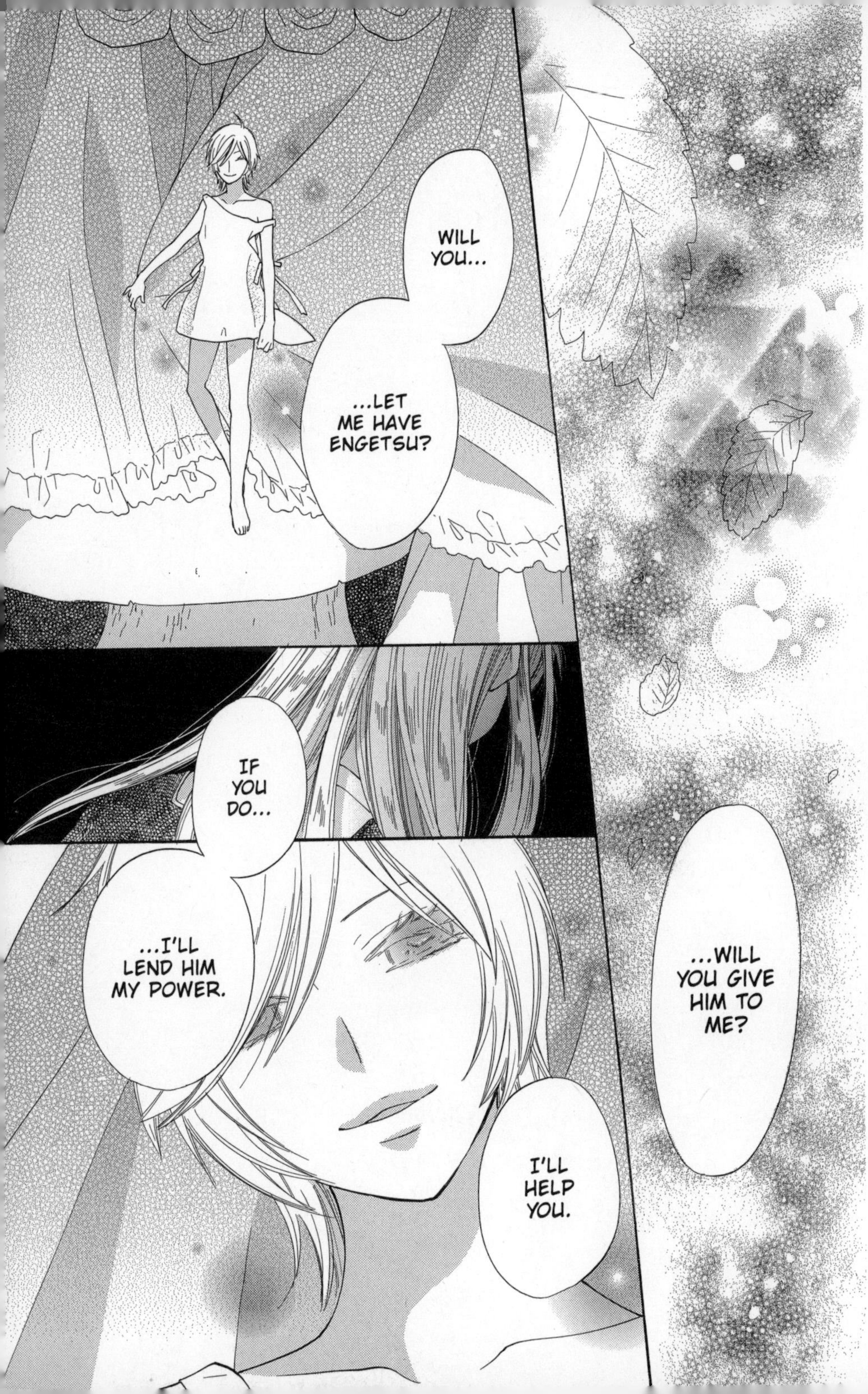
WILL YOU...
...LET ME HAVE ENGETSU?
IF YOU DO...
...I'LL LEND HIM MY POWER.
...WILL YOU GIVE HIM TO ME?
I'LL HELP YOU.

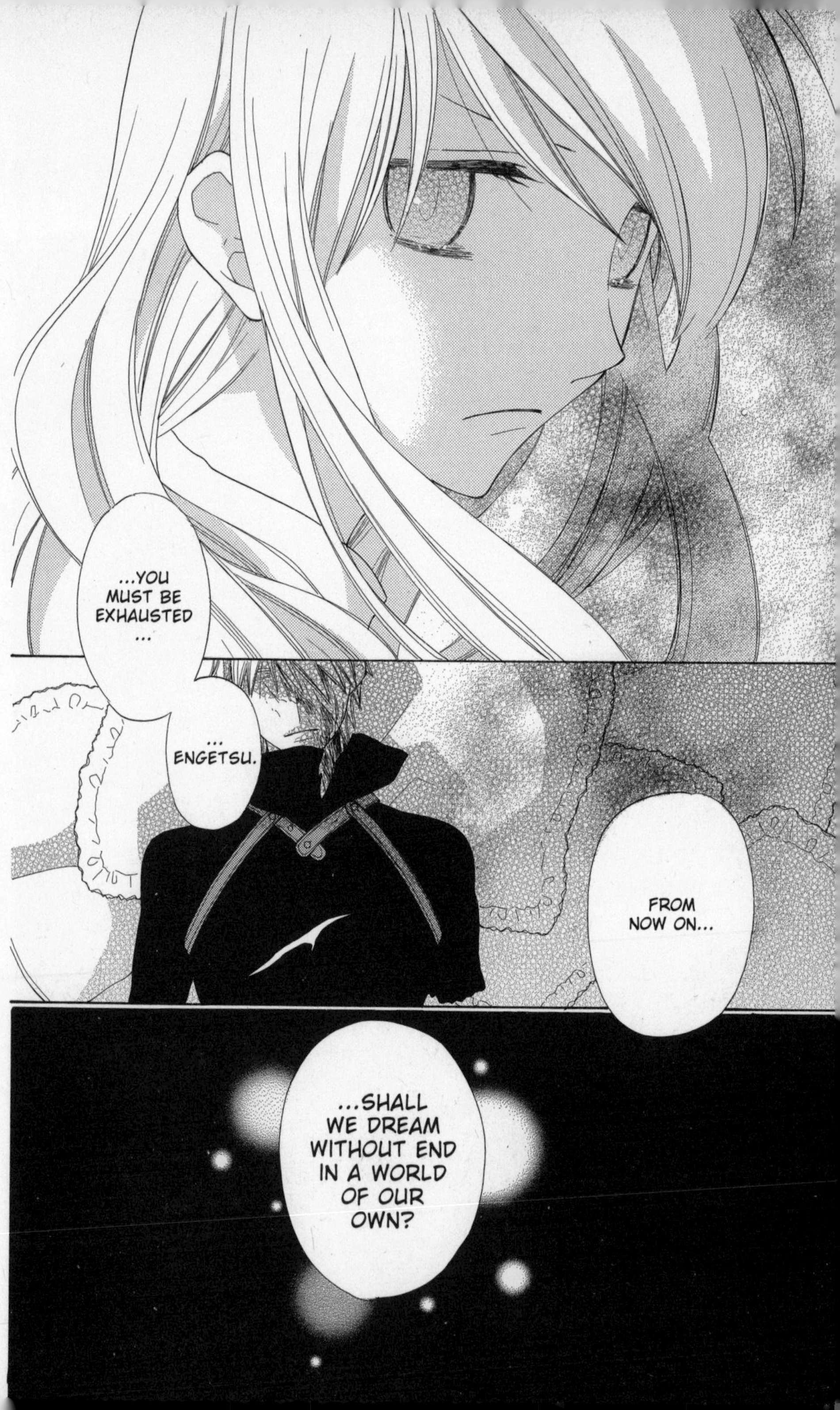
...YOU MUST BE EXHAUSTED ...
... ENGETSU.
FROM NOW ON...
...SHALL WE DREAM WITHOUT END IN A WORLD OF OUR OWN?

Chapter 13

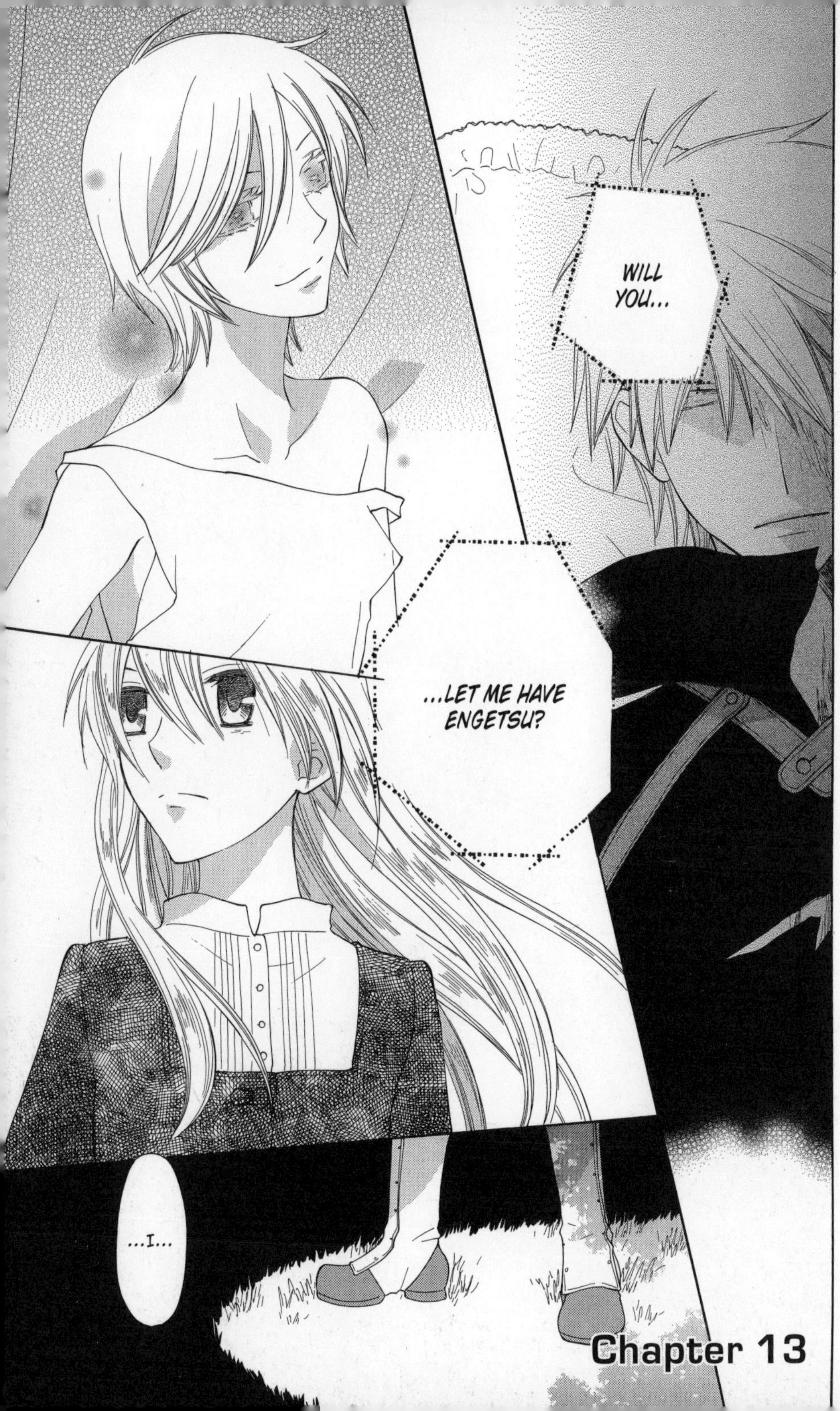
WILL YOU...
...LET ME HAVE ENGETSU?
...I...

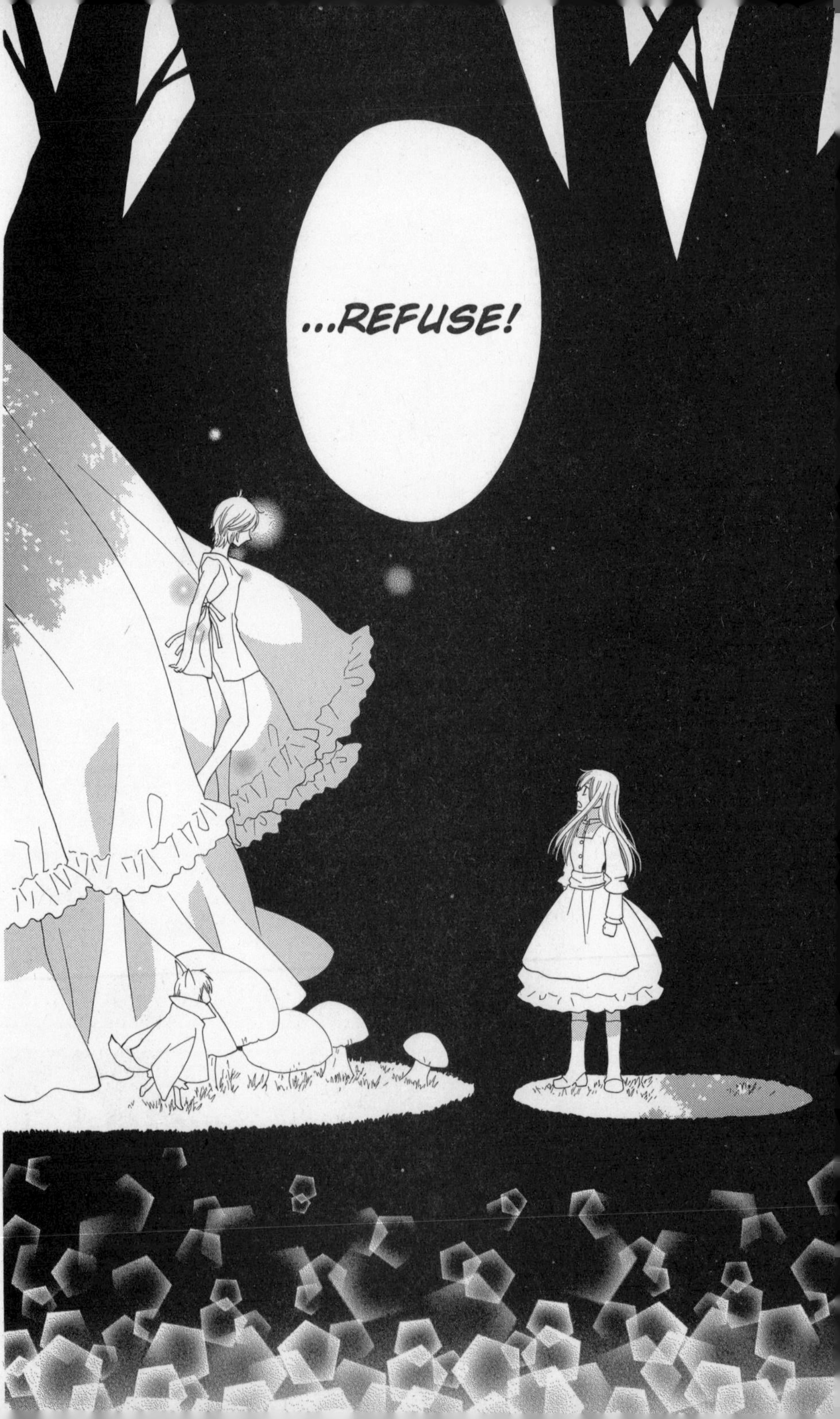
...REFUSE!

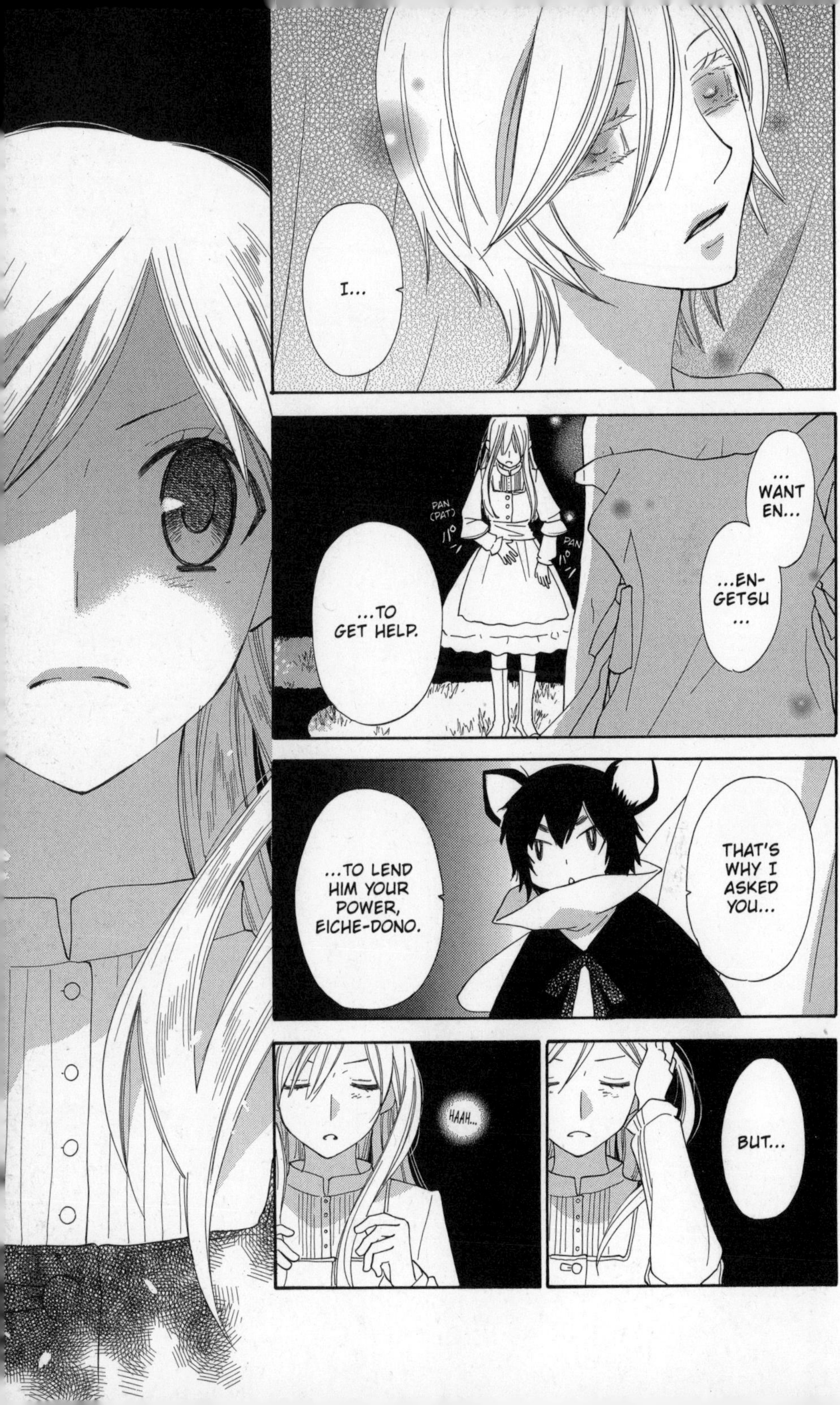
I...
...WANT EN...
...EN-GETSU...
PAN
PAN (PAT)
...TO GET HELP.
THAT'S WHY I ASKED YOU...
...TO LEND HIM YOUR POWER, EICHE-DONO.
BUT...
HAAH...

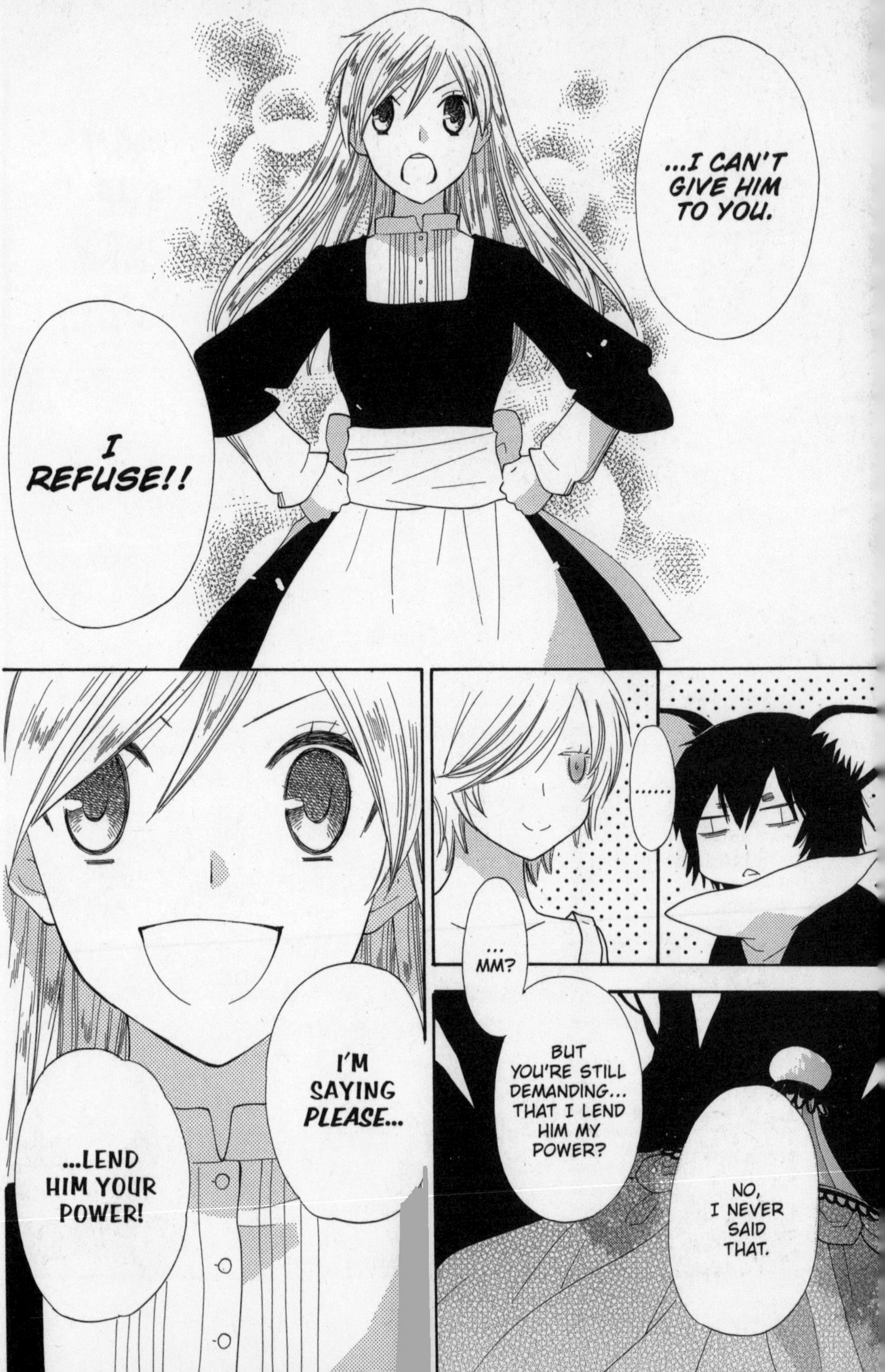
...I CAN'T GIVE HIM TO YOU.
I REFUSE!!
......
... MM?
BUT YOU'RE STILL DEMANDING... THAT I LEND HIM MY POWER?
NO, I NEVER SAID THAT.
I'M SAYING *PLEASE*...
...LEND HIM YOUR POWER!

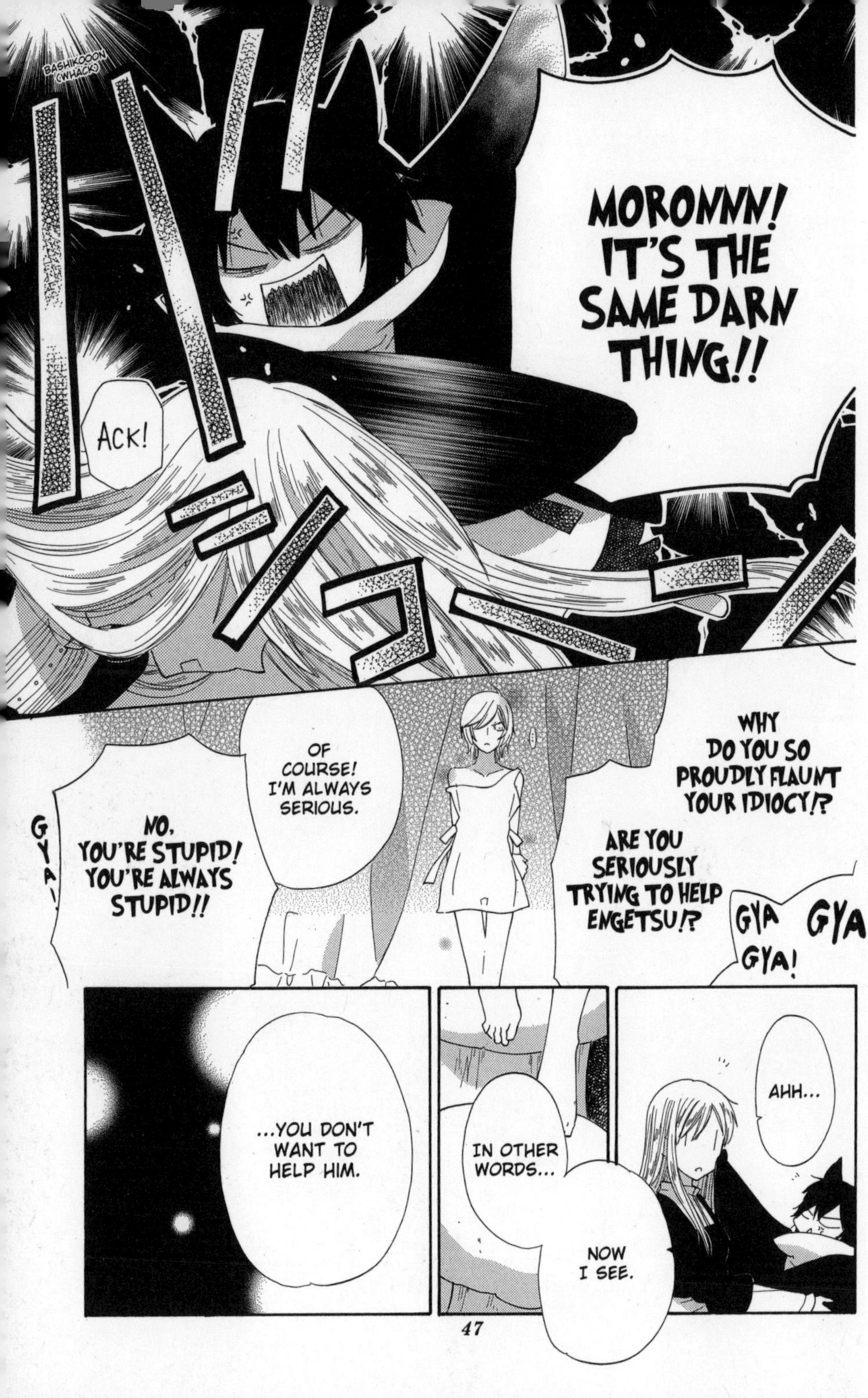
MORONNN! IT'S THE SAME DARN THING!!
BASHIKOOON (WHACK)
ACK!
WHY DO YOU SO PROUDLY FLAUNT YOUR IDIOCY!?
ARE YOU SERIOUSLY TRYING TO HELP ENGETSU!?
GYA GYA GYA!
OF COURSE! I'M ALWAYS SERIOUS.
NO. YOU'RE STUPID! YOU'RE ALWAYS STUPID!!
GYA!
AHH...
NOW I SEE.
IN OTHER WORDS...
...YOU DON'T WANT TO HELP HIM.

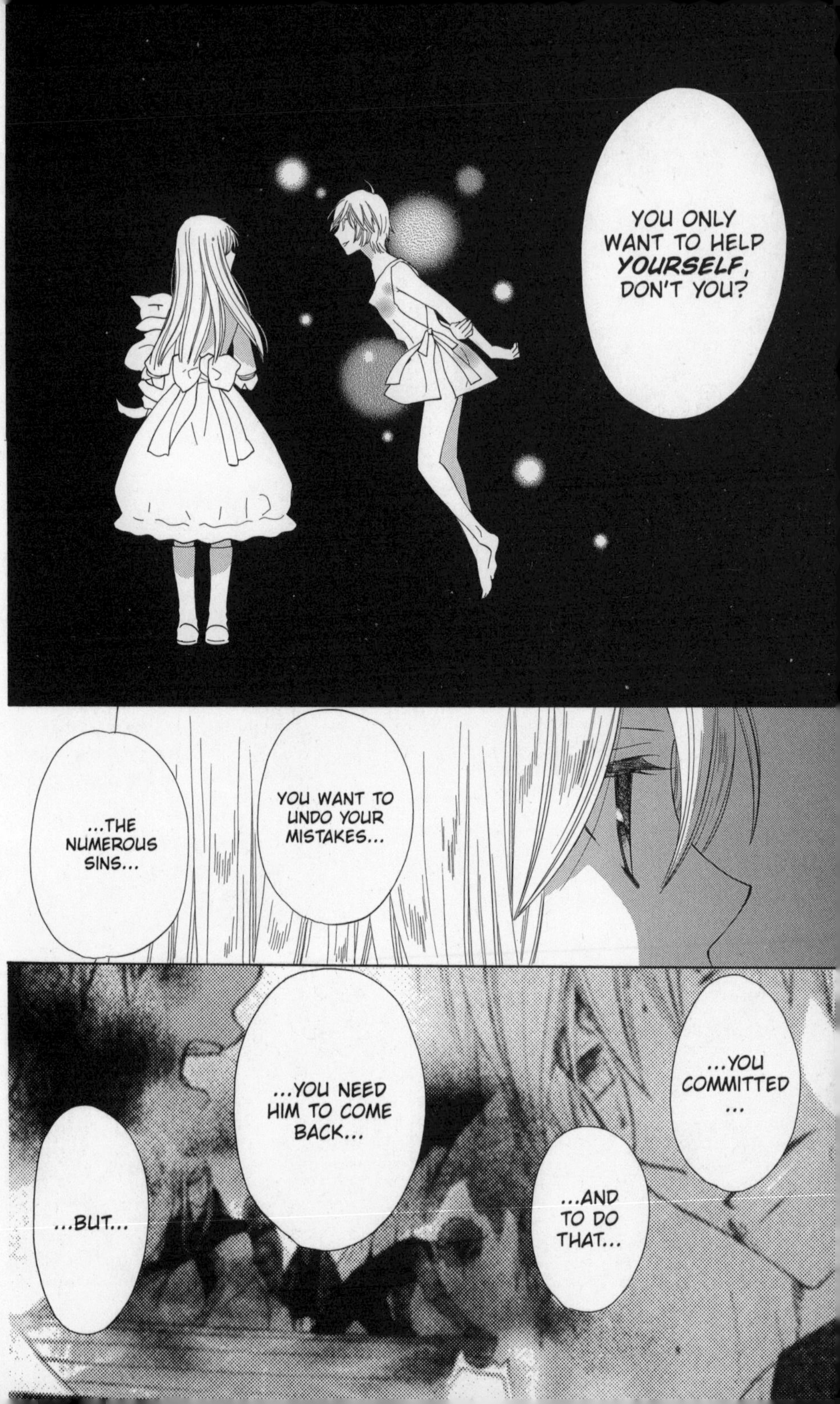
YOU ONLY WANT TO HELP *YOURSELF*, DON'T YOU?
YOU WANT TO UNDO YOUR MISTAKES...
...THE NUMEROUS SINS...
...YOU COMMITTED...
...AND TO DO THAT...
...YOU NEED HIM TO COME BACK...
...BUT...

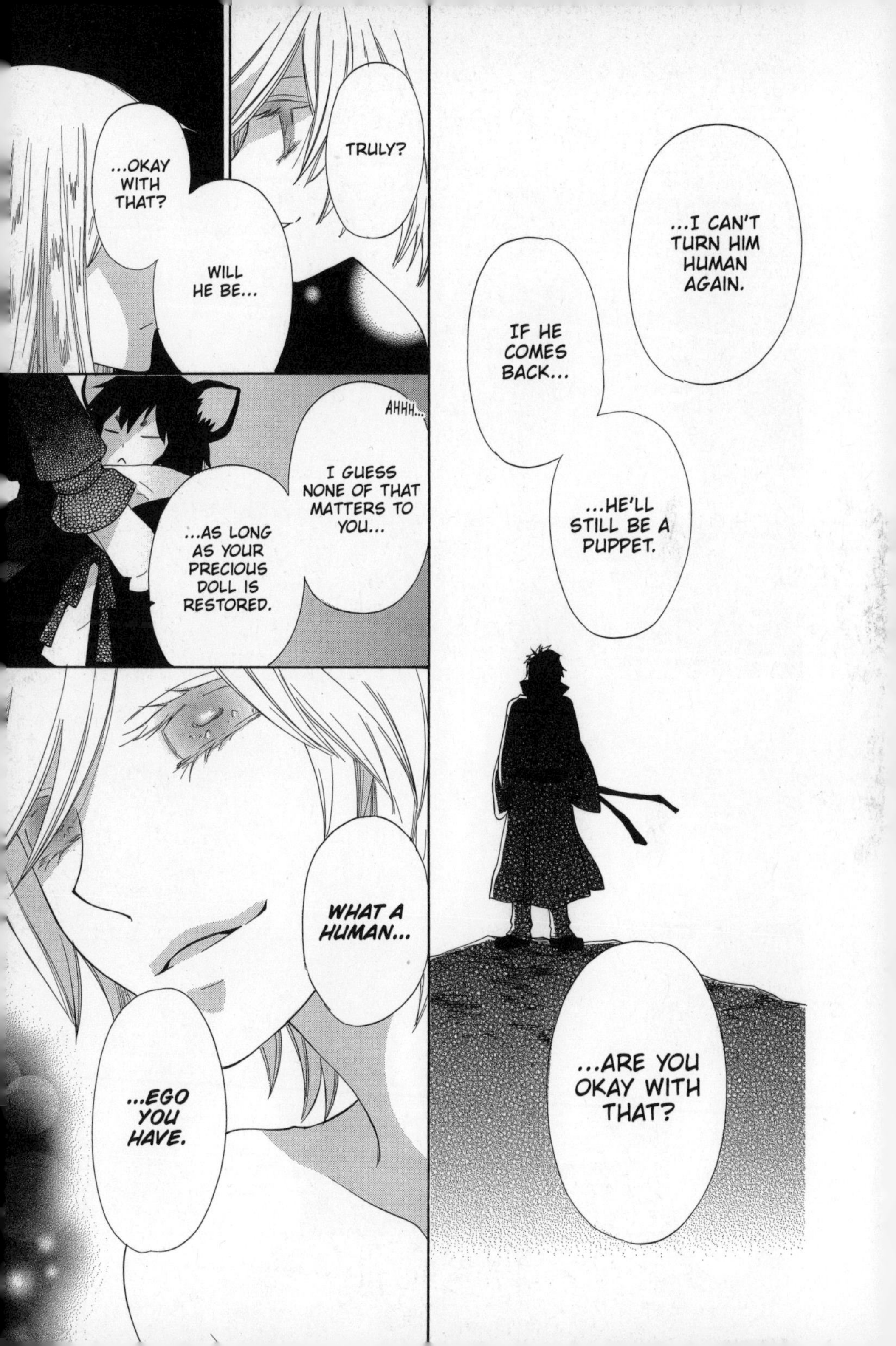
...I CAN'T TURN HIM HUMAN AGAIN.
IF HE COMES BACK...
...HE'LL STILL BE A PUPPET.
...ARE YOU OKAY WITH THAT?
TRULY?
WILL HE BE...
...OKAY WITH THAT?
AHHH...
I GUESS NONE OF THAT MATTERS TO YOU...
...AS LONG AS YOUR PRECIOUS DOLL IS RESTORED.
WHAT A HUMAN...
...EGO YOU HAVE.

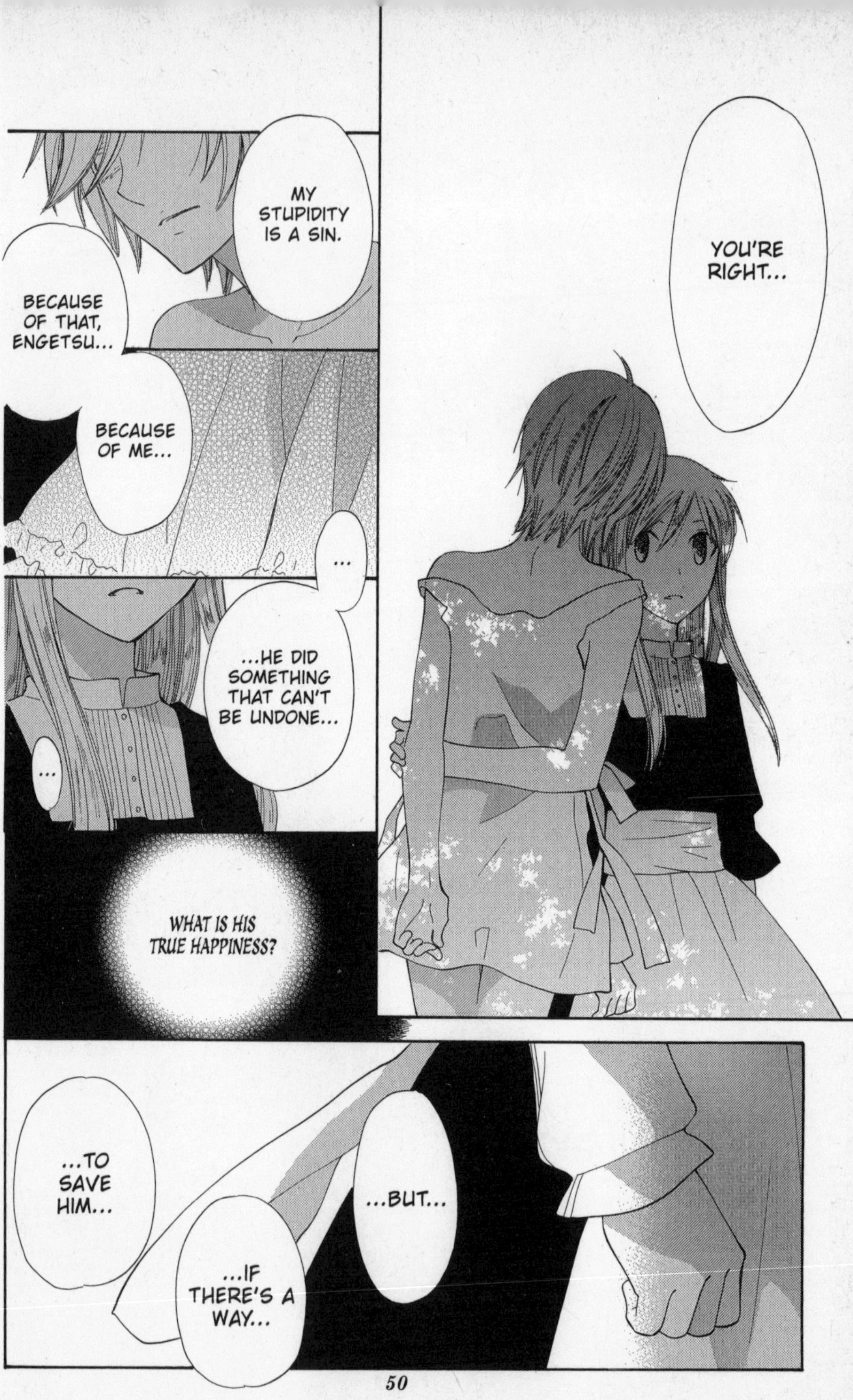
YOU'RE RIGHT...
MY STUPIDITY IS A SIN.
BECAUSE OF THAT, ENGETSU...
BECAUSE OF ME...
...
...HE DID SOMETHING THAT CAN'T BE UNDONE...
...
WHAT IS HIS TRUE HAPPINESS?
...BUT...
...IF THERE'S A WAY...
...TO SAVE HIM...

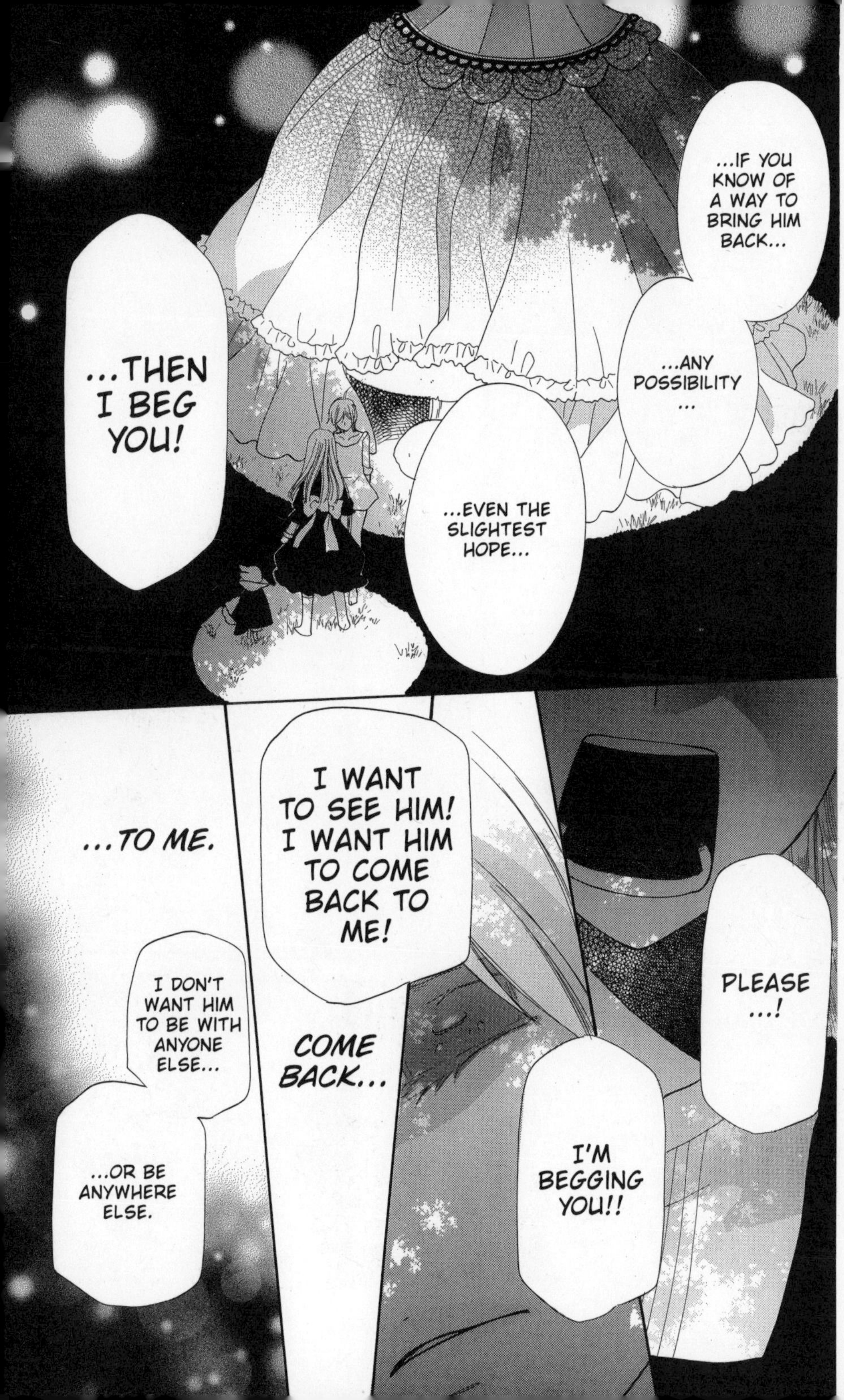
...IF YOU KNOW OF A WAY TO BRING HIM BACK...
...ANY POSSIBILITY...
...EVEN THE SLIGHTEST HOPE...
...THEN I BEG YOU!
PLEASE...!
I'M BEGGING YOU!!
I WANT TO SEE HIM! I WANT HIM TO COME BACK TO ME!
COME BACK...
...TO ME.
I DON'T WANT HIM TO BE WITH ANYONE ELSE...
...OR BE ANYWHERE ELSE.

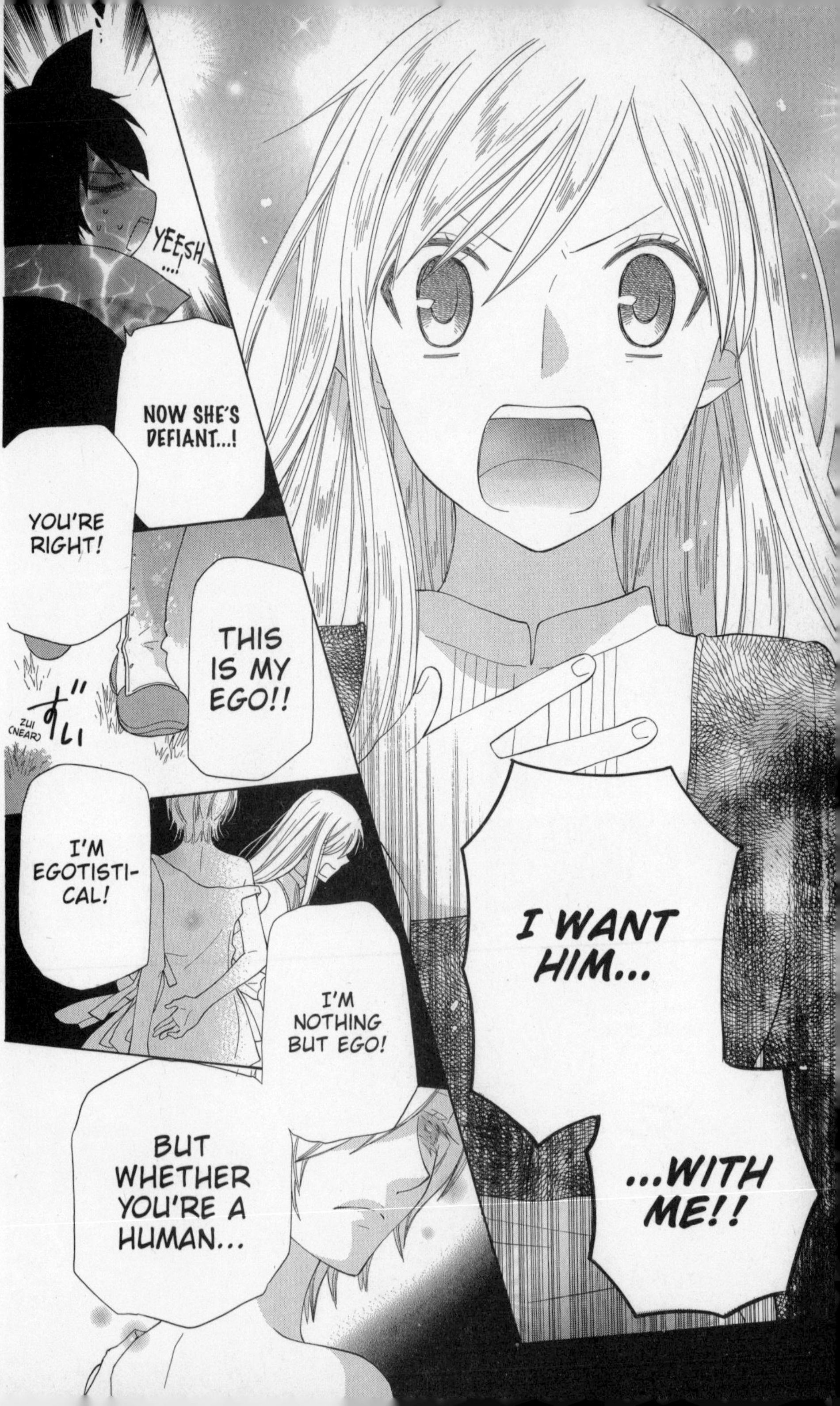
I WANT HIM...
...WITH ME!!
YEESH ...!
NOW SHE'S DEFIANT...!
YOU'RE RIGHT!
THIS IS MY EGO!!
ZUI (NEAR)
I'M EGOTISTICAL!
I'M NOTHING BUT EGO!
BUT WHETHER YOU'RE A HUMAN...

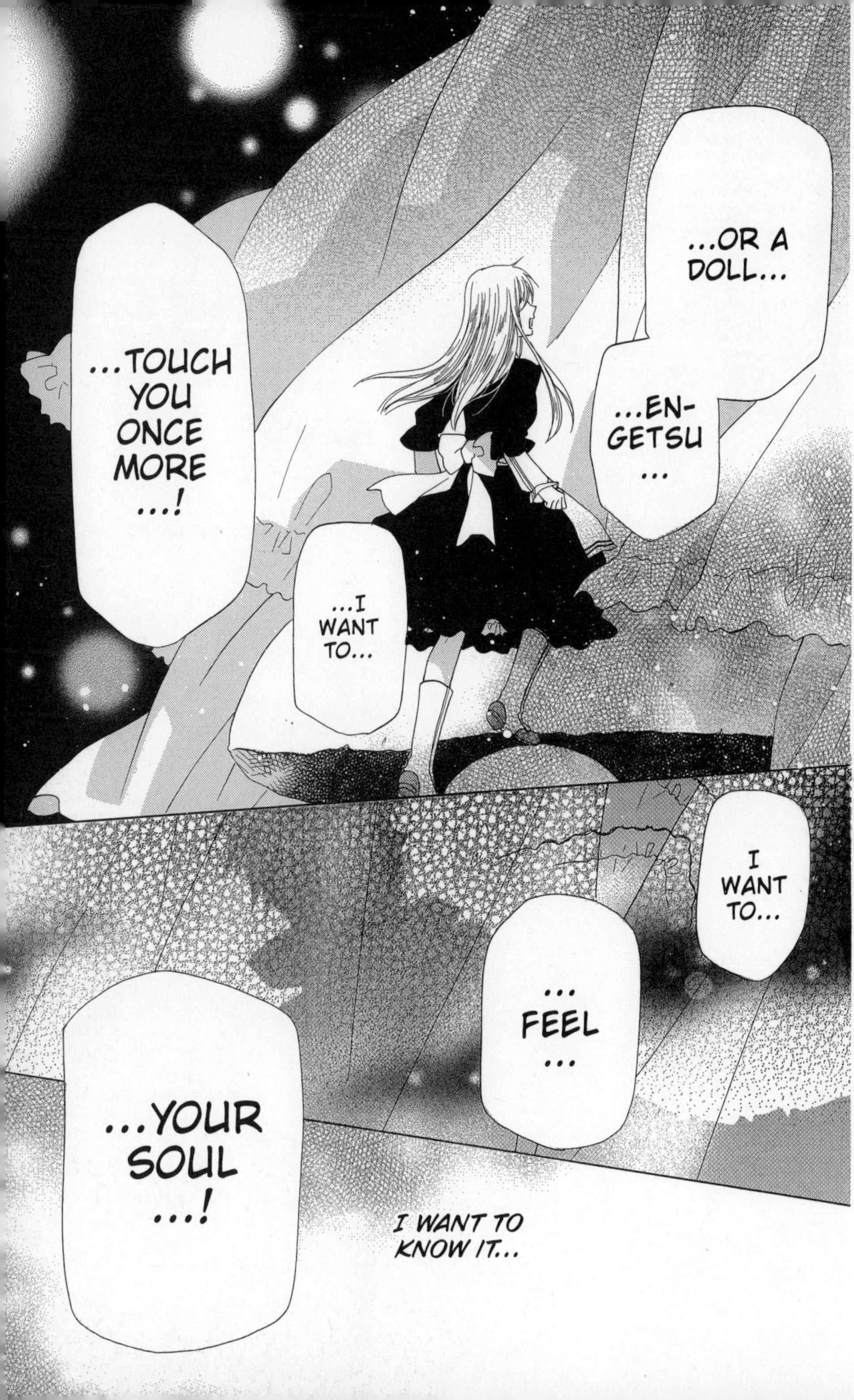
...OR A DOLL...
...EN-GETSU...
...I WANT TO...
...TOUCH YOU ONCE MORE...!
I WANT TO...
...FEEL...
...YOUR SOUL...!
I WANT TO KNOW IT...

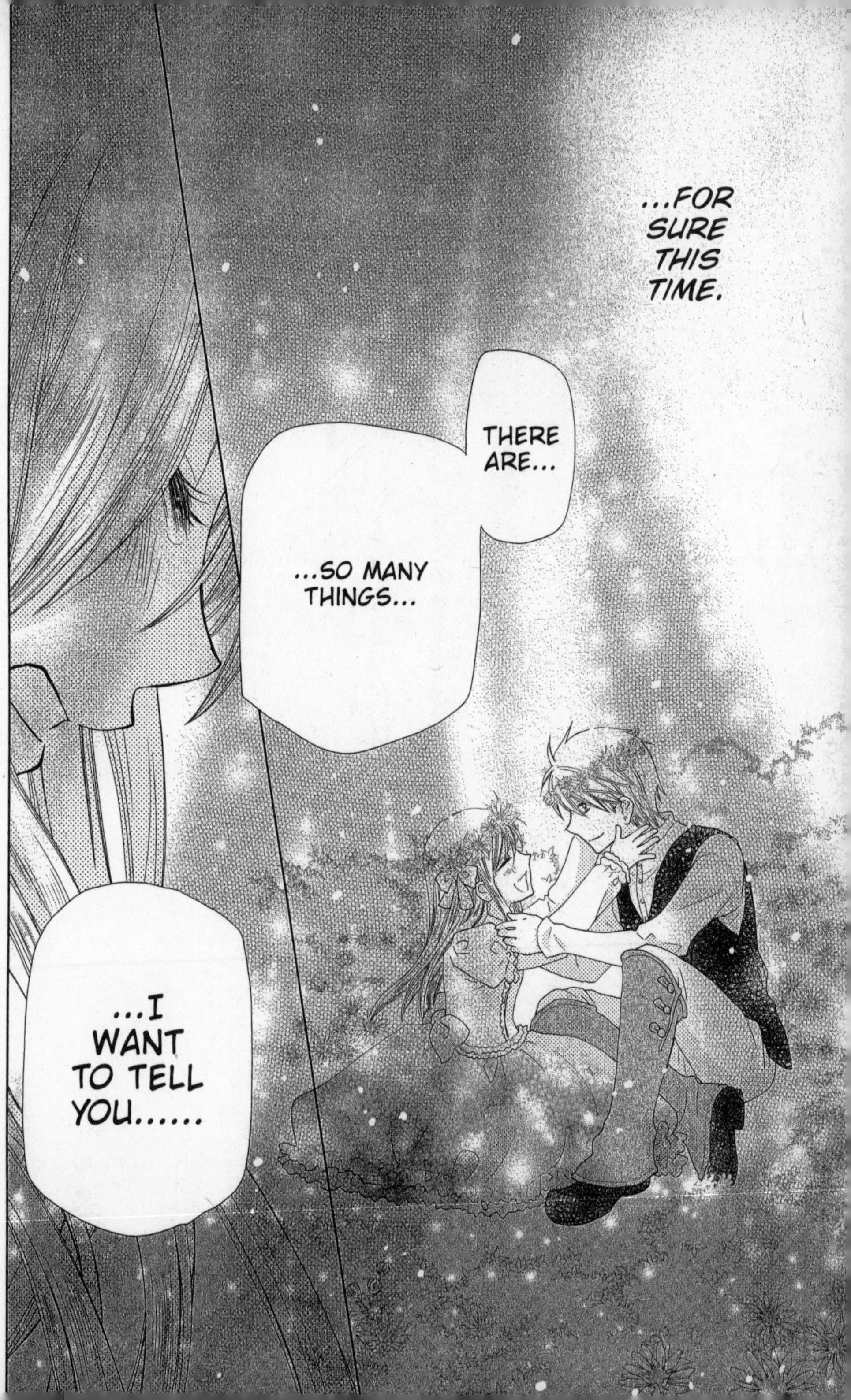
...FOR SURE THIS TIME.
THERE ARE...
...SO MANY THINGS...
...I WANT TO TELL YOU......

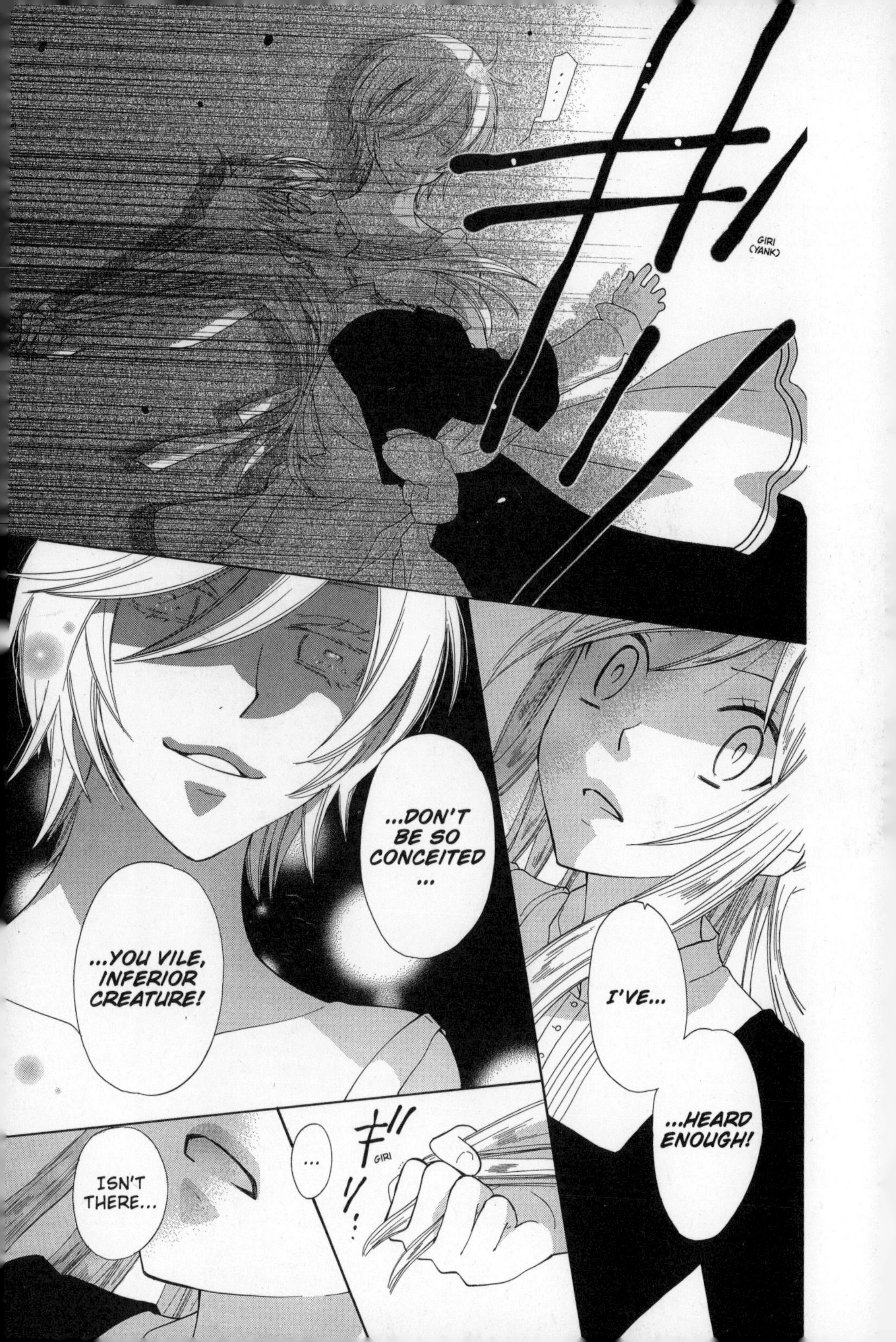
!...
GIRI (YANK)
I'VE...
...HEARD ENOUGH!
...DON'T BE SO CONCEITED ...
...YOU VILE, INFERIOR CREATURE!
GIRI
...
ISN'T THERE...

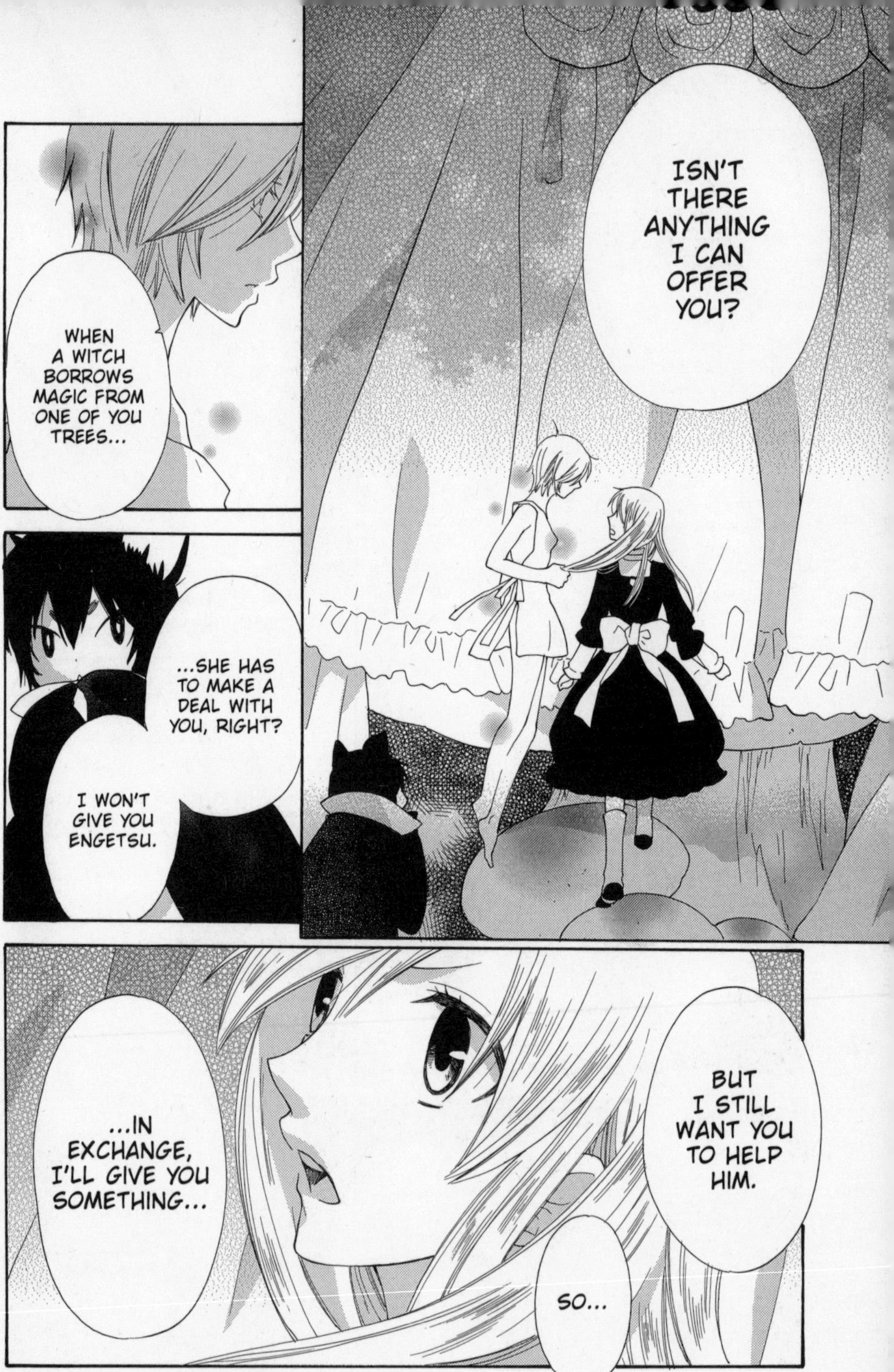
ISN'T THERE ANYTHING I CAN OFFER YOU?
WHEN A WITCH BORROWS MAGIC FROM ONE OF YOU TREES...
...SHE HAS TO MAKE A DEAL WITH YOU, RIGHT?
I WON'T GIVE YOU ENGETSU.
BUT I STILL WANT YOU TO HELP HIM.
SO...
...IN EXCHANGE, I'LL GIVE YOU SOMETHING...

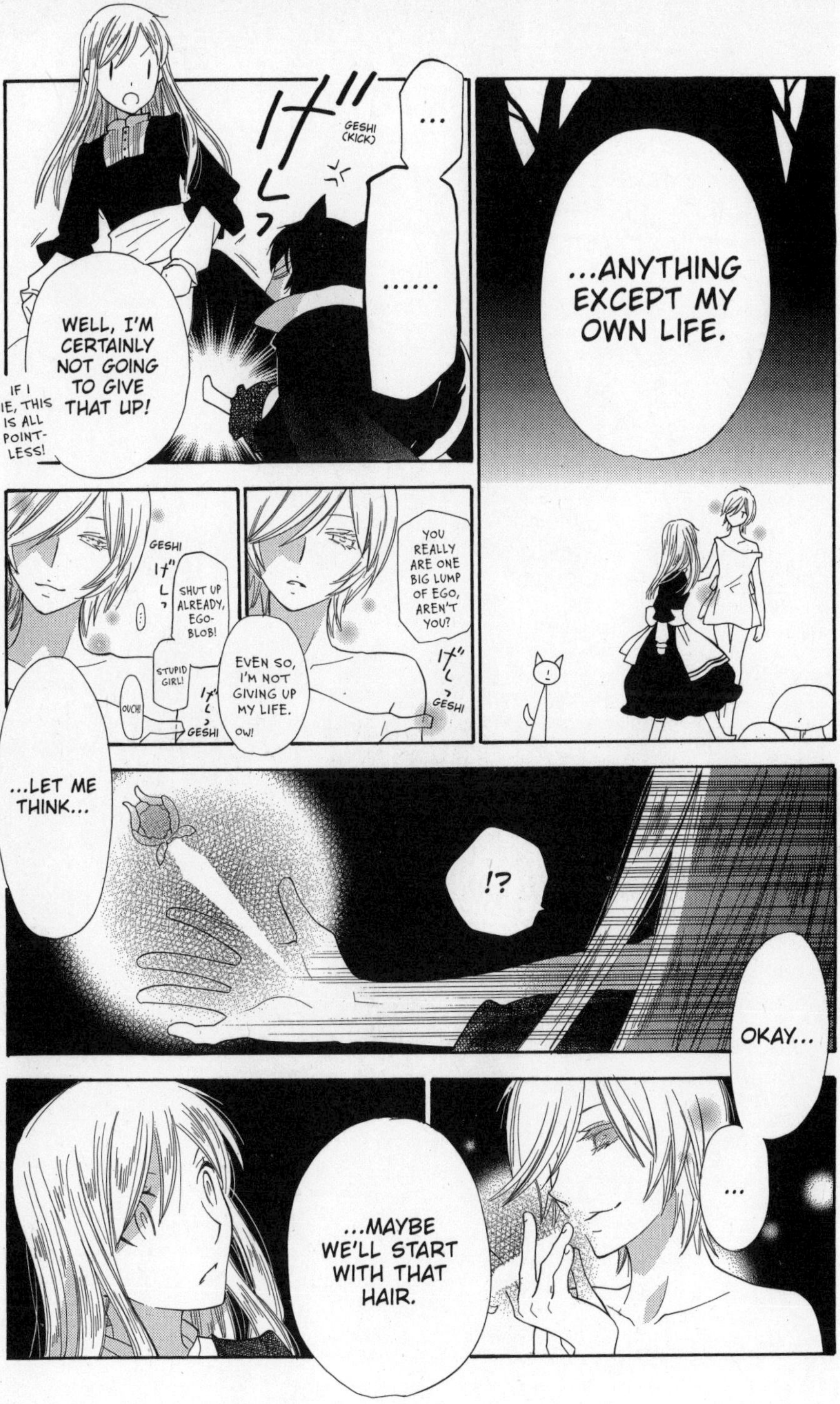
...ANYTHING EXCEPT MY OWN LIFE.
...
......
GESHI (KICK)
WELL, I'M CERTAINLY NOT GOING TO GIVE THAT UP!
IF I DIE, THIS IS ALL POINTLESS!
YOU REALLY ARE ONE BIG LUMP OF EGO, AREN'T YOU?
GESHI
EVEN SO, I'M NOT GIVING UP MY LIFE.
OW!
GESHI
SHUT UP ALREADY, EGO-BLOB!
...
GESHI
STUPID GIRL!
OUCH!
GESHI
...LET ME THINK...
!?
OKAY...
...
...MAYBE WE'LL START WITH THAT HAIR.

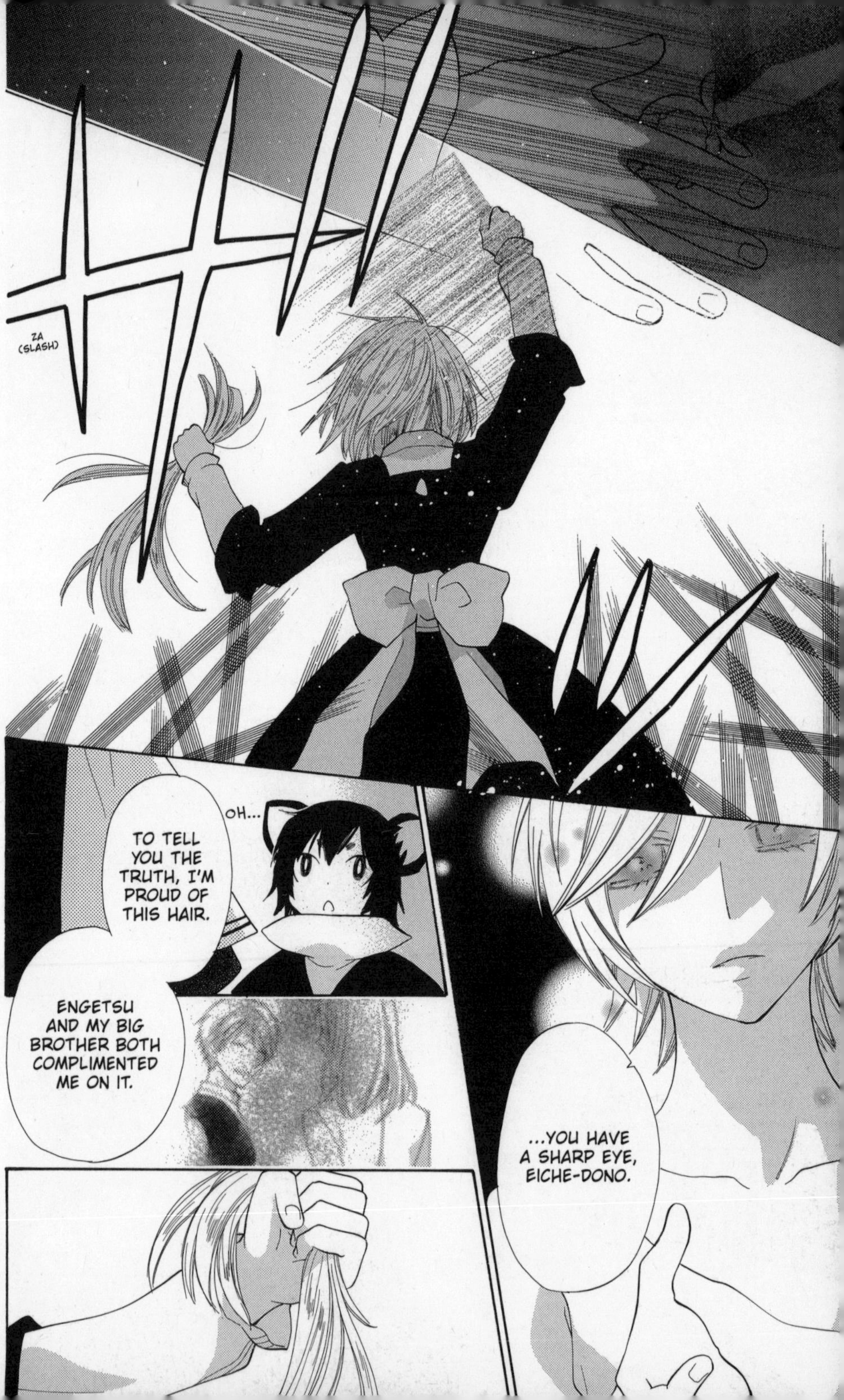
ZA (SLASH)
...YOU HAVE A SHARP EYE, EICHE-DONO.
TO TELL YOU THE TRUTH, I'M PROUD OF THIS HAIR.
OH...
ENGETSU AND MY BIG BROTHER BOTH COMPLIMENTED ME ON IT.

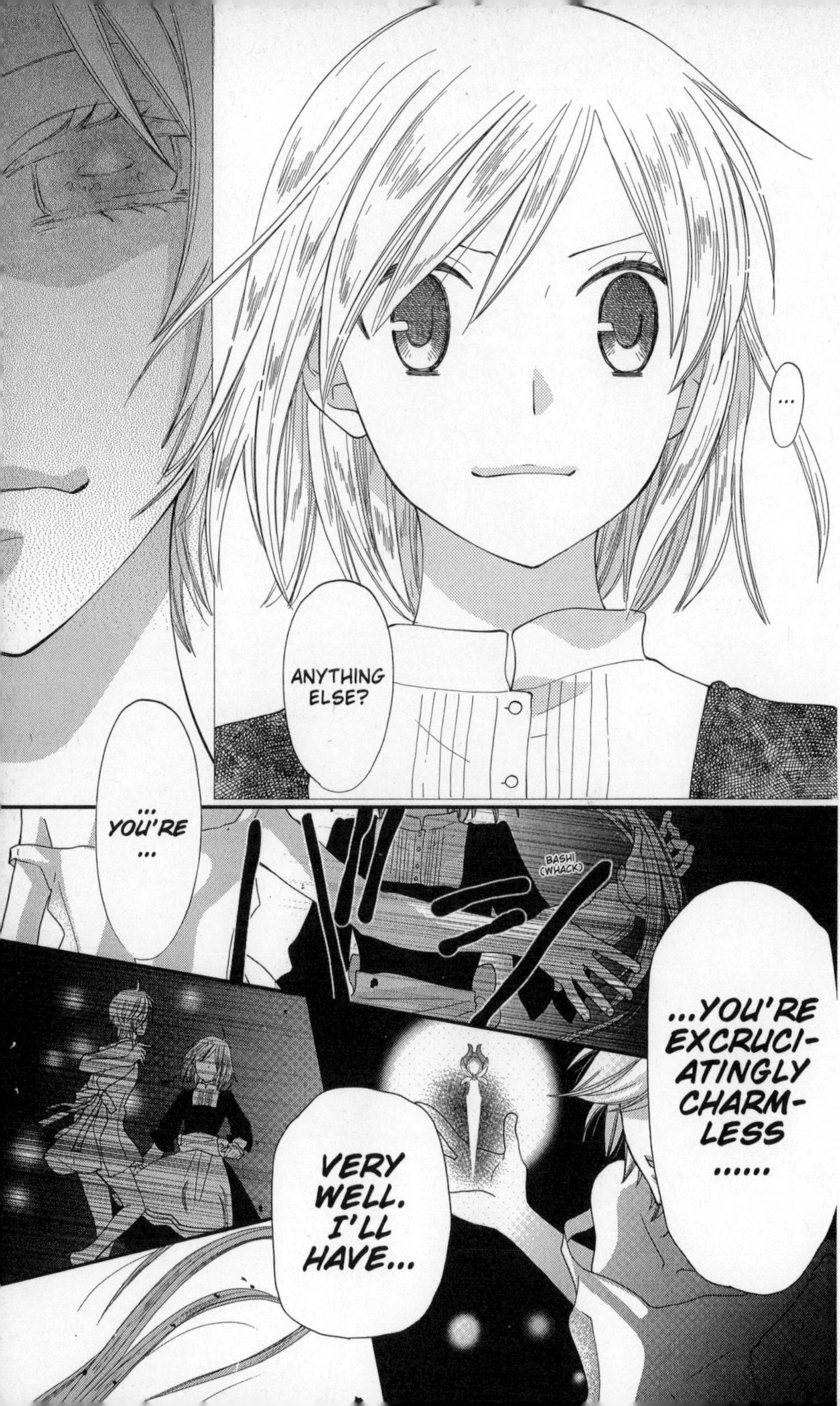
...
ANYTHING ELSE?
...YOU'RE ...
BASHI (WHACK)
...YOU'RE EXCRUCI-ATINGLY CHARM-LESS ......
VERY WELL. I'LL HAVE...

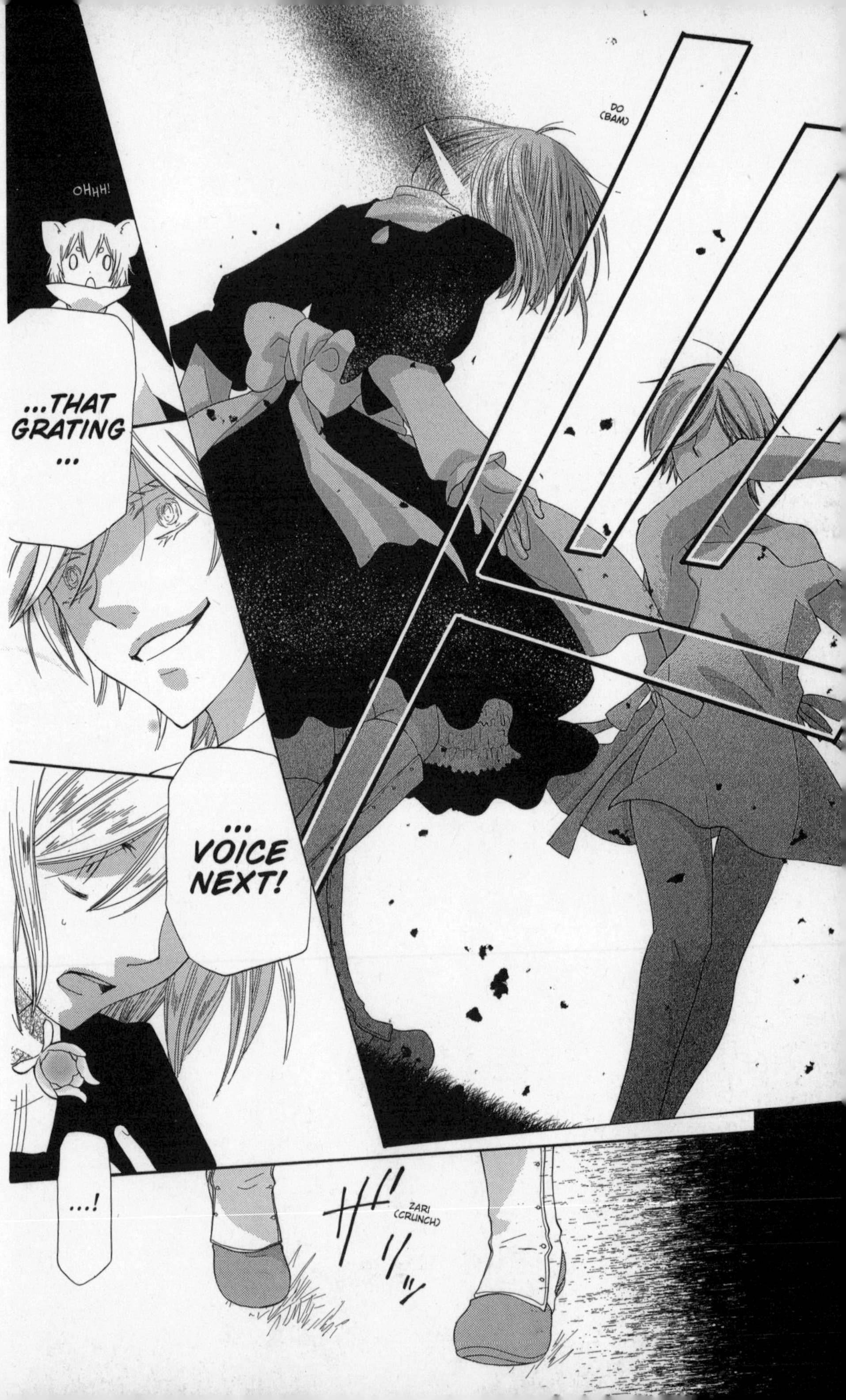
DO
(BAM)
OHHH!
...THAT GRATING ...
... VOICE NEXT!
ZARI
(CRUNCH)
...!

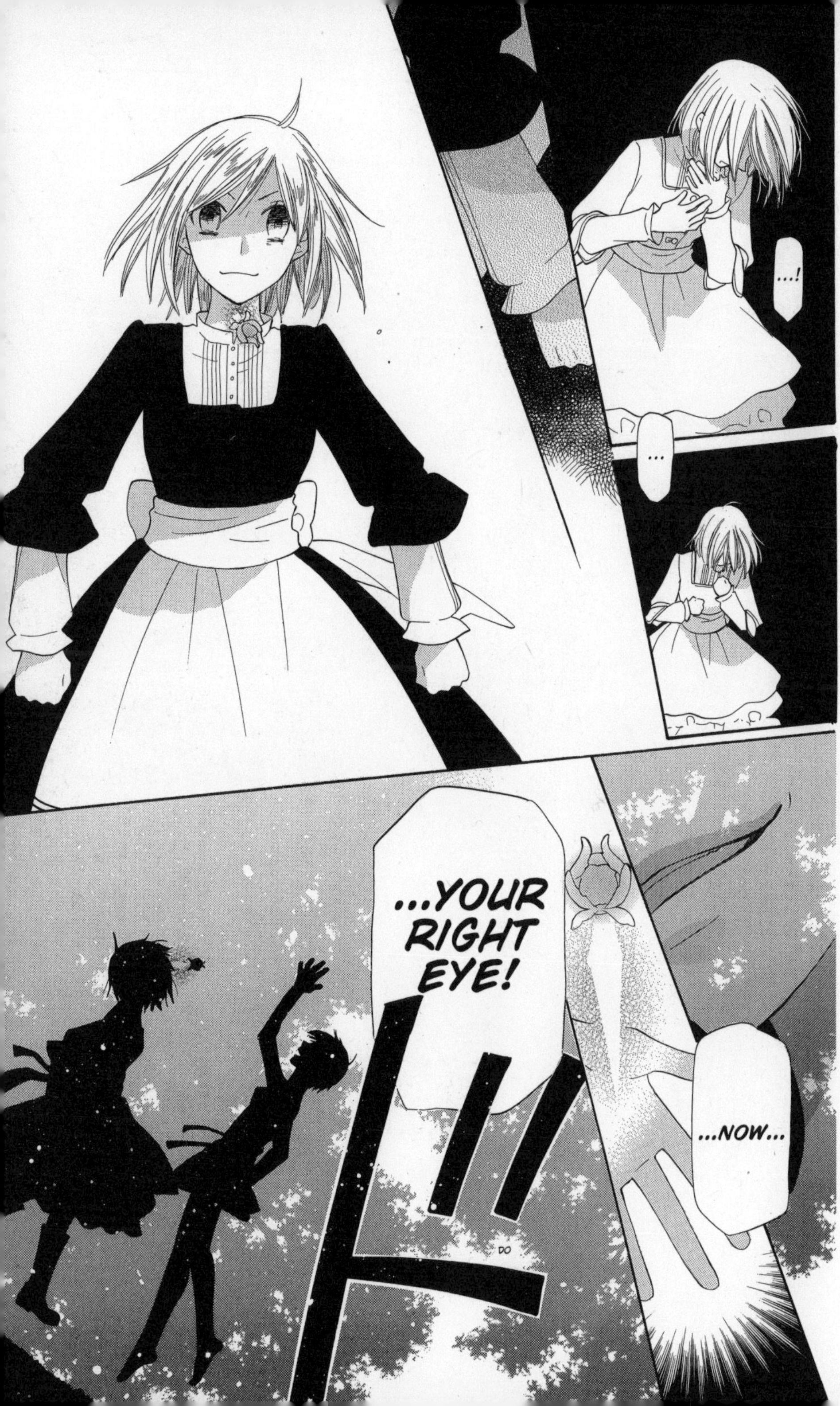

...!
...
...NOW...
...YOUR RIGHT EYE!
DO

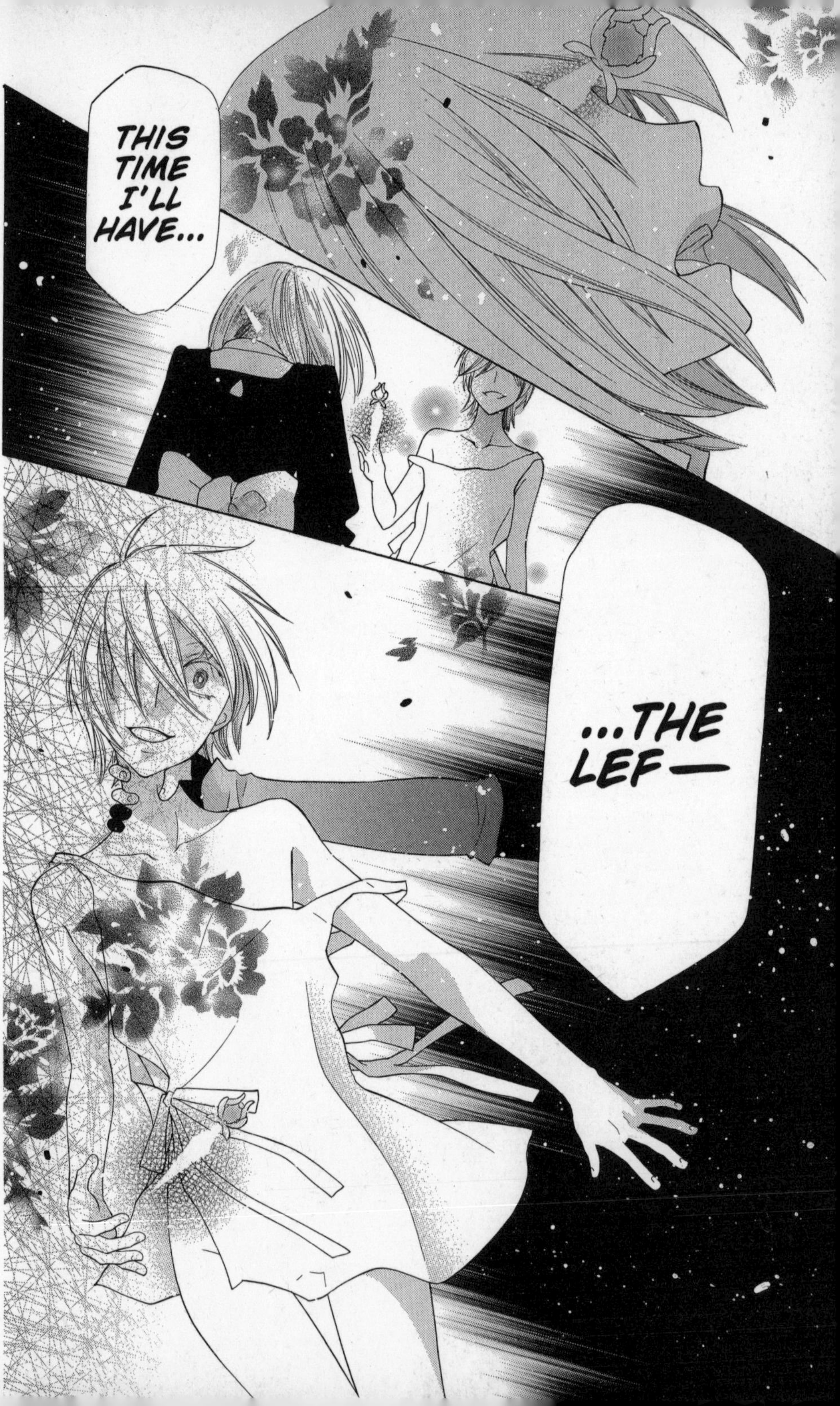
THIS TIME I'LL HAVE...
...THE LEF—

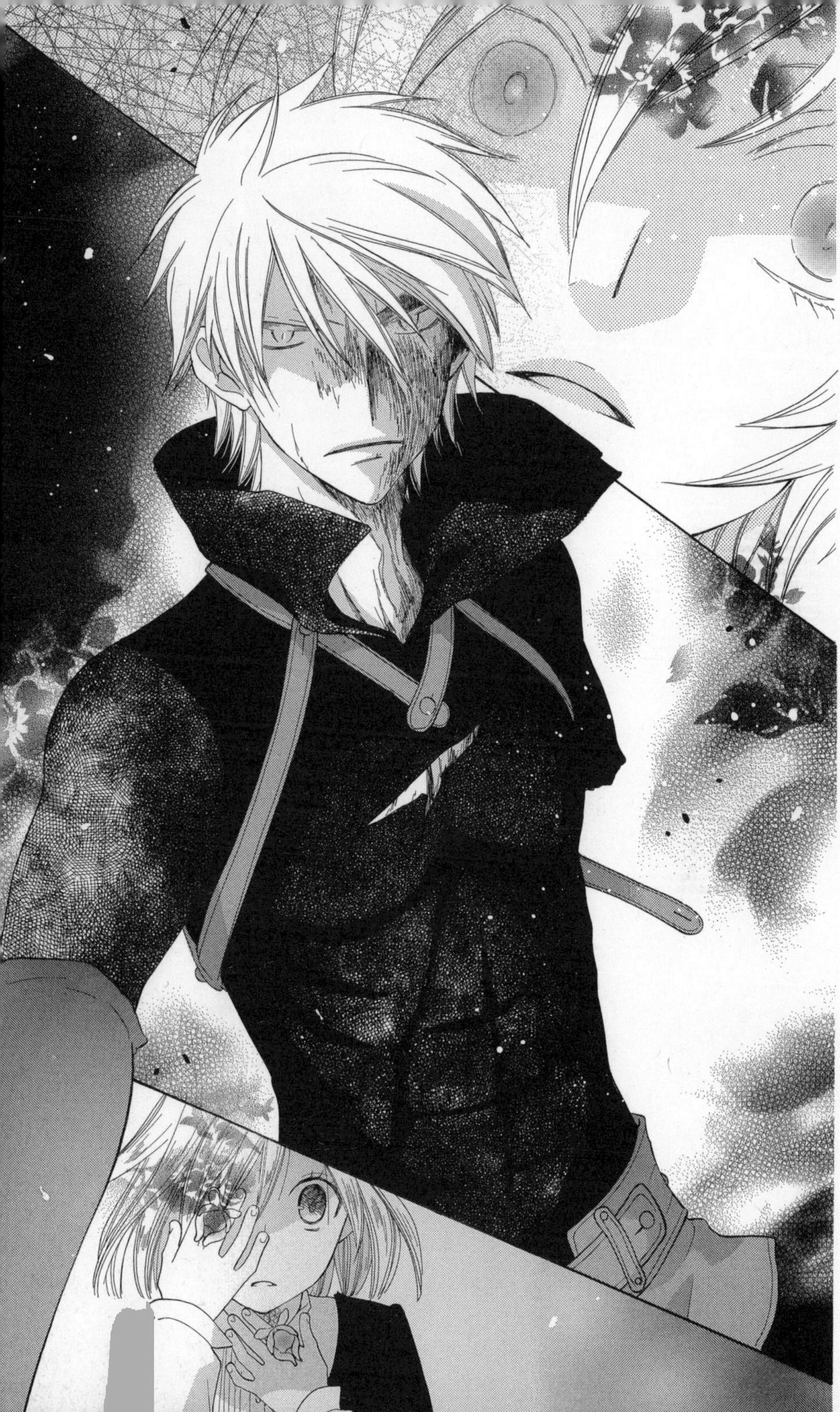

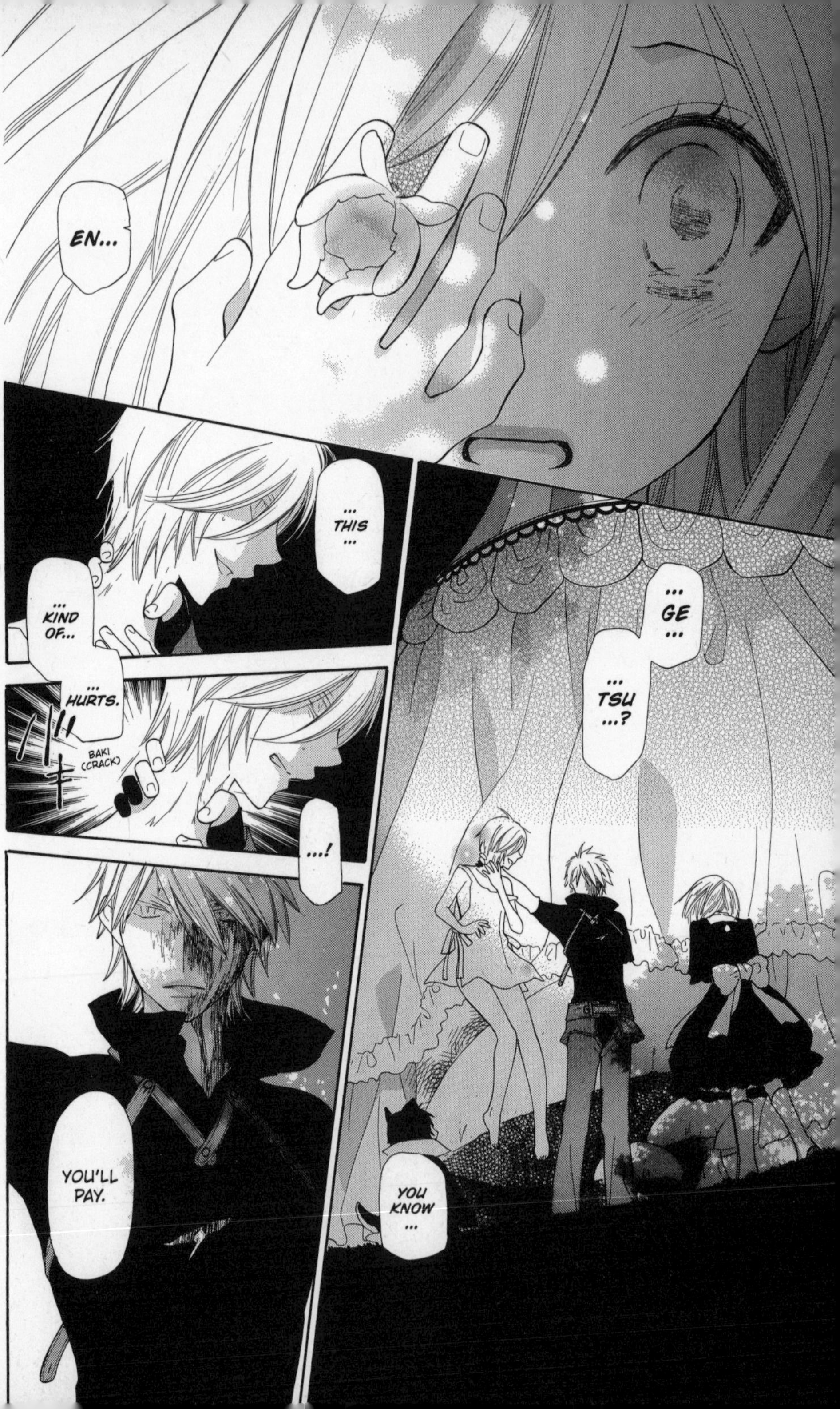
EN...
...GE...
...TSU...?
YOU KNOW...
...THIS...
...KIND OF...
...HURTS.
BAKI (CRACK)
...!
YOU'LL PAY.

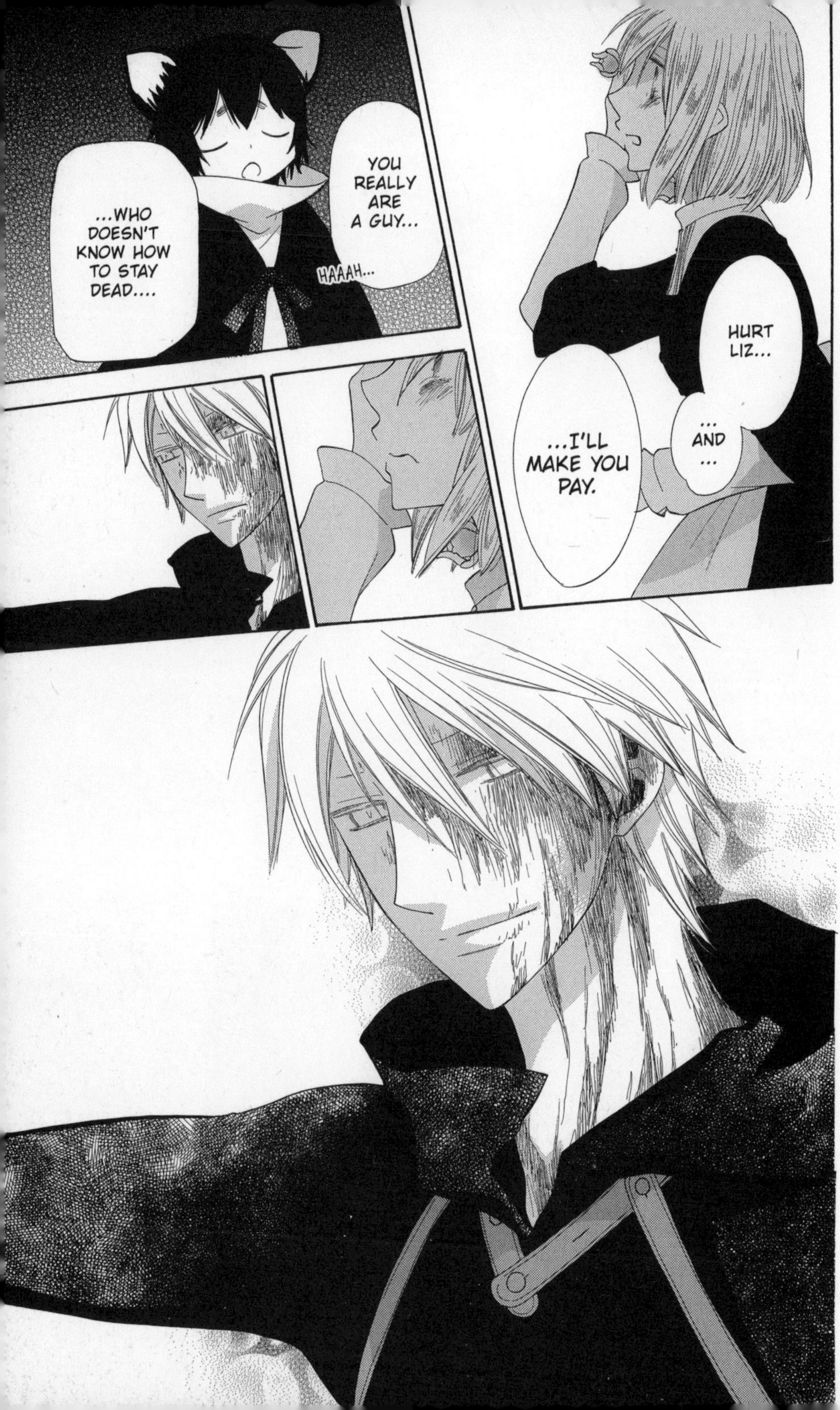
HURT LIZ...
...AND...
...I'LL MAKE YOU PAY.
YOU REALLY ARE A GUY...
HAAAH...
...WHO DOESN'T KNOW HOW TO STAY DEAD....

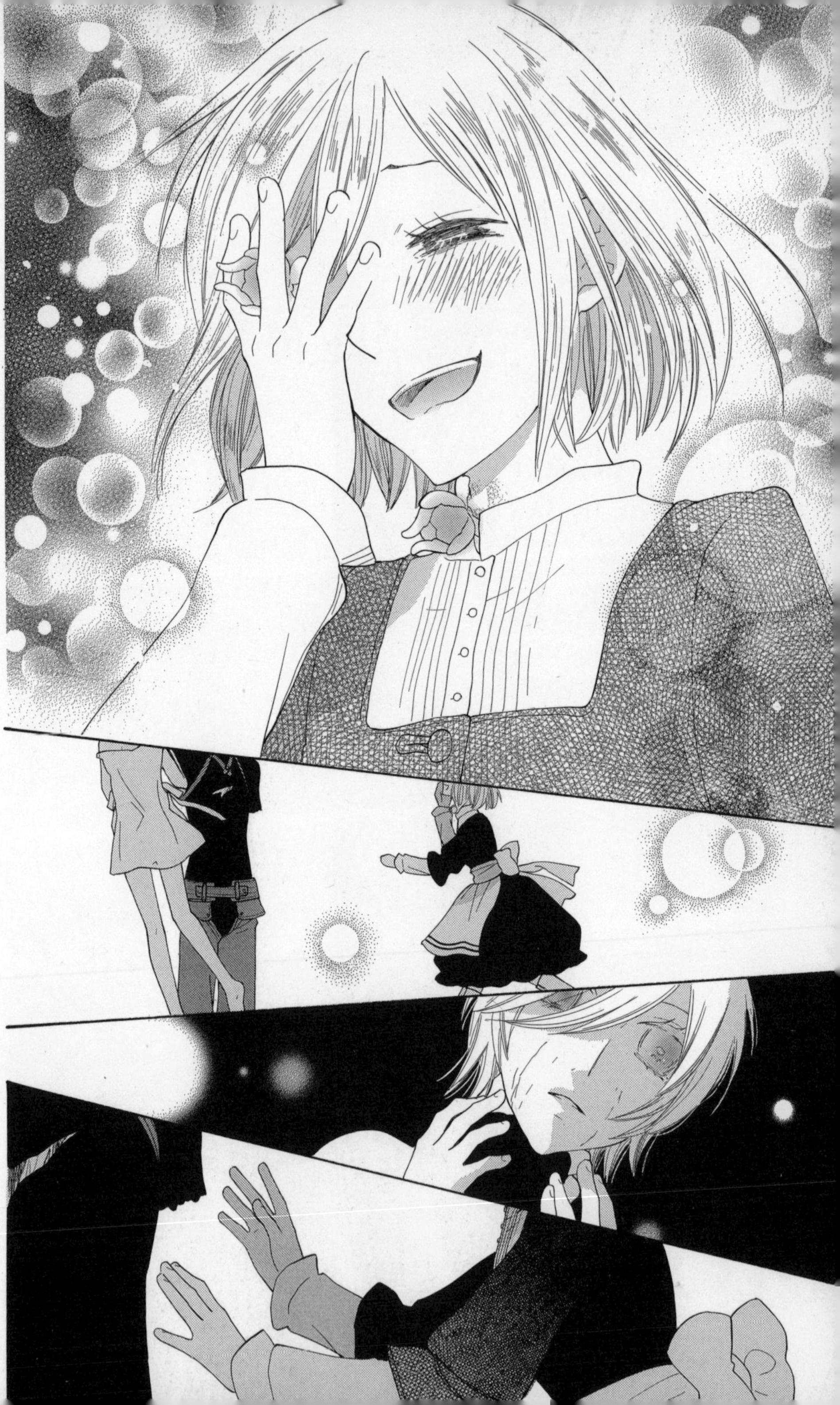

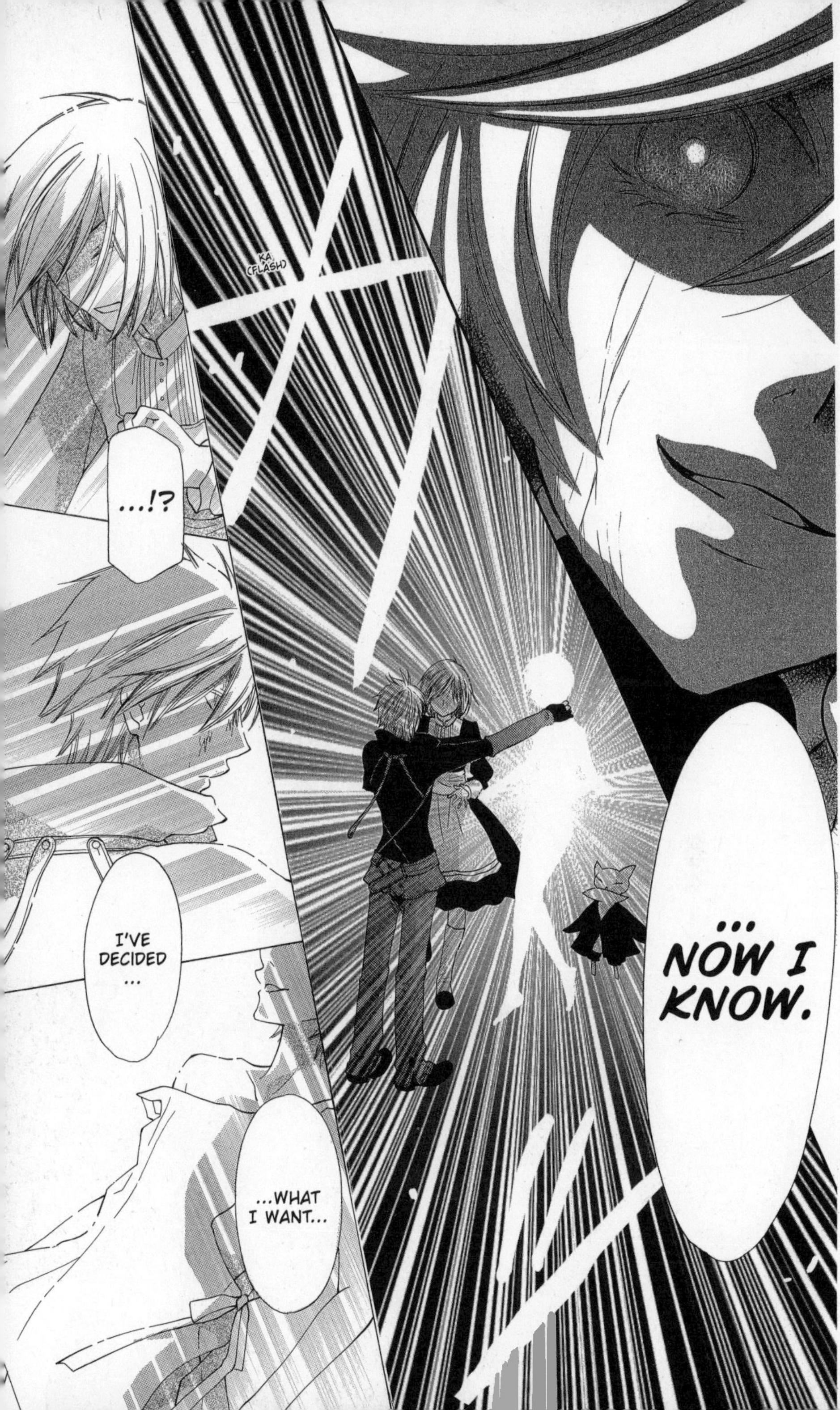
KA (FLASH)
...NOW I KNOW.
...!?
I'VE DECIDED ...
...WHAT I WANT...

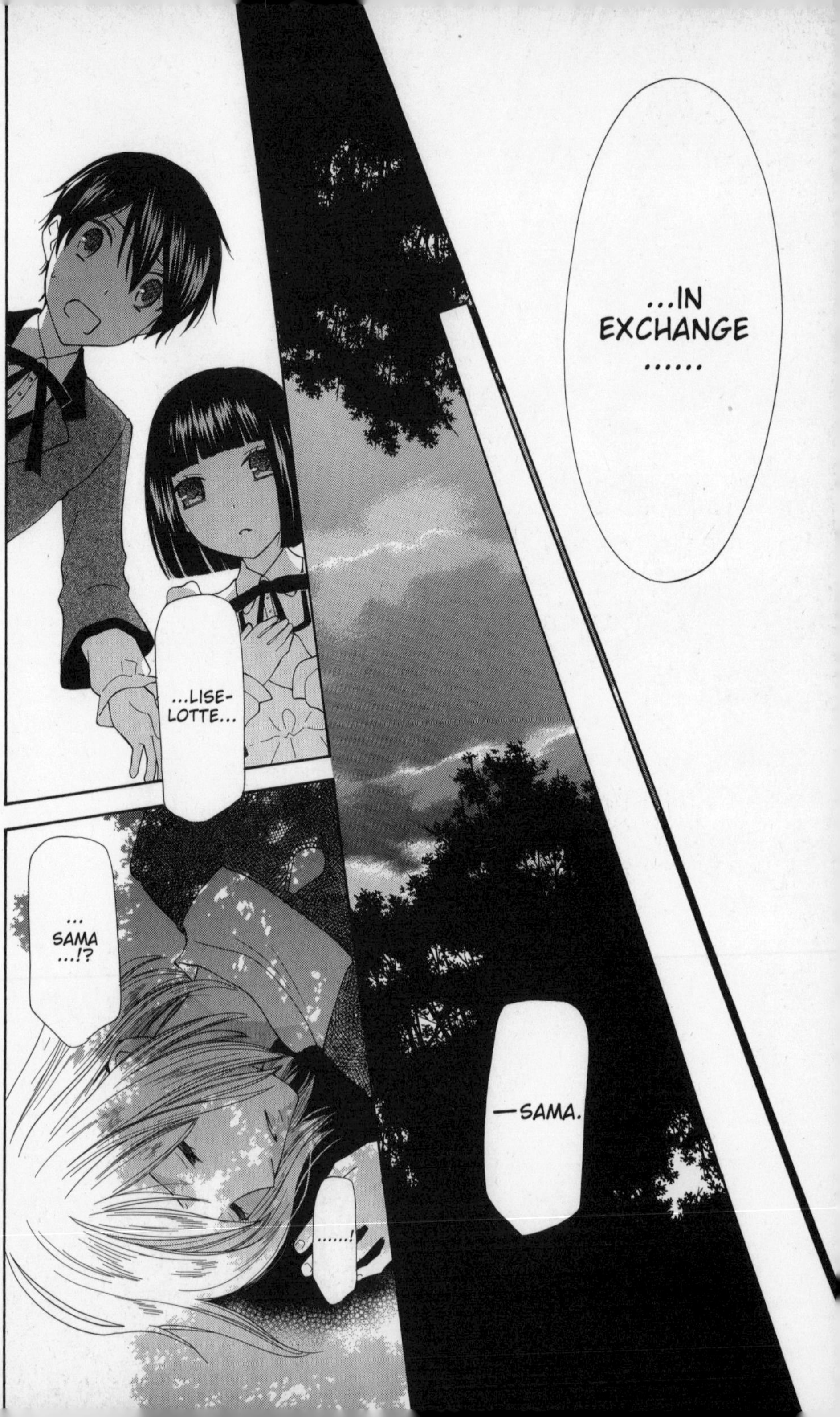
...IN EXCHANGE ......
—SAMA.
...LISE-LOTTE...
... SAMA ...!?
......!

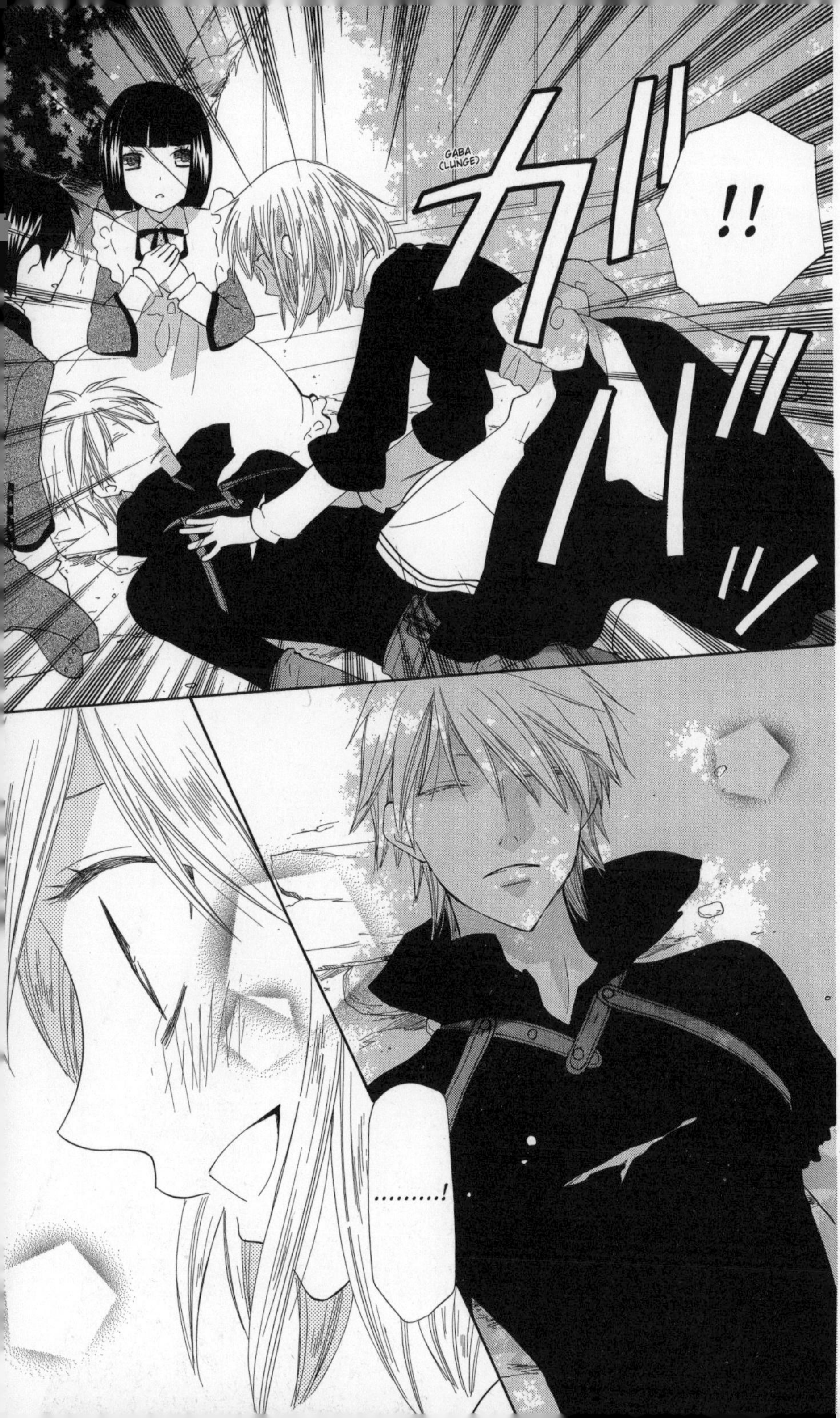
GABA (LUNGE)
!!
.........!

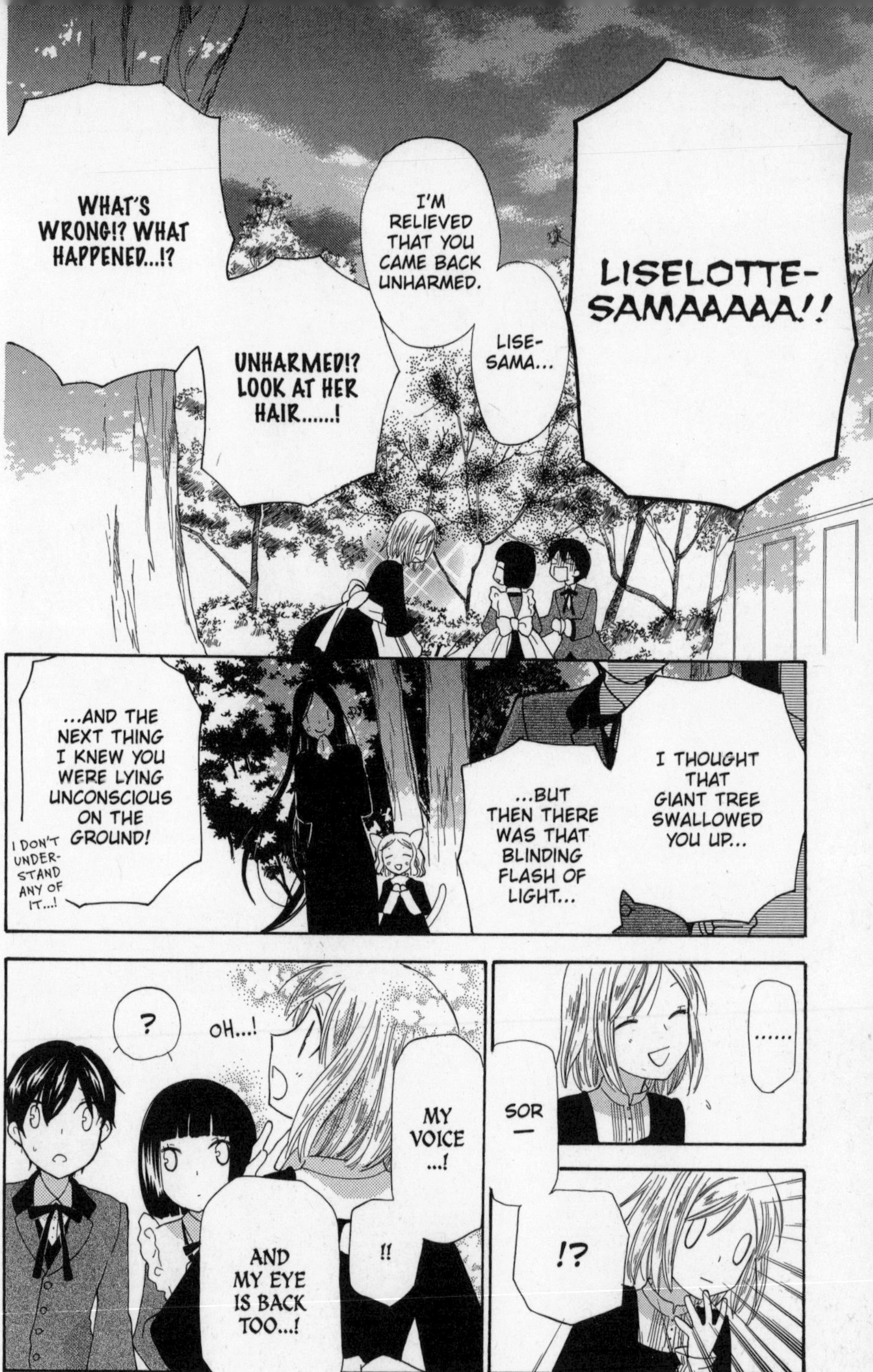

LISELOTTE-SAMAAAAA!!
I'M RELIEVED THAT YOU CAME BACK UNHARMED.
LISE-SAMA...
WHAT'S WRONG!? WHAT HAPPENED...!?
UNHARMED!? LOOK AT HER HAIR......!
I THOUGHT THAT GIANT TREE SWALLOWED YOU UP...
...BUT THEN THERE WAS THAT BLINDING FLASH OF LIGHT...
...AND THE NEXT THING I KNEW YOU WERE LYING UNCONSCIOUS ON THE GROUND!
I DON'T UNDERSTAND ANY OF IT...!
......
SOR—
!?
MY VOICE...!
OH...!
?
!!
AND MY EYE IS BACK TOO...!

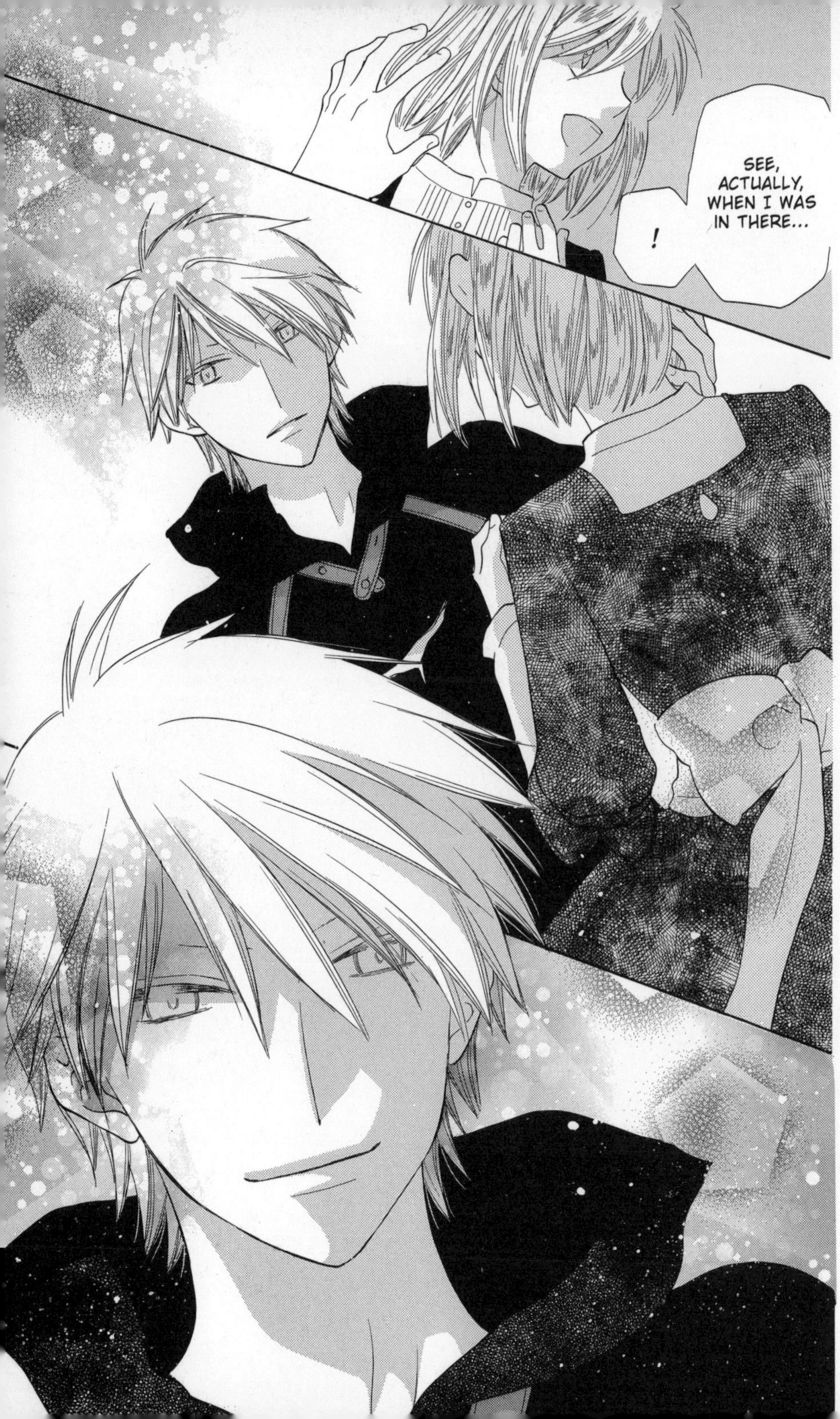
SEE, ACTUALLY, WHEN I WAS IN THERE...
!

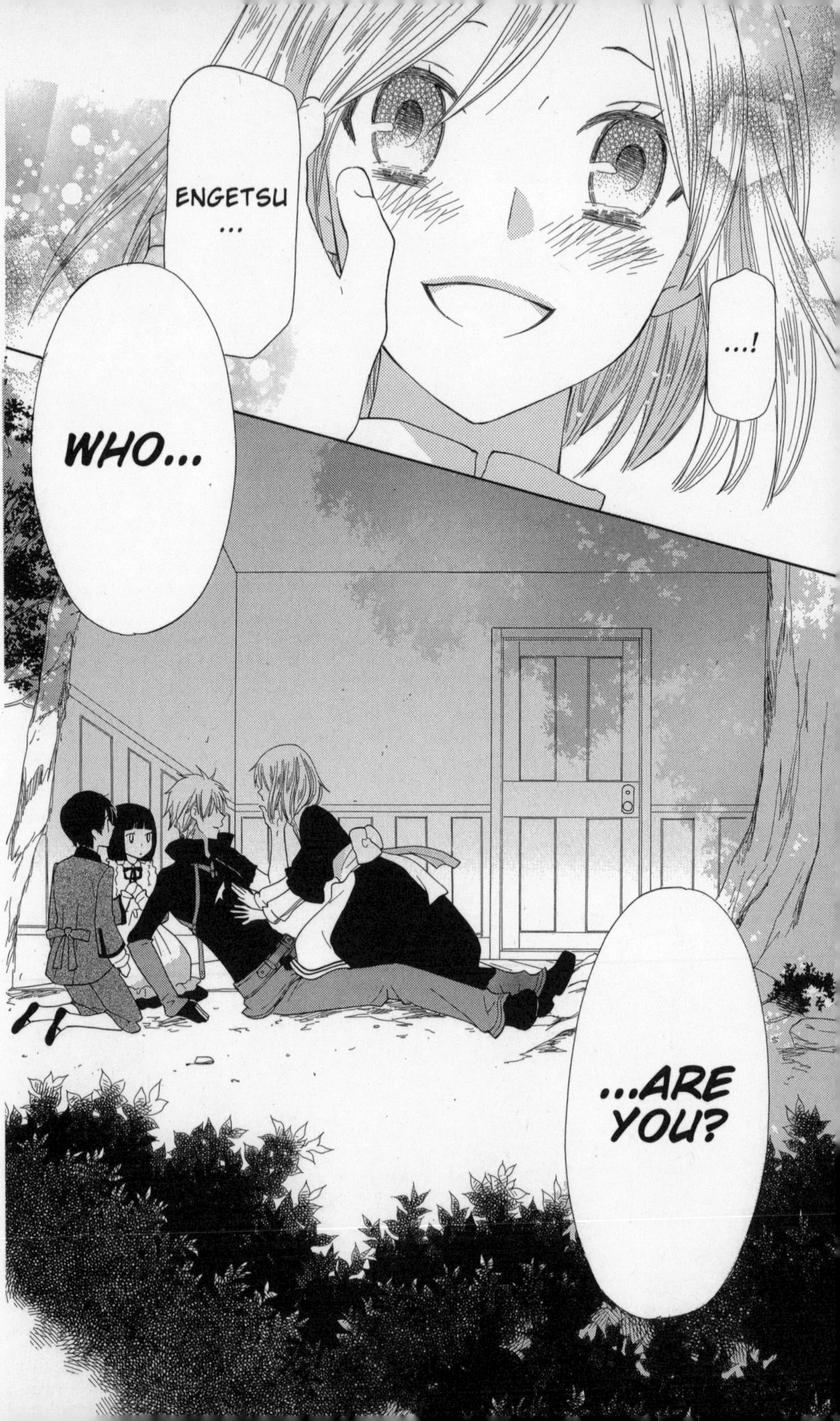
...!
ENGETSU ...
WHO...
...ARE YOU?

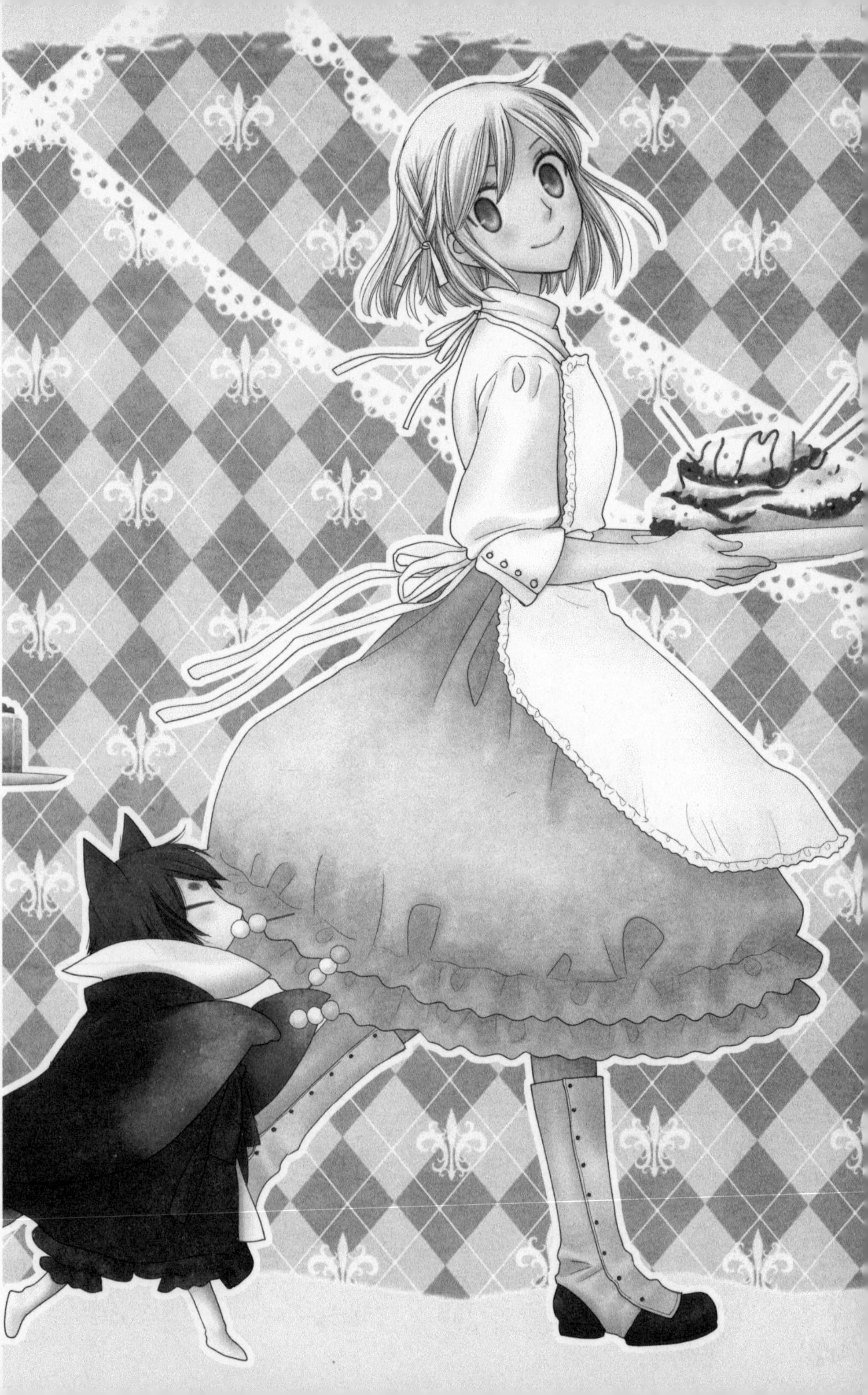

Chapter 14

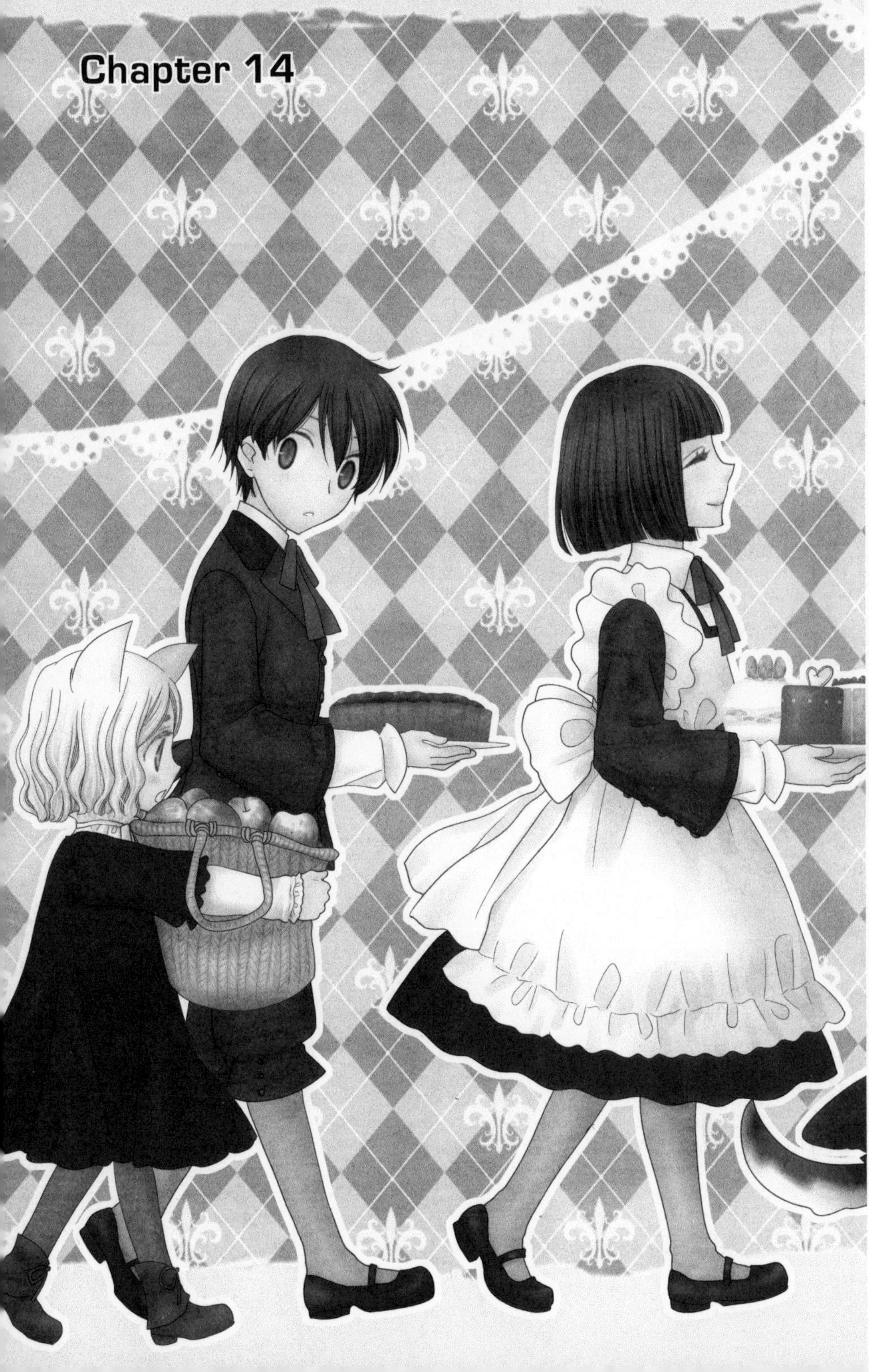

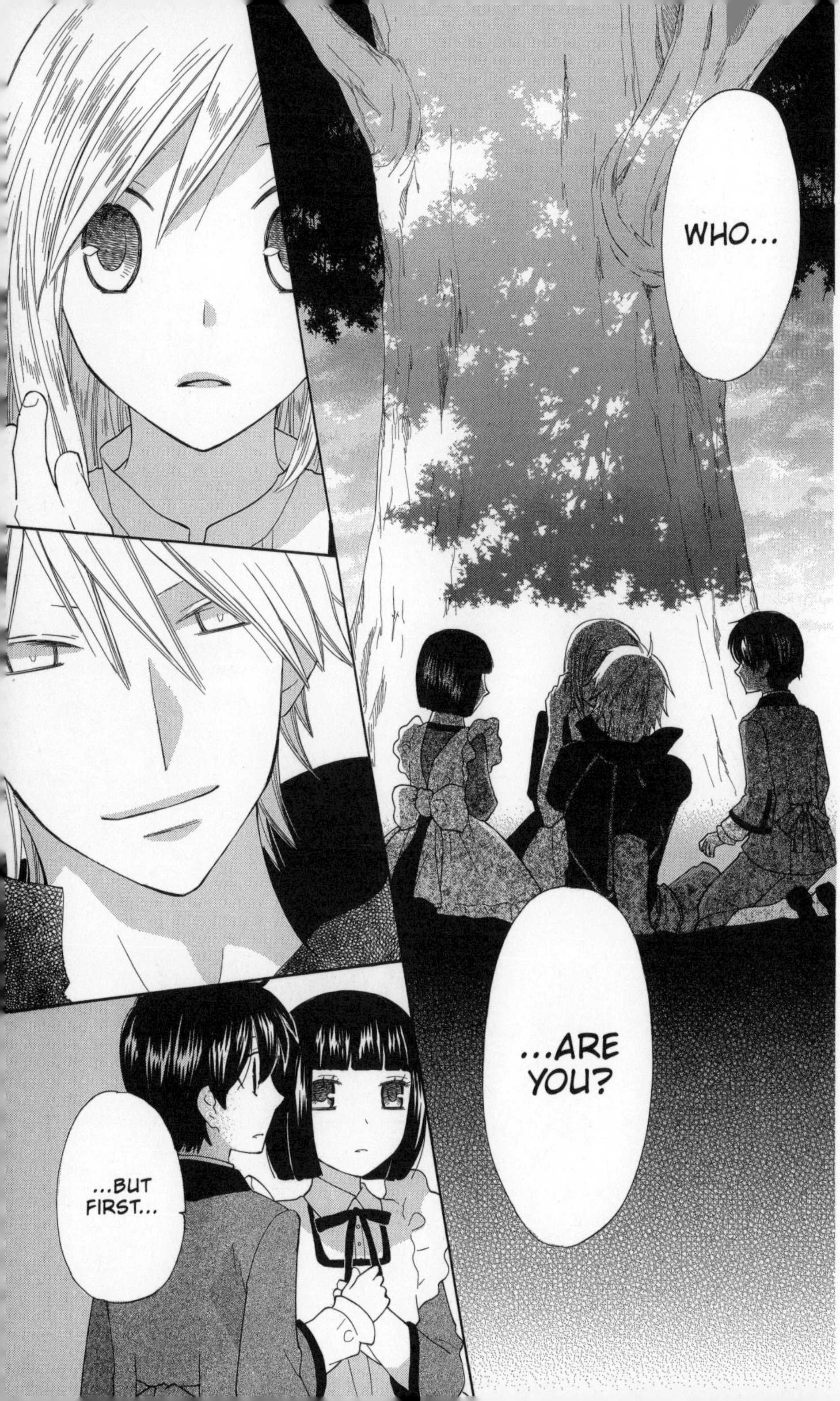
WHO...
...ARE YOU?
...BUT FIRST...

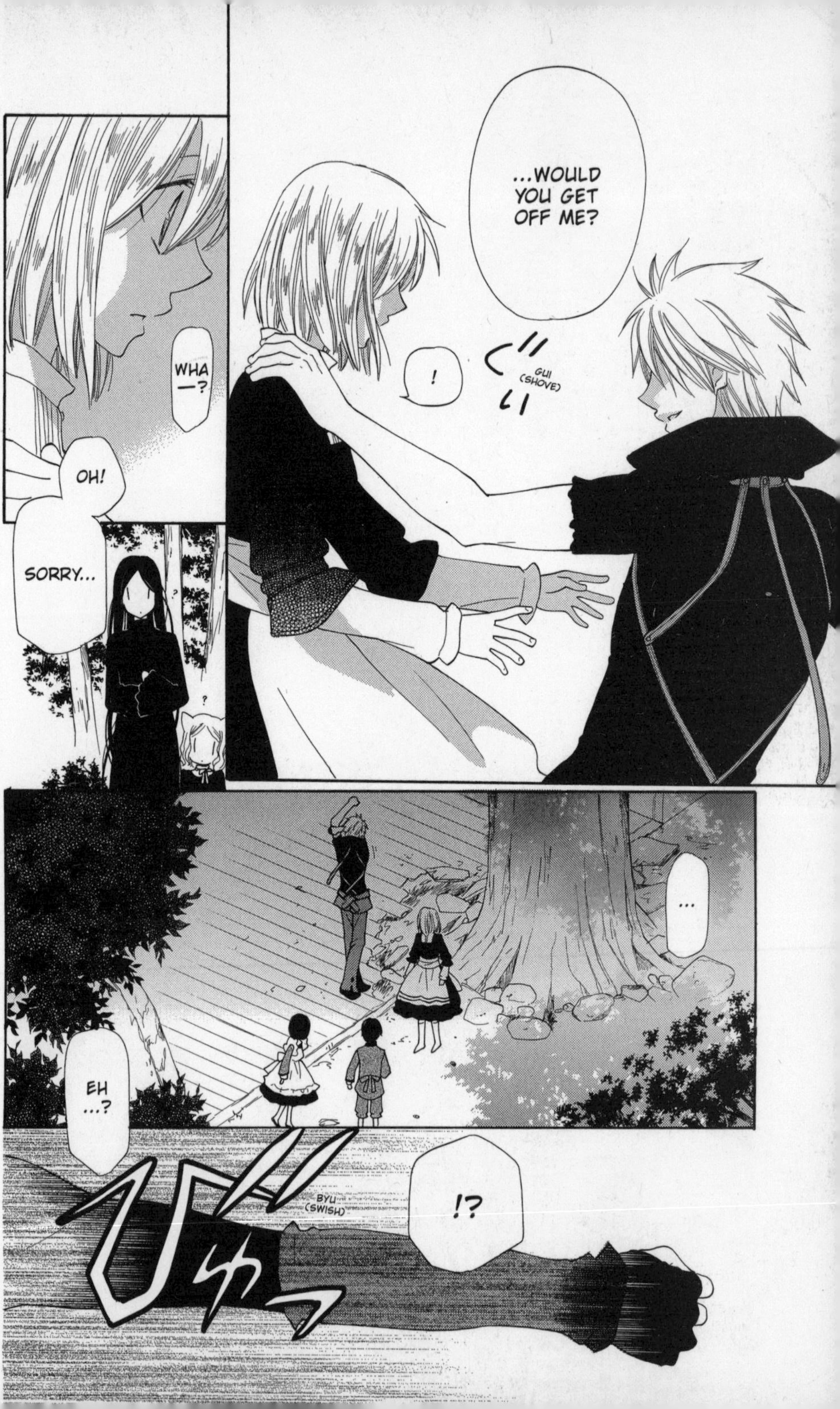
...WOULD YOU GET OFF ME?
GUI (SHOVE)
!
WHA—?
OH!
SORRY...
...
EH ...?
!?
BYU (SWISH)

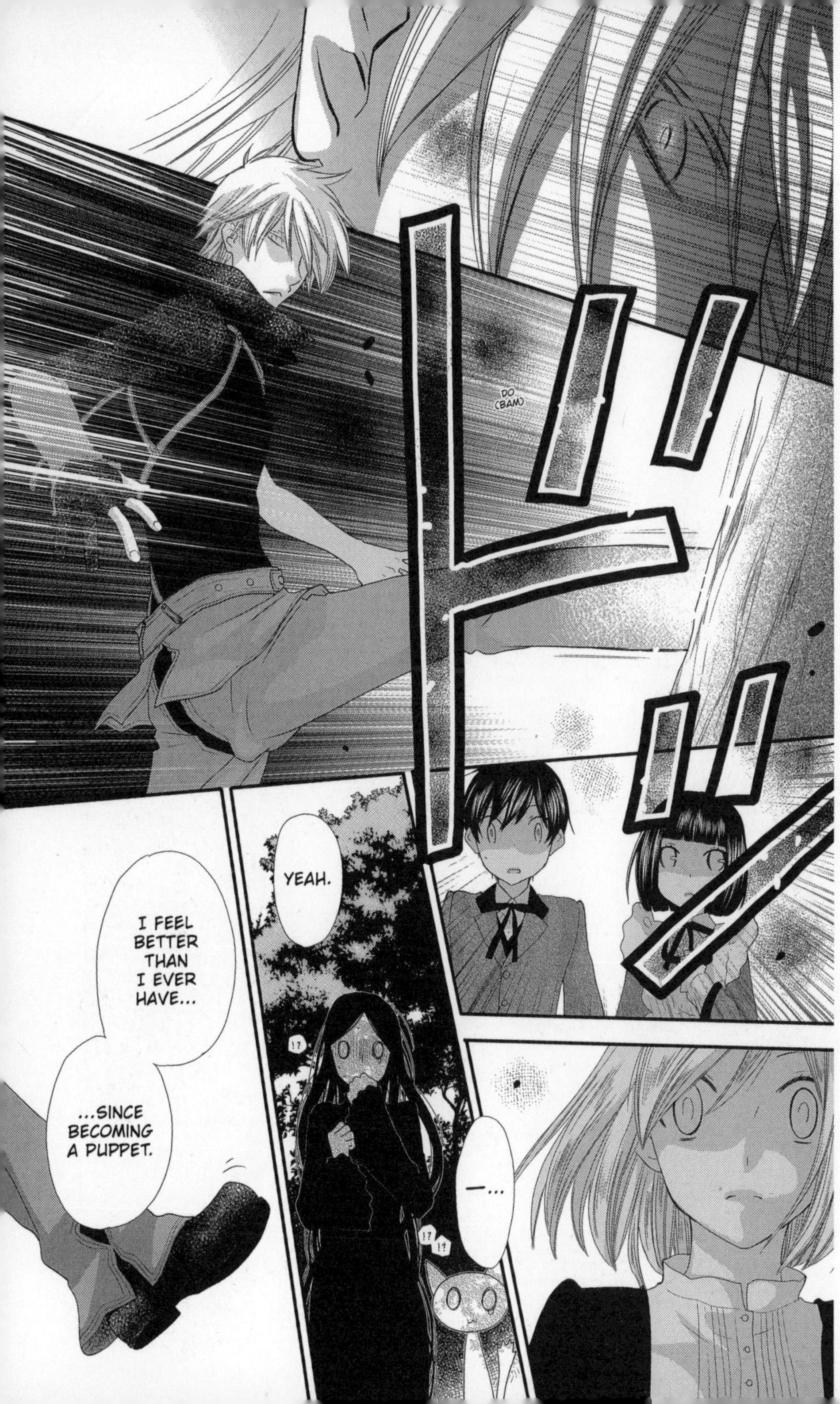
DO
(BAM)
—...
!?
!?
!?
YEAH.
I FEEL BETTER THAN I EVER HAVE...
...SINCE BECOMING A PUPPET.

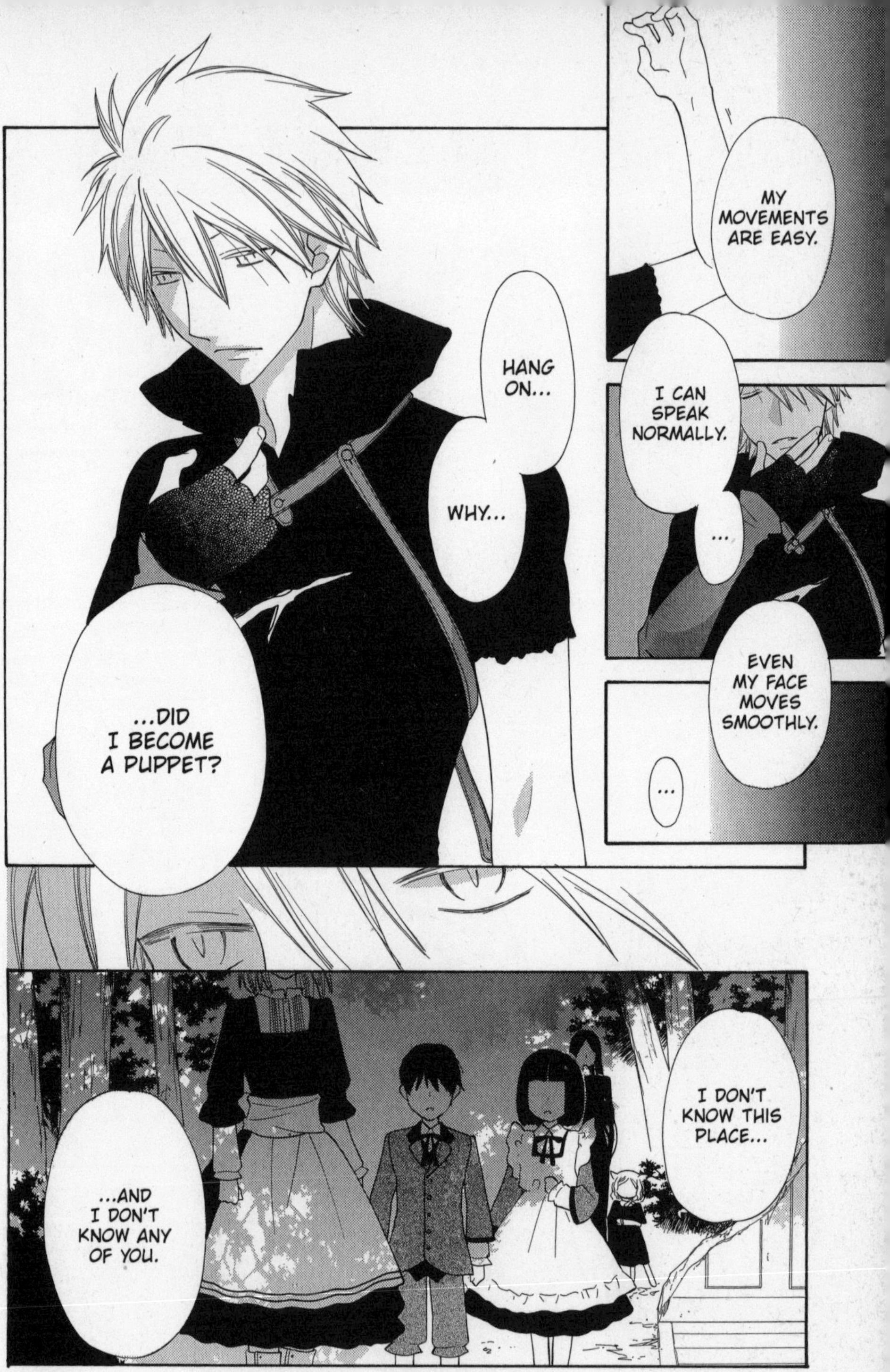
MY MOVEMENTS ARE EASY.
I CAN SPEAK NORMALLY.
...
EVEN MY FACE MOVES SMOOTHLY.
...
HANG ON...
WHY...
...DID I BECOME A PUPPET?
I DON'T KNOW THIS PLACE...
...AND I DON'T KNOW ANY OF YOU.

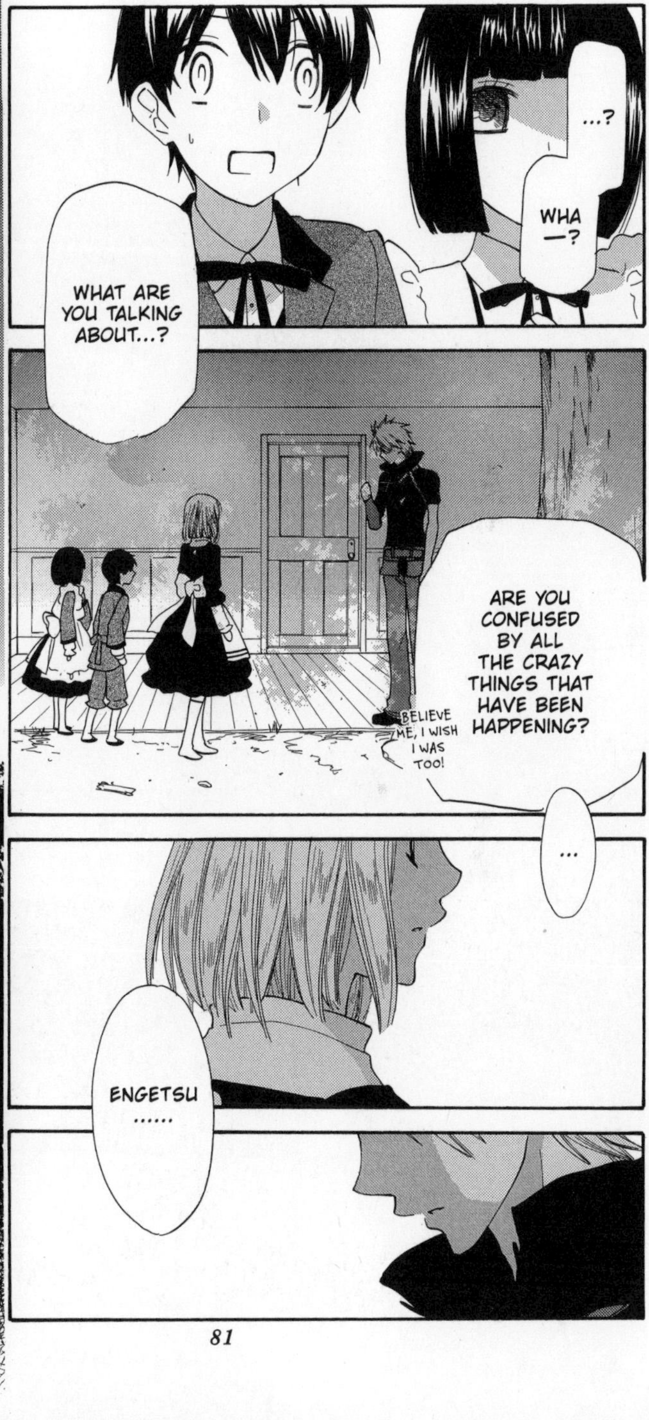
...?
WHA—?
WHAT ARE YOU TALKING ABOUT...?
ARE YOU CONFUSED BY ALL THE CRAZY THINGS THAT HAVE BEEN HAPPENING?
BELIEVE ME, I WISH I WAS TOO!
...
ENGETSU ......
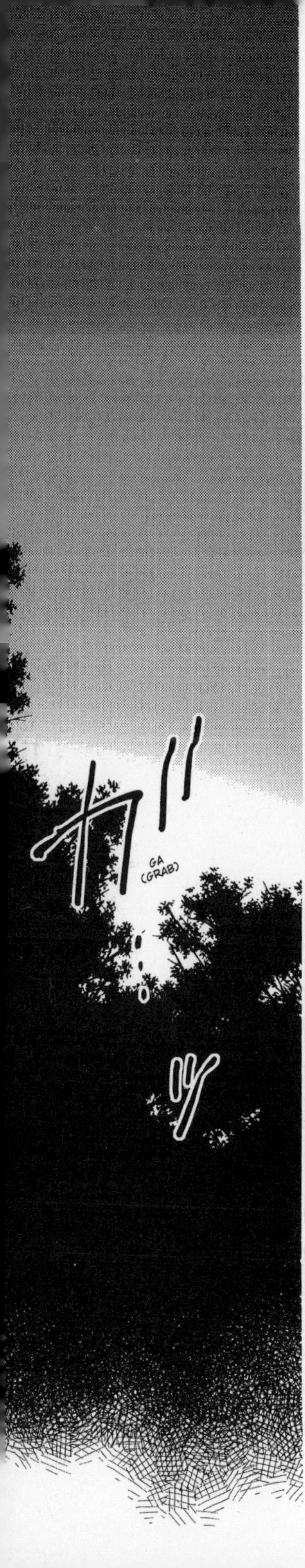
GA (GRAB)

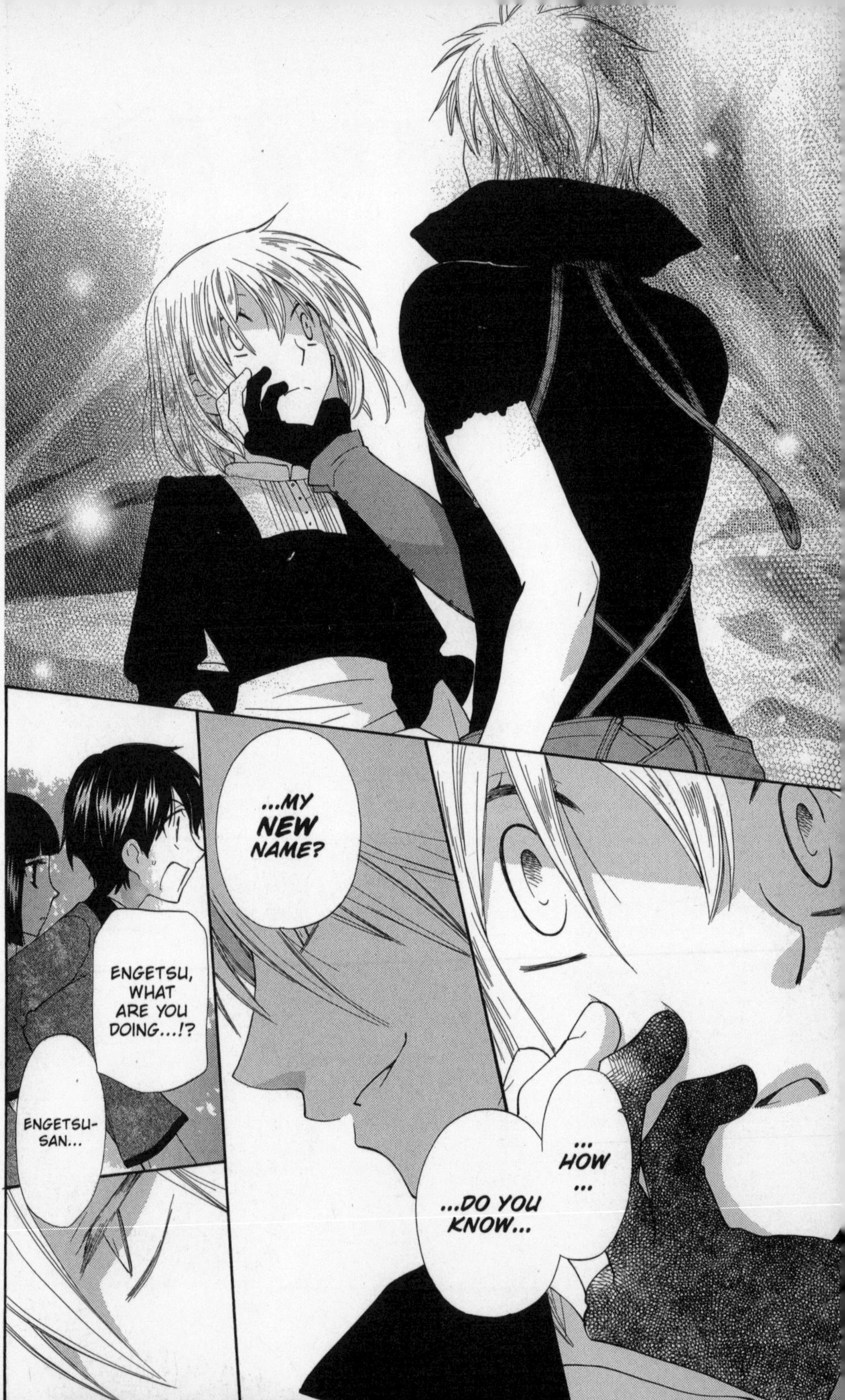
... HOW ...
...DO YOU KNOW...
...MY NEW NAME?
ENGETSU, WHAT ARE YOU DOING...!?
ENGETSU-SAN...

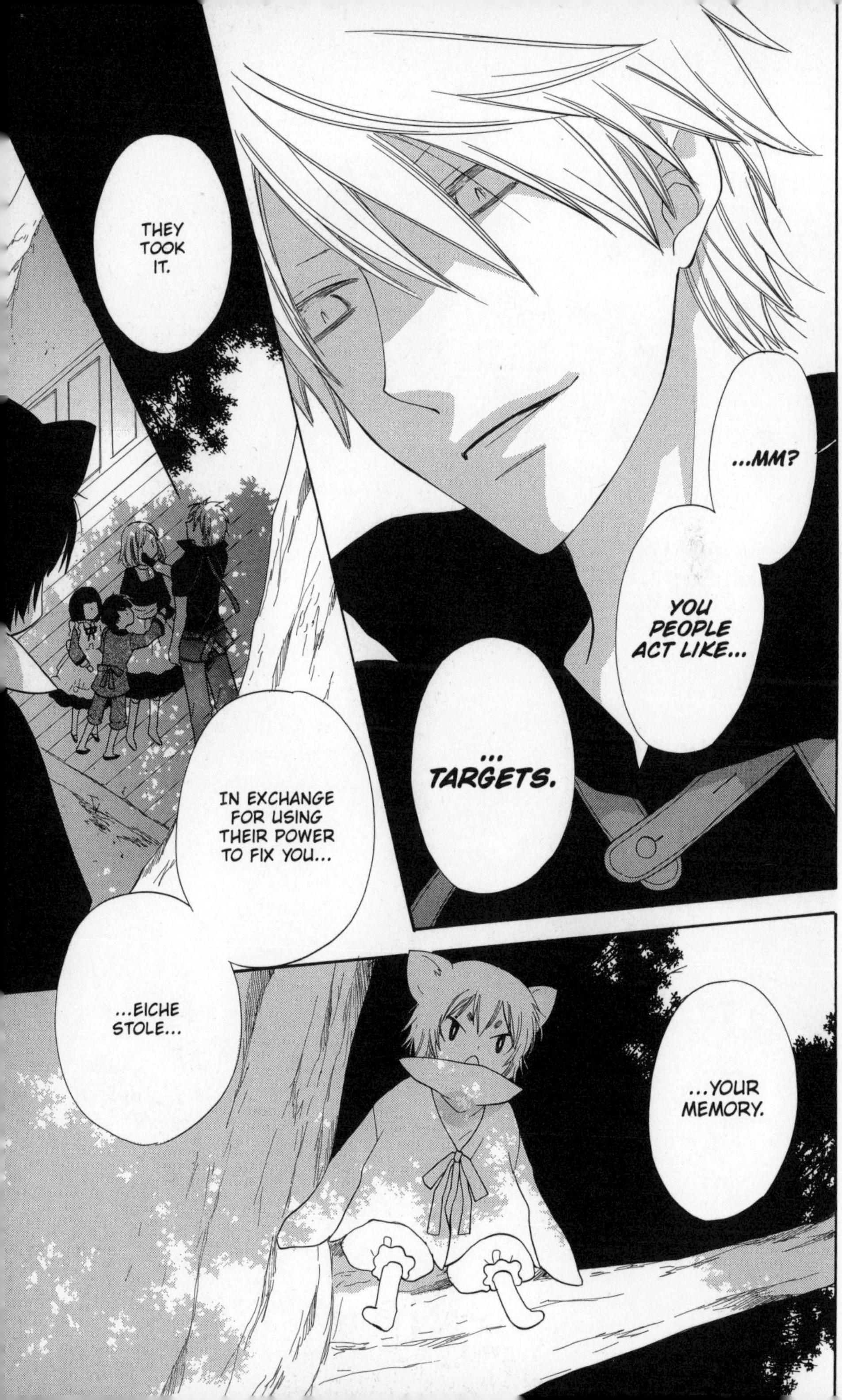
...MM?
YOU PEOPLE ACT LIKE...
...TARGETS.
THEY TOOK IT.
IN EXCHANGE FOR USING THEIR POWER TO FIX YOU...
...EICHE STOLE...
...YOUR MEMORY.

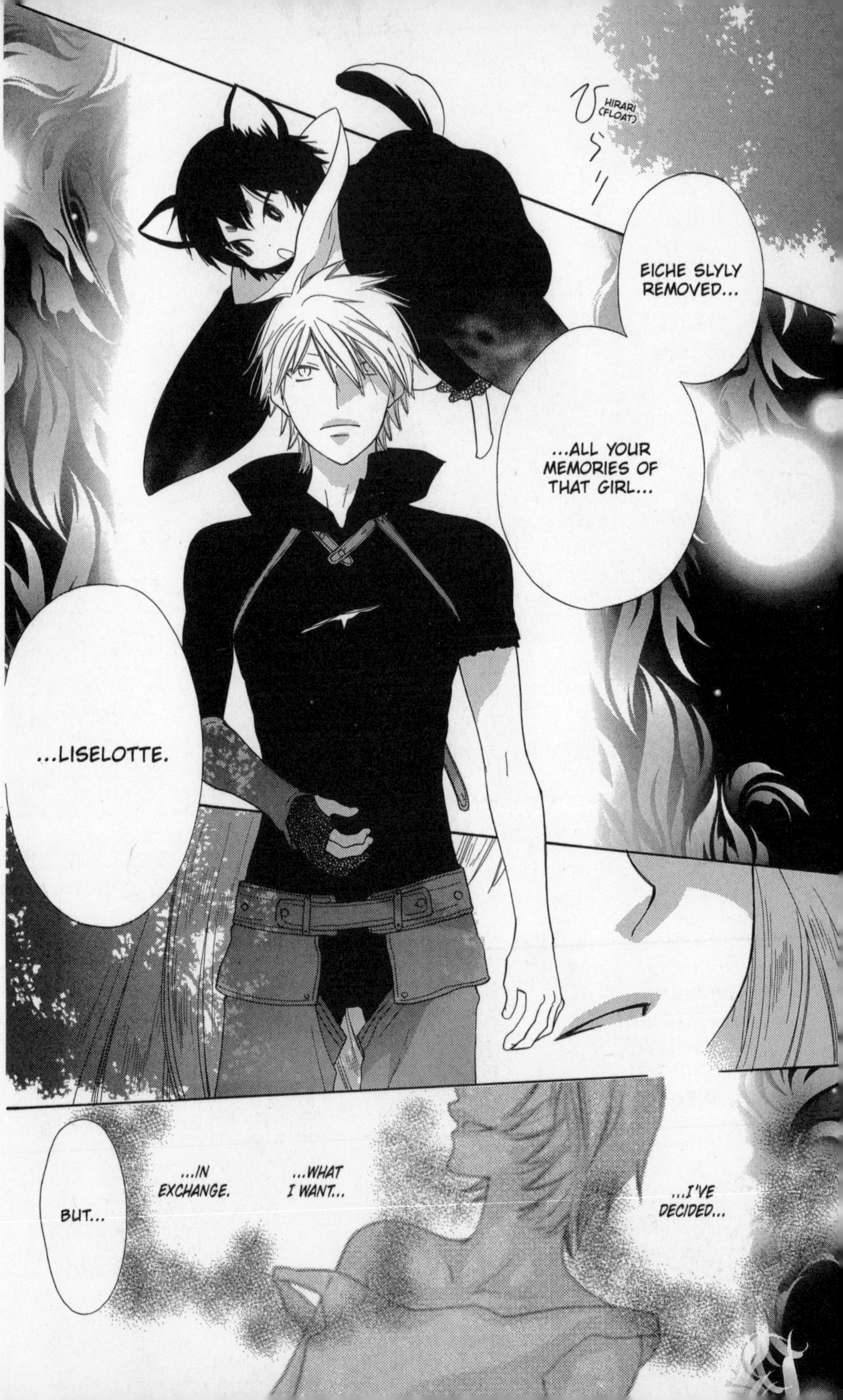
HIRARI (FLOAT)
EICHE SLYLY REMOVED...
...ALL YOUR MEMORIES OF THAT GIRL...
...LISELOTTE.
...I'VE DECIDED...
...WHAT I WANT...
...IN EXCHANGE.
BUT...

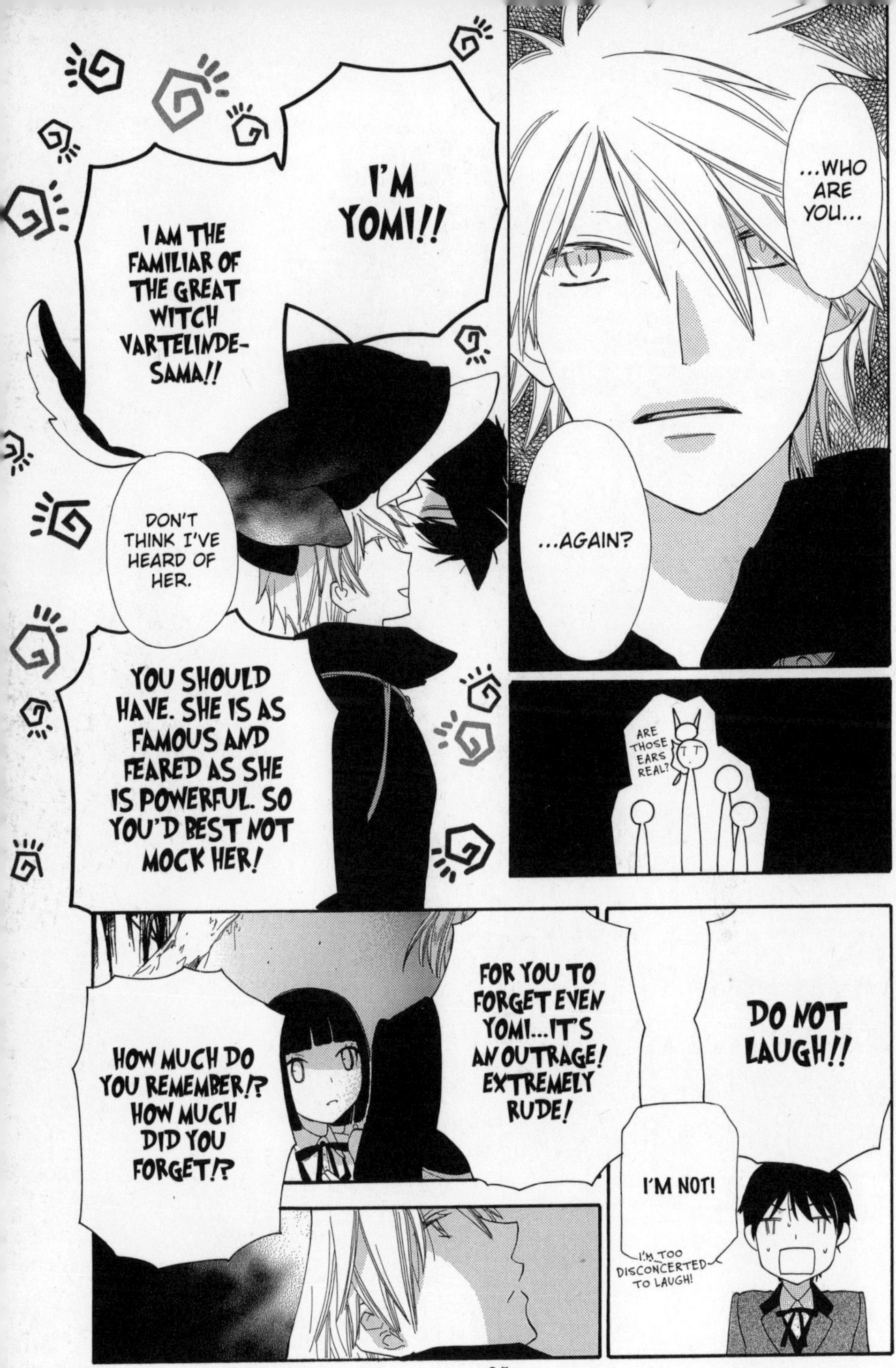
...WHO ARE YOU...
...AGAIN?
ARE THOSE EARS REAL?
I'M YOMI!!
I AM THE FAMILIAR OF THE GREAT WITCH VARTELINDE-SAMA!!
DON'T THINK I'VE HEARD OF HER.
YOU SHOULD HAVE. SHE IS AS FAMOUS AND FEARED AS SHE IS POWERFUL. SO YOU'D BEST NOT MOCK HER!
DO NOT LAUGH!!
I'M NOT!
I'M TOO DISCONCERTED TO LAUGH!
FOR YOU TO FORGET EVEN YOMI...IT'S AN OUTRAGE! EXTREMELY RUDE!
HOW MUCH DO YOU REMEMBER!? HOW MUCH DID YOU FORGET!?

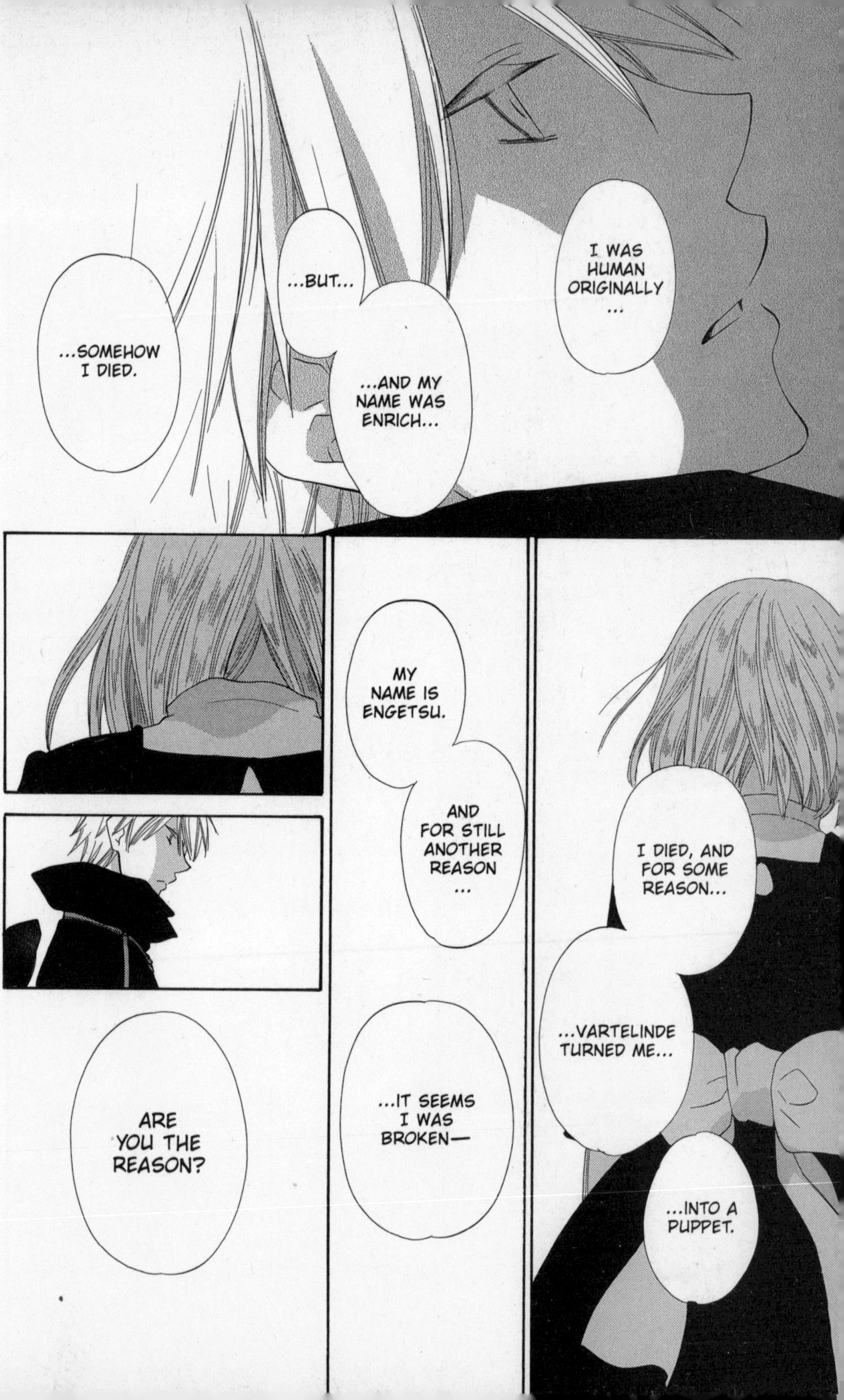
I WAS HUMAN ORIGINALLY ...
...AND MY NAME WAS ENRICH...
...BUT...
...SOMEHOW I DIED.
I DIED, AND FOR SOME REASON...
...VARTELINDE TURNED ME...
...INTO A PUPPET.
MY NAME IS ENGETSU.
AND FOR STILL ANOTHER REASON ...
...IT SEEMS I WAS BROKEN—
ARE YOU THE REASON?

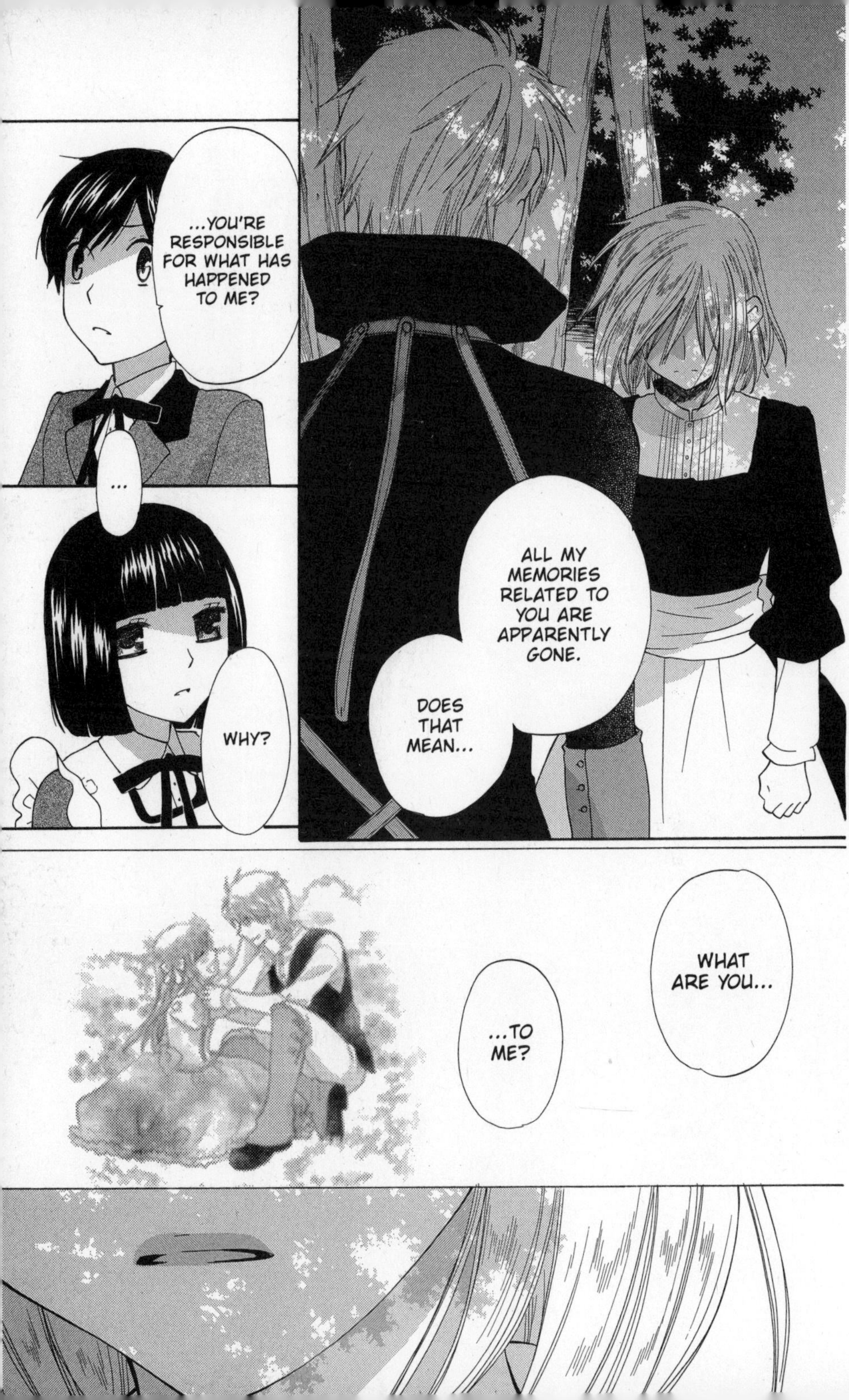
ALL MY MEMORIES RELATED TO YOU ARE APPARENTLY GONE.
DOES THAT MEAN...
...YOU'RE RESPONSIBLE FOR WHAT HAS HAPPENED TO ME?
...
WHY?
WHAT ARE YOU...
...TO ME?

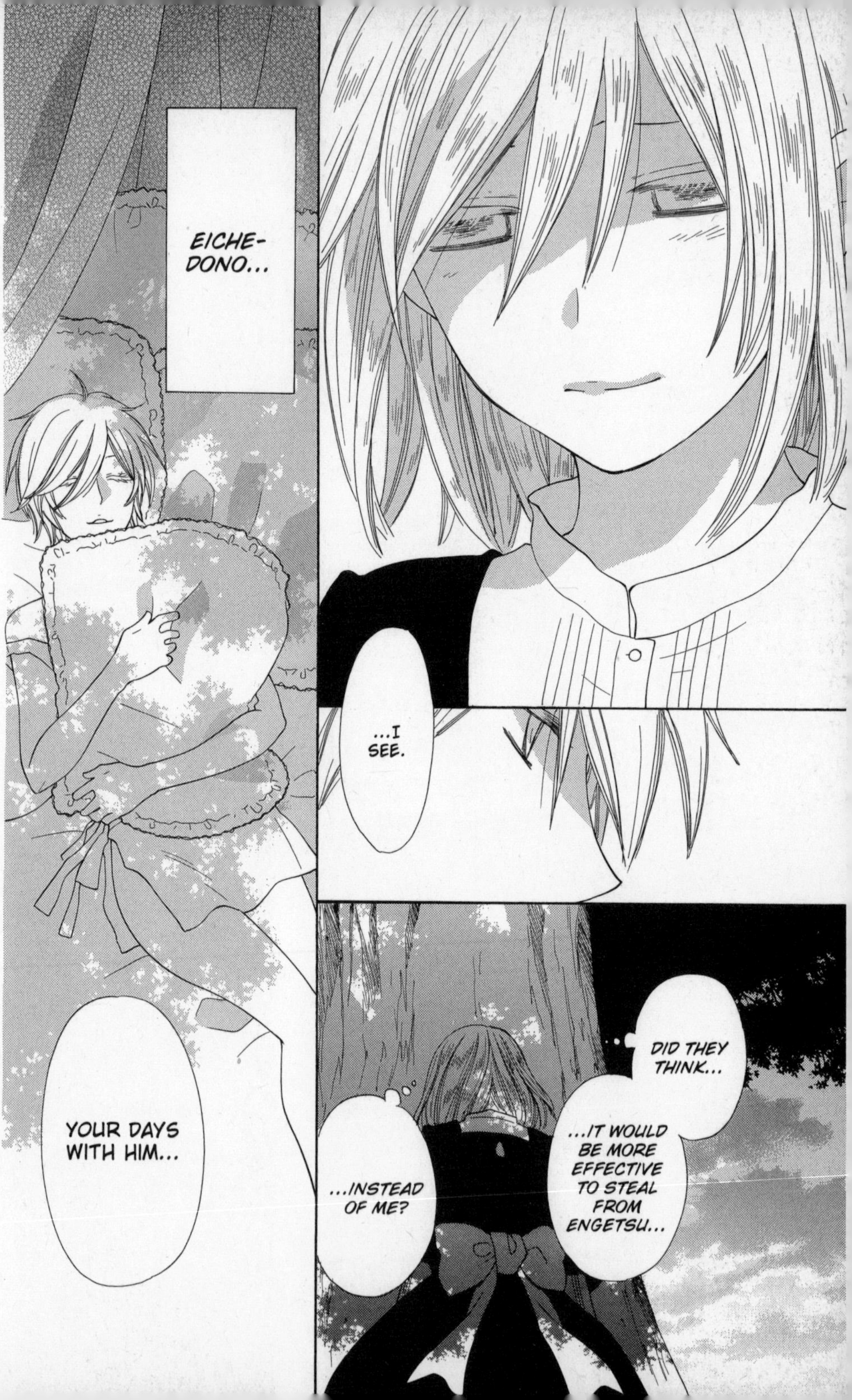
...I SEE.
DID THEY THINK...
...IT WOULD BE MORE EFFECTIVE TO STEAL FROM ENGETSU...
...INSTEAD OF ME?
EICHE-DONO...
YOUR DAYS WITH HIM...

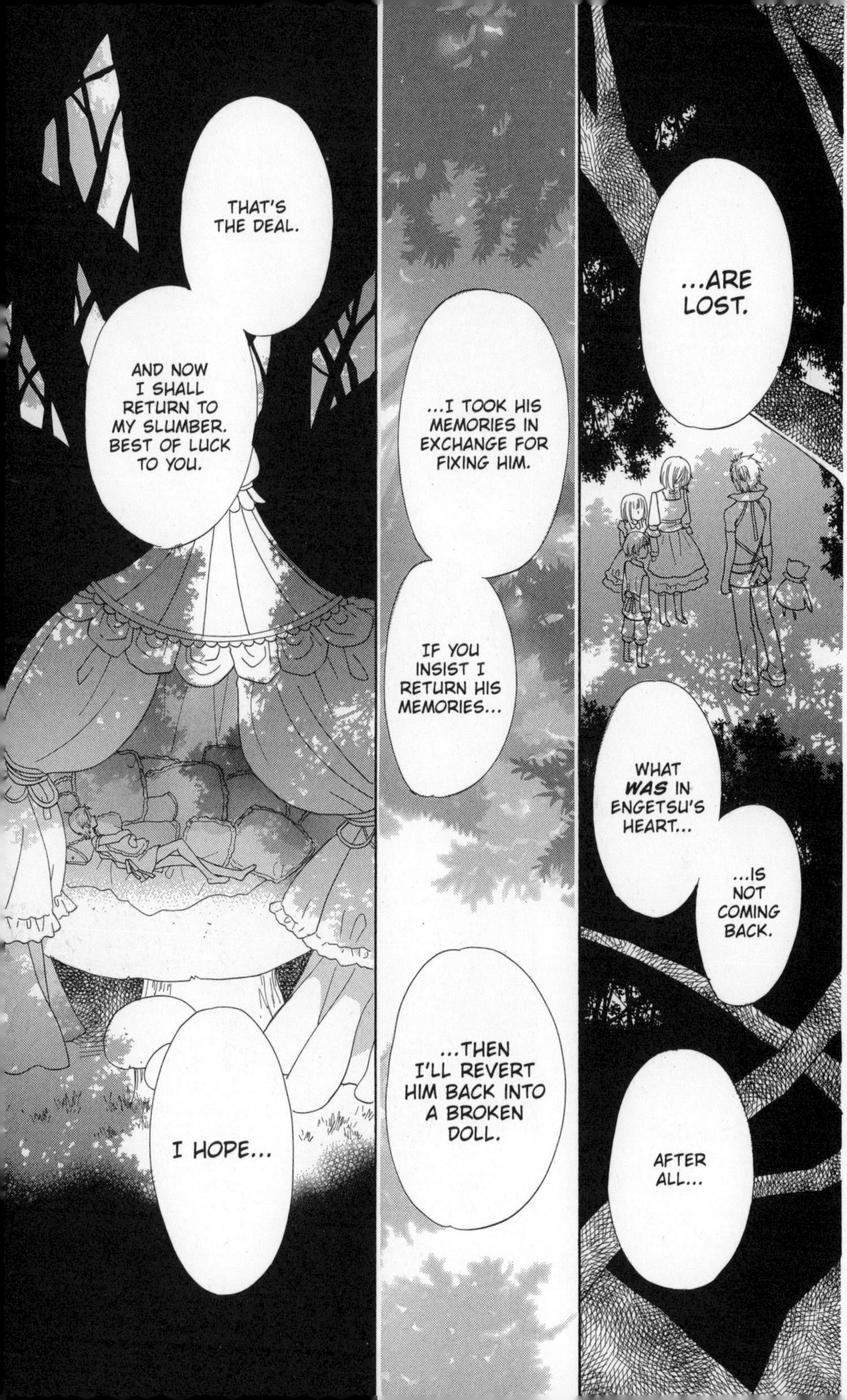
...ARE LOST.
WHAT *WAS* IN ENGETSU'S HEART...
...IS NOT COMING BACK.
AFTER ALL...
...I TOOK HIS MEMORIES IN EXCHANGE FOR FIXING HIM.
IF YOU INSIST I RETURN HIS MEMORIES...
...THEN I'LL REVERT HIM BACK INTO A BROKEN DOLL.
THAT'S THE DEAL.
AND NOW I SHALL RETURN TO MY SLUMBER. BEST OF LUCK TO YOU.
I HOPE...

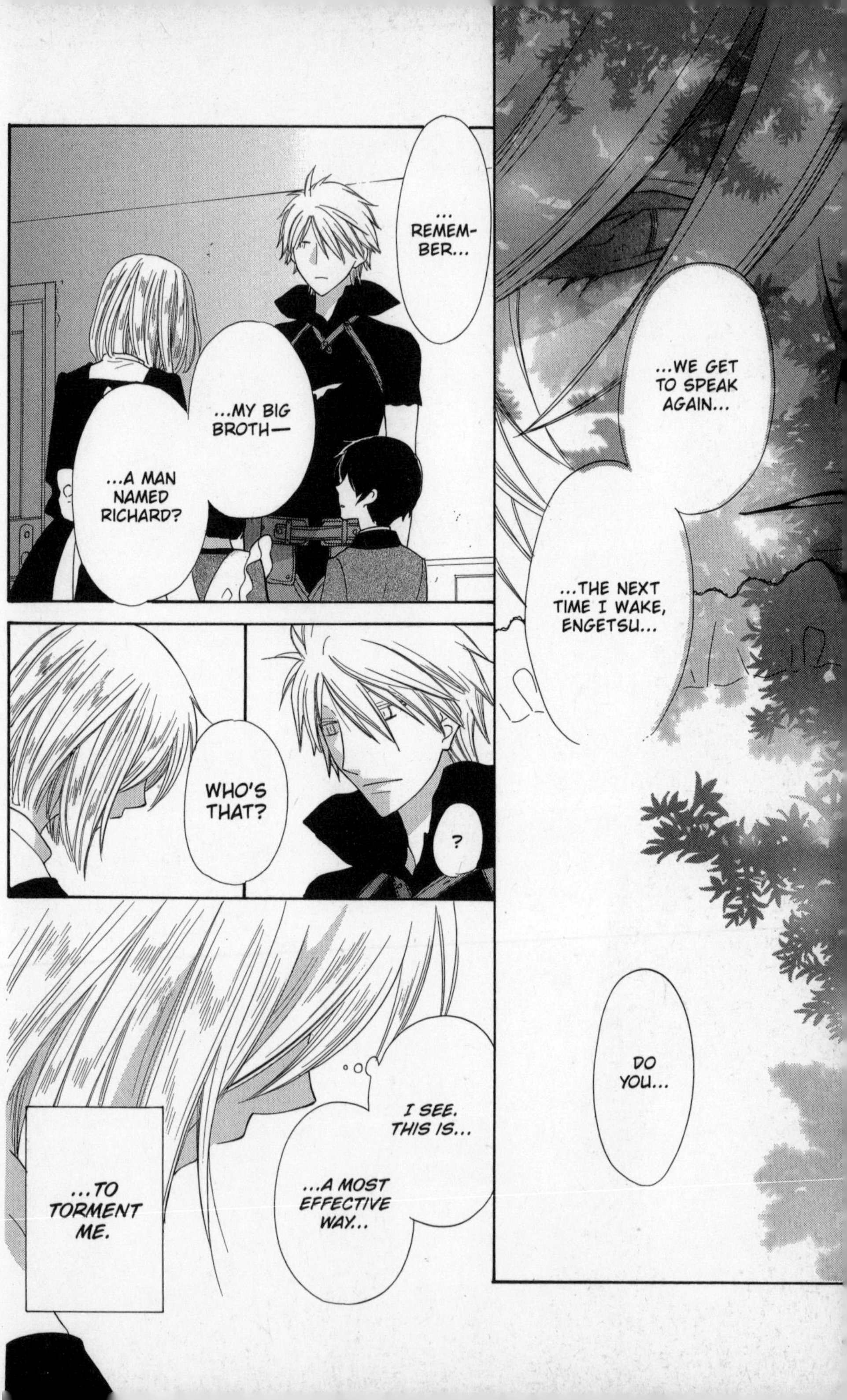
...THE NEXT TIME I WAKE, ENGETSU...
...WE GET TO SPEAK AGAIN...
DO YOU...
...REMEMBER...
...MY BIG BROTH—
...A MAN NAMED RICHARD?
WHO'S THAT?
?
I SEE. THIS IS...
...A MOST EFFECTIVE WAY...
...TO TORMENT ME.

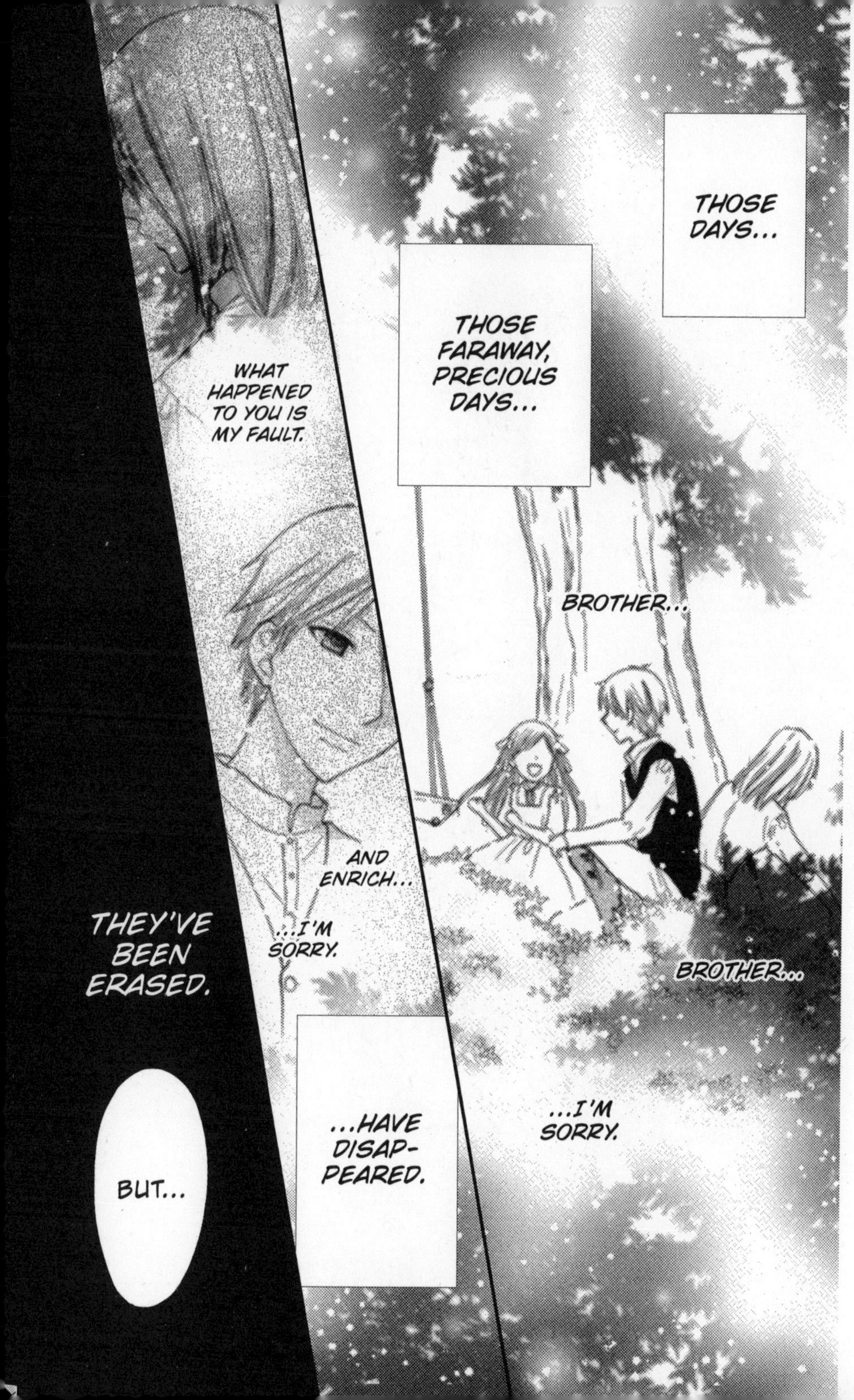
THOSE DAYS...
THOSE FARAWAY, PRECIOUS DAYS...
BROTHER...
BROTHER...
...I'M SORRY.
...HAVE DISAP-PEARED.
WHAT HAPPENED TO YOU IS MY FAULT.
AND ENRICH...
...I'M SORRY.
THEY'VE BEEN ERASED.
BUT...

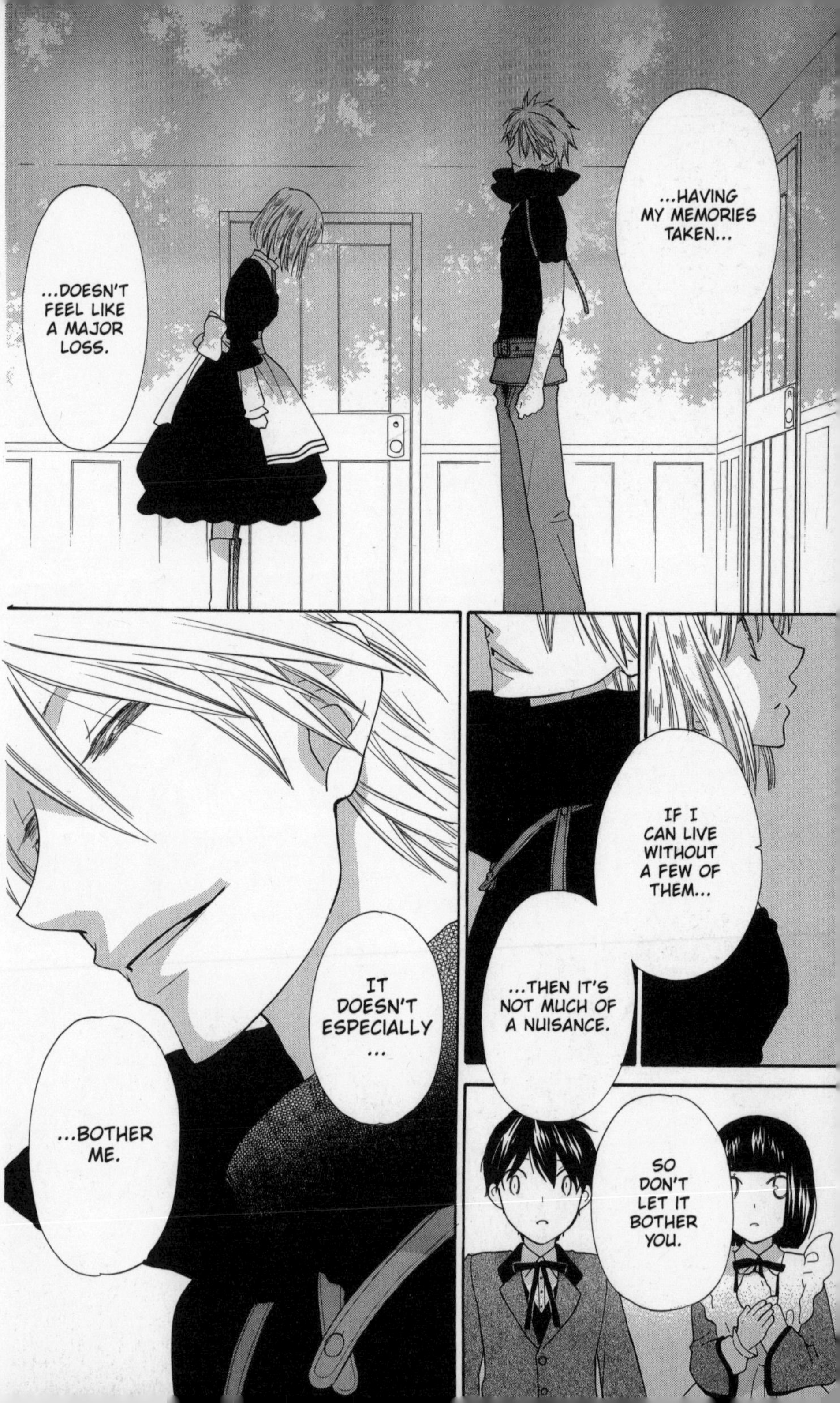
...HAVING MY MEMORIES TAKEN...
...DOESN'T FEEL LIKE A MAJOR LOSS.
IF I CAN LIVE WITHOUT A FEW OF THEM...
...THEN IT'S NOT MUCH OF A NUISANCE.
SO DON'T LET IT BOTHER YOU.
IT DOESN'T ESPECIALLY ...
...BOTHER ME.

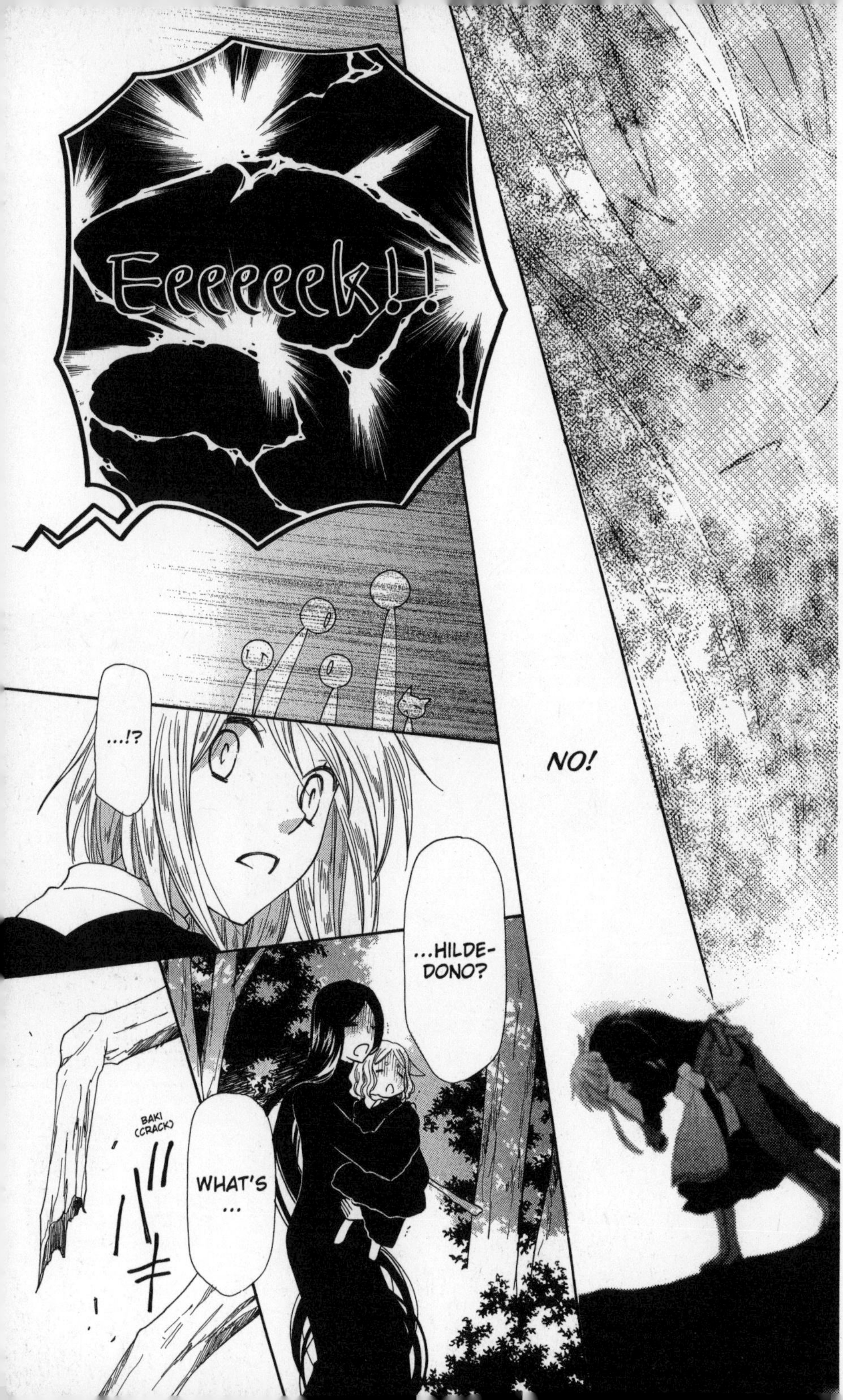
NO!
Eeeeeek!!
...!?
...HILDE-DONO?
BAKI (CRACK)
WHAT'S ...

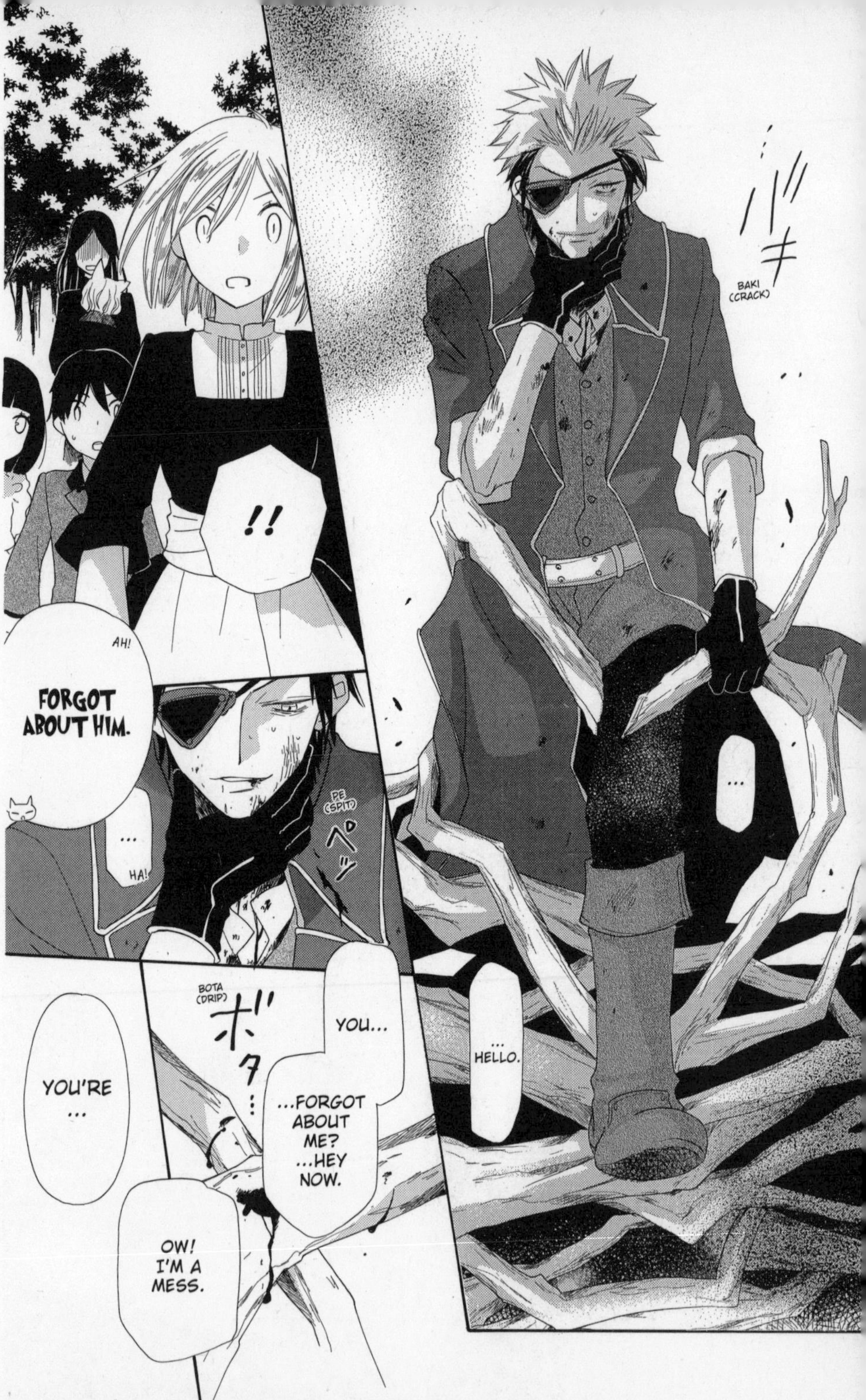
BAKI (CRACK)
...
... HELLO.
!!
AH!
FORGOT ABOUT HIM.
PE (SPIT)
...
HA!
BOTA (DRIP)
YOU...
...FORGOT ABOUT ME? ...HEY NOW.
YOU'RE ...
OW! I'M A MESS.

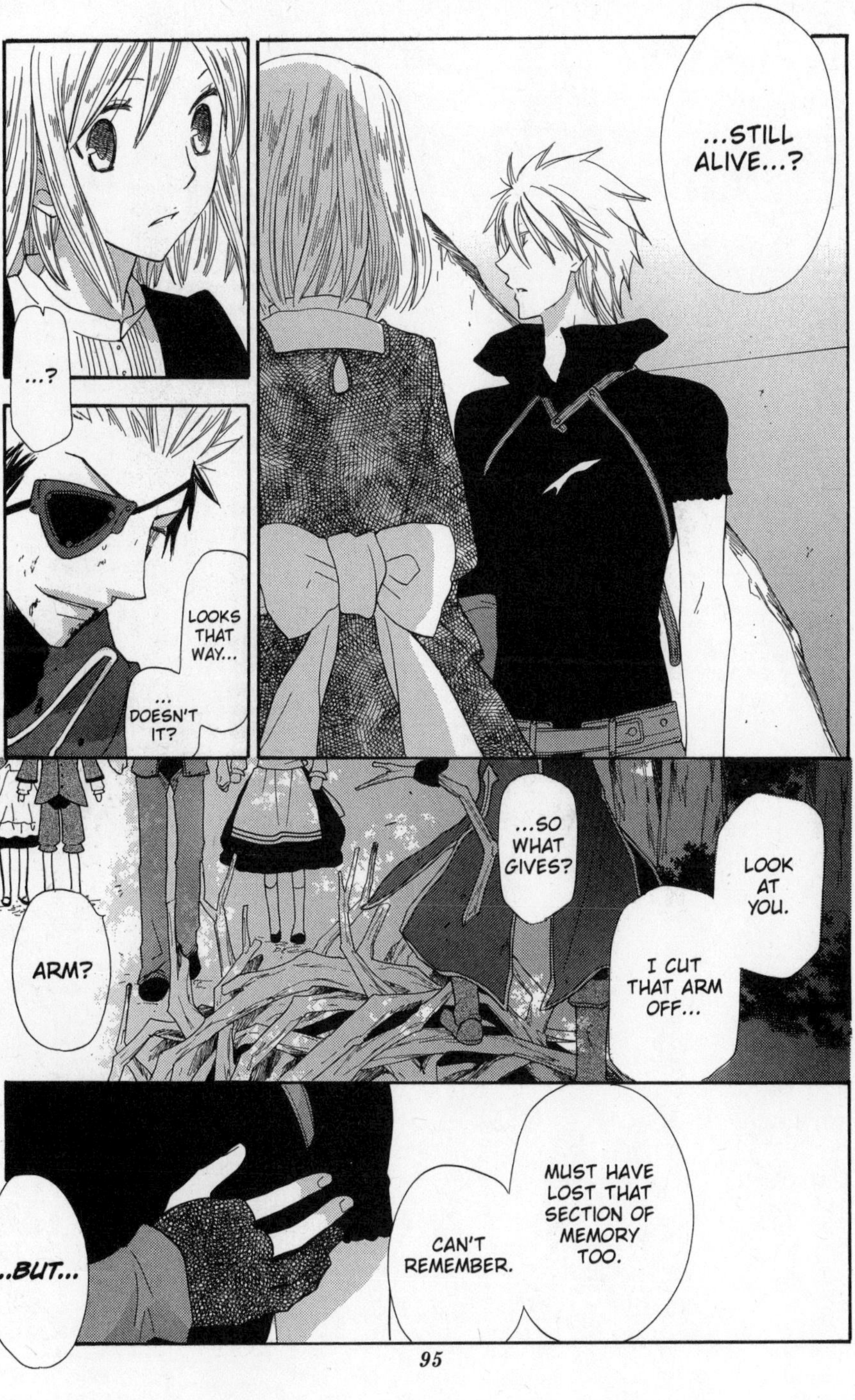
...STILL ALIVE...?
...?
LOOKS THAT WAY...
...DOESN'T IT?
LOOK AT YOU.
I CUT THAT ARM OFF...
...SO WHAT GIVES?
ARM?
MUST HAVE LOST THAT SECTION OF MEMORY TOO.
CAN'T REMEMBER.
...BUT...

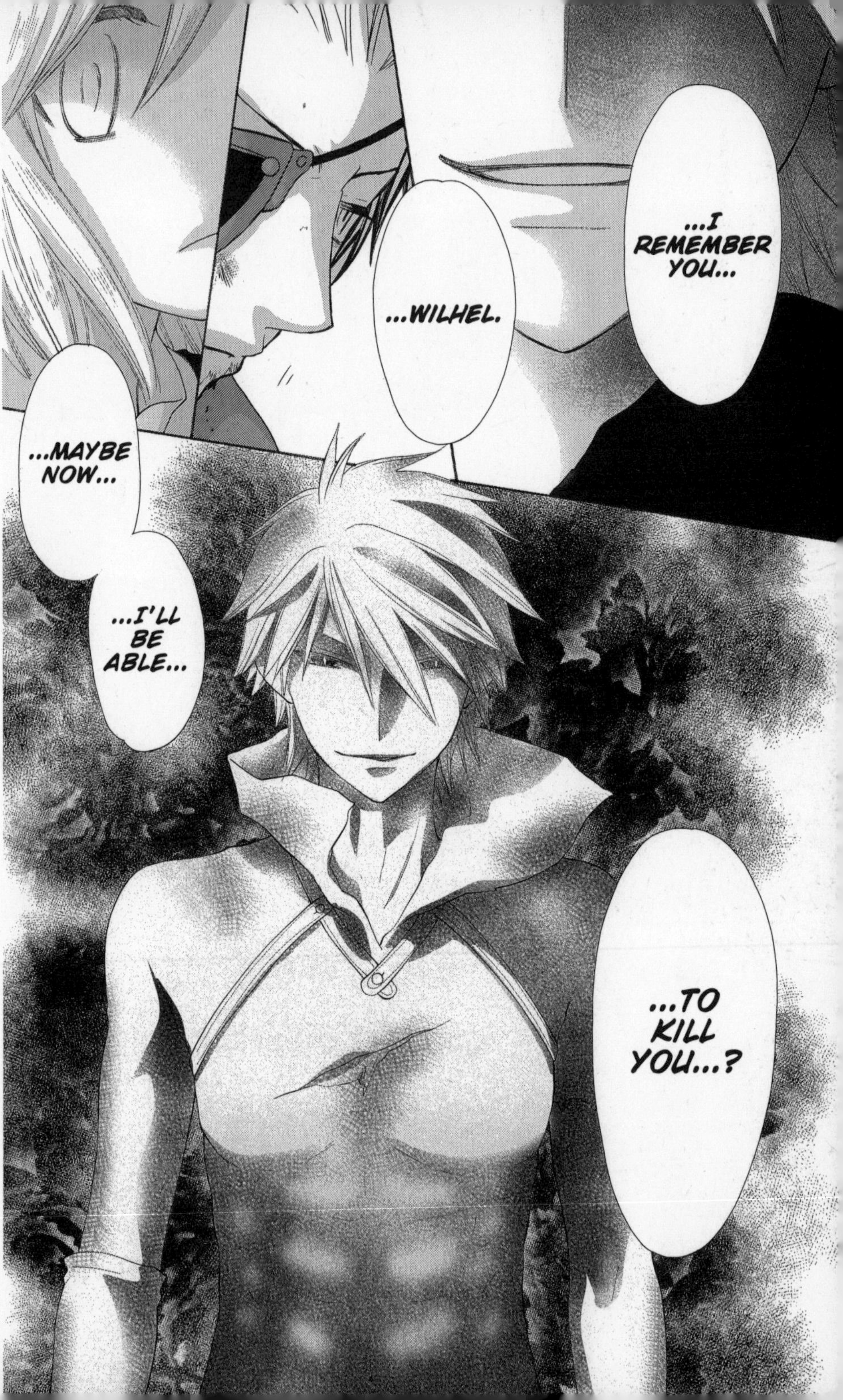
...I REMEMBER YOU...
...WILHEL.
...MAYBE NOW...
...I'LL BE ABLE...
...TO KILL YOU...?

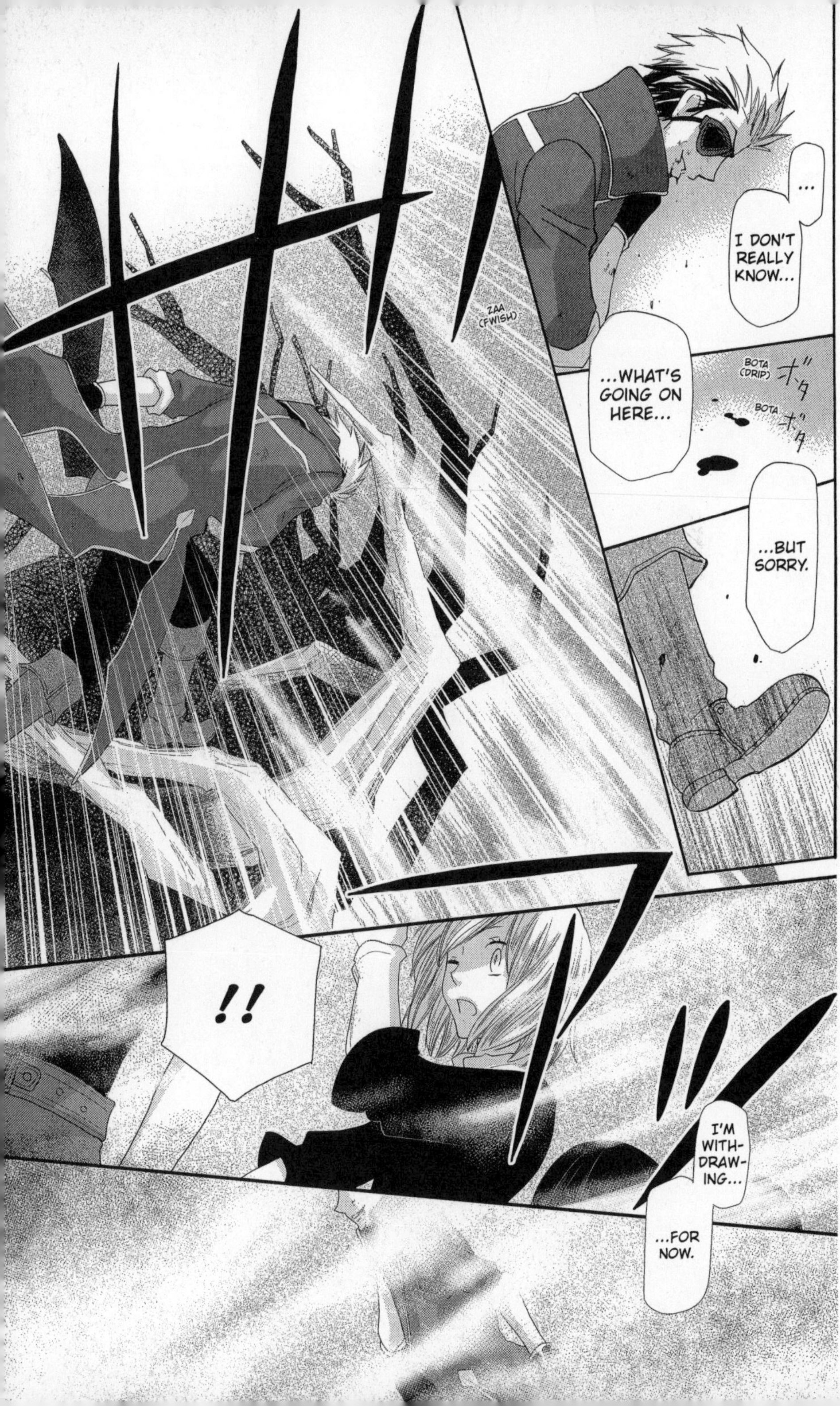
...
I DON'T REALLY KNOW...
...WHAT'S GOING ON HERE...
BOTA (DRIP) ボタ
BOTA ボタ
...BUT SORRY.
ZAA (FWISH)
!!
I'M WITH-DRAW-ING...
...FOR NOW.

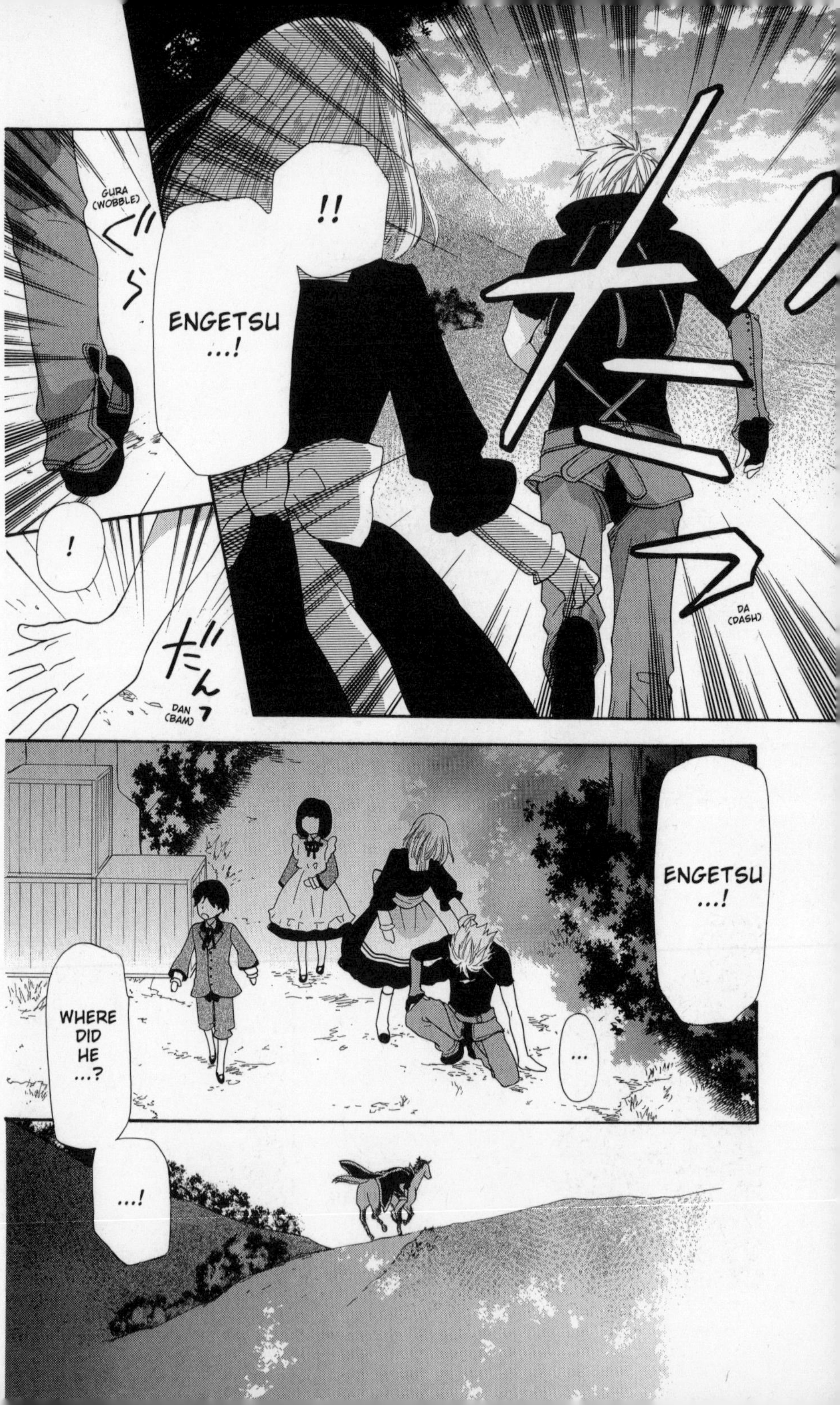

!!
ENGETSU ...!
DA (DASH)
GURA (WOBBLE)
ぐら
!
だん
DAN (BAM)
ENGETSU ...!
...
WHERE DID HE ...?
...!

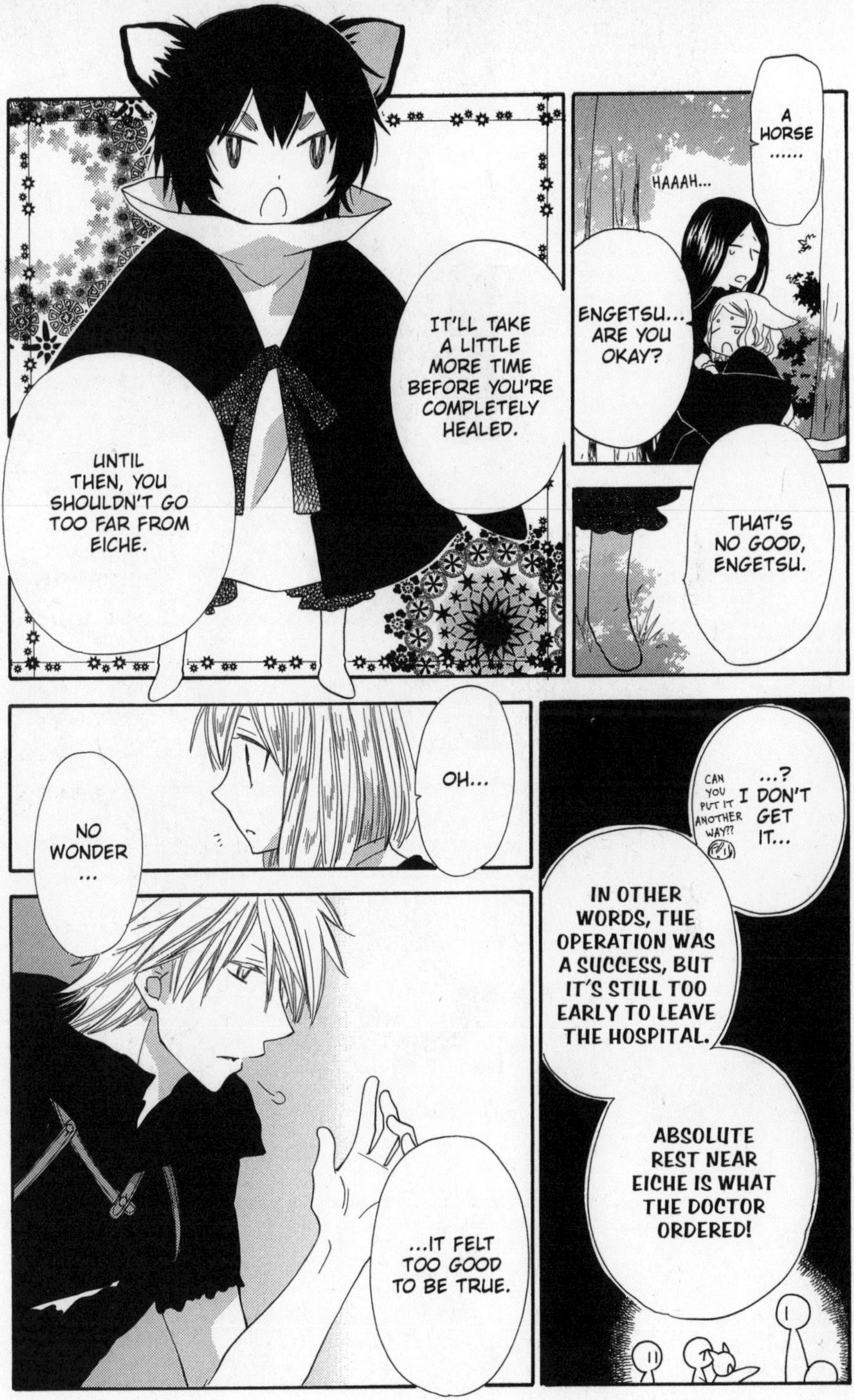
A HORSE......
HAAAH...
ENGETSU... ARE YOU OKAY?
THAT'S NO GOOD, ENGETSU.
IT'LL TAKE A LITTLE MORE TIME BEFORE YOU'RE COMPLETELY HEALED.
UNTIL THEN, YOU SHOULDN'T GO TOO FAR FROM EICHE.
...? I DON'T GET IT...
CAN YOU PUT IT ANOTHER WAY??
IN OTHER WORDS, THE OPERATION WAS A SUCCESS, BUT IT'S STILL TOO EARLY TO LEAVE THE HOSPITAL.
ABSOLUTE REST NEAR EICHE IS WHAT THE DOCTOR ORDERED!
OH...
NO WONDER...
...IT FELT TOO GOOD TO BE TRUE.

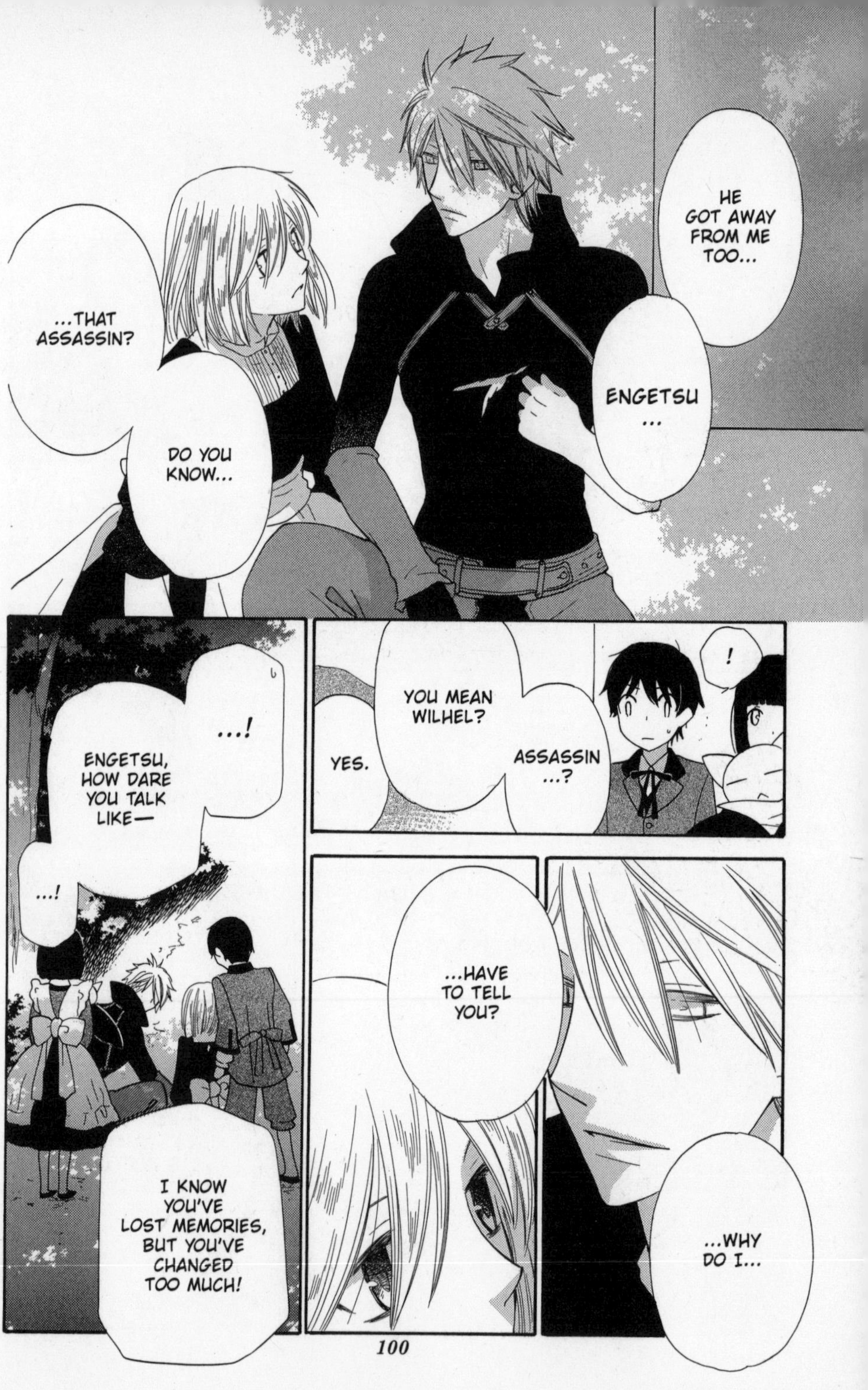
HE GOT AWAY FROM ME TOO...
ENGETSU ...
DO YOU KNOW...
...THAT ASSASSIN?
!
ASSASSIN ...?
YOU MEAN WILHEL?
YES.
...WHY DO I...
...HAVE TO TELL YOU?
...!
ENGETSU, HOW DARE YOU TALK LIKE—
...!
I KNOW YOU'VE LOST MEMORIES, BUT YOU'VE CHANGED TOO MUCH!

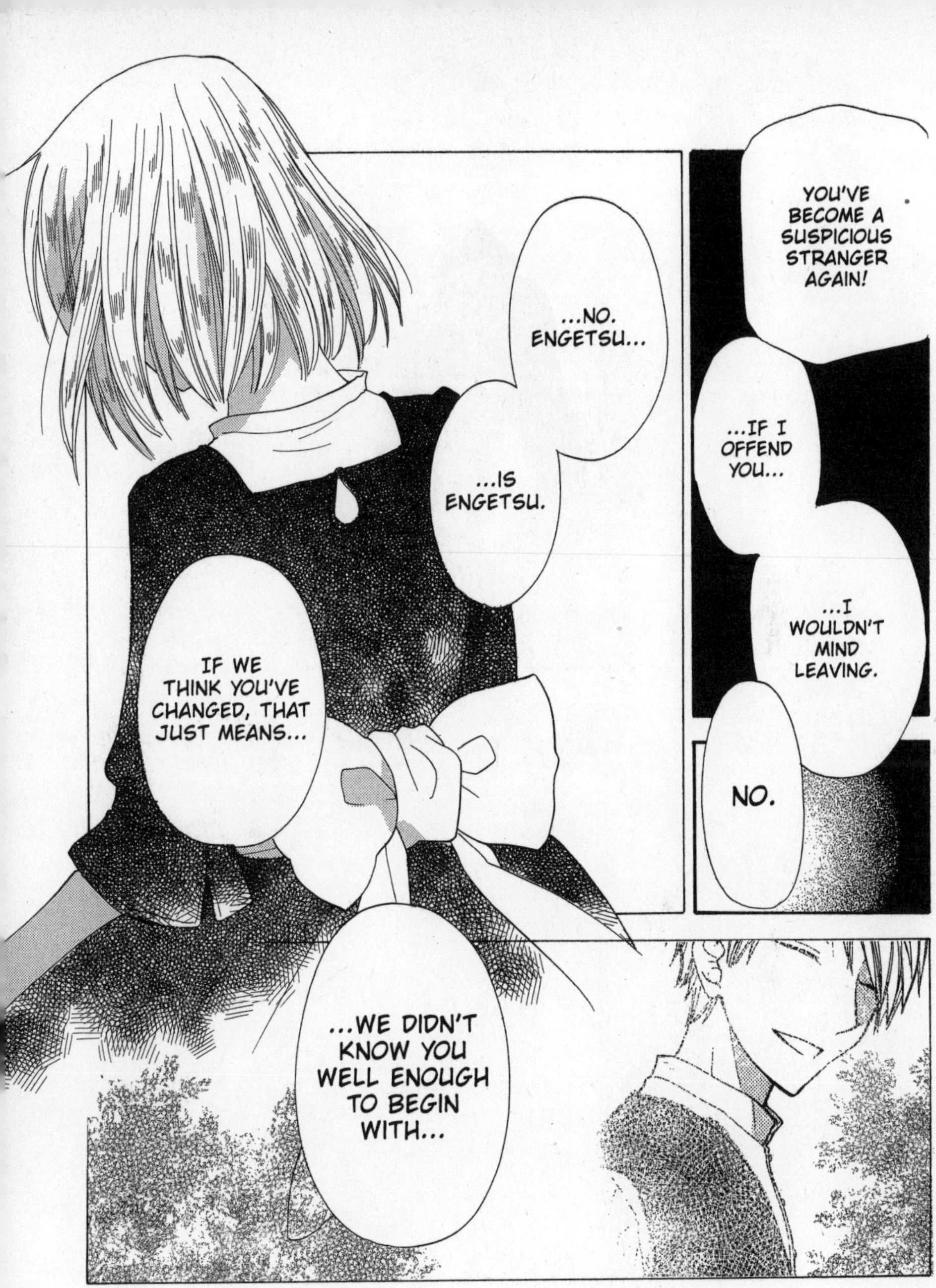
YOU'VE BECOME A SUSPICIOUS STRANGER AGAIN!
...IF I OFFEND YOU...
...I WOULDN'T MIND LEAVING.
NO.
...NO. ENGETSU...
...IS ENGETSU.
IF WE THINK YOU'VE CHANGED, THAT JUST MEANS...
...WE DIDN'T KNOW YOU WELL ENOUGH TO BEGIN WITH...

THAT'S RIGHT.

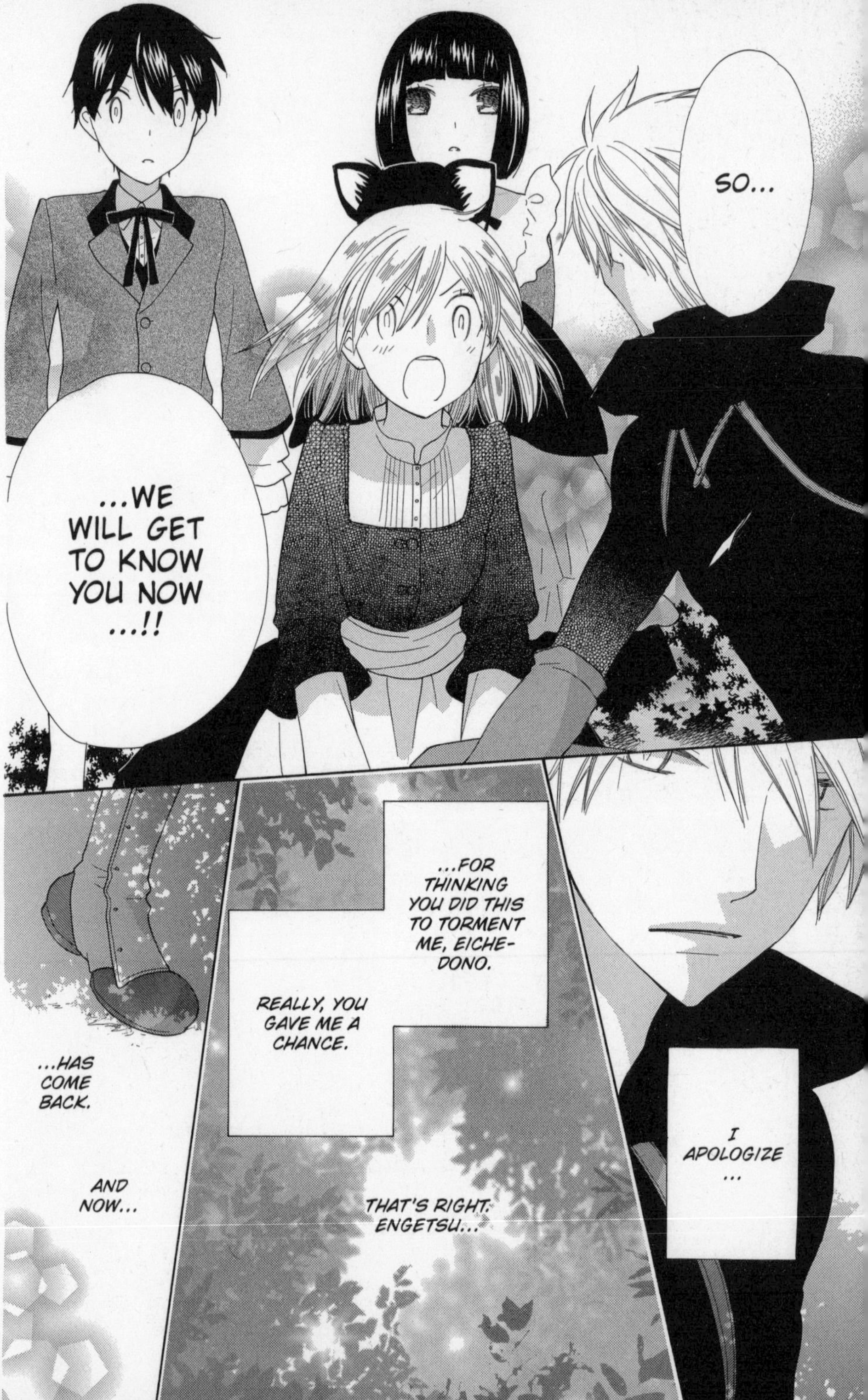
SO...
...WE WILL GET TO KNOW YOU NOW...!!
I APOLOGIZE...
...FOR THINKING YOU DID THIS TO TORMENT ME, EICHE-DONO.
REALLY, YOU GAVE ME A CHANCE.
THAT'S RIGHT. ENGETSU...
...HAS COME BACK.
AND NOW...

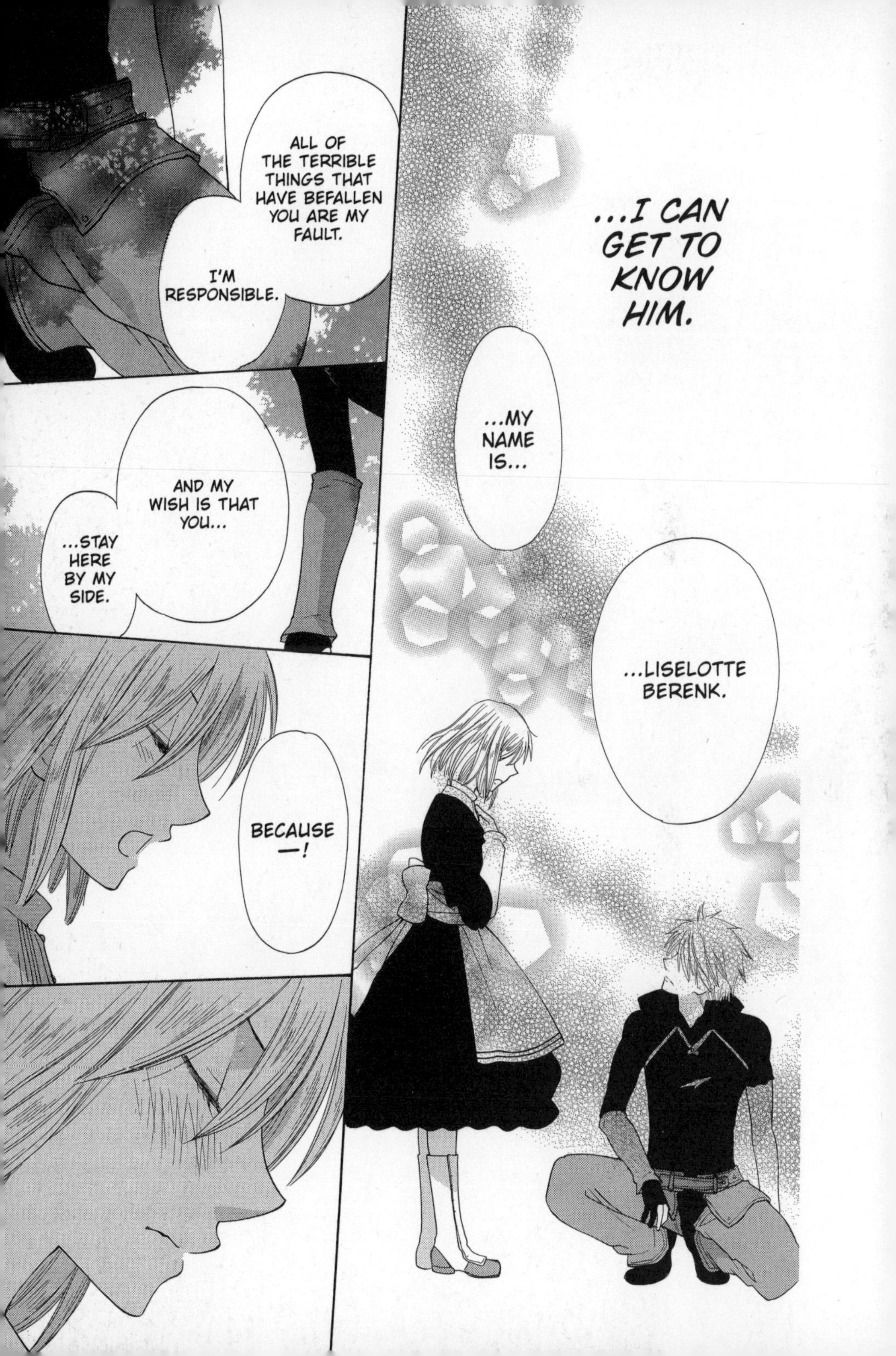
...I CAN GET TO KNOW HIM.
...MY NAME IS...
...LISELOTTE BERENK.
ALL OF THE TERRIBLE THINGS THAT HAVE BEFALLEN YOU ARE MY FAULT.
I'M RESPONSIBLE.
AND MY WISH IS THAT YOU...
...STAY HERE BY MY SIDE.
BECAUSE—!

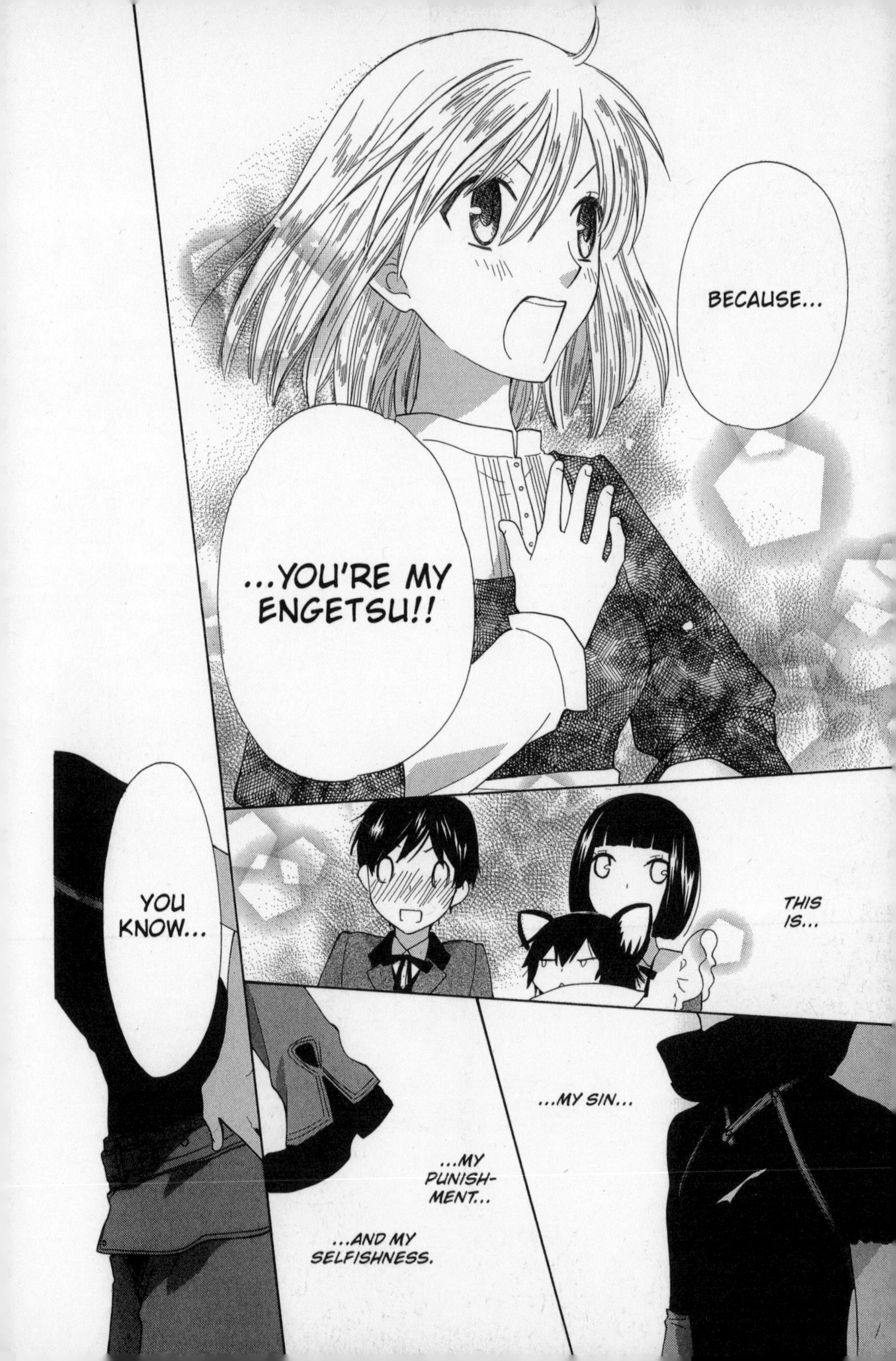
BECAUSE...
...YOU'RE MY ENGETSU!!
THIS IS...
...MY SIN...
...MY PUNISHMENT...
...AND MY SELFISHNESS.
YOU KNOW...

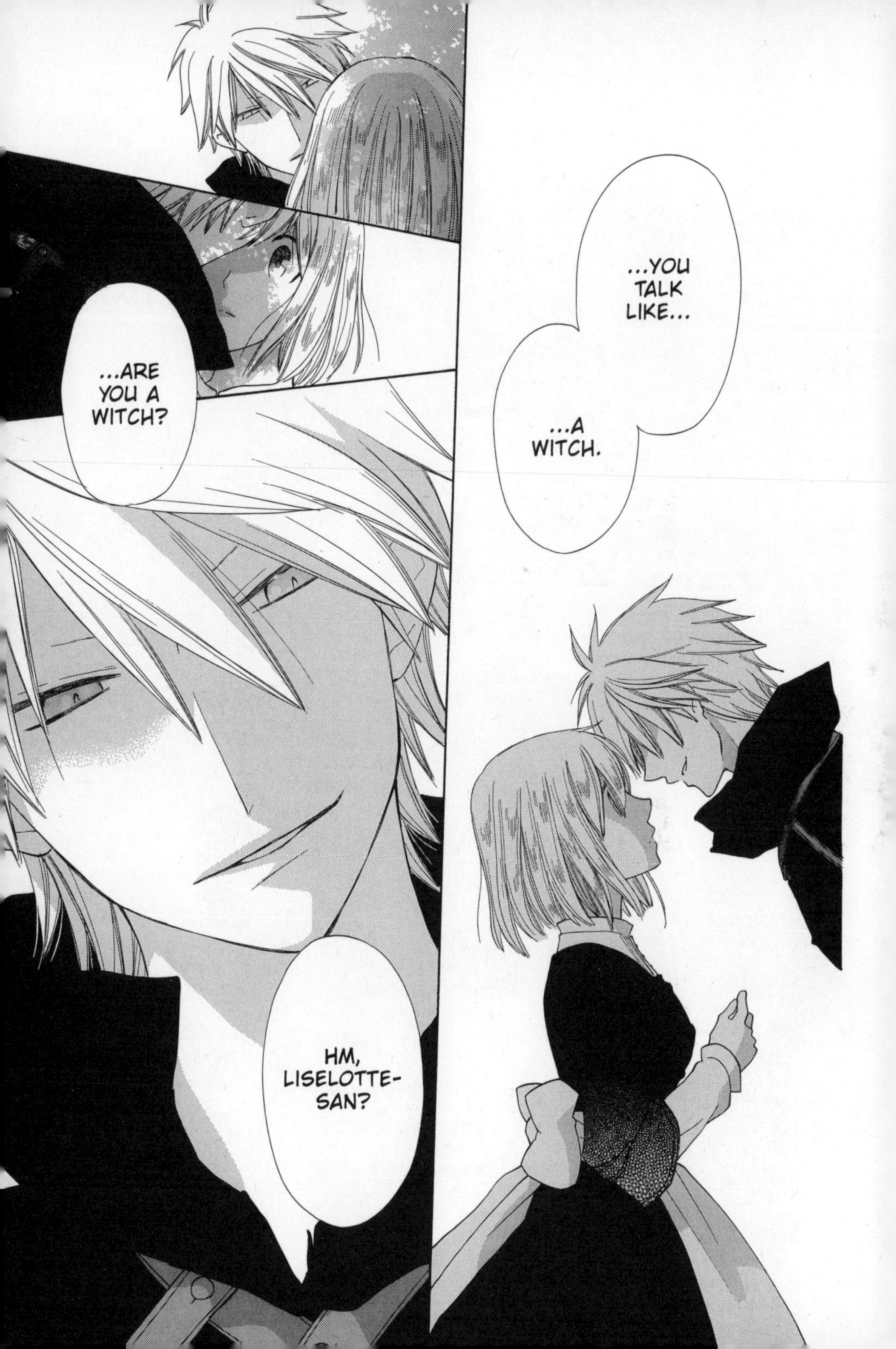
...YOU TALK LIKE...
...A WITCH.
...ARE YOU A WITCH?
HM, LISELOTTE-SAN?

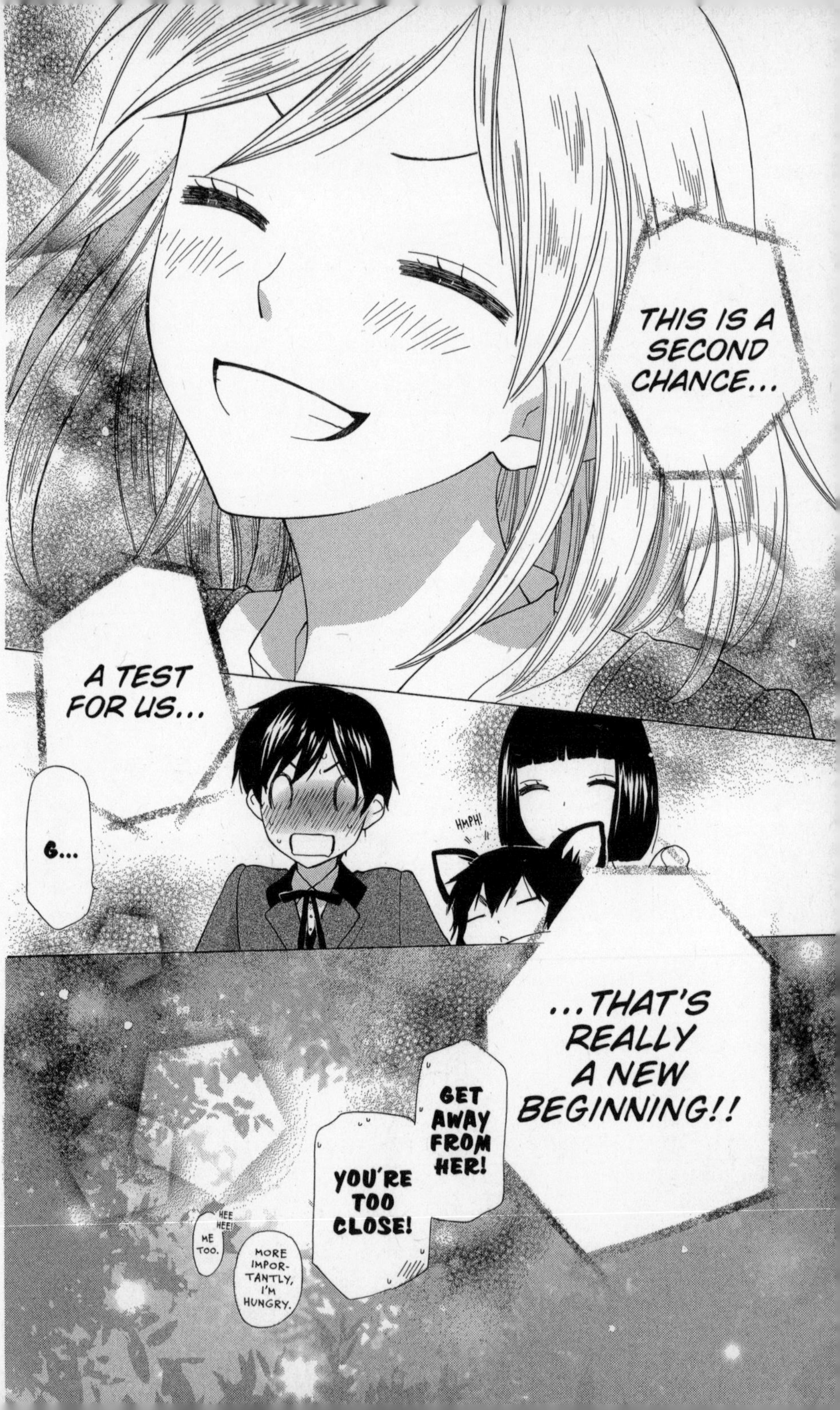
THIS IS A SECOND CHANCE...
A TEST FOR US...
HMPH!
G...
...THAT'S REALLY A NEW BEGINNING!!
GET AWAY FROM HER!
YOU'RE TOO CLOSE!
HEE HEE!
MORE IMPOR-TANTLY, I'M HUNGRY.
ME TOO.

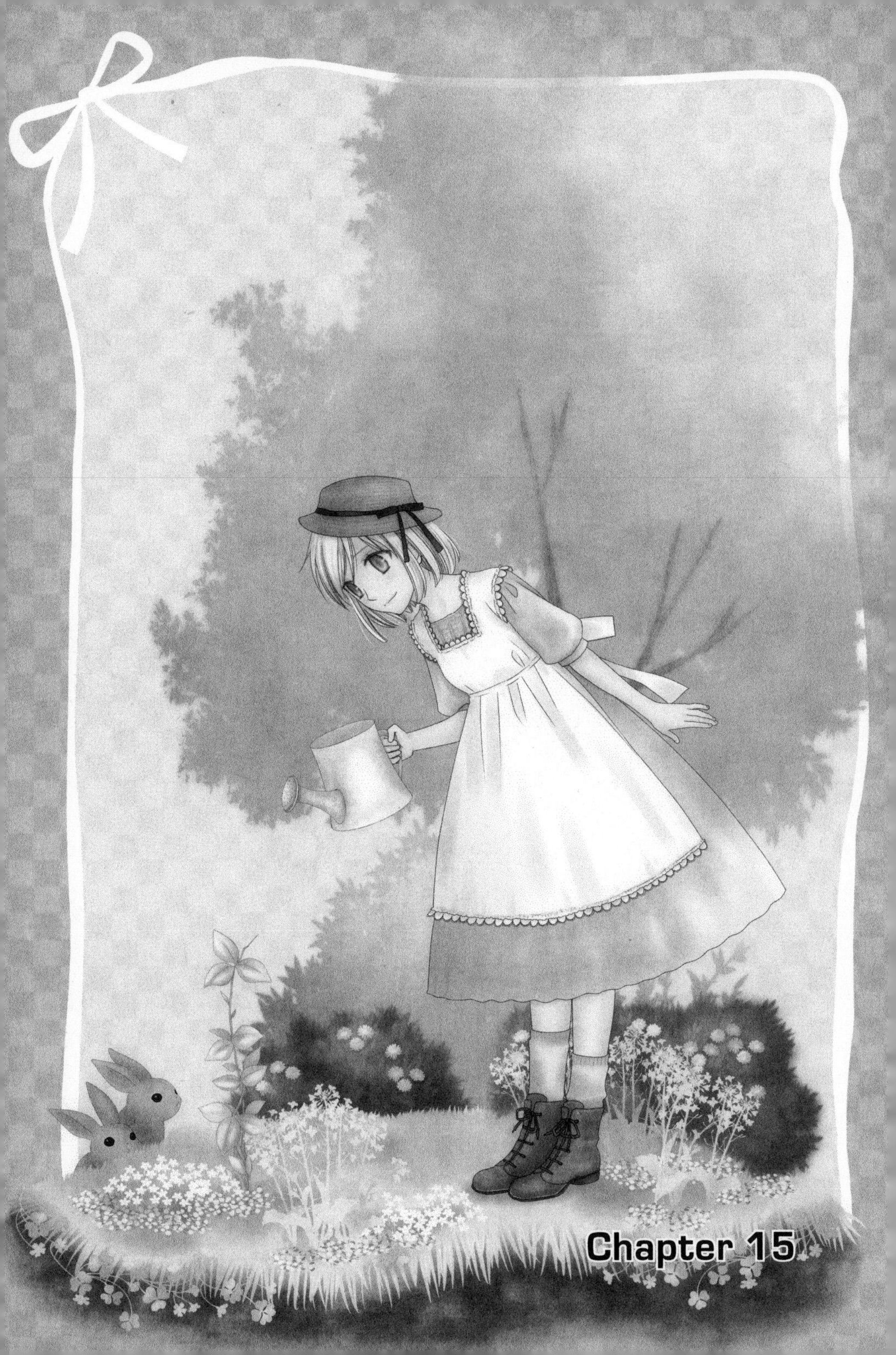
Chapter 15

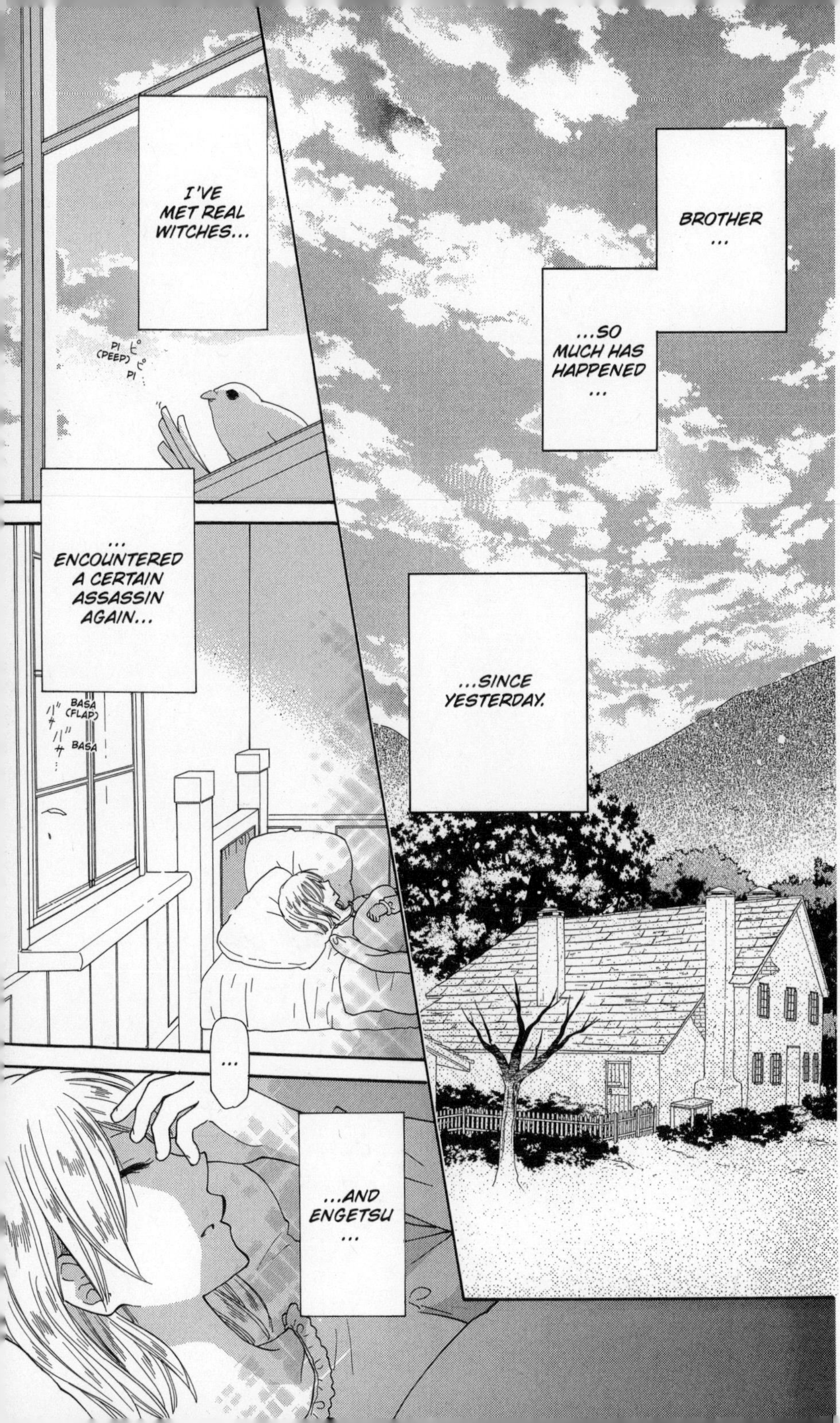
BROTHER ...
...SO MUCH HAS HAPPENED ...
...SINCE YESTERDAY.
I'VE MET REAL WITCHES...
PI ピ (PEEP) ピ PI
... ENCOUNTERED A CERTAIN ASSASSIN AGAIN...
バサ BASA (FLAP) バサ BASA
...
...AND ENGETSU ...

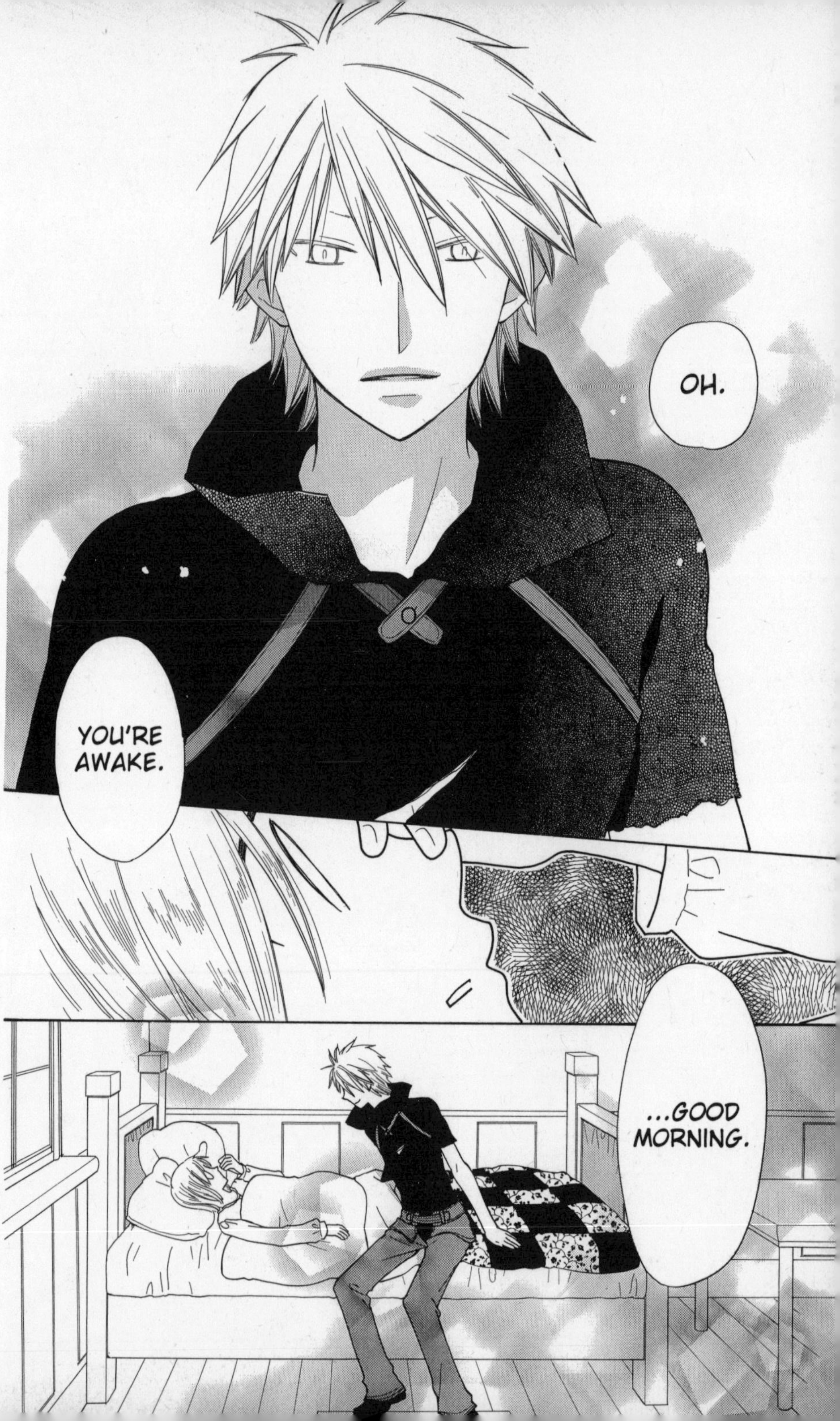
OH.
YOU'RE AWAKE.
...GOOD MORNING.

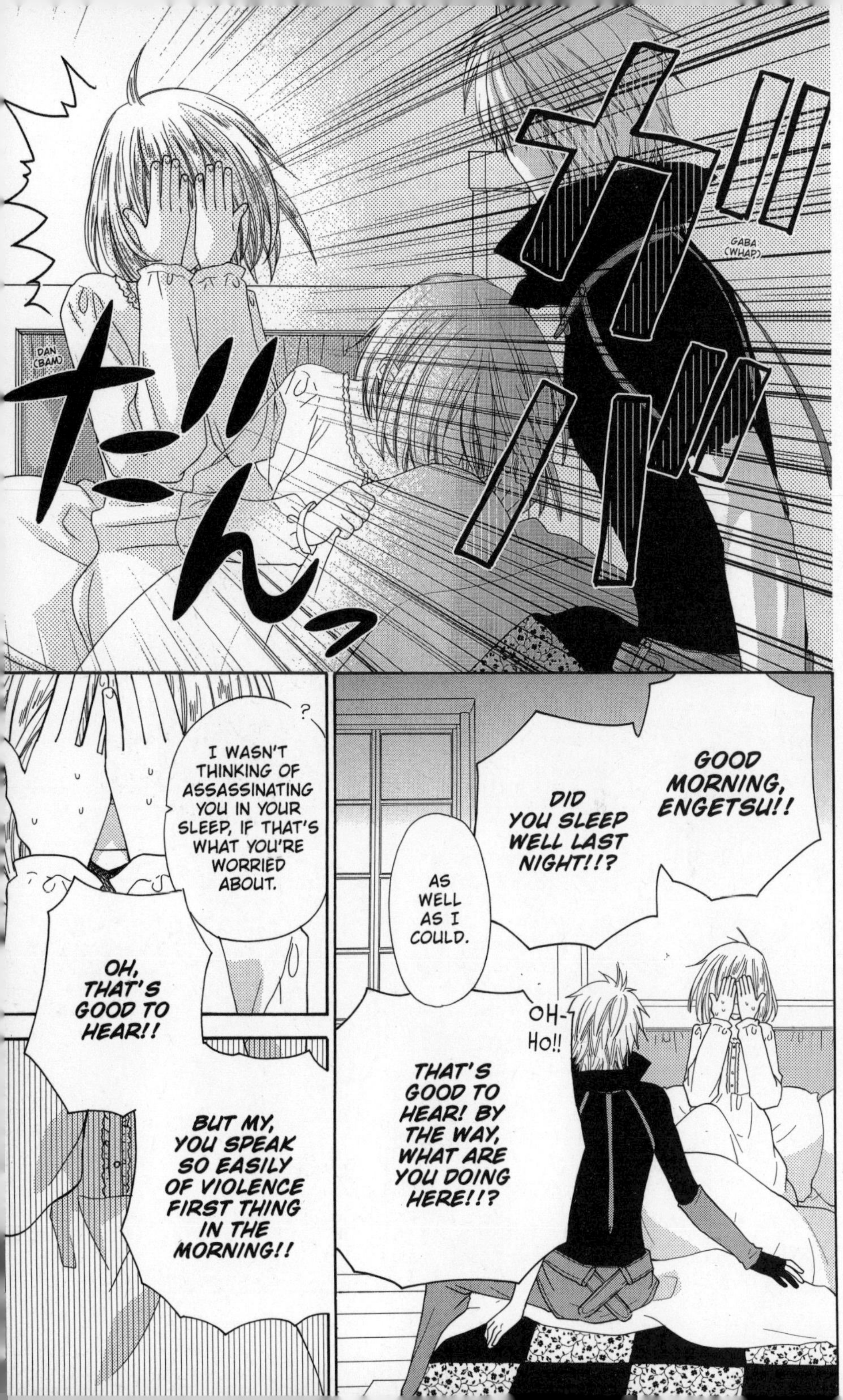
GABA (WHAP)
DAN (BAM)
GOOD MORNING, ENGETSU!!
DID YOU SLEEP WELL LAST NIGHT!!?
AS WELL AS I COULD.
OH-HO!!
THAT'S GOOD TO HEAR! BY THE WAY, WHAT ARE YOU DOING HERE!!?
?
I WASN'T THINKING OF ASSASSINATING YOU IN YOUR SLEEP, IF THAT'S WHAT YOU'RE WORRIED ABOUT.
OH, THAT'S GOOD TO HEAR!!
BUT MY, YOU SPEAK SO EASILY OF VIOLENCE FIRST THING IN THE MORNING!!

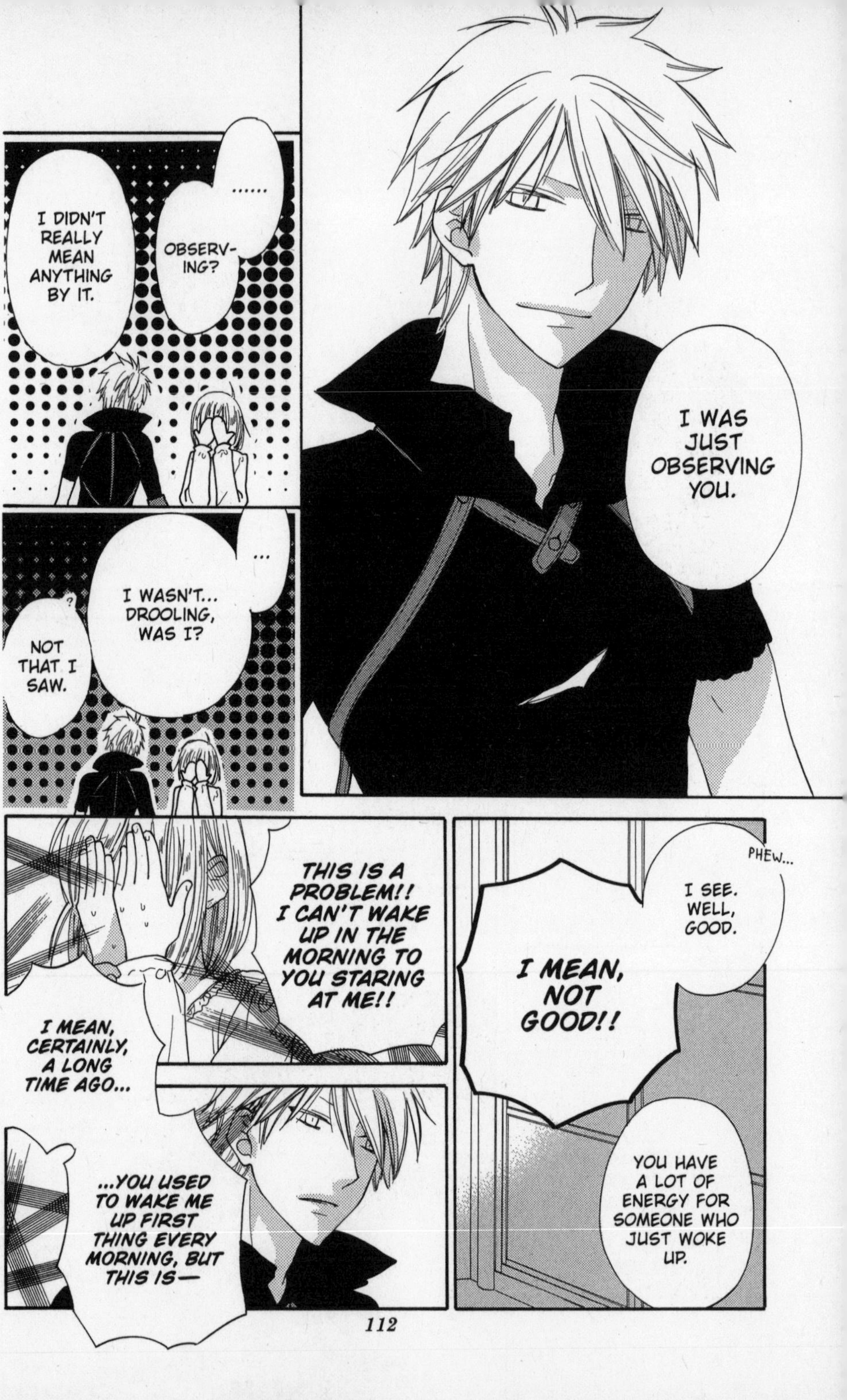
I WAS JUST OBSERVING YOU.
......
OBSERVING?
I DIDN'T REALLY MEAN ANYTHING BY IT.
...
I WASN'T... DROOLING, WAS I?
NOT THAT I SAW.
PHEW...
I SEE. WELL, GOOD.
I MEAN, NOT GOOD!!
YOU HAVE A LOT OF ENERGY FOR SOMEONE WHO JUST WOKE UP.
THIS IS A PROBLEM!! I CAN'T WAKE UP IN THE MORNING TO YOU STARING AT ME!!
I MEAN, CERTAINLY, A LONG TIME AGO...
...YOU USED TO WAKE ME UP FIRST THING EVERY MORNING, BUT THIS IS—

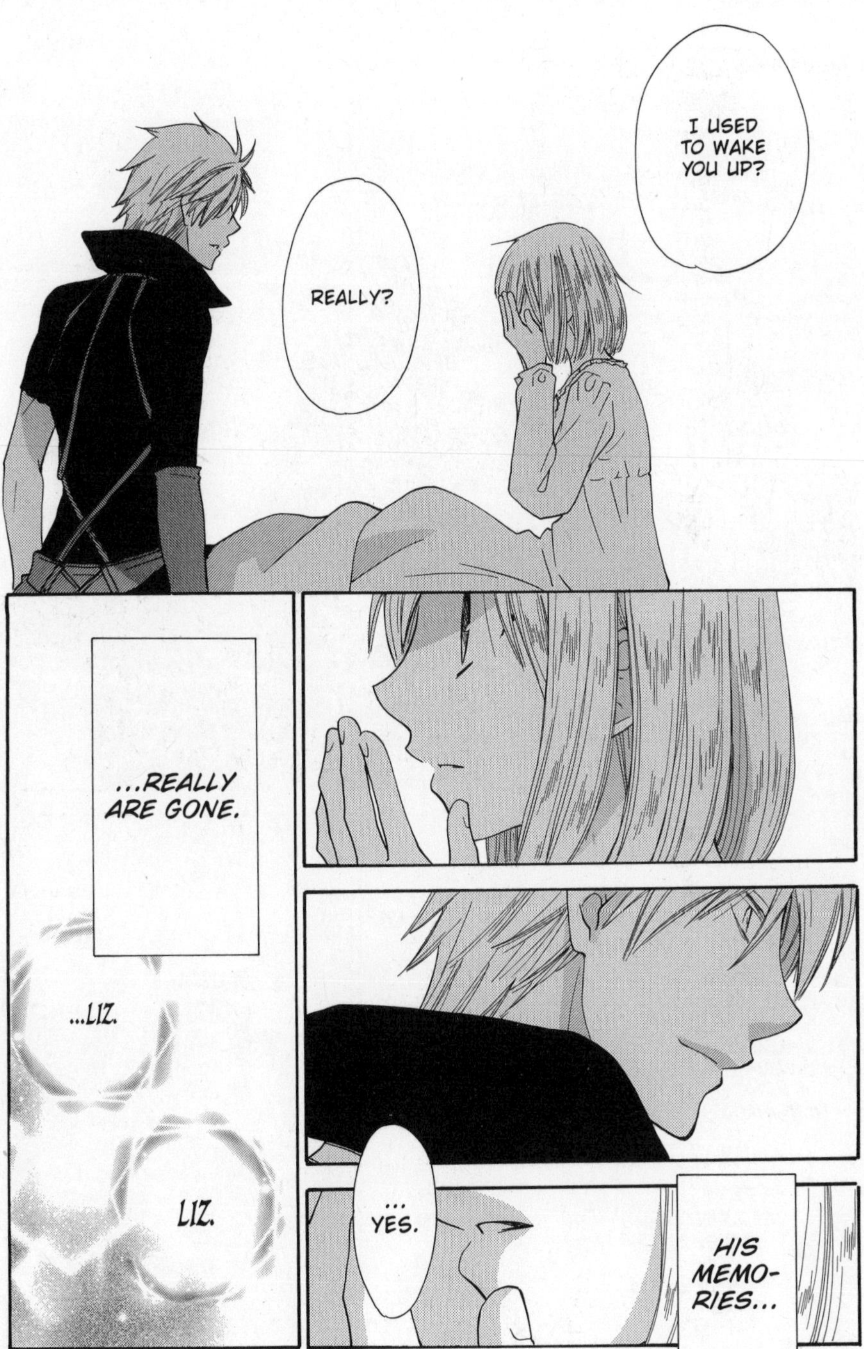
I USED TO WAKE YOU UP?
REALLY?
HIS MEMO-RIES...
... YES.
...REALLY ARE GONE.
...LIZ.
LIZ.

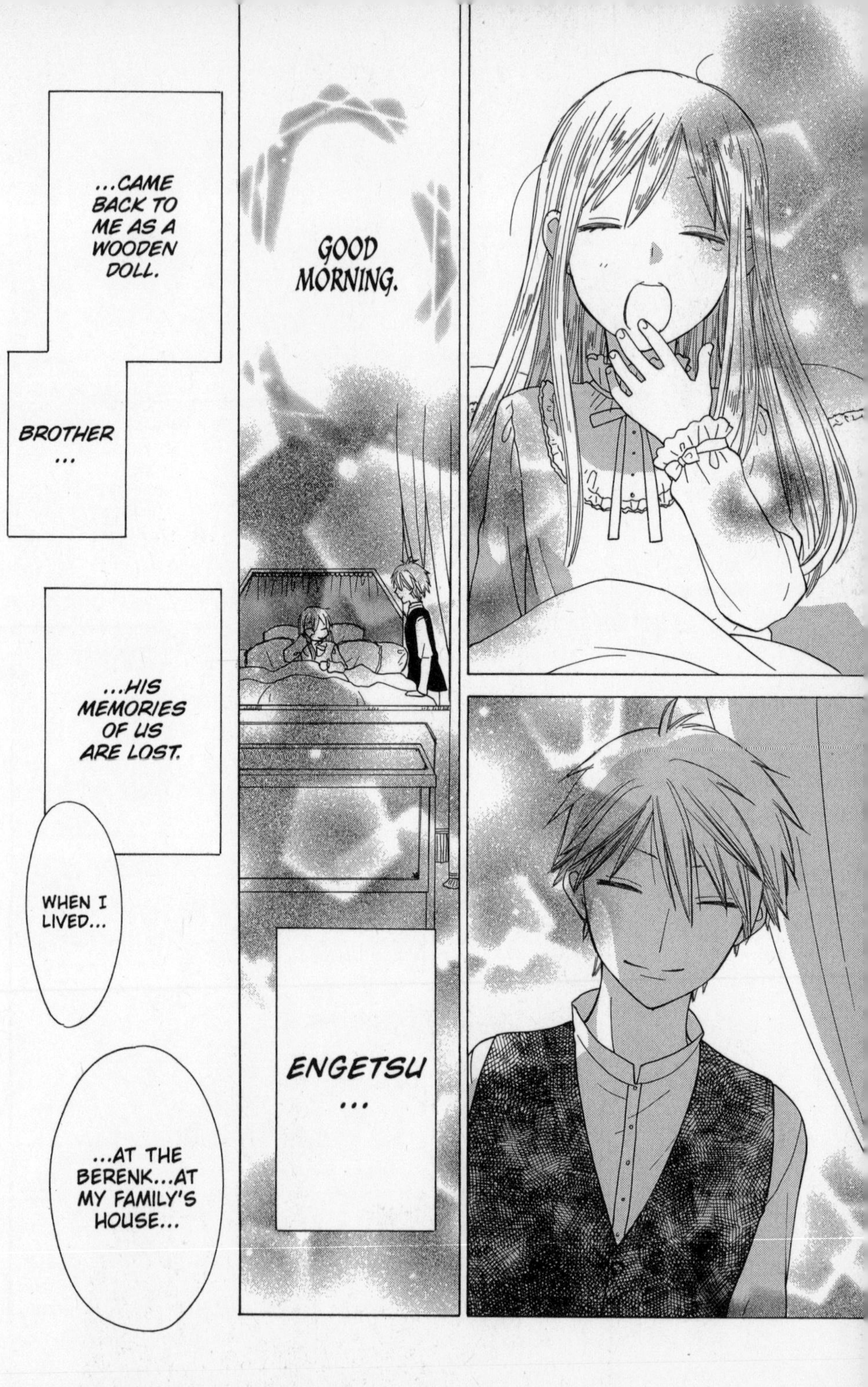
GOOD MORNING.
ENGETSU ...
...CAME BACK TO ME AS A WOODEN DOLL.
BROTHER ...
...HIS MEMORIES OF US ARE LOST.
WHEN I LIVED...
...AT THE BERENK...AT MY FAMILY'S HOUSE...

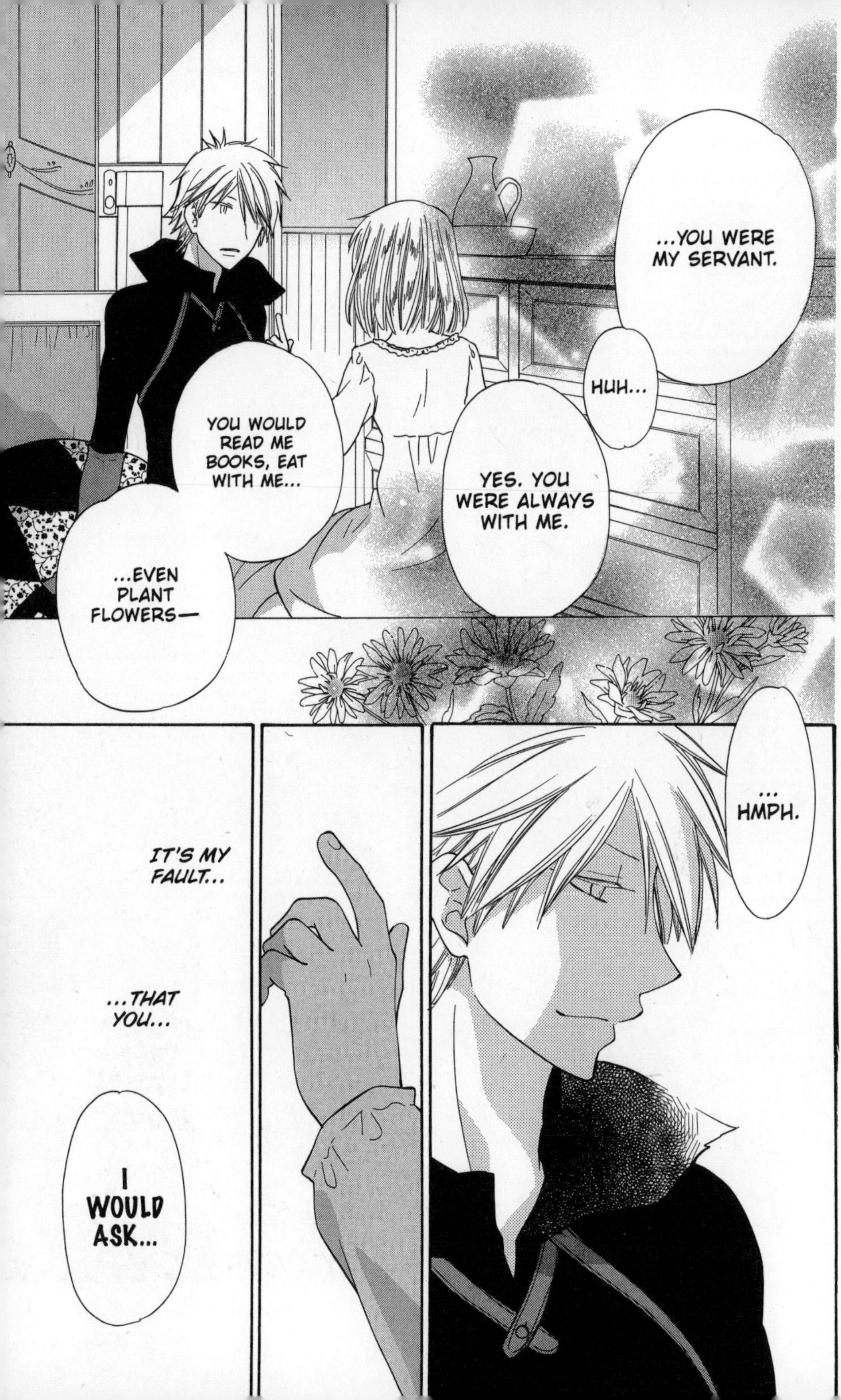
...YOU WERE MY SERVANT.
HUH...
YES. YOU WERE ALWAYS WITH ME.
YOU WOULD READ ME BOOKS, EAT WITH ME...
...EVEN PLANT FLOWERS—
... HMPH.
IT'S MY FAULT...
...THAT YOU...
I WOULD ASK...

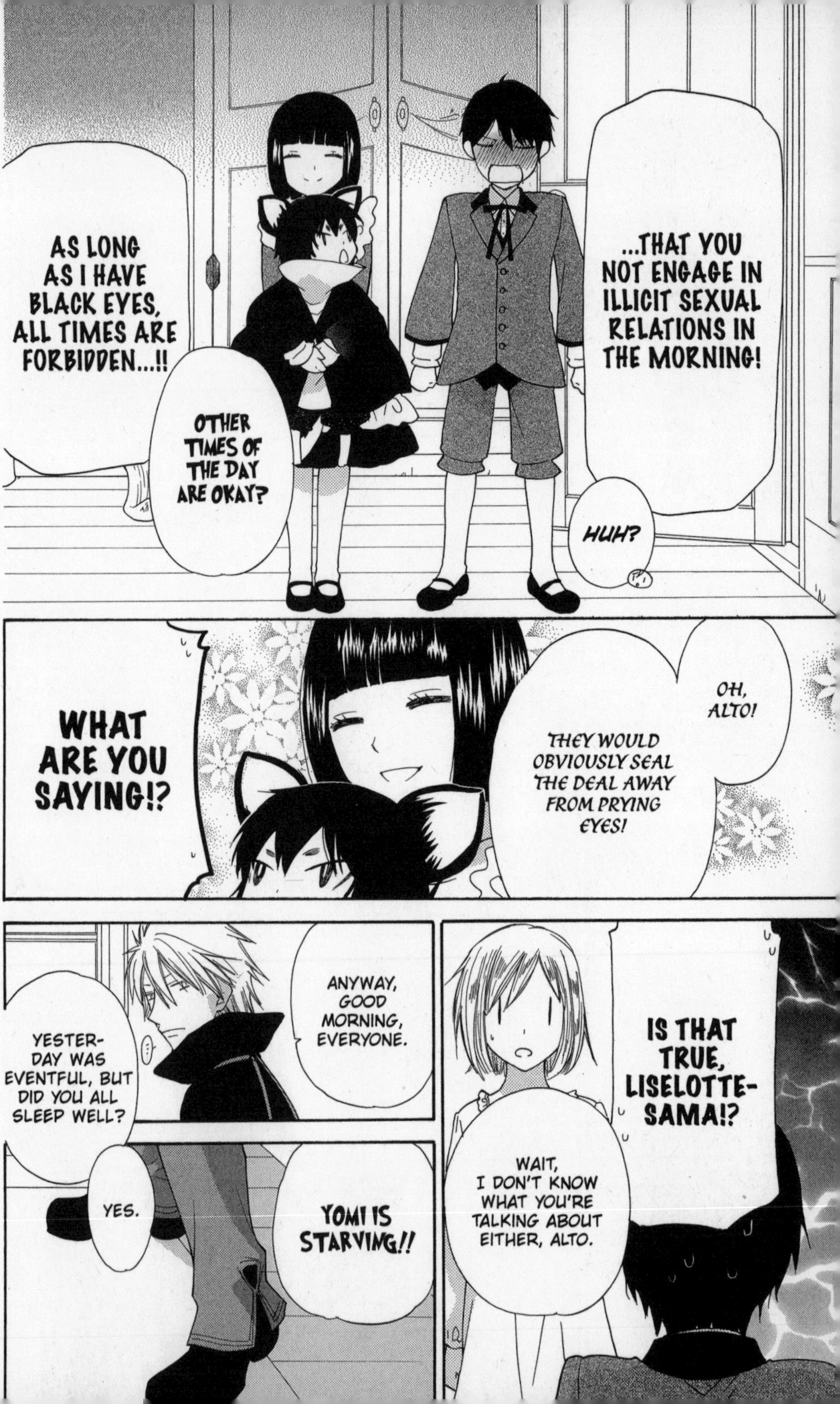
...THAT YOU NOT ENGAGE IN ILLICIT SEXUAL RELATIONS IN THE MORNING!
OTHER TIMES OF THE DAY ARE OKAY?
AS LONG AS I HAVE BLACK EYES, ALL TIMES ARE FORBIDDEN...!!
HUH?
OH, ALTO!
THEY WOULD OBVIOUSLY SEAL THE DEAL AWAY FROM PRYING EYES!
WHAT ARE YOU SAYING!?
IS THAT TRUE, LISELOTTE-SAMA!?
WAIT, I DON'T KNOW WHAT YOU'RE TALKING ABOUT EITHER, ALTO.
ANYWAY, GOOD MORNING, EVERYONE.
YESTER-DAY WAS EVENTFUL, BUT DID YOU ALL SLEEP WELL?
YOMI IS STARVING!!
YES.

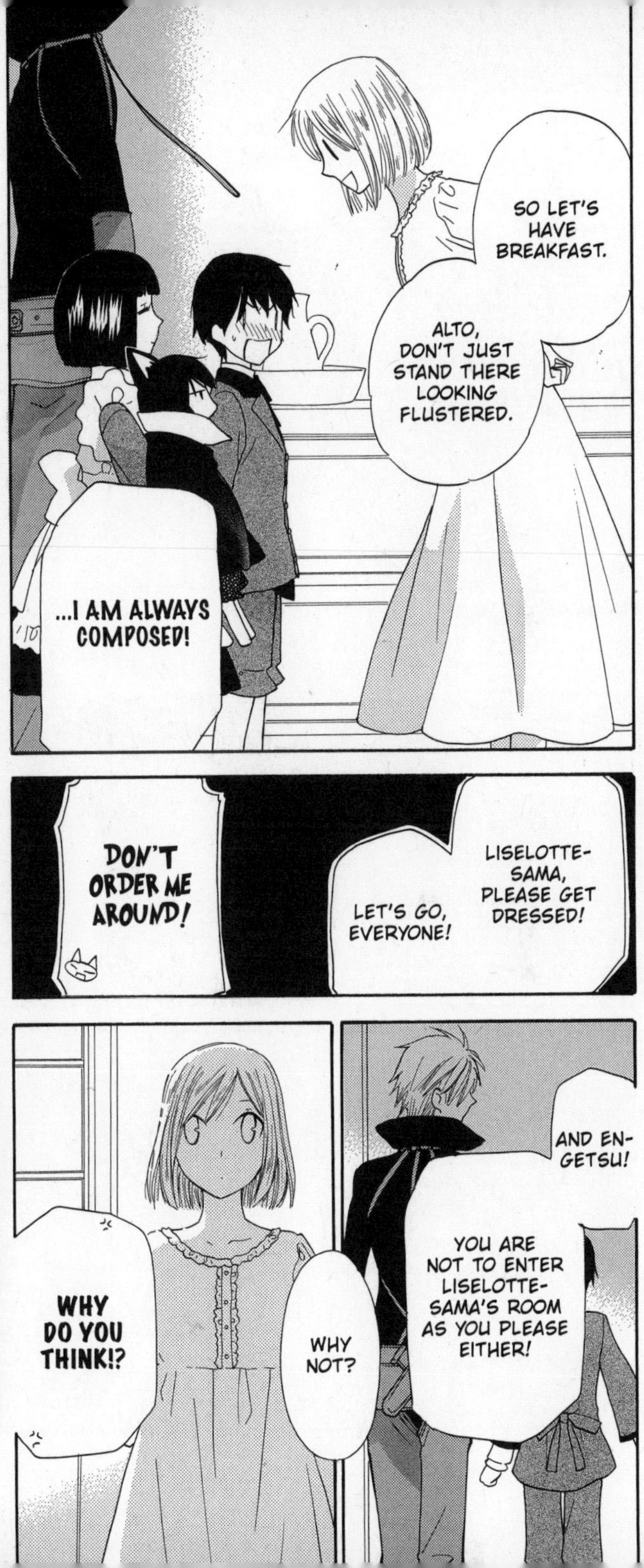
SO LET'S HAVE BREAKFAST.
ALTO, DON'T JUST STAND THERE LOOKING FLUSTERED.
...I AM ALWAYS COMPOSED!
LISELOTTE-SAMA, PLEASE GET DRESSED!
LET'S GO, EVERYONE!
DON'T ORDER ME AROUND!
AND EN-GETSU!
YOU ARE NOT TO ENTER LISELOTTE-SAMA'S ROOM AS YOU PLEASE EITHER!
WHY NOT?
WHY DO YOU THINK!?

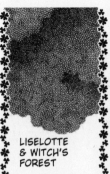

LISELOTTE & WITCH'S FOREST

NICE TO MEET YOU & HELLO. I'M TAKAYA, AND THIS IS VOLUME 3 OF LISE & WITCH.

A FAIR AMOUNT HAPPENS IN THIS VOLUME, BUT I HOPE YOU WATCH OVER LISELOTTE AS SHE BOLDLY YET CHEERFULLY GOES DOWN HER PATH.

THIS IS THE BEGINNING OF THAT KIND OF LISE & WITCH.

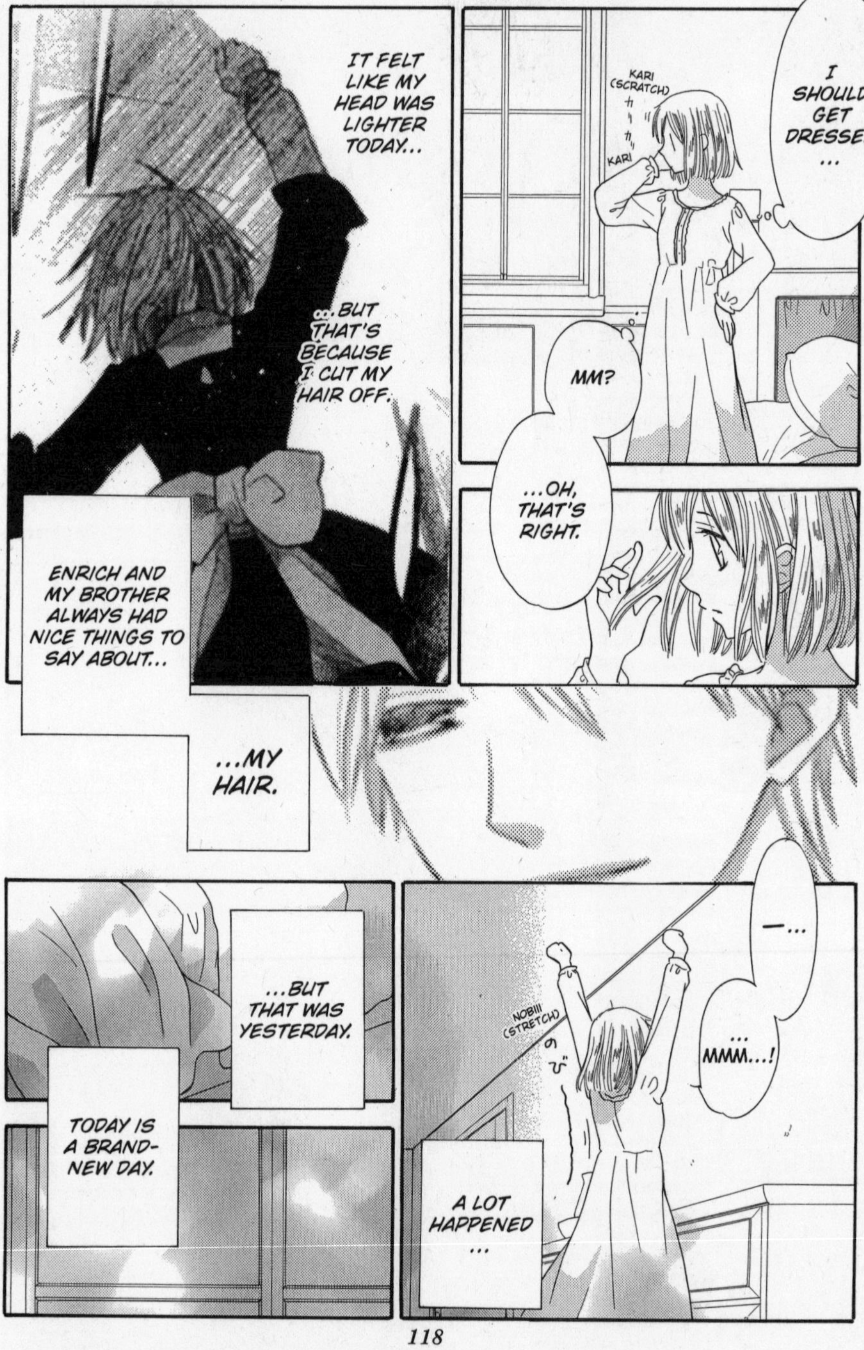
I SHOULD GET DRESSED ...
KARI (SCRATCH)
KARI
MM?
...OH, THAT'S RIGHT.
IT FELT LIKE MY HEAD WAS LIGHTER TODAY...
...BUT THAT'S BECAUSE I CUT MY HAIR OFF.
ENRICH AND MY BROTHER ALWAYS HAD NICE THINGS TO SAY ABOUT...
...MY HAIR.
—...
...MMM...!
NOBIII (STRETCH)
A LOT HAPPENED ...
...BUT THAT WAS YESTERDAY.
TODAY IS A BRAND-NEW DAY.

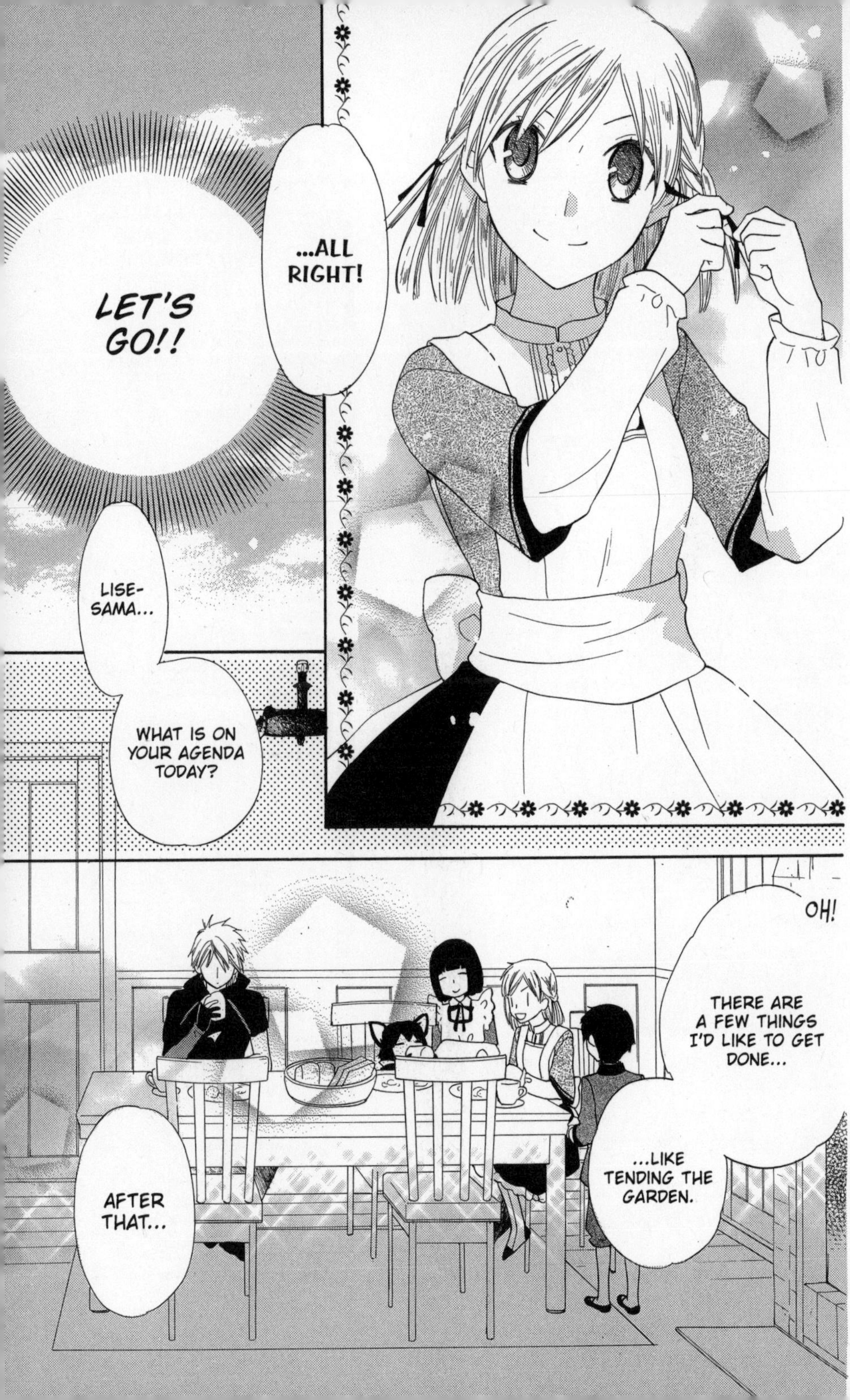
...ALL RIGHT!
LET'S GO!!
LISE-SAMA...
WHAT IS ON YOUR AGENDA TODAY?
OH!
THERE ARE A FEW THINGS I'D LIKE TO GET DONE...
...LIKE TENDING THE GARDEN.
AFTER THAT...

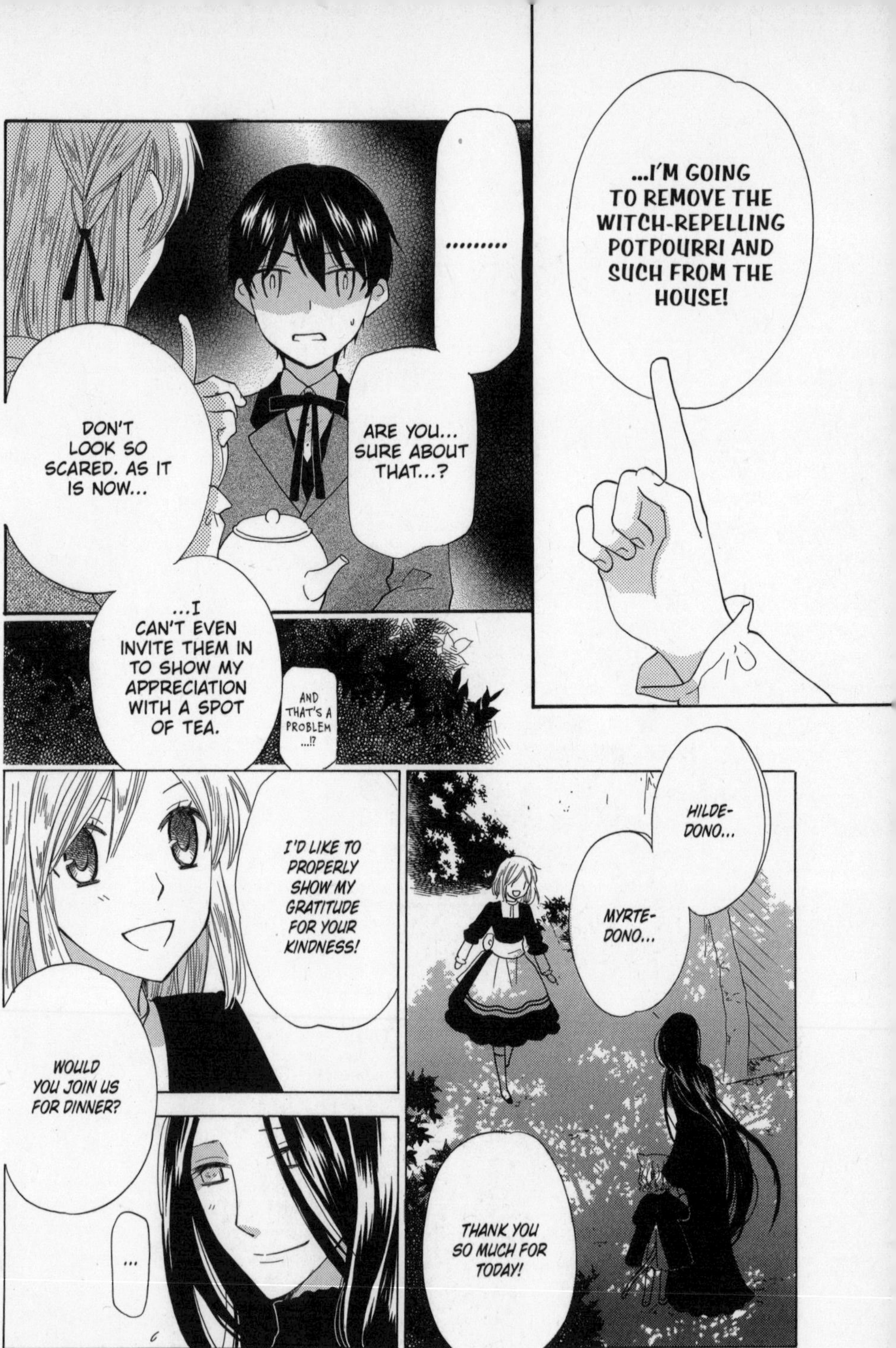
...I'M GOING TO REMOVE THE WITCH-REPELLING POTPOURRI AND SUCH FROM THE HOUSE!
....
ARE YOU... SURE ABOUT THAT...?
DON'T LOOK SO SCARED. AS IT IS NOW...
...I CAN'T EVEN INVITE THEM IN TO SHOW MY APPRECIATION WITH A SPOT OF TEA.
AND THAT'S A PROBLEM ...!?
HILDE-DONO...
MYRTE-DONO...
THANK YOU SO MUCH FOR TODAY!
I'D LIKE TO PROPERLY SHOW MY GRATITUDE FOR YOUR KINDNESS!
WOULD YOU JOIN US FOR DINNER?
...

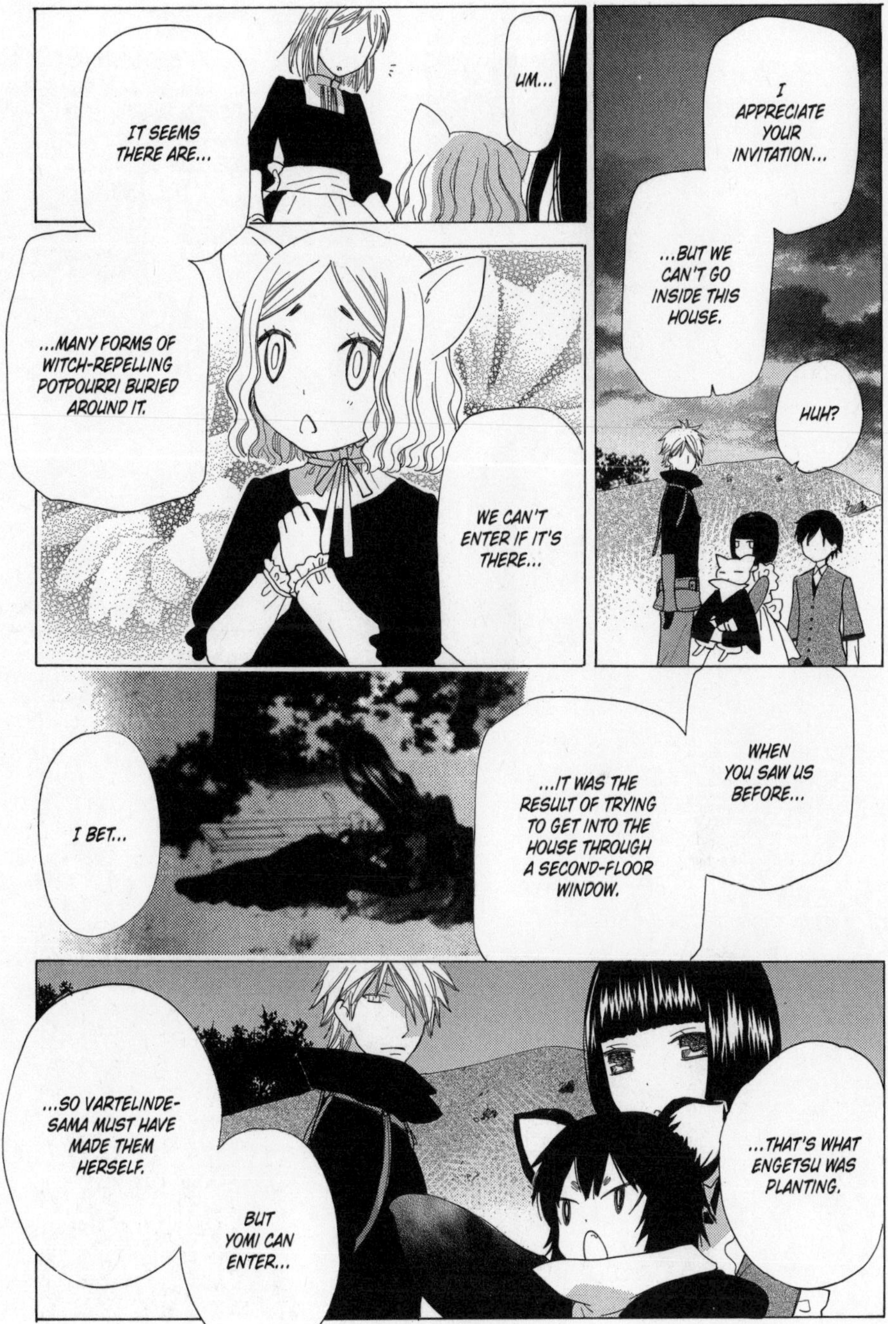
I APPRECIATE YOUR INVITATION...
...BUT WE CAN'T GO INSIDE THIS HOUSE.
HUH?
UM...
IT SEEMS THERE ARE...
...MANY FORMS OF WITCH-REPELLING POTPOURRI BURIED AROUND IT.
WE CAN'T ENTER IF IT'S THERE...
WHEN YOU SAW US BEFORE...
...IT WAS THE RESULT OF TRYING TO GET INTO THE HOUSE THROUGH A SECOND-FLOOR WINDOW.
I BET...
...THAT'S WHAT ENGETSU WAS PLANTING.
...SO VARTELINDE-SAMA MUST HAVE MADE THEM HERSELF.
BUT YOMI CAN ENTER...

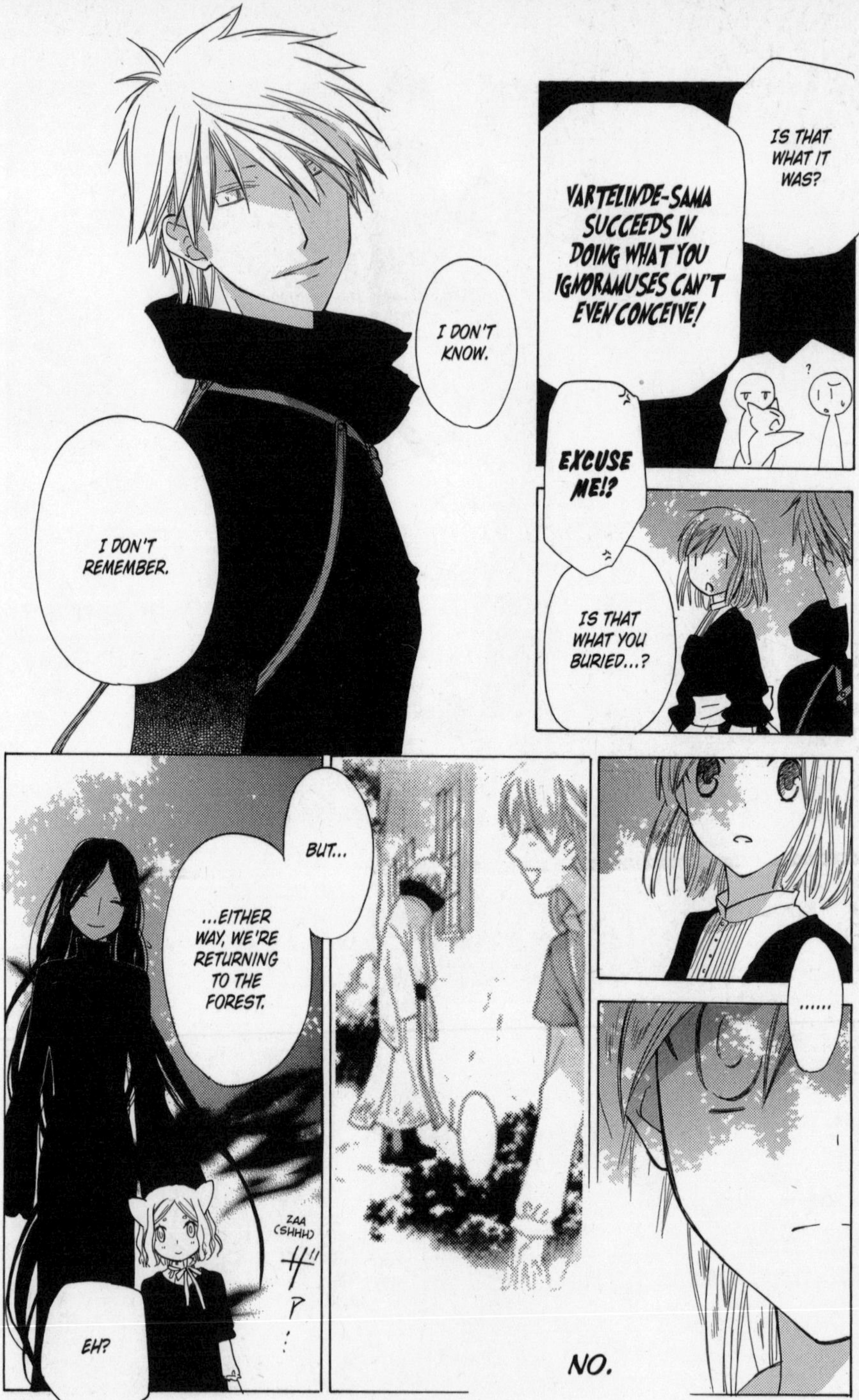
?
IS THAT WHAT IT WAS?
VARTELINDE-SAMA SUCCEEDS IN DOING WHAT YOU IGNORAMUSES CAN'T EVEN CONCEIVE!
EXCUSE ME!?
IS THAT WHAT YOU BURIED...?
I DON'T KNOW.
I DON'T REMEMBER.
......
NO.
BUT...
...EITHER WAY, WE'RE RETURNING TO THE FOREST.
ZAA (SHHH)
EH?

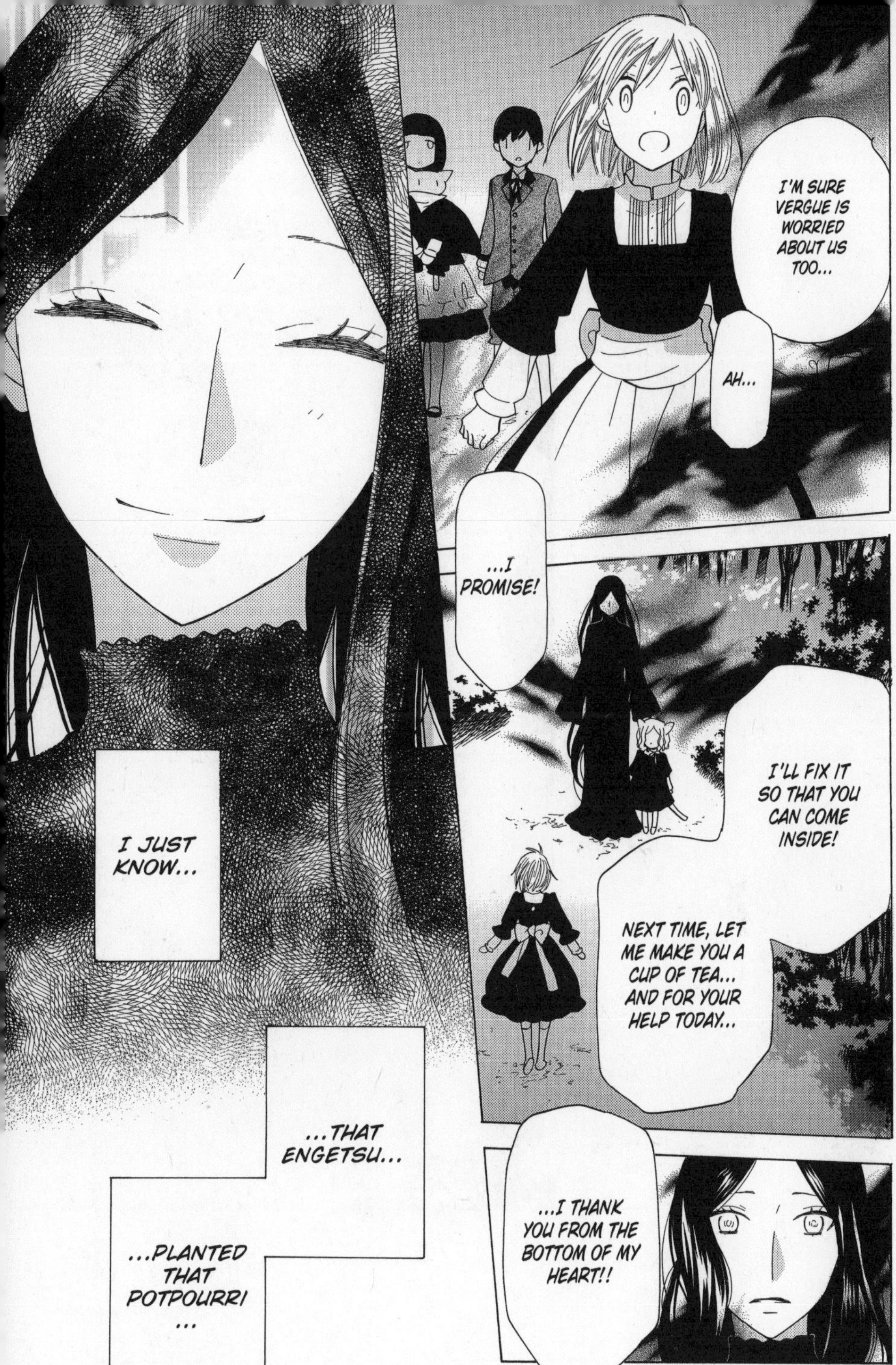
I'M SURE VERGUE IS WORRIED ABOUT US TOO...
AH...
...I PROMISE!
I'LL FIX IT SO THAT YOU CAN COME INSIDE!
NEXT TIME, LET ME MAKE YOU A CUP OF TEA... AND FOR YOUR HELP TODAY...
...I THANK YOU FROM THE BOTTOM OF MY HEART!!
I JUST KNOW...
...THAT ENGETSU...
...PLANTED THAT POTPOURRI ...

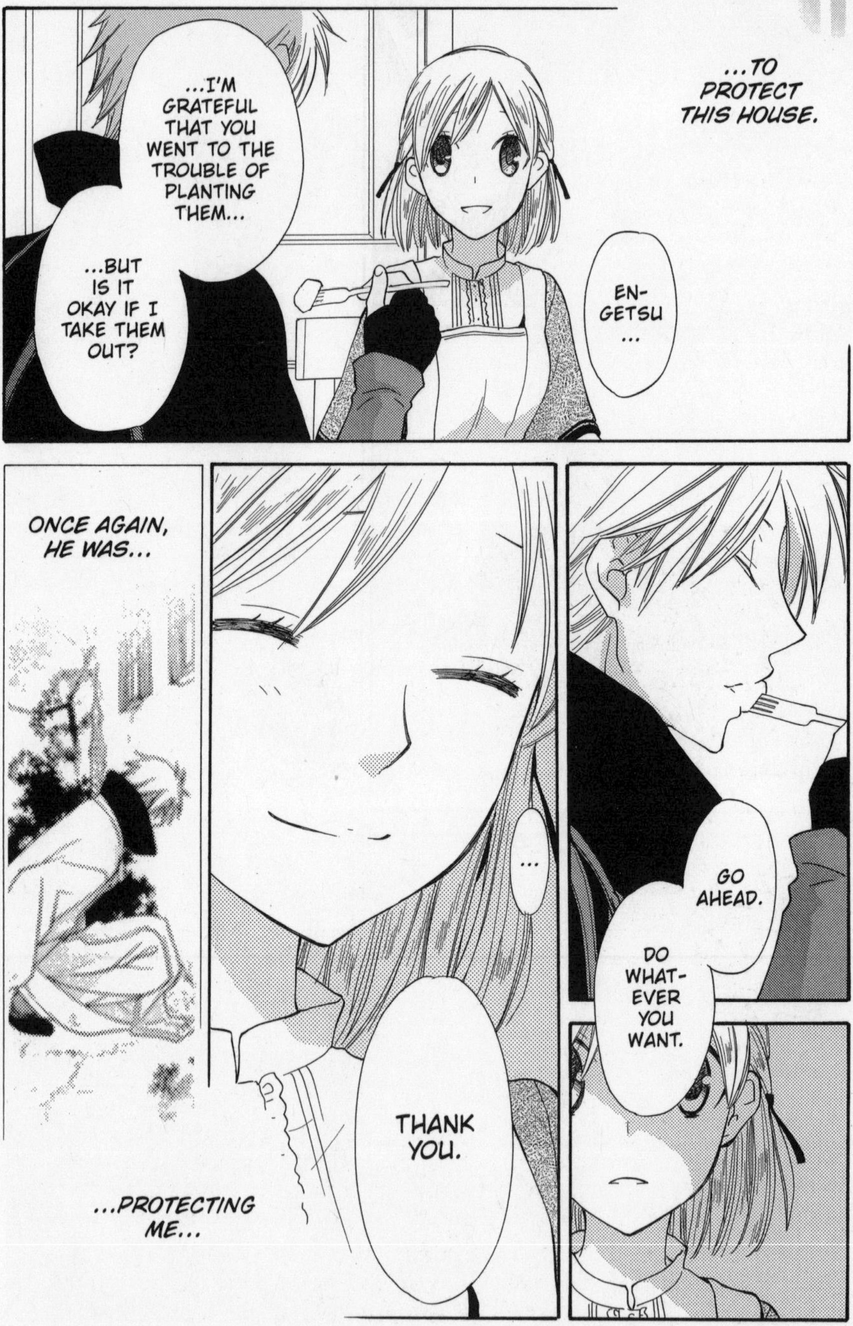
...TO PROTECT THIS HOUSE.
EN-GETSU...
...I'M GRATEFUL THAT YOU WENT TO THE TROUBLE OF PLANTING THEM...
...BUT IS IT OKAY IF I TAKE THEM OUT?
GO AHEAD.
DO WHAT-EVER YOU WANT.
...
THANK YOU.
ONCE AGAIN, HE WAS...
...PROTECTING ME...

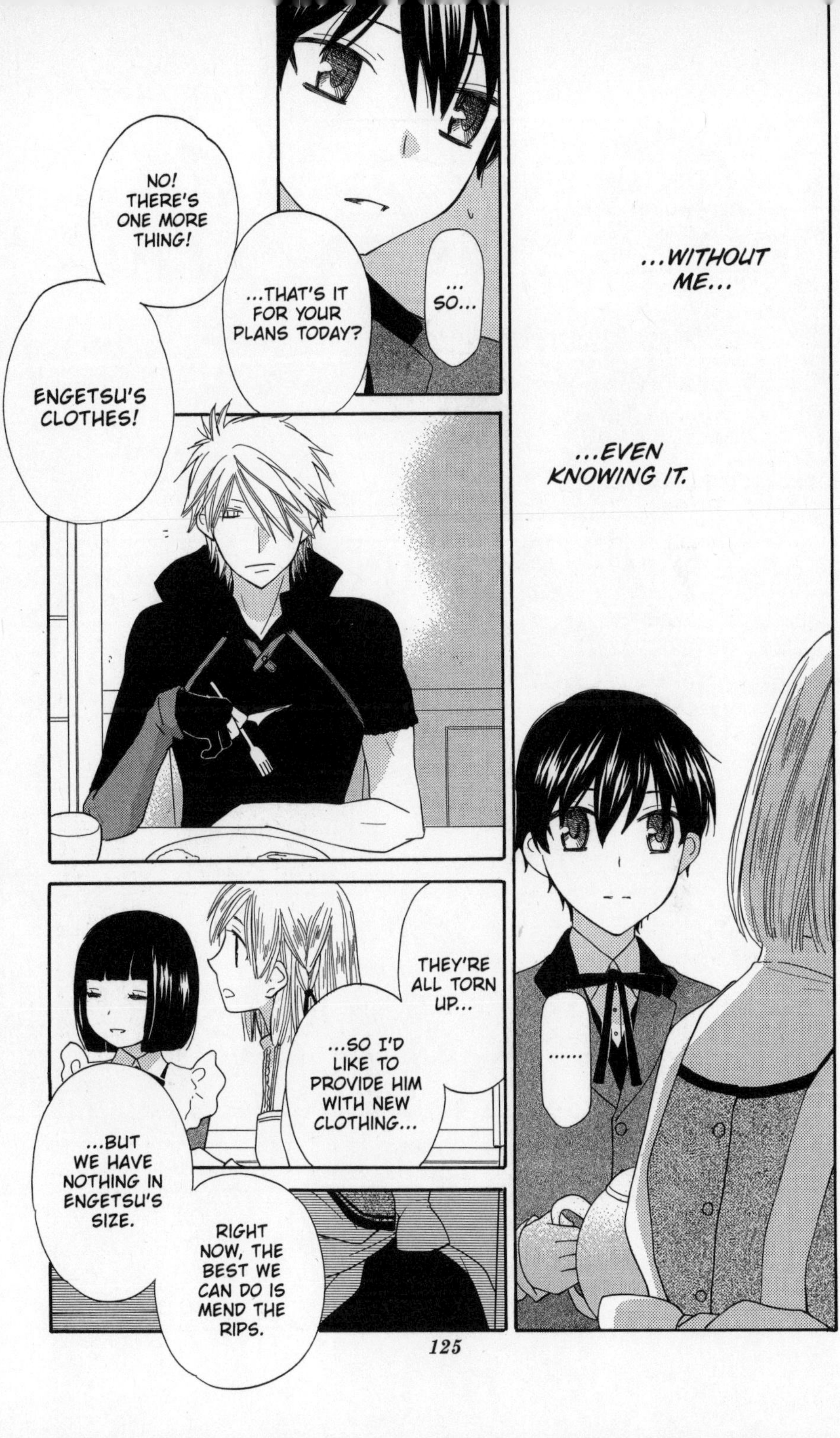
...WITHOUT ME...
...EVEN KNOWING IT.
......
... SO...
...THAT'S IT FOR YOUR PLANS TODAY?
NO! THERE'S ONE MORE THING!
ENGETSU'S CLOTHES!
THEY'RE ALL TORN UP...
...SO I'D LIKE TO PROVIDE HIM WITH NEW CLOTHING...
...BUT WE HAVE NOTHING IN ENGETSU'S SIZE.
RIGHT NOW, THE BEST WE CAN DO IS MEND THE RIPS.

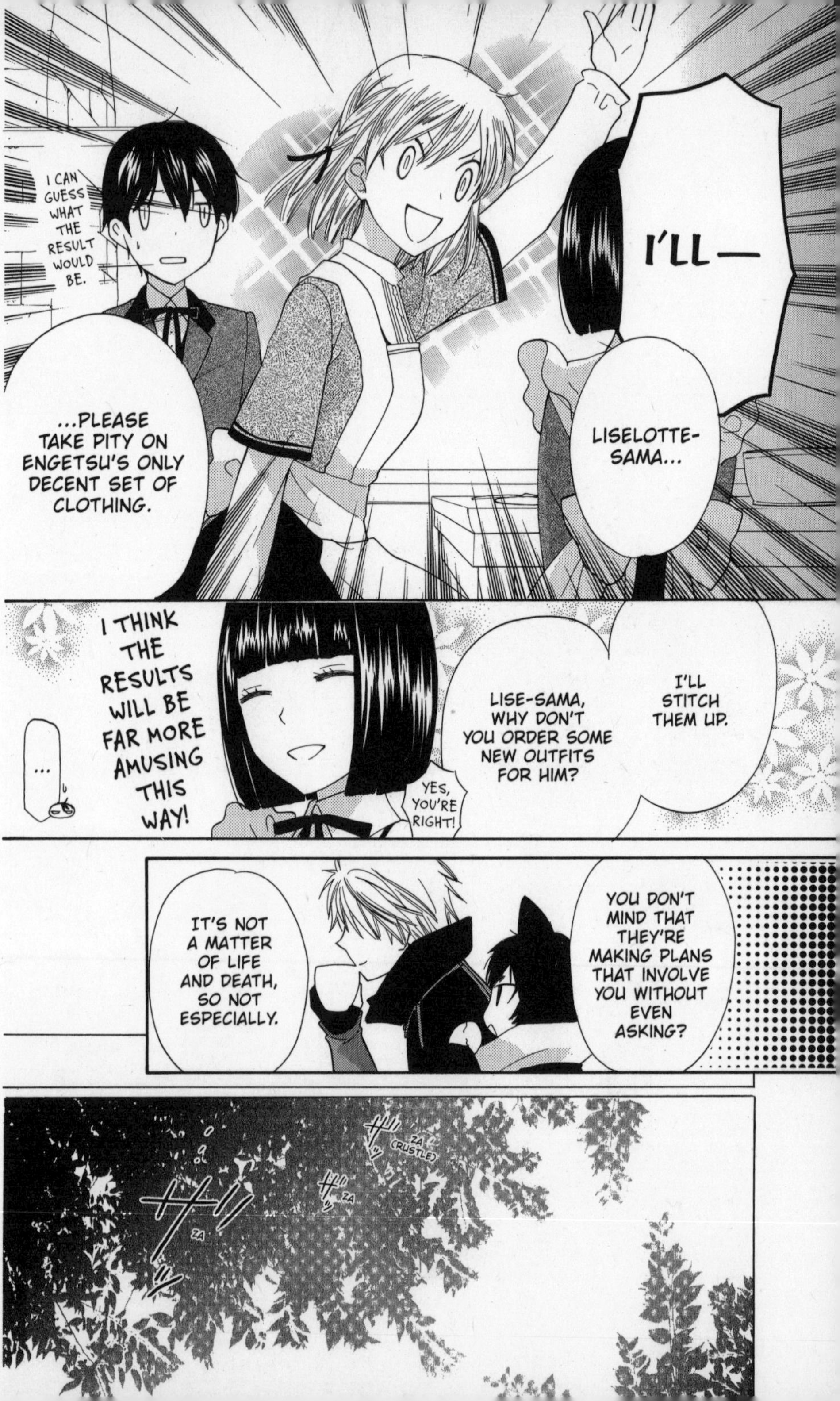
I'LL—
LISELOTTE-SAMA...
I CAN GUESS WHAT THE RESULT WOULD BE.
...PLEASE TAKE PITY ON ENGETSU'S ONLY DECENT SET OF CLOTHING.
I'LL STITCH THEM UP.
LISE-SAMA, WHY DON'T YOU ORDER SOME NEW OUTFITS FOR HIM?
YES, YOU'RE RIGHT!
I THINK THE RESULTS WILL BE FAR MORE AMUSING THIS WAY!
...
YOU DON'T MIND THAT THEY'RE MAKING PLANS THAT INVOLVE YOU WITHOUT EVEN ASKING?
IT'S NOT A MATTER OF LIFE AND DEATH, SO NOT ESPECIALLY.
ZA (RUSTLE)
ZA
ZA

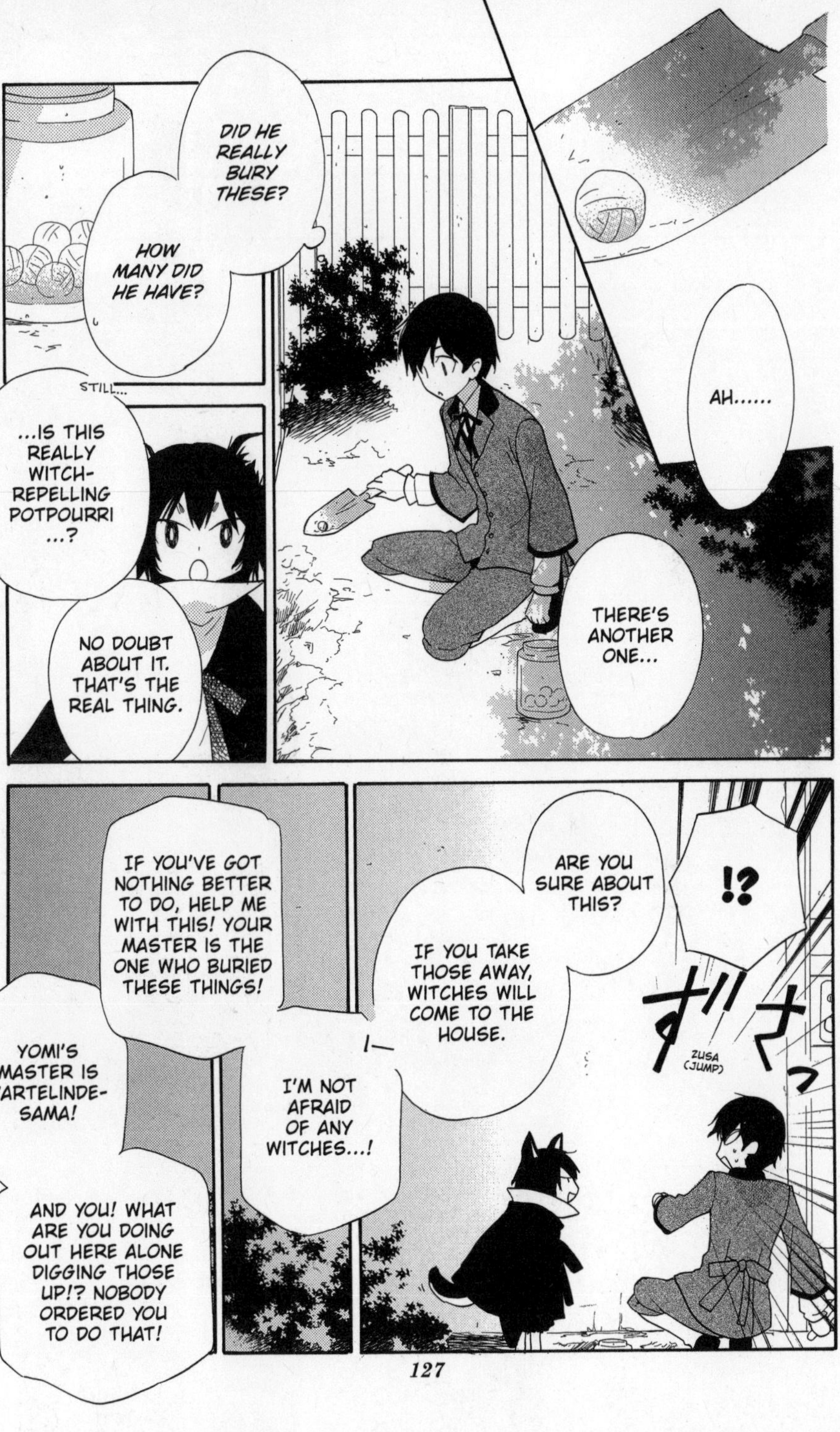
AH......
THERE'S ANOTHER ONE...
DID HE REALLY BURY THESE?
HOW MANY DID HE HAVE?
STILL...
...IS THIS REALLY WITCH-REPELLING POTPOURRI ...?
NO DOUBT ABOUT IT. THAT'S THE REAL THING.
!?
ZUSA (JUMP)
ARE YOU SURE ABOUT THIS?
IF YOU TAKE THOSE AWAY, WITCHES WILL COME TO THE HOUSE.
I—
I'M NOT AFRAID OF ANY WITCHES...!
IF YOU'VE GOT NOTHING BETTER TO DO, HELP ME WITH THIS! YOUR MASTER IS THE ONE WHO BURIED THESE THINGS!
YOMI'S MASTER IS VARTELINDE-SAMA!
AND YOU! WHAT ARE YOU DOING OUT HERE ALONE DIGGING THOSE UP!? NOBODY ORDERED YOU TO DO THAT!

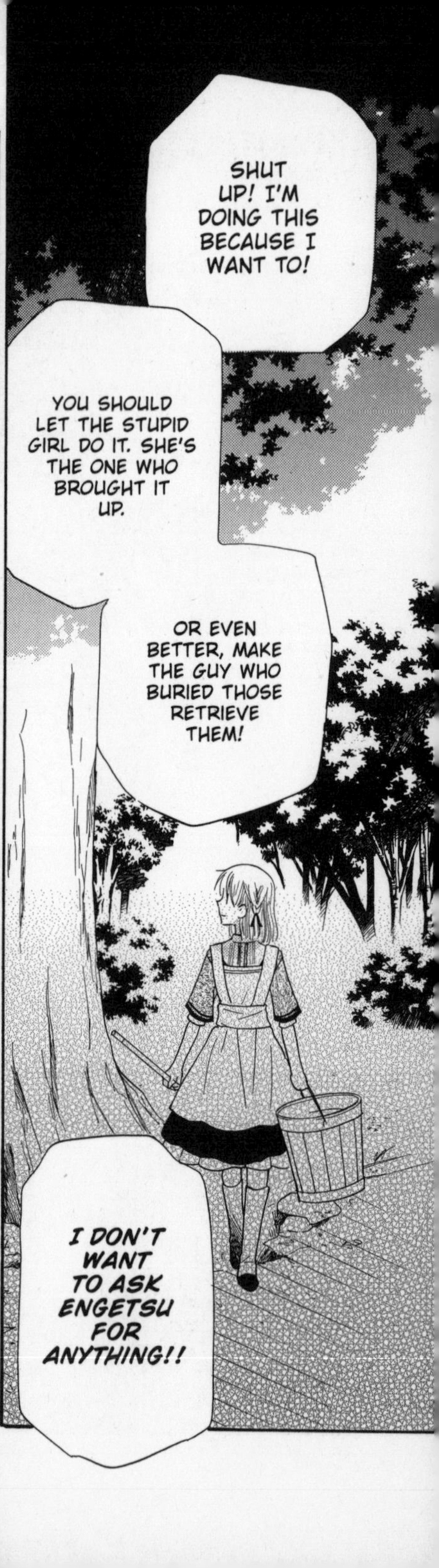
SHUT UP! I'M DOING THIS BECAUSE I WANT TO!
YOU SHOULD LET THE STUPID GIRL DO IT. SHE'S THE ONE WHO BROUGHT IT UP.
OR EVEN BETTER, MAKE THE GUY WHO BURIED THOSE RETRIEVE THEM!
I DON'T WANT TO ASK ENGETSU FOR ANYTHING!!

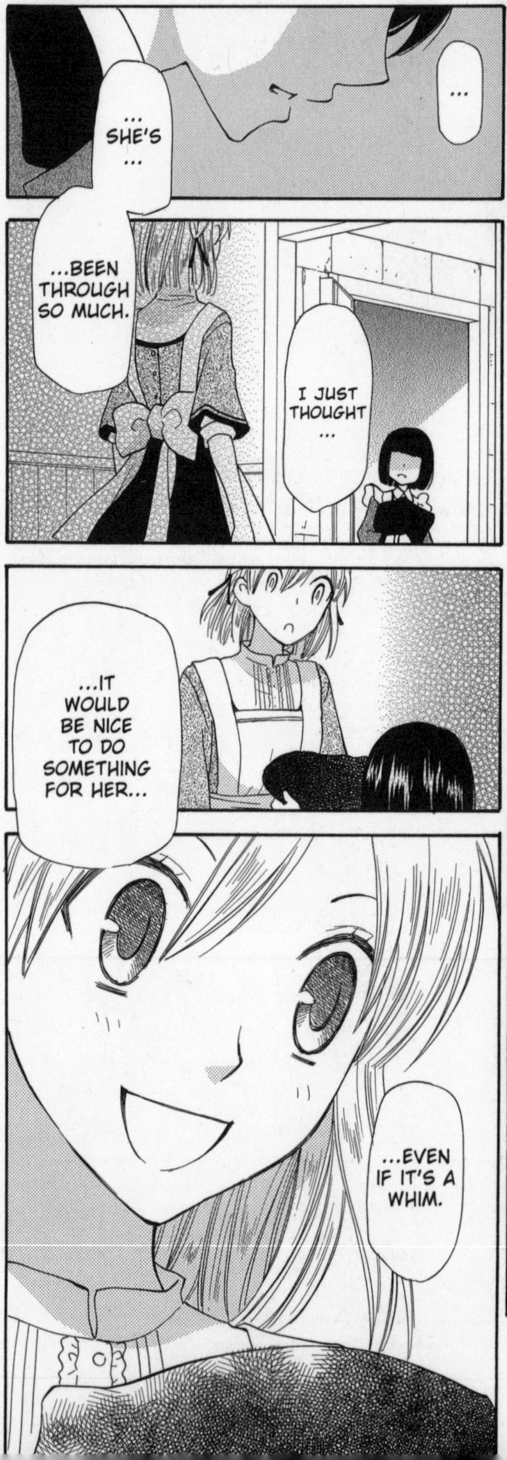
...
...SHE'S...
...BEEN THROUGH SO MUCH.
I JUST THOUGHT...
...IT WOULD BE NICE TO DO SOMETHING FOR HER...
...EVEN IF IT'S A WHIM.

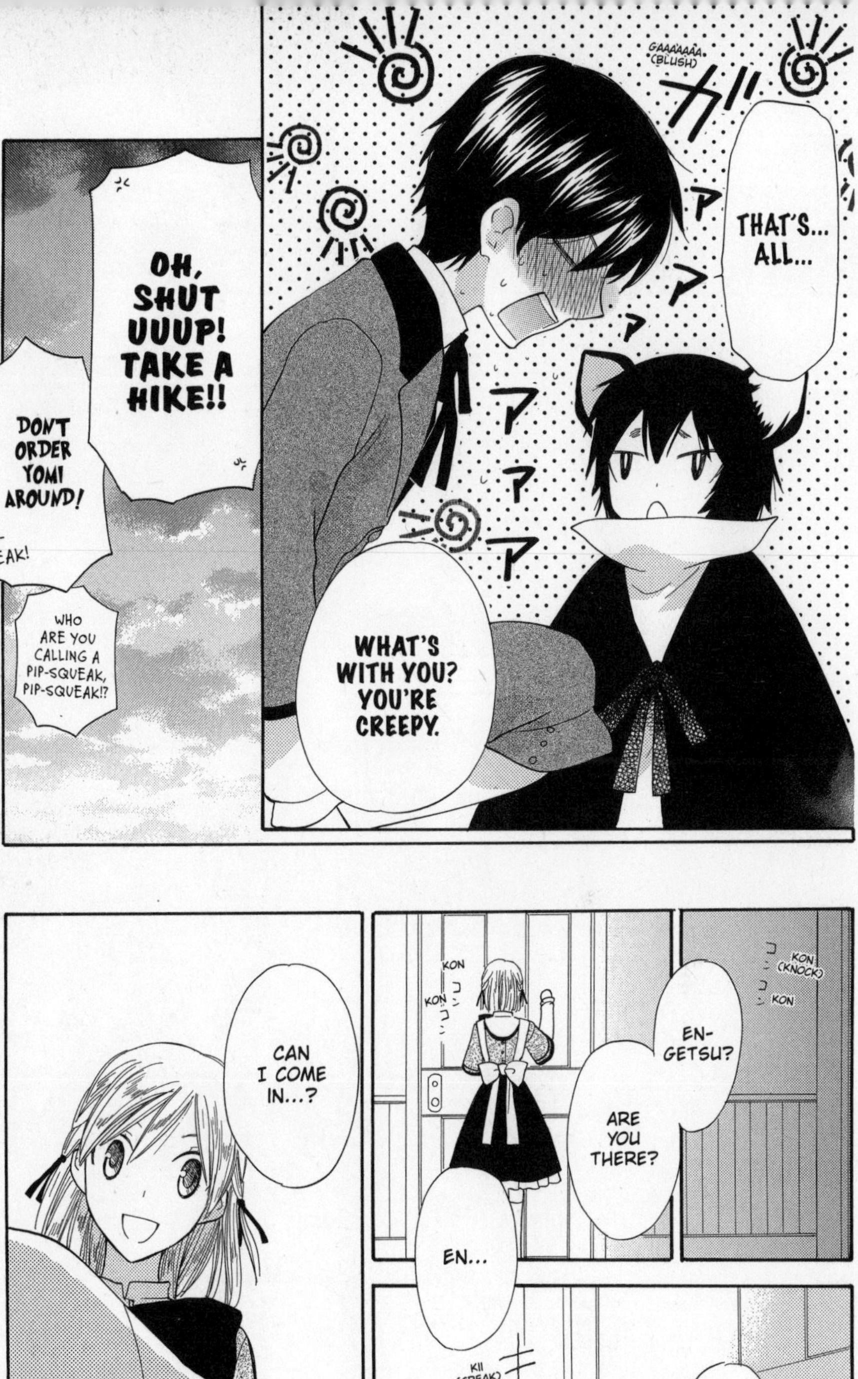
GAAAAAAA (BLUSH)
THAT'S... ALL...
WHAT'S WITH YOU? YOU'RE CREEPY.
OH, SHUT UUUP! TAKE A HIKE!!
DON'T ORDER YOMI AROUND!
PIP-SQUEAK!
WHO ARE YOU CALLING A PIP-SQUEAK, PIP-SQUEAK!?
KON (KNOCK)
KON
KON
KON
EN-GETSU?
ARE YOU THERE?
EN...
KII (CREAK)
OH...
CAN I COME IN...?

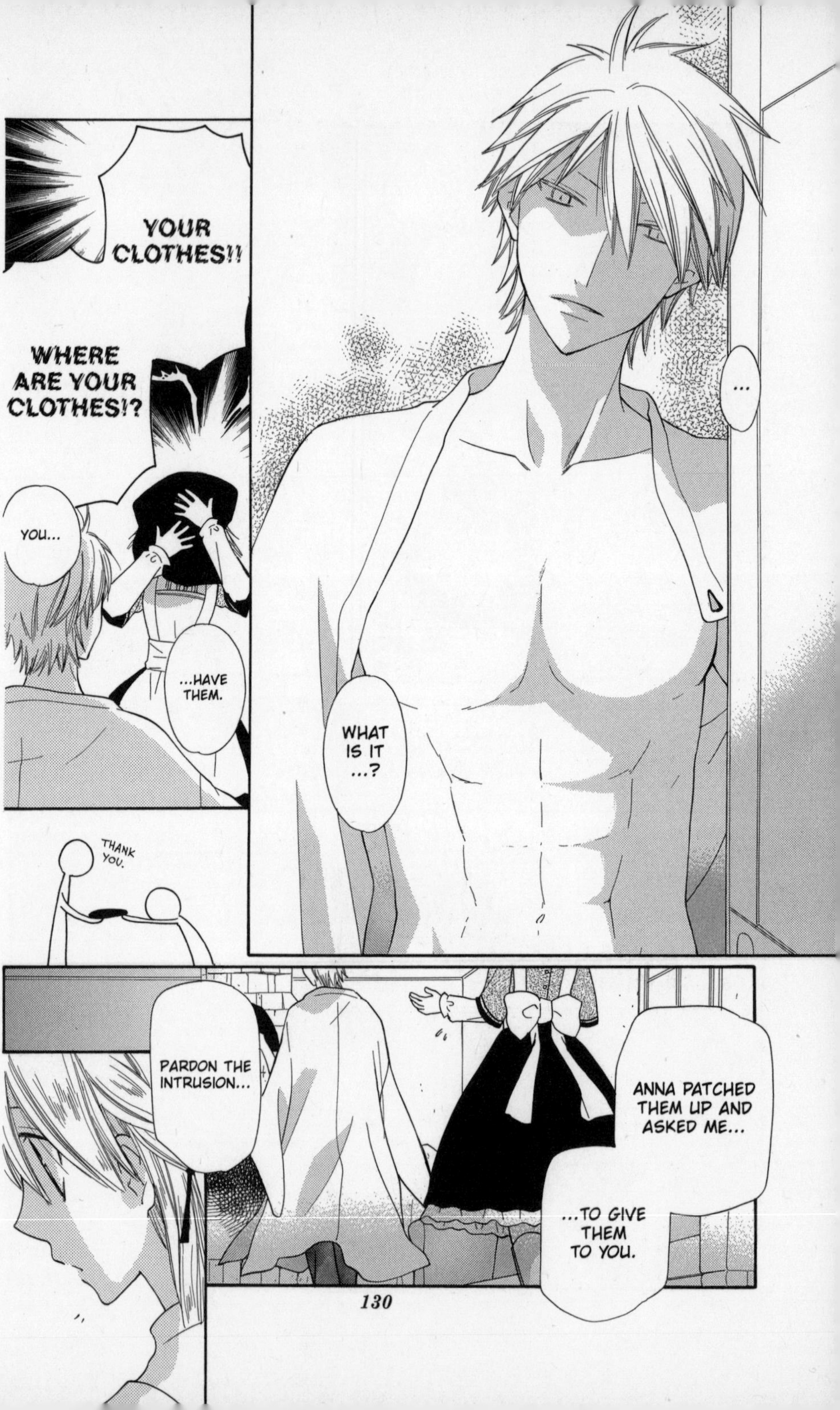
...
WHAT IS IT ...?
YOUR CLOTHES!!
WHERE ARE YOUR CLOTHES!?
YOU...
...HAVE THEM.
THANK YOU.
ANNA PATCHED THEM UP AND ASKED ME...
...TO GIVE THEM TO YOU.
PARDON THE INTRUSION...

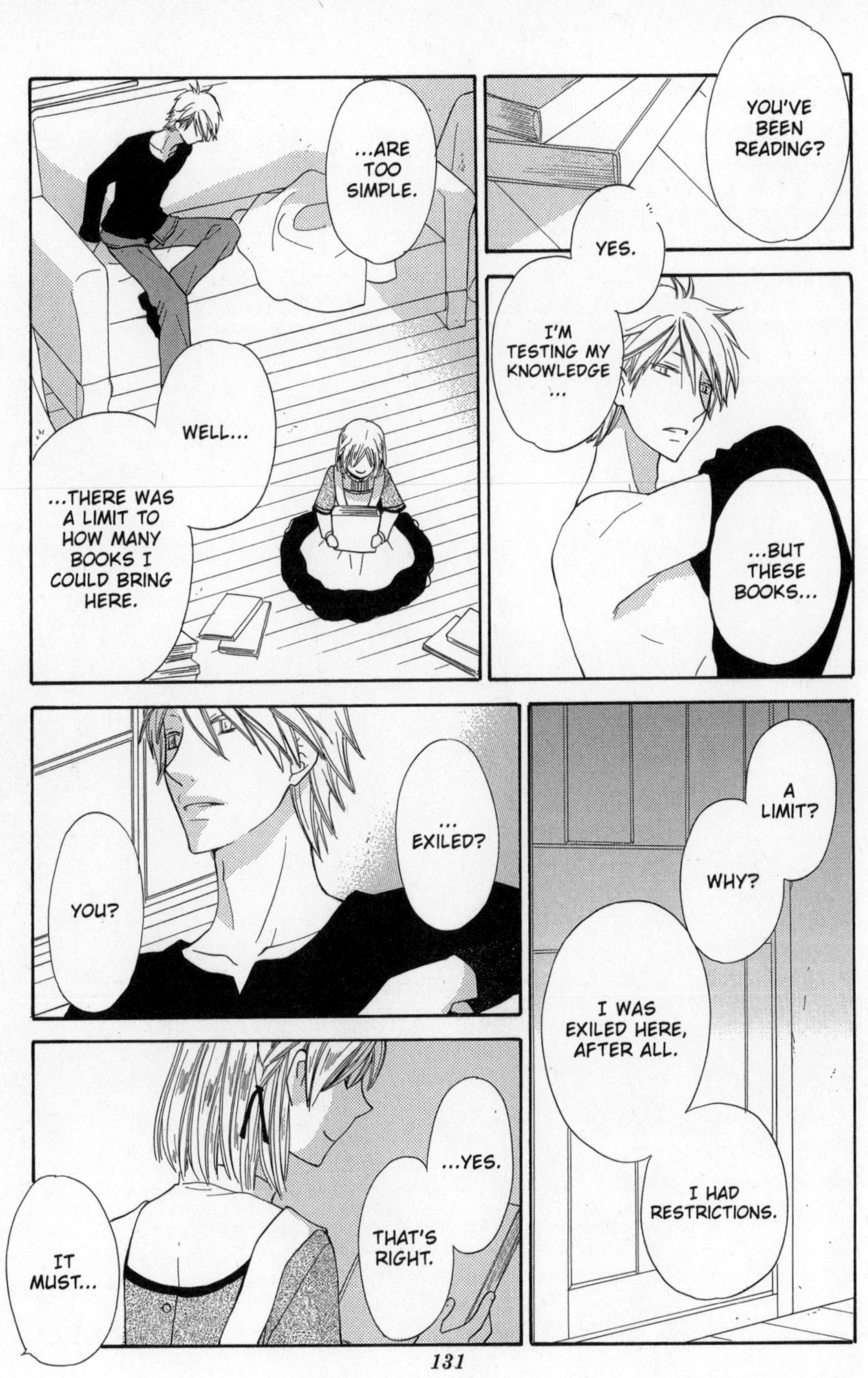
YOU'VE BEEN READING?
YES.
I'M TESTING MY KNOWLEDGE ...
...BUT THESE BOOKS...
...ARE TOO SIMPLE.
WELL...
...THERE WAS A LIMIT TO HOW MANY BOOKS I COULD BRING HERE.
A LIMIT?
WHY?
I WAS EXILED HERE, AFTER ALL.
I HAD RESTRICTIONS.
... EXILED?
YOU?
...YES.
THAT'S RIGHT.
IT MUST...

...BE ROUGH.

...

HOW CAN I...

KARI (SCRATCH)

...GET TO KNOW YOU?

HOW CAN YOU...

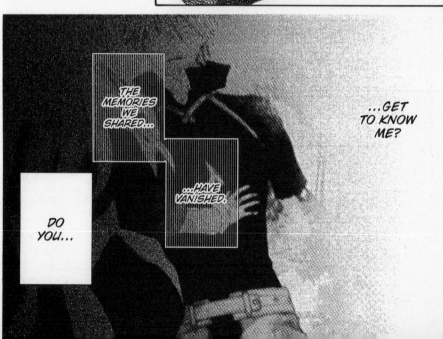

THE MEMORIES WE SHARED...

...HAVE VANISHED.

...GET TO KNOW ME?

DO YOU...

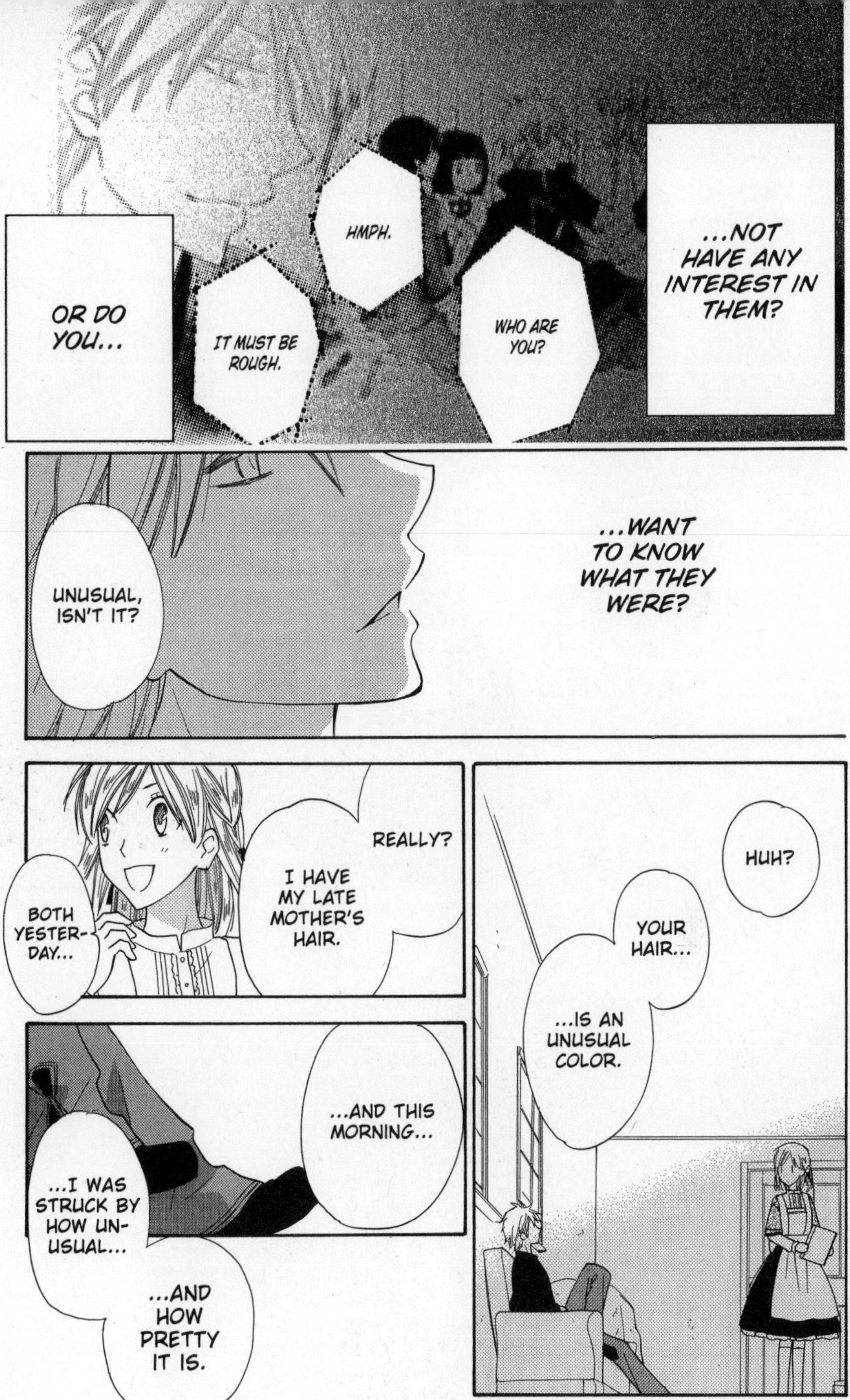
...NOT HAVE ANY INTEREST IN THEM?
WHO ARE YOU?
HMPH.
IT MUST BE ROUGH.
OR DO YOU...
...WANT TO KNOW WHAT THEY WERE?
UNUSUAL, ISN'T IT?
HUH?
YOUR HAIR...
...IS AN UNUSUAL COLOR.
REALLY?
I HAVE MY LATE MOTHER'S HAIR.
BOTH YESTER-DAY...
...AND THIS MORNING...
...I WAS STRUCK BY HOW UN-USUAL...
...AND HOW PRETTY IT IS.

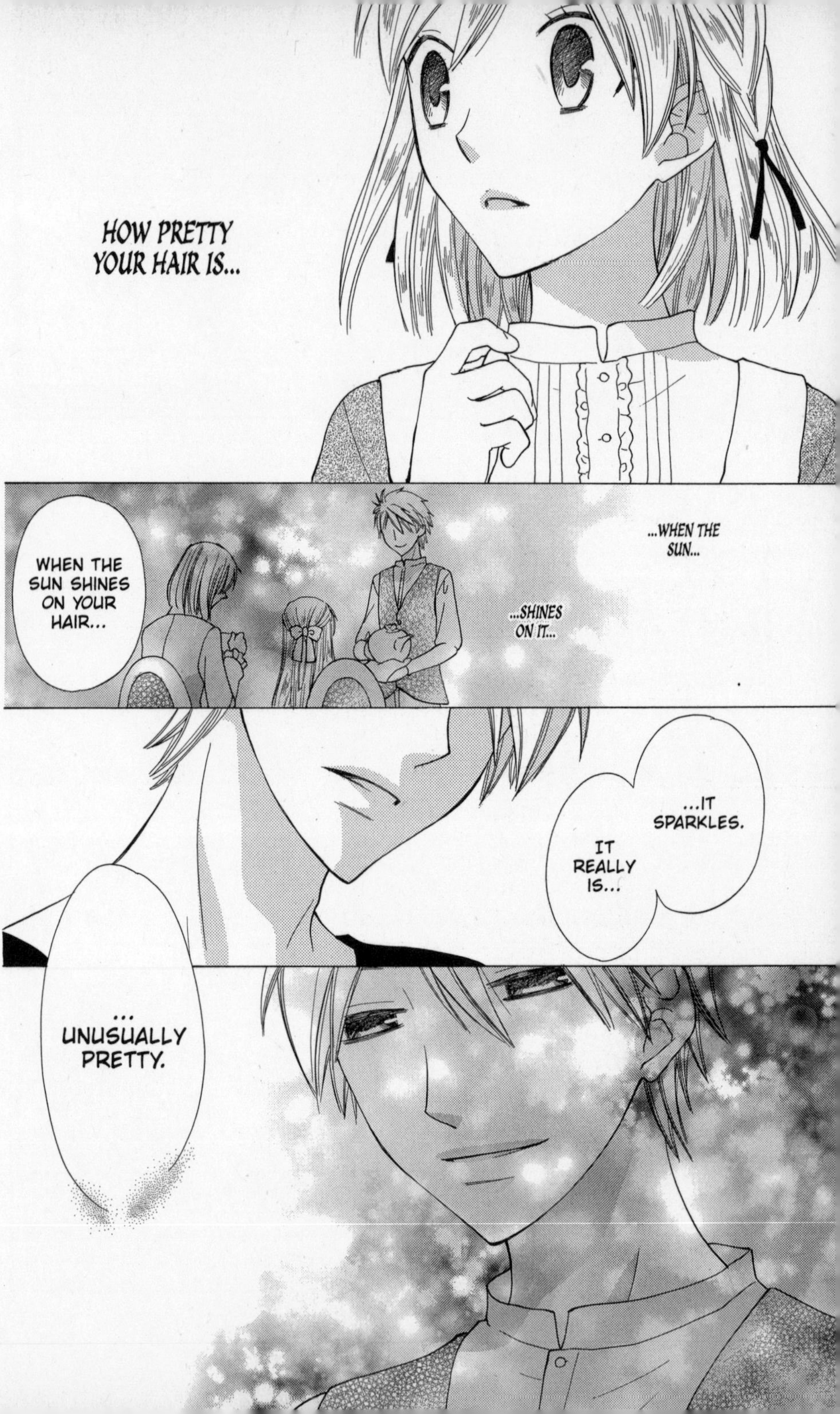
HOW PRETTY YOUR HAIR IS...
...WHEN THE SUN...
...SHINES ON IT...
WHEN THE SUN SHINES ON YOUR HAIR...
...IT SPARKLES.
IT REALLY IS...
... UNUSUALLY PRETTY.

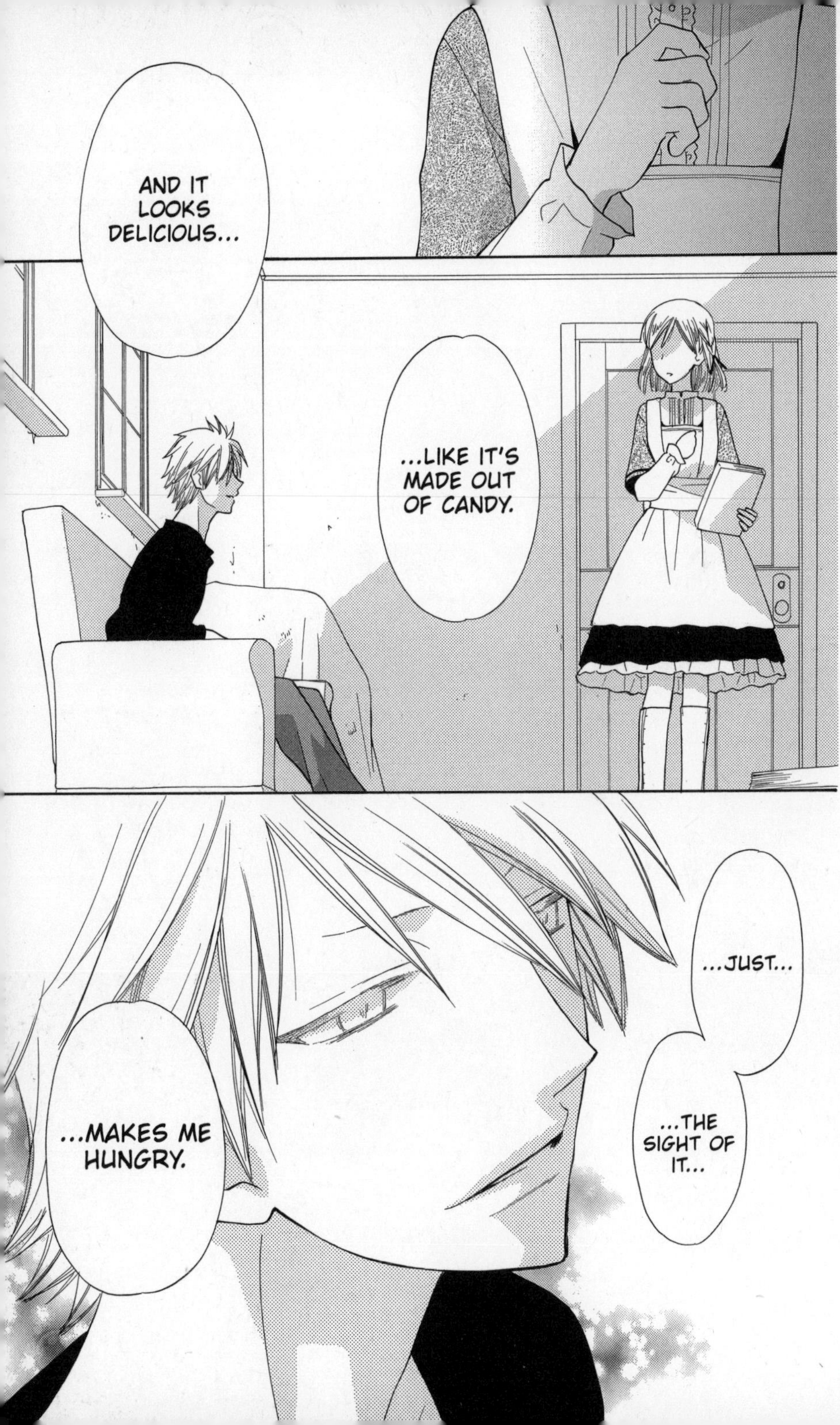
AND IT LOOKS DELICIOUS...
...LIKE IT'S MADE OUT OF CANDY.
...JUST...
...THE SIGHT OF IT...
...MAKES ME HUNGRY.

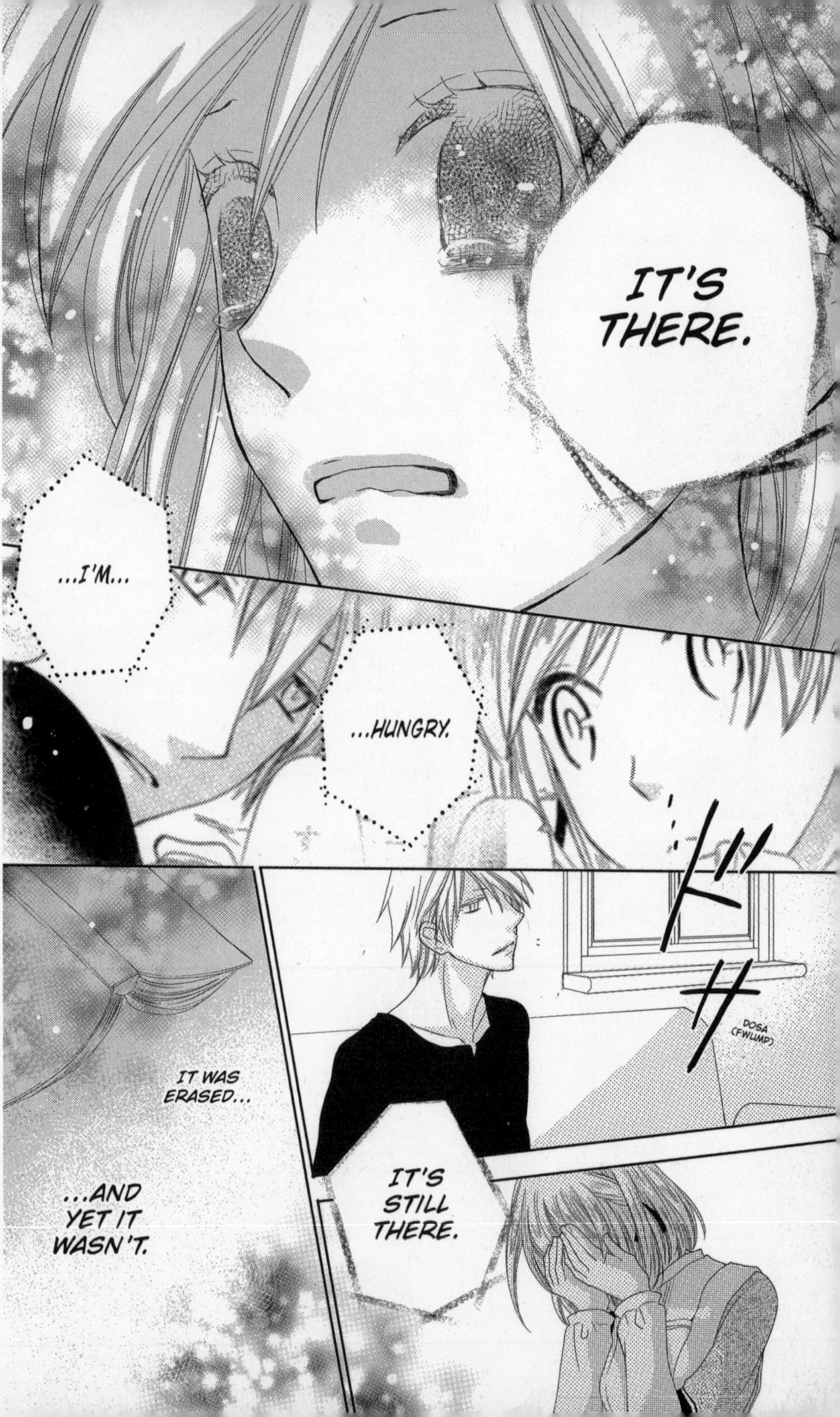
IT'S THERE.
...I'M...
...HUNGRY.
ドサ
DOSA (FWUMP)
IT'S STILL THERE.
IT WAS ERASED...
...AND YET IT WASN'T.

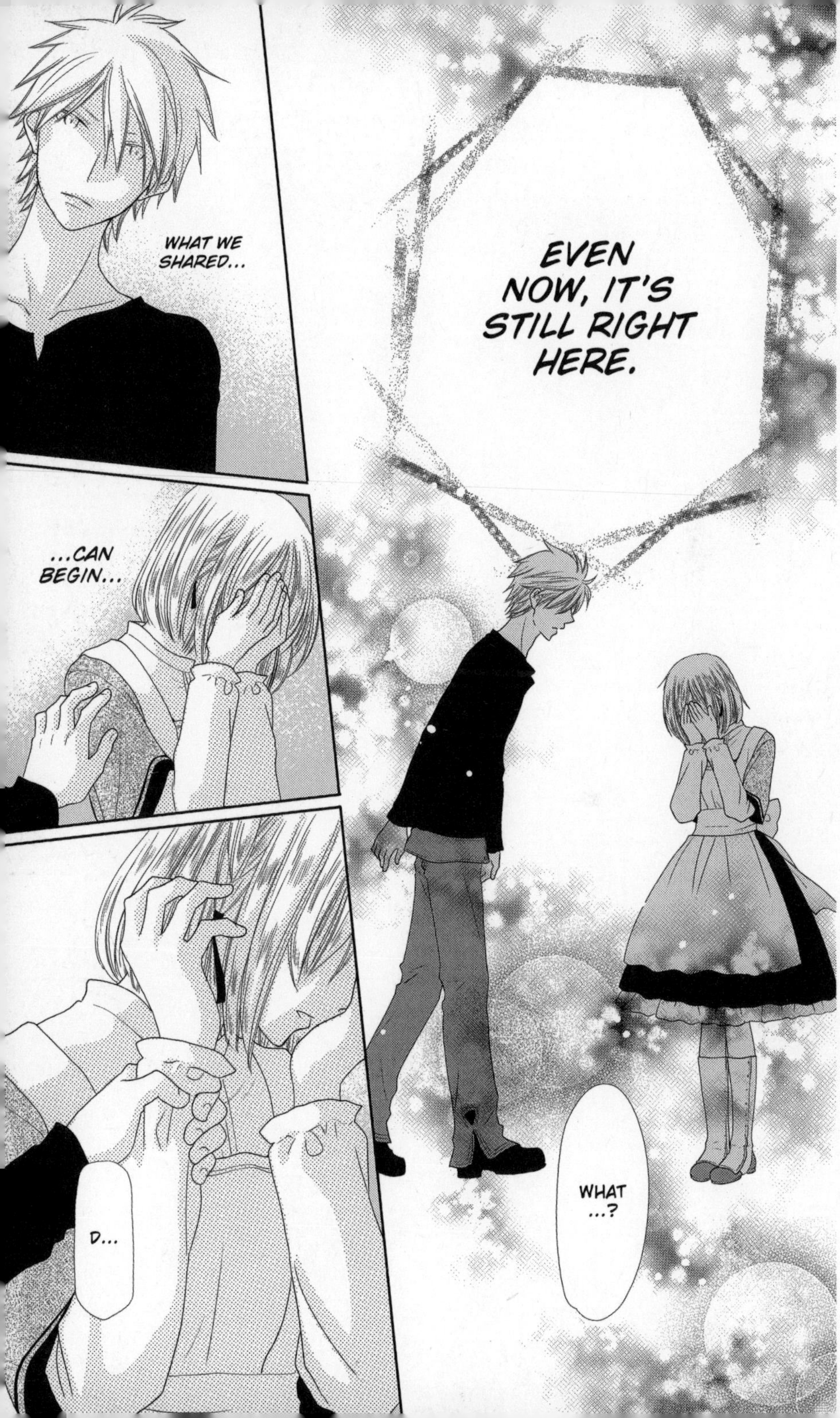
EVEN NOW, IT'S STILL RIGHT HERE.
WHAT ...?
WHAT WE SHARED...
...CAN BEGIN...
D...

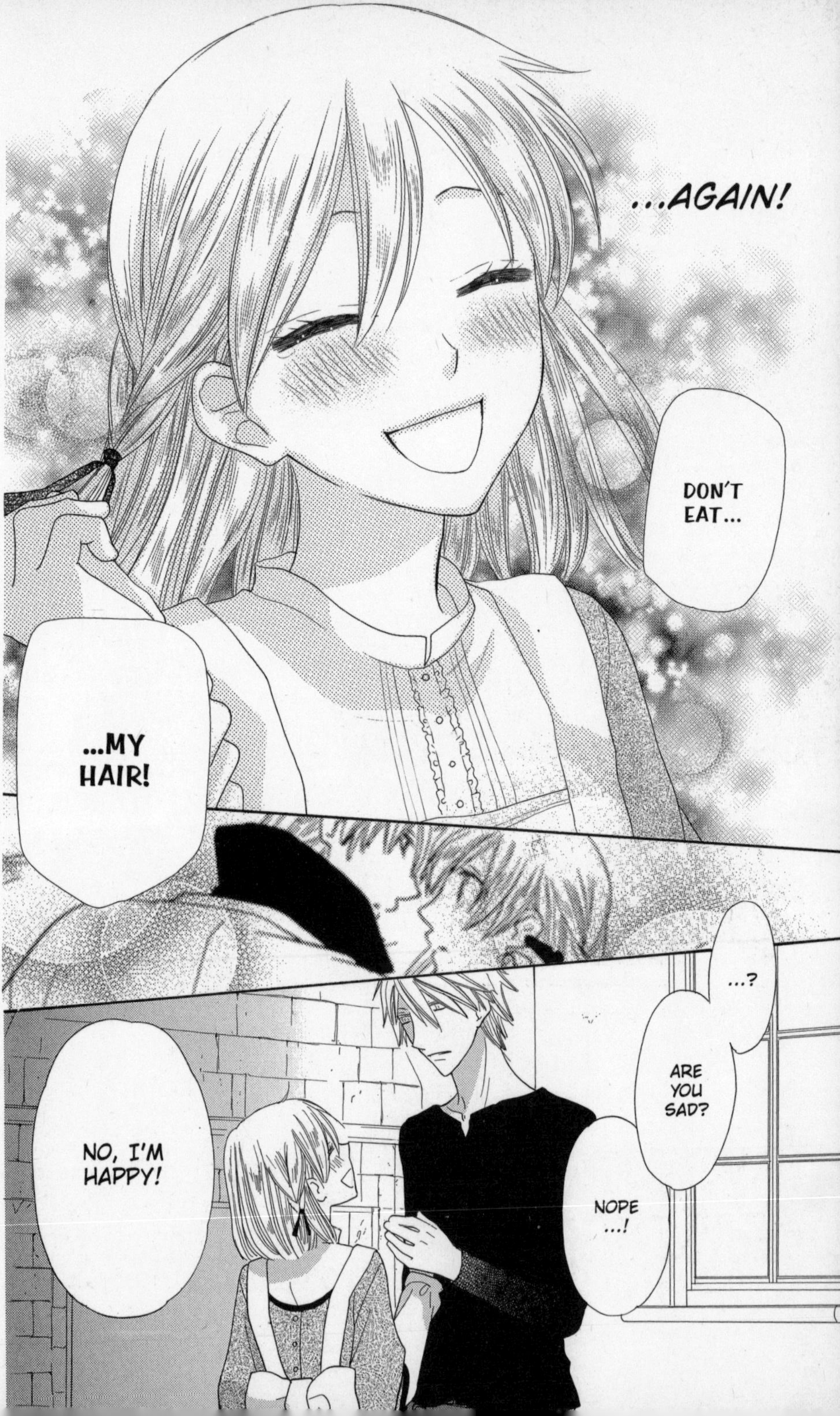
...AGAIN!
DON'T EAT...
...MY HAIR!
...?
ARE YOU SAD?
NOPE ...!
NO, I'M HAPPY!

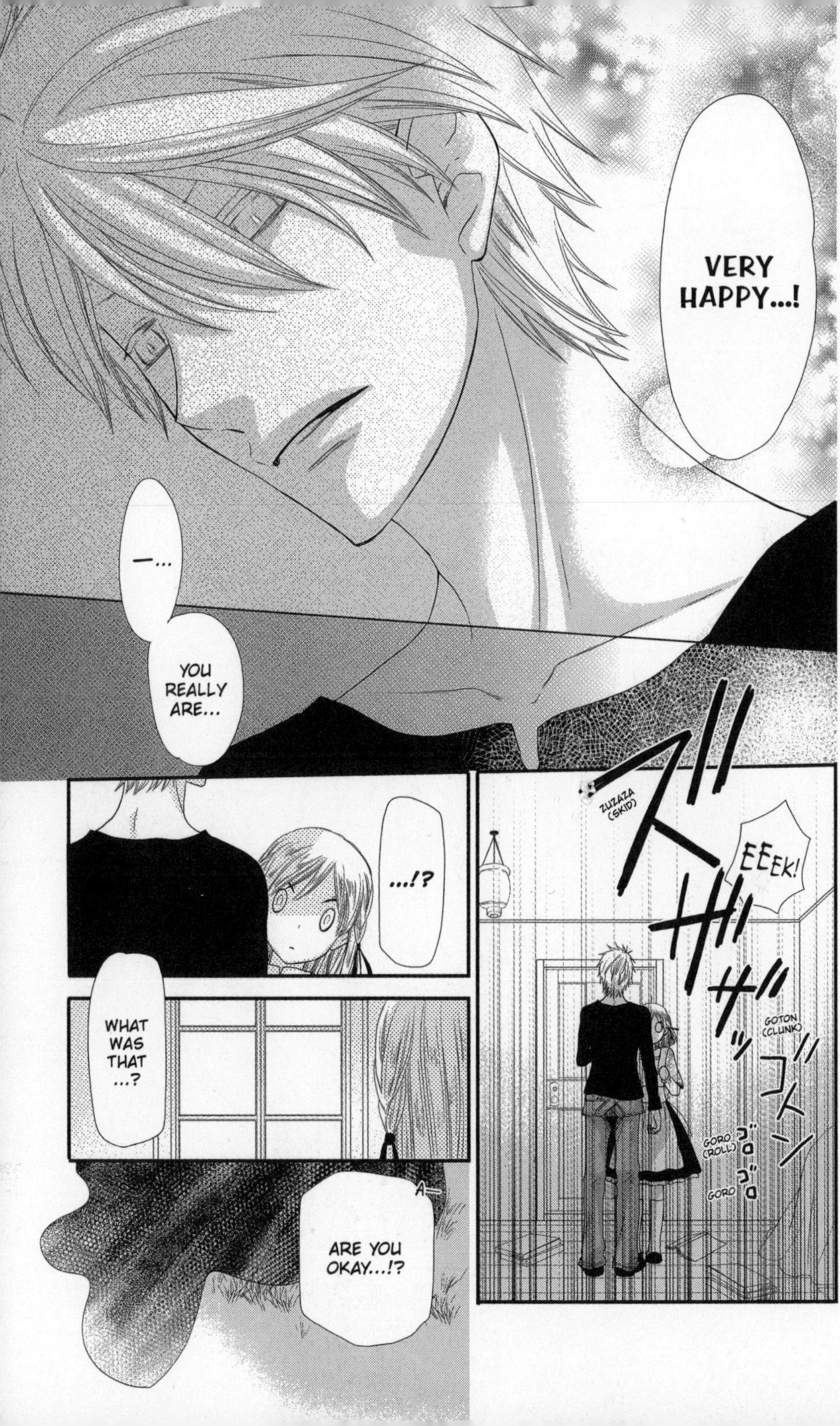
VERY HAPPY...!
—...
YOU REALLY ARE...
ZUZAZA (SKID)
EEEK!
GOTON (CLUNK)
GORO (ROLL)
GORO
...!?
WHAT WAS THAT ...?
A—
ARE YOU OKAY...!?

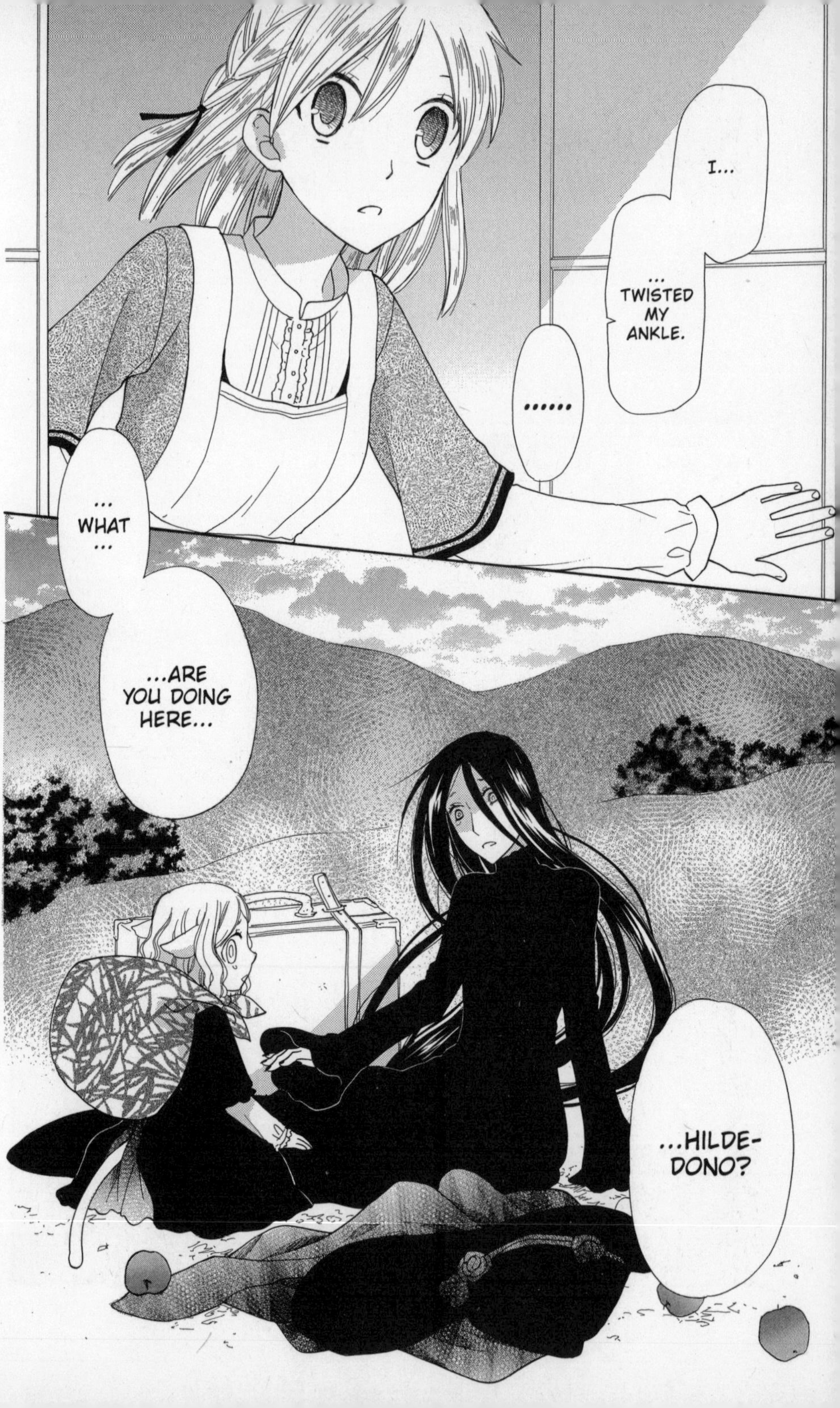
I...
...TWISTED MY ANKLE.
......
... WHAT ...
...ARE YOU DOING HERE...
...HILDE-DONO?

Chapter 16

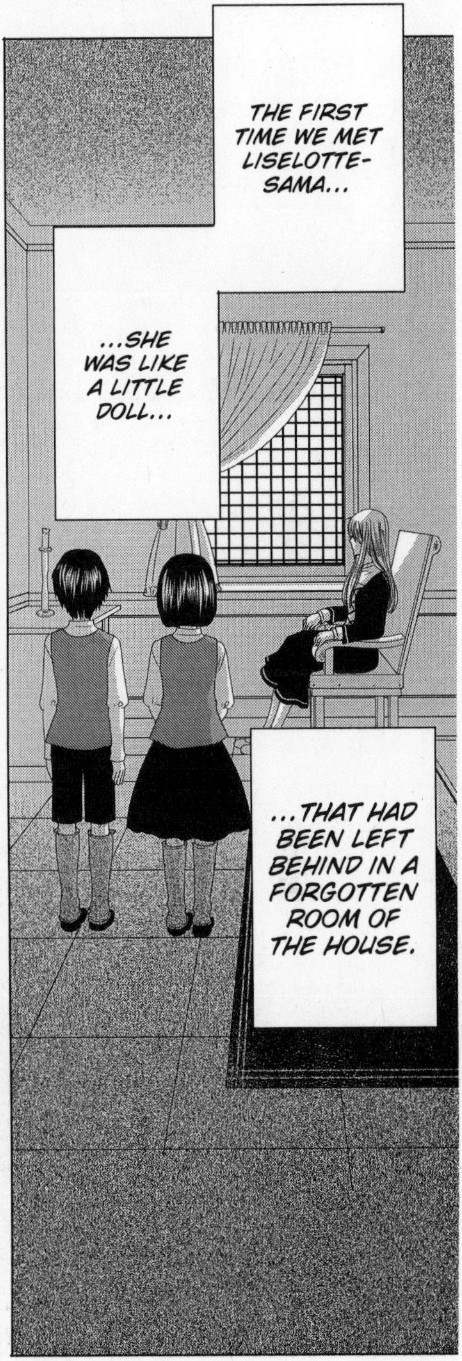
THE FIRST TIME WE MET LISELOTTE-SAMA...
...SHE WAS LIKE A LITTLE DOLL...
...THAT HAD BEEN LEFT BEHIND IN A FORGOTTEN ROOM OF THE HOUSE.

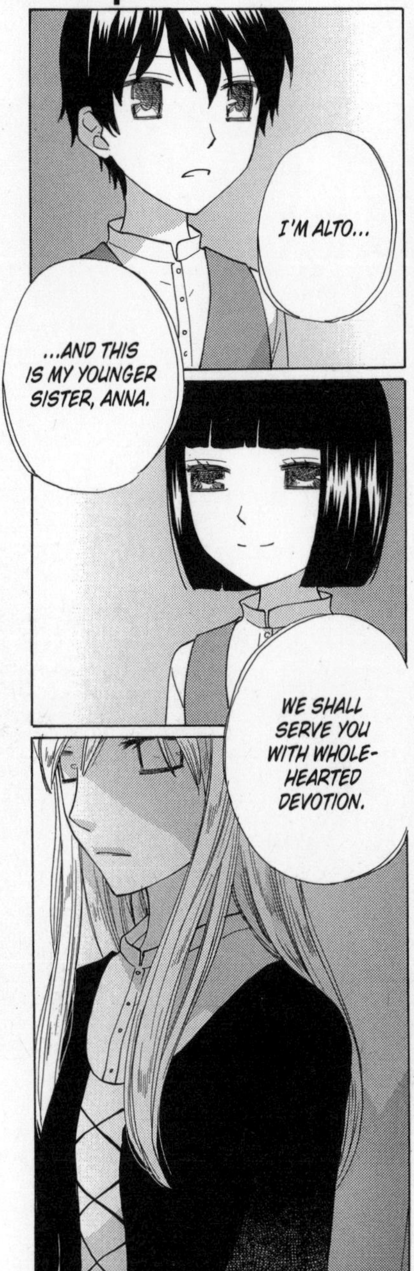
I'M ALTO...
...AND THIS IS MY YOUNGER SISTER, ANNA.
WE SHALL SERVE YOU WITH WHOLE-HEARTED DEVOTION.

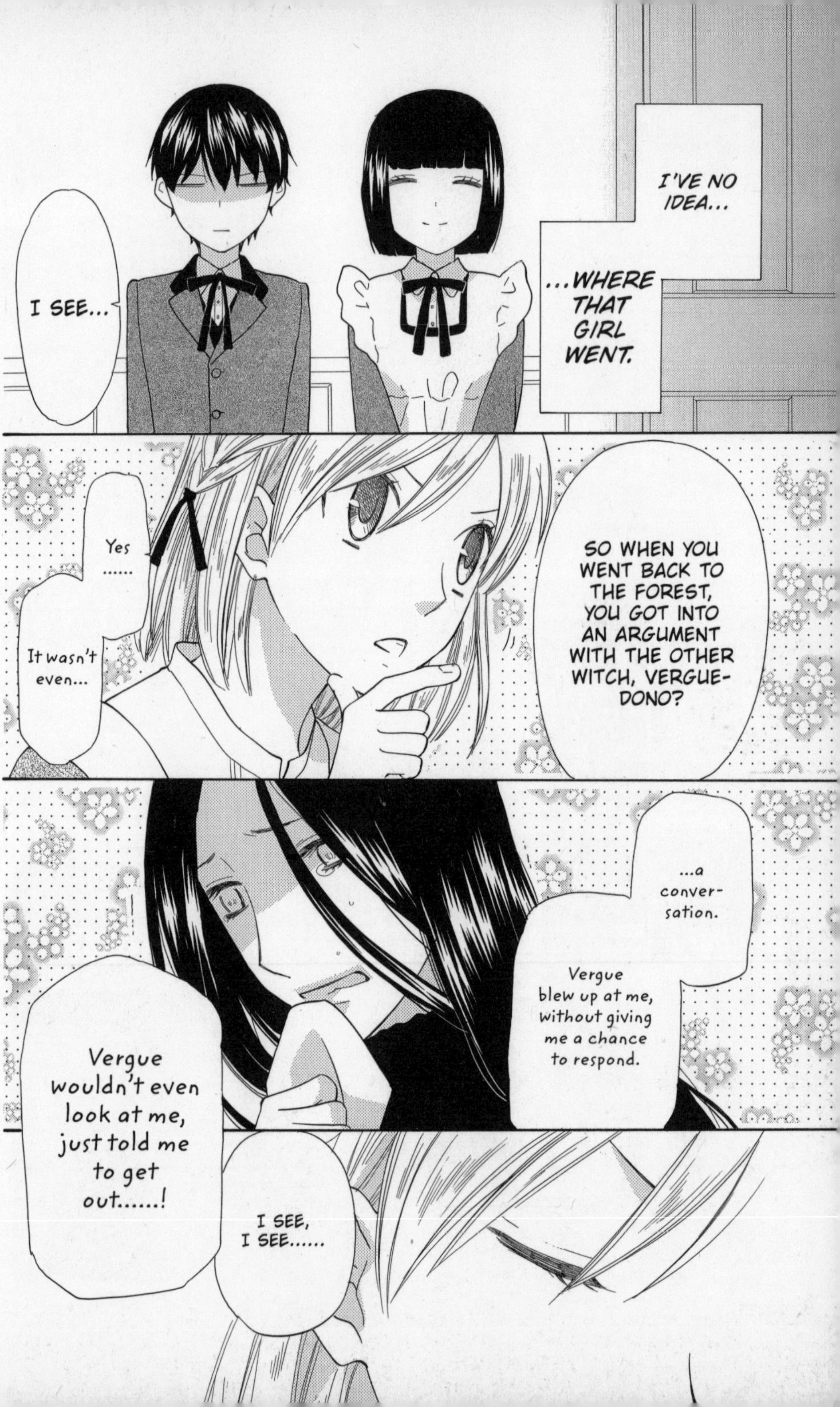
I'VE NO IDEA...
...WHERE THAT GIRL WENT.
I SEE...
SO WHEN YOU WENT BACK TO THE FOREST, YOU GOT INTO AN ARGUMENT WITH THE OTHER WITCH, VERGUE-DONO?
Yes ......
It wasn't even...
...a conver-sation.
Vergue blew up at me, without giving me a chance to respond.
Vergue wouldn't even look at me, just told me to get out......!
I SEE, I SEE......

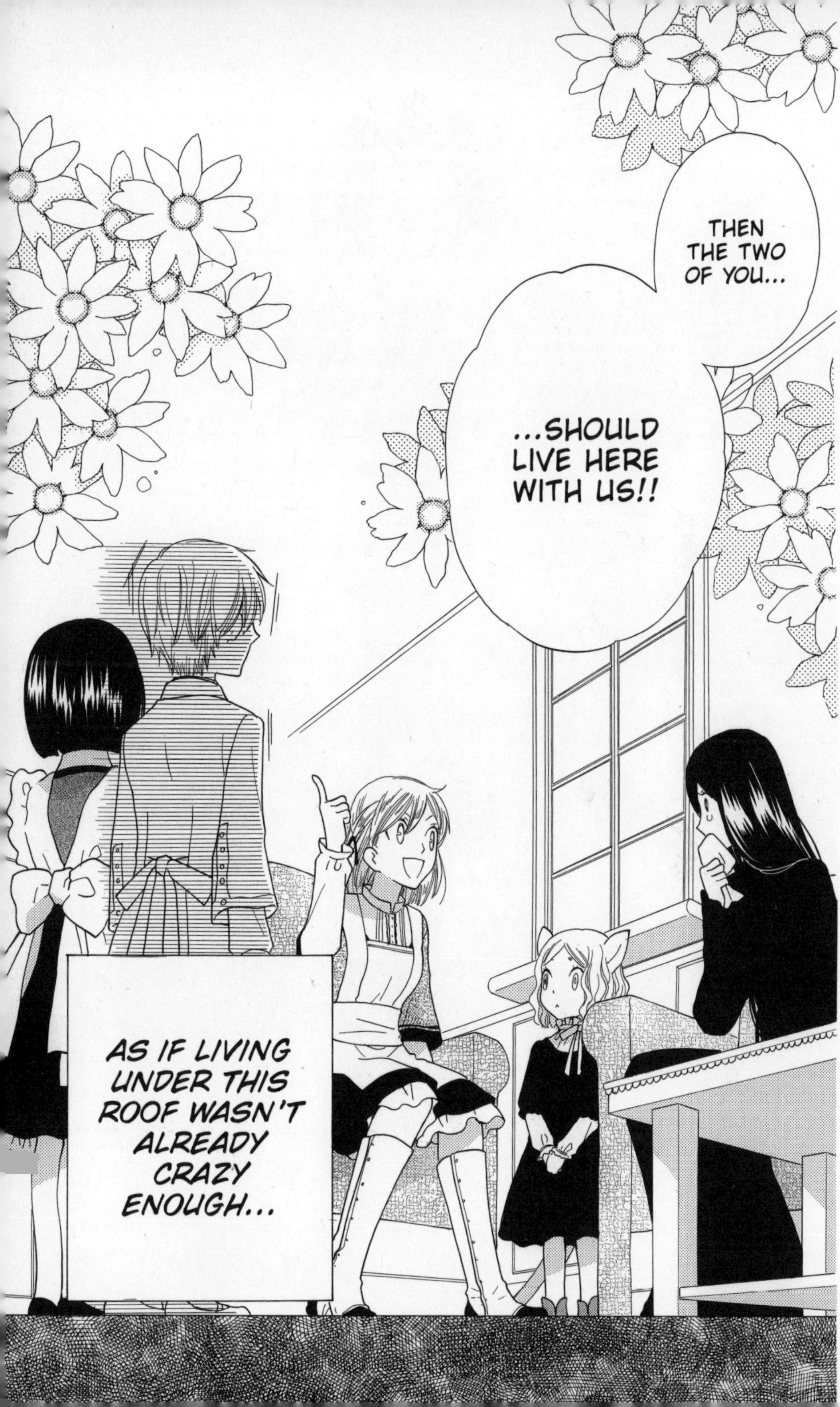
THEN THE TWO OF YOU...
...SHOULD LIVE HERE WITH US!!
AS IF LIVING UNDER THIS ROOF WASN'T ALREADY CRAZY ENOUGH...

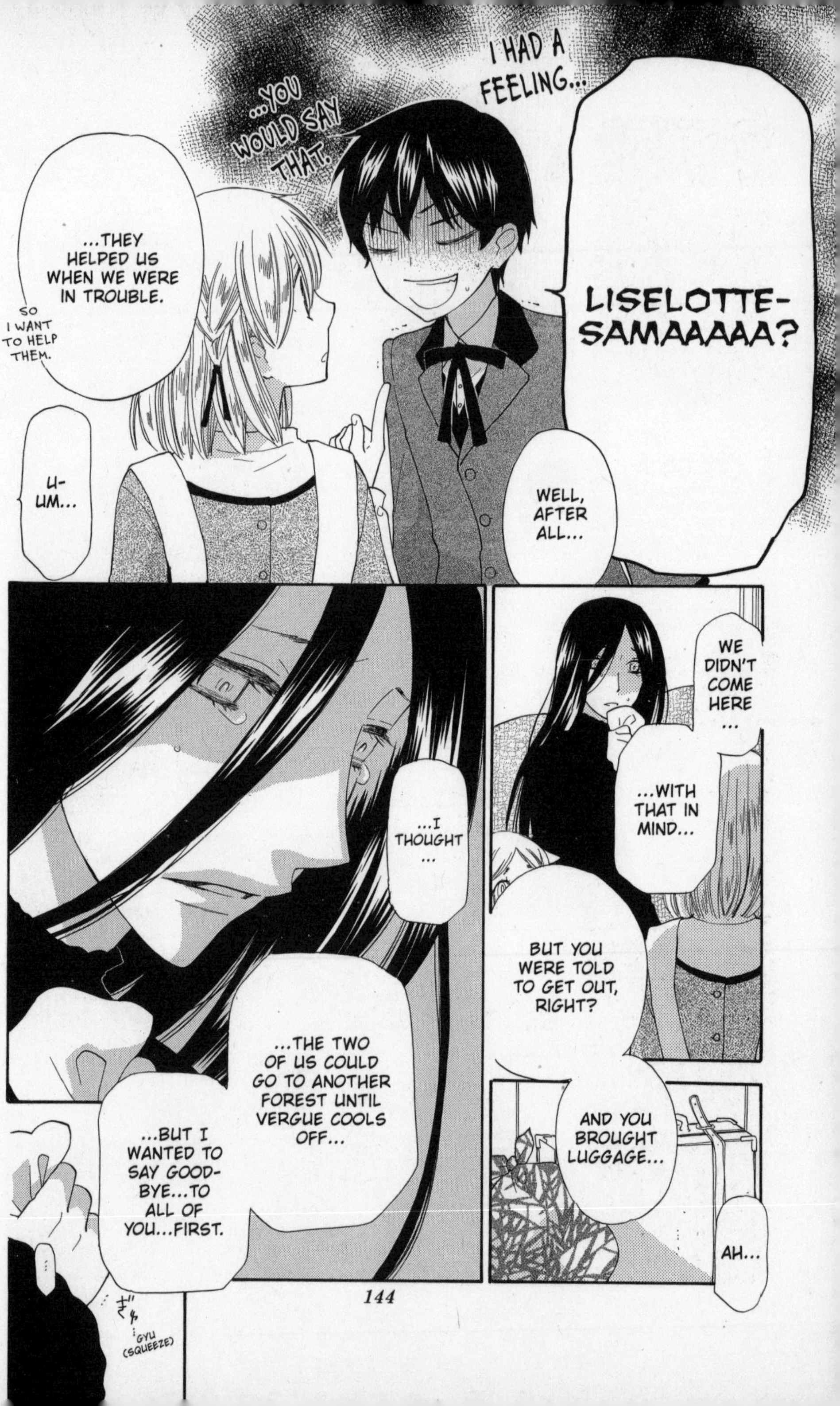
I HAD A FEELING...
...YOU WOULD SAY THAT.
LISELOTTE-SAMAAAAA?
WELL, AFTER ALL...
...THEY HELPED US WHEN WE WERE IN TROUBLE.
SO I WANT TO HELP THEM.
U-UM...
WE DIDN'T COME HERE...
...WITH THAT IN MIND...
BUT YOU WERE TOLD TO GET OUT, RIGHT?
AND YOU BROUGHT LUGGAGE...
...
AH...
...I THOUGHT...
...THE TWO OF US COULD GO TO ANOTHER FOREST UNTIL VERGUE COOLS OFF...
...BUT I WANTED TO SAY GOOD-BYE...TO ALL OF YOU...FIRST.
...
ぎゅ
GYU (SQUEEZE)

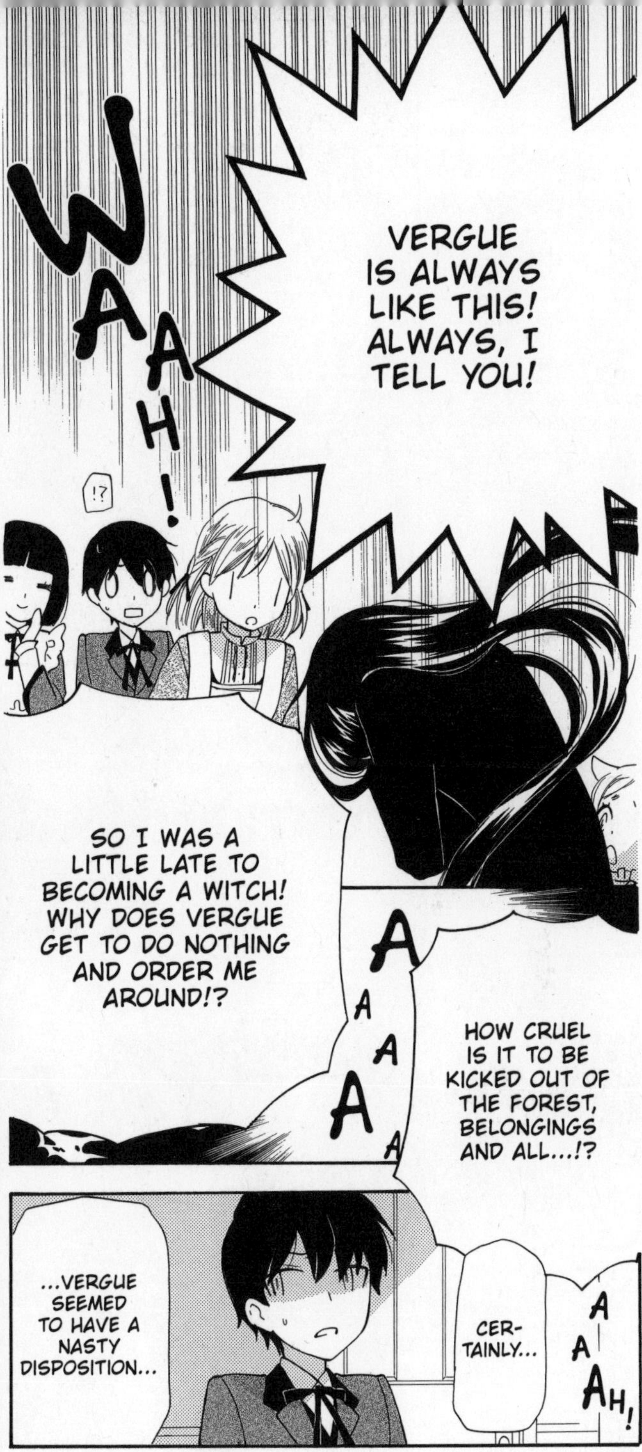
VERGUE IS ALWAYS LIKE THIS! ALWAYS, I TELL YOU!
WAAAH!
!?
HOW CRUEL IS IT TO BE KICKED OUT OF THE FOREST, BELONGINGS AND ALL...!?
AAAAAA
SO I WAS A LITTLE LATE TO BECOMING A WITCH! WHY DOES VERGUE GET TO DO NOTHING AND ORDER ME AROUND!?
AAAAH!
CER-TAINLY...
...VERGUE SEEMED TO HAVE A NASTY DISPOSITION...

EICHE OF THE EICHE TREE IS NEITHER MALE NOR FEMALE. THAT'S THE IMAGE I HAD ANYWAY. I'VE ALWAYS LOVED DRAWING THAT KIND OF CHARACTER, SO IT WAS FUN.

I DON'T KNOW WHEN EICHE WILL MAKE ANOTHER APPEARANCE THOUGH......

I DON'T KNOW WHEN WE'LL SEE WILHEL-SAN AGAIN EITHER... (LOL)

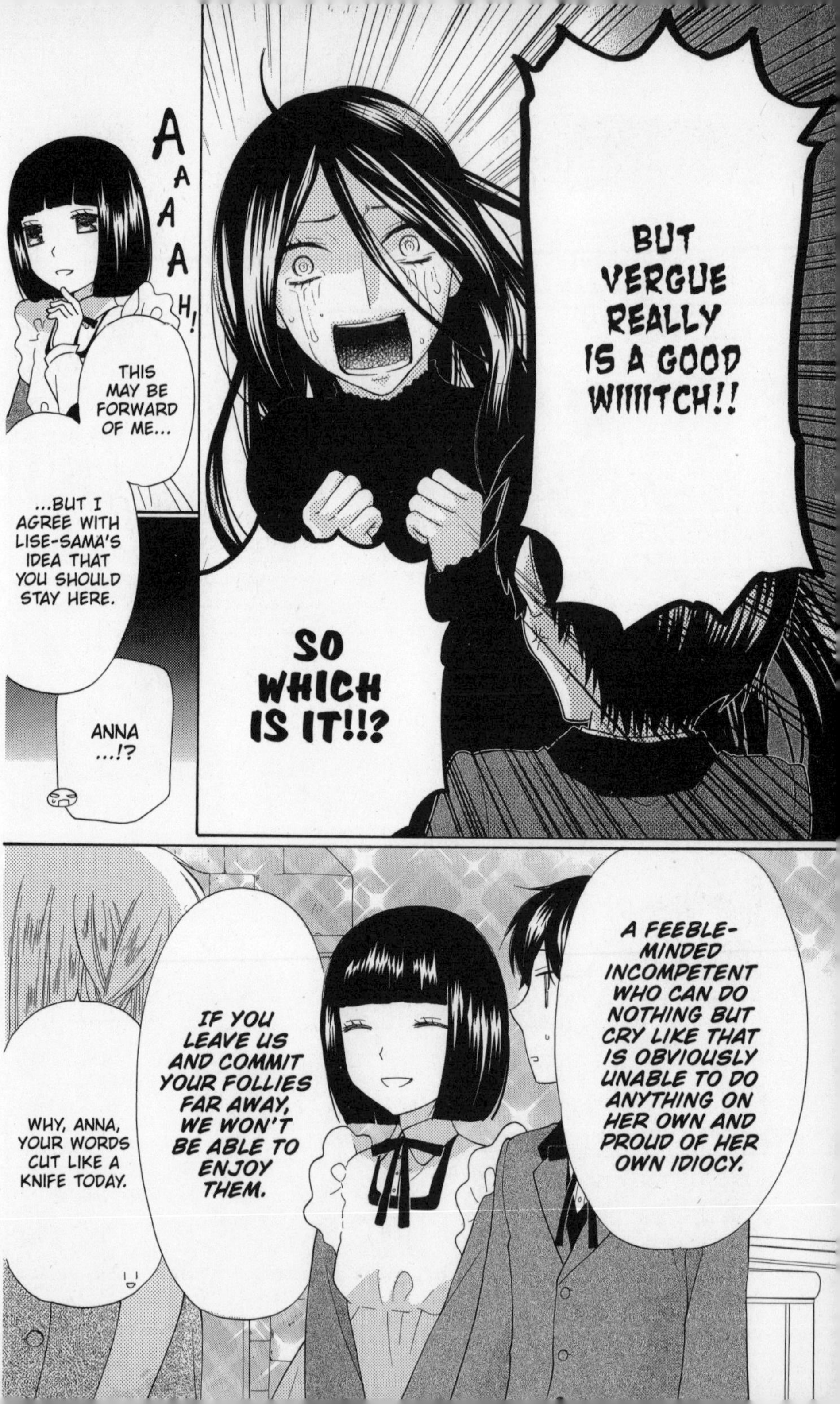
BUT VERGUE REALLY IS A GOOD WIIIITCH!!
SO WHICH IS IT!!?
AAAAH!
THIS MAY BE FORWARD OF ME...
...BUT I AGREE WITH LISE-SAMA'S IDEA THAT YOU SHOULD STAY HERE.
ANNA ...!?
A FEEBLE-MINDED INCOMPETENT WHO CAN DO NOTHING BUT CRY LIKE THAT IS OBVIOUSLY UNABLE TO DO ANYTHING ON HER OWN AND PROUD OF HER OWN IDIOCY.
IF YOU LEAVE US AND COMMIT YOUR FOLLIES FAR AWAY, WE WON'T BE ABLE TO ENJOY THEM.
WHY, ANNA, YOUR WORDS CUT LIKE A KNIFE TODAY.

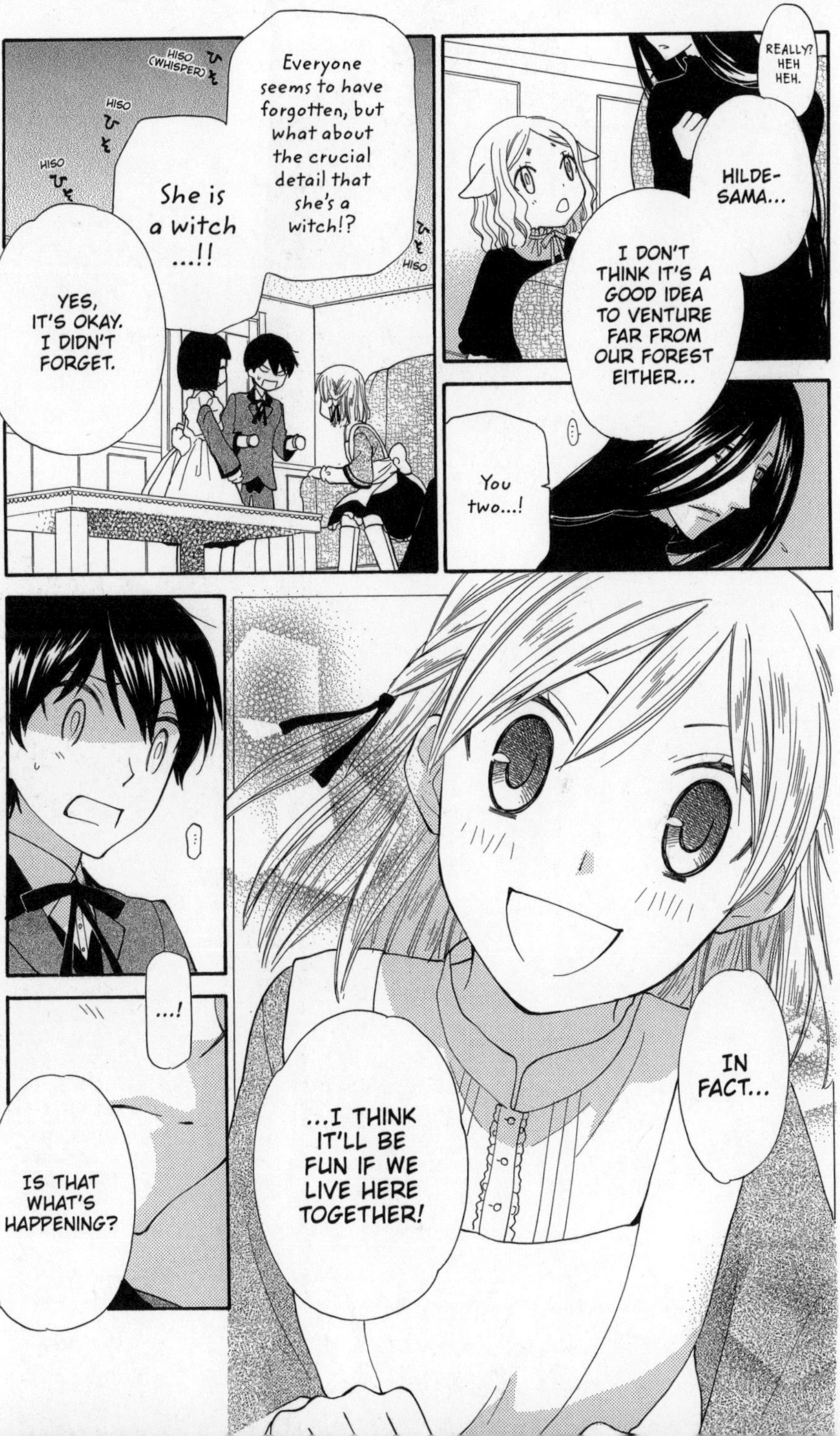
REALLY? HEH HEH.
HILDE-SAMA...
I DON'T THINK IT'S A GOOD IDEA TO VENTURE FAR FROM OUR FOREST EITHER...
...
You two...!
HISO (WHISPER)
HISO
HISO
HISO
Everyone seems to have forgotten, but what about the crucial detail that she's a witch!?
She is a witch ...!!
YES, IT'S OKAY. I DIDN'T FORGET.
IN FACT...
...I THINK IT'LL BE FUN IF WE LIVE HERE TOGETHER!
...
...!
IS THAT WHAT'S HAPPENING?

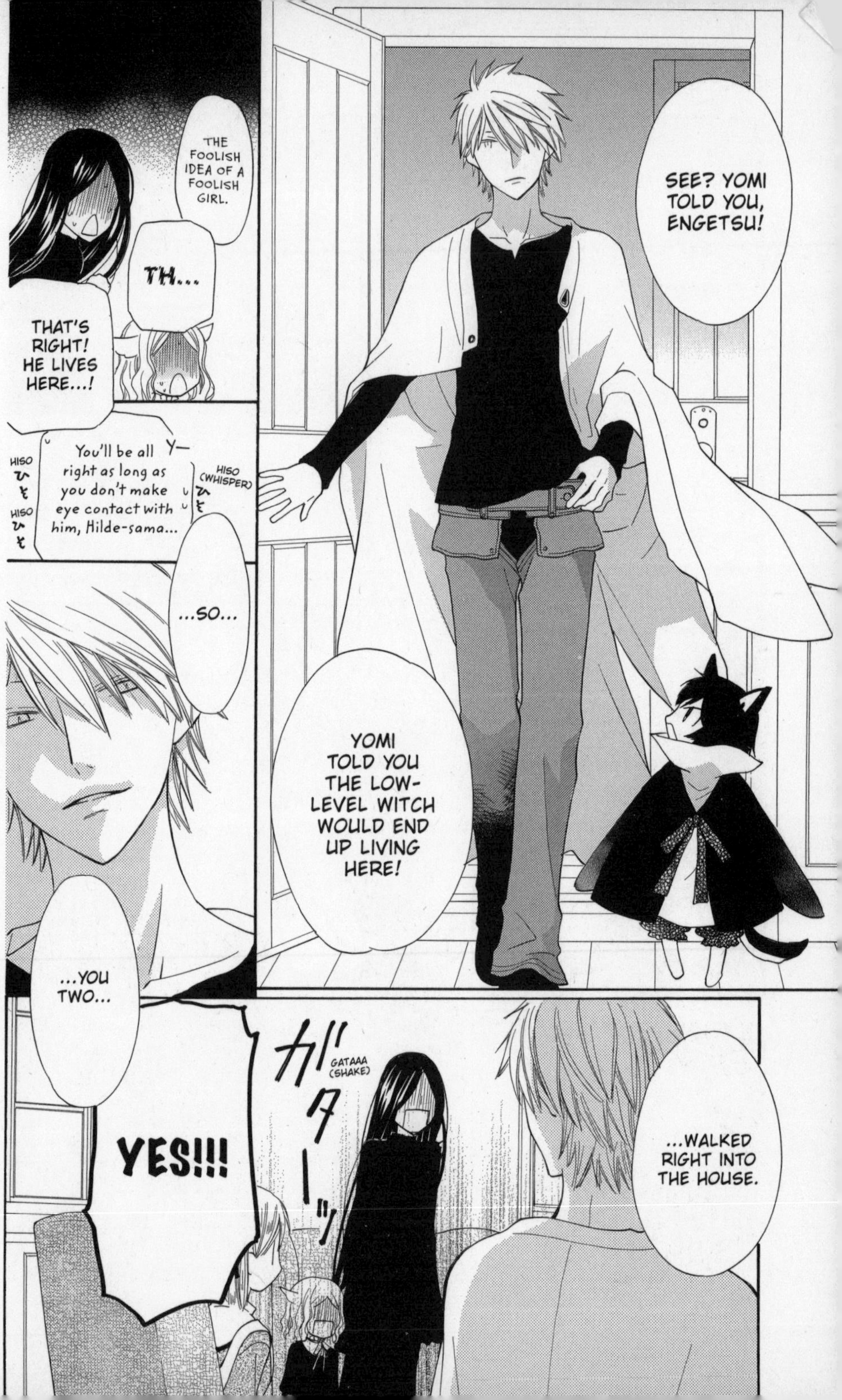
SEE? YOMI TOLD YOU, ENGETSU!
YOMI TOLD YOU THE LOW-LEVEL WITCH WOULD END UP LIVING HERE!
THE FOOLISH IDEA OF A FOOLISH GIRL.
TH...
THAT'S RIGHT! HE LIVES HERE...!
Y—
HISO (WHISPER)
You'll be all right as long as you don't make eye contact with him, Hilde-sama...
HISO
HISO
...SO...
...YOU TWO...
...WALKED RIGHT INTO THE HOUSE.
GATAAA (SHAKE)
YES!!!

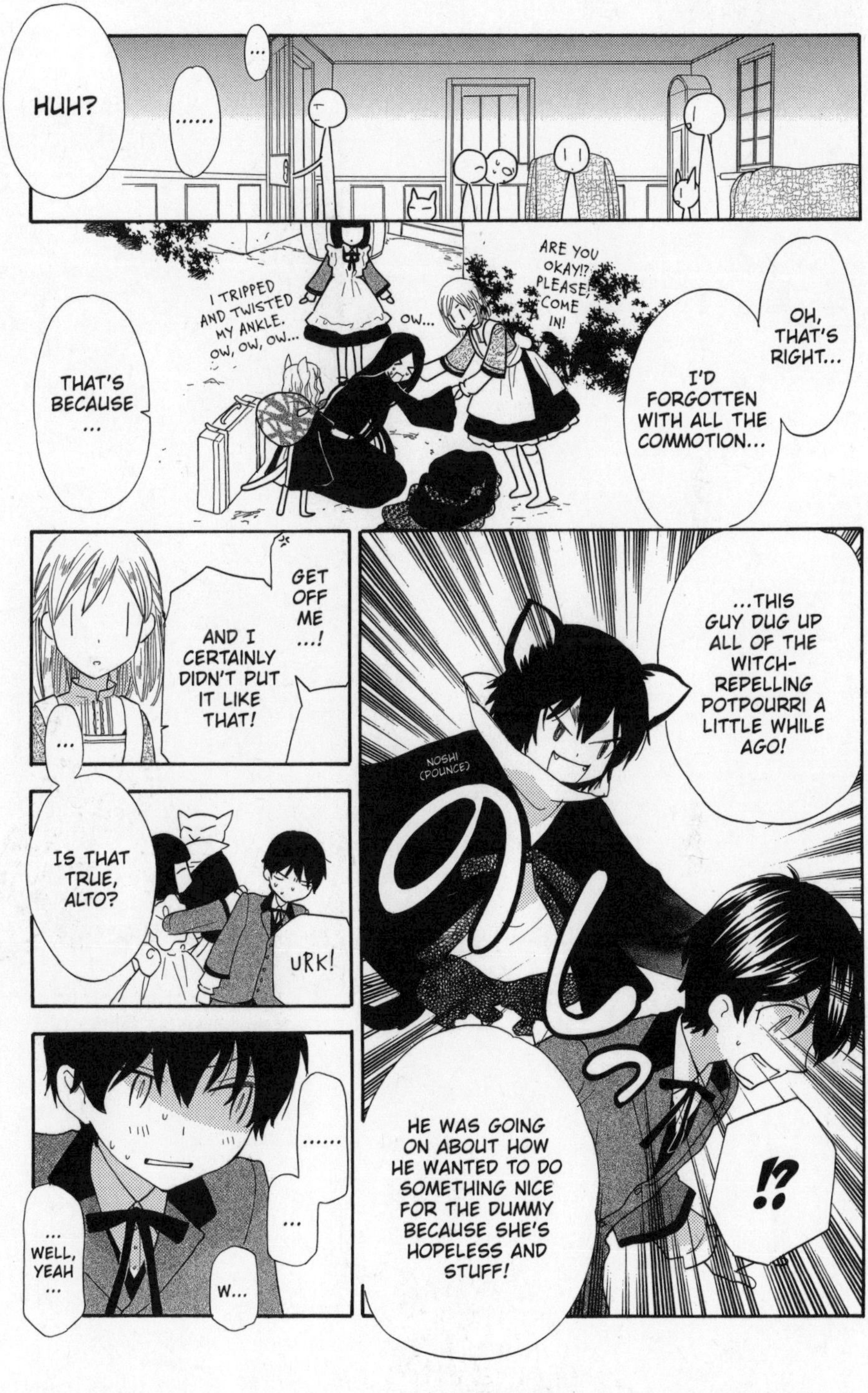
...
......
HUH?
OH, THAT'S RIGHT...
I'D FORGOTTEN WITH ALL THE COMMOTION...
ARE YOU OKAY!? PLEASE, COME IN!
OW...
I TRIPPED AND TWISTED MY ANKLE. OW, OW, OW...
THAT'S BECAUSE ...
...THIS GUY DUG UP ALL OF THE WITCH-REPELLING POTPOURRI A LITTLE WHILE AGO!
NOSHI (POUNCE)
!?
HE WAS GOING ON ABOUT HOW HE WANTED TO DO SOMETHING NICE FOR THE DUMMY BECAUSE SHE'S HOPELESS AND STUFF!
GET OFF ME ...!
AND I CERTAINLY DIDN'T PUT IT LIKE THAT!
...
IS THAT TRUE, ALTO?
URK!
......
...
W...
... WELL, YEAH ...

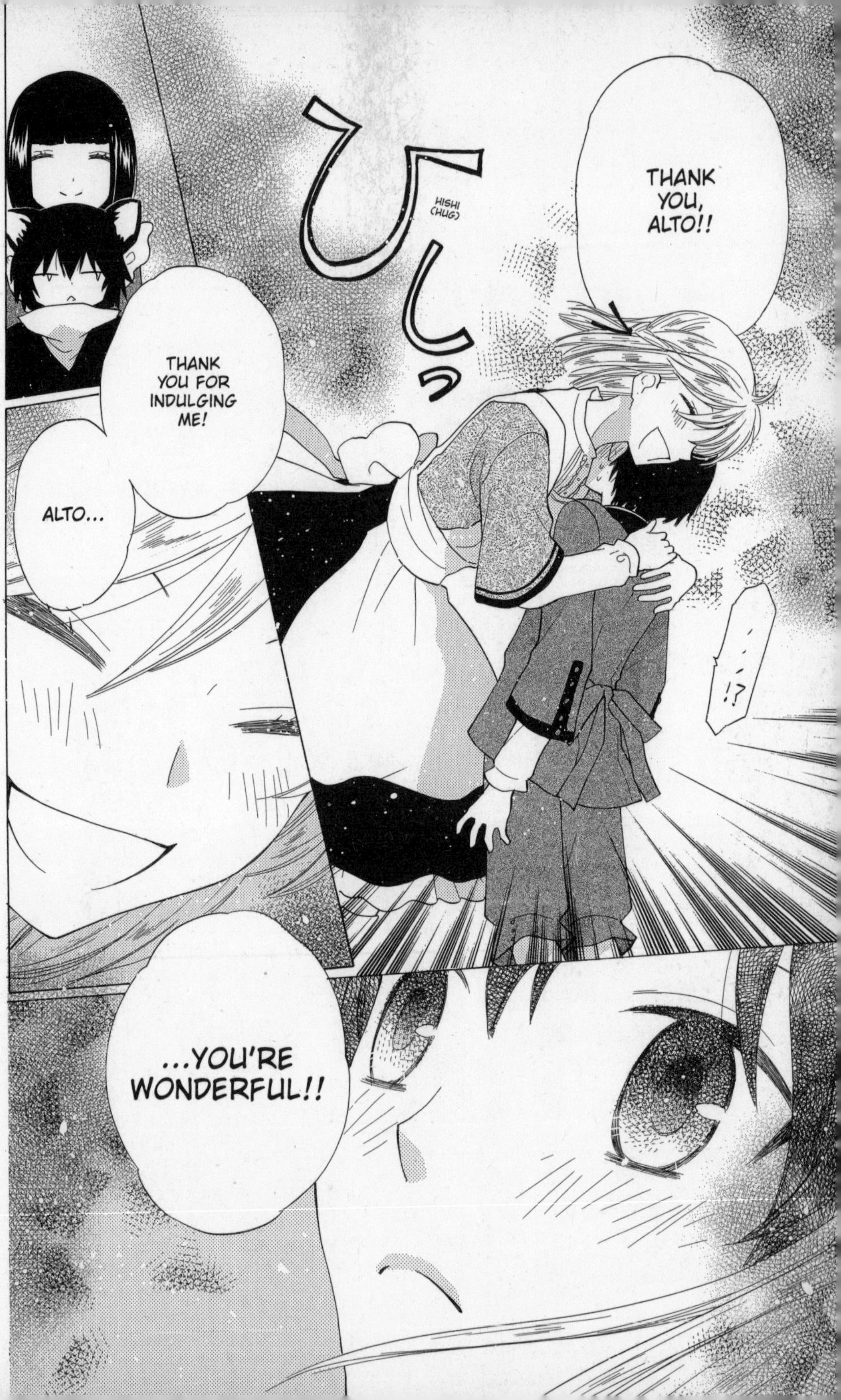
THANK YOU, ALTO!!
HISHI (HUG)
...!?
THANK YOU FOR INDULGING ME!
ALTO...
...YOU'RE WONDERFUL!!

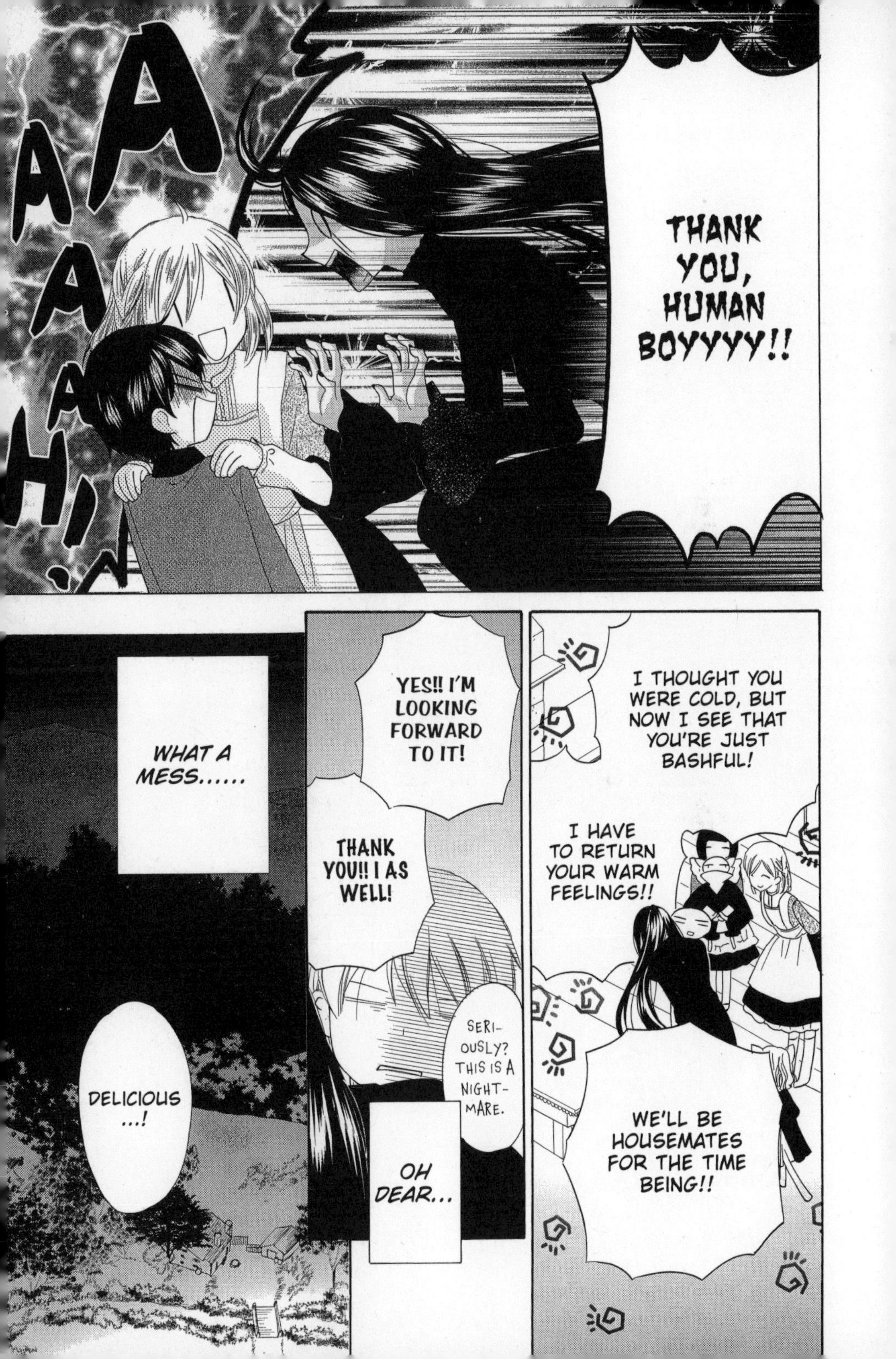
THANK YOU, HUMAN BOYYYY!!
AAAAH!
I THOUGHT YOU WERE COLD, BUT NOW I SEE THAT YOU'RE JUST BASHFUL!
I HAVE TO RETURN YOUR WARM FEELINGS!!
WE'LL BE HOUSEMATES FOR THE TIME BEING!!
YES!! I'M LOOKING FORWARD TO IT!
THANK YOU!! I AS WELL!
SERI-OUSLY? THIS IS A NIGHT-MARE.
OH DEAR...
WHAT A MESS......
DELICIOUS ...!

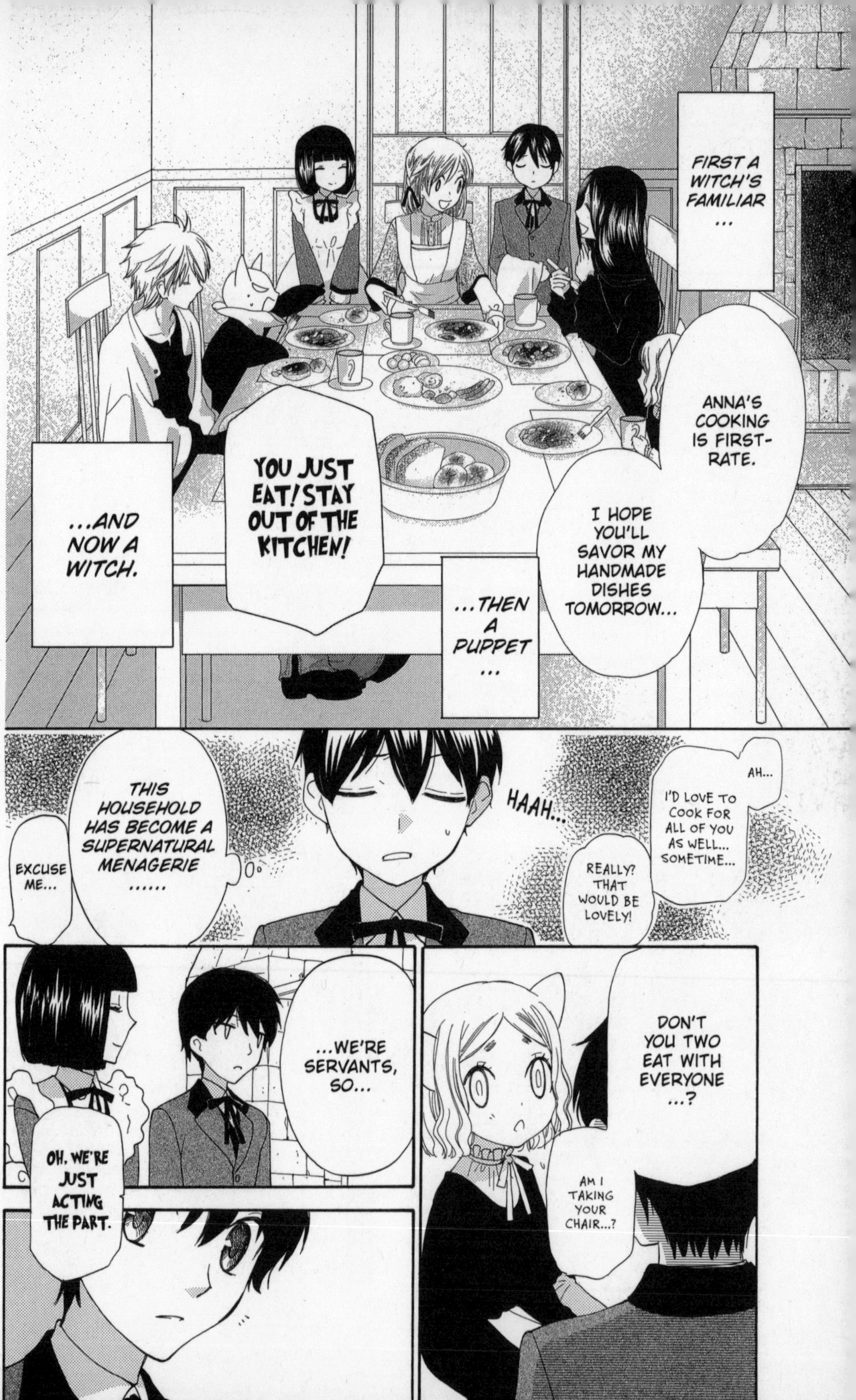
FIRST A WITCH'S FAMILIAR ...
ANNA'S COOKING IS FIRST-RATE.
I HOPE YOU'LL SAVOR MY HANDMADE DISHES TOMORROW...
...THEN A PUPPET ...
YOU JUST EAT! STAY OUT OF THE KITCHEN!
...AND NOW A WITCH.
AH... I'D LOVE TO COOK FOR ALL OF YOU AS WELL... SOMETIME...
REALLY? THAT WOULD BE LOVELY!
HAAH...
THIS HOUSEHOLD HAS BECOME A SUPERNATURAL MENAGERIE ......
EXCUSE ME...
DON'T YOU TWO EAT WITH EVERYONE ...?
AM I TAKING YOUR CHAIR...?
...WE'RE SERVANTS, SO...
OH. WE'RE JUST ACTING THE PART.

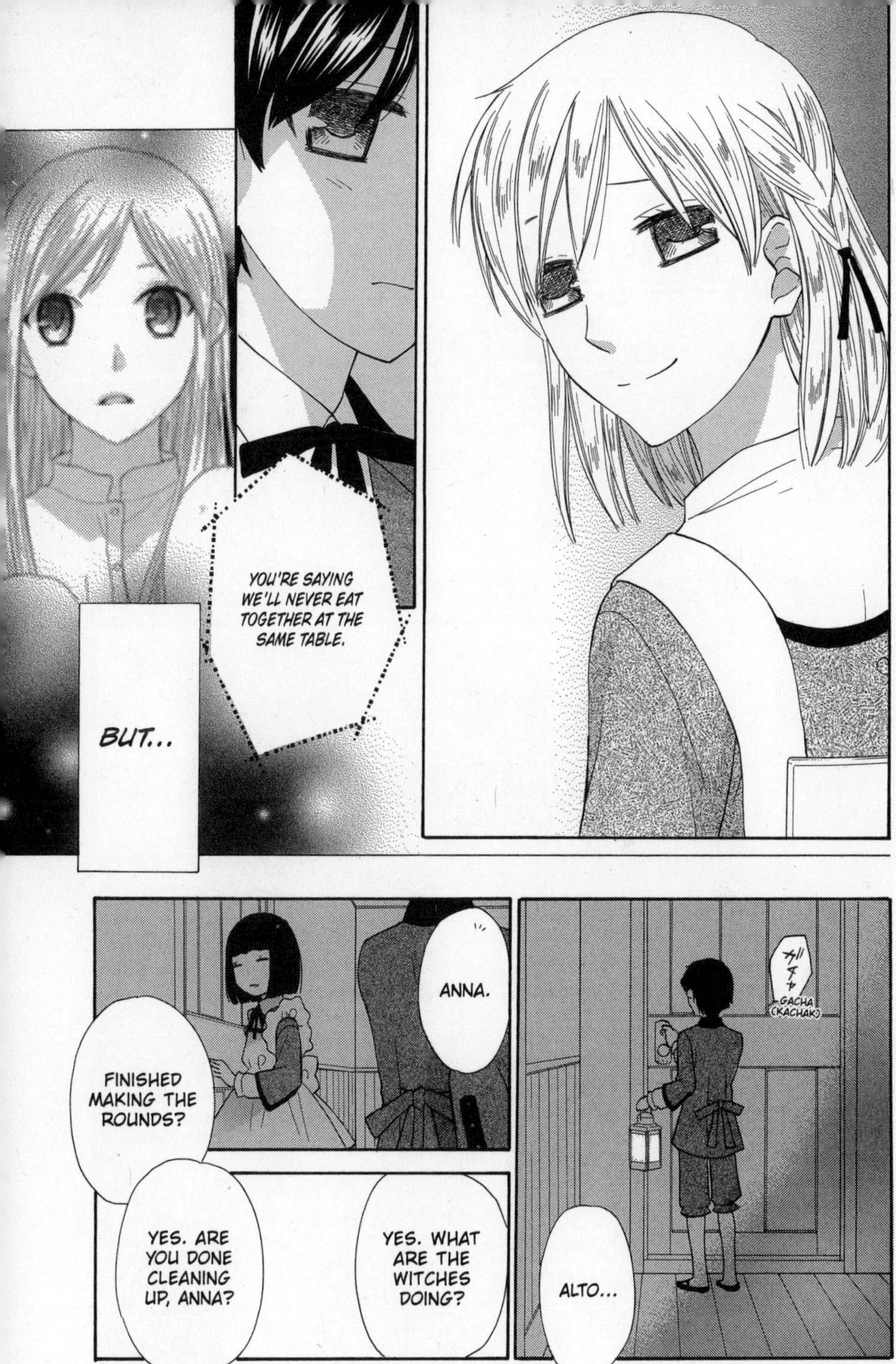
YOU'RE SAYING WE'LL NEVER EAT TOGETHER AT THE SAME TABLE.
BUT...
GACHA (KACHAK)
ALTO...
ANNA.
FINISHED MAKING THE ROUNDS?
YES. ARE YOU DONE CLEANING UP, ANNA?
YES. WHAT ARE THE WITCHES DOING?

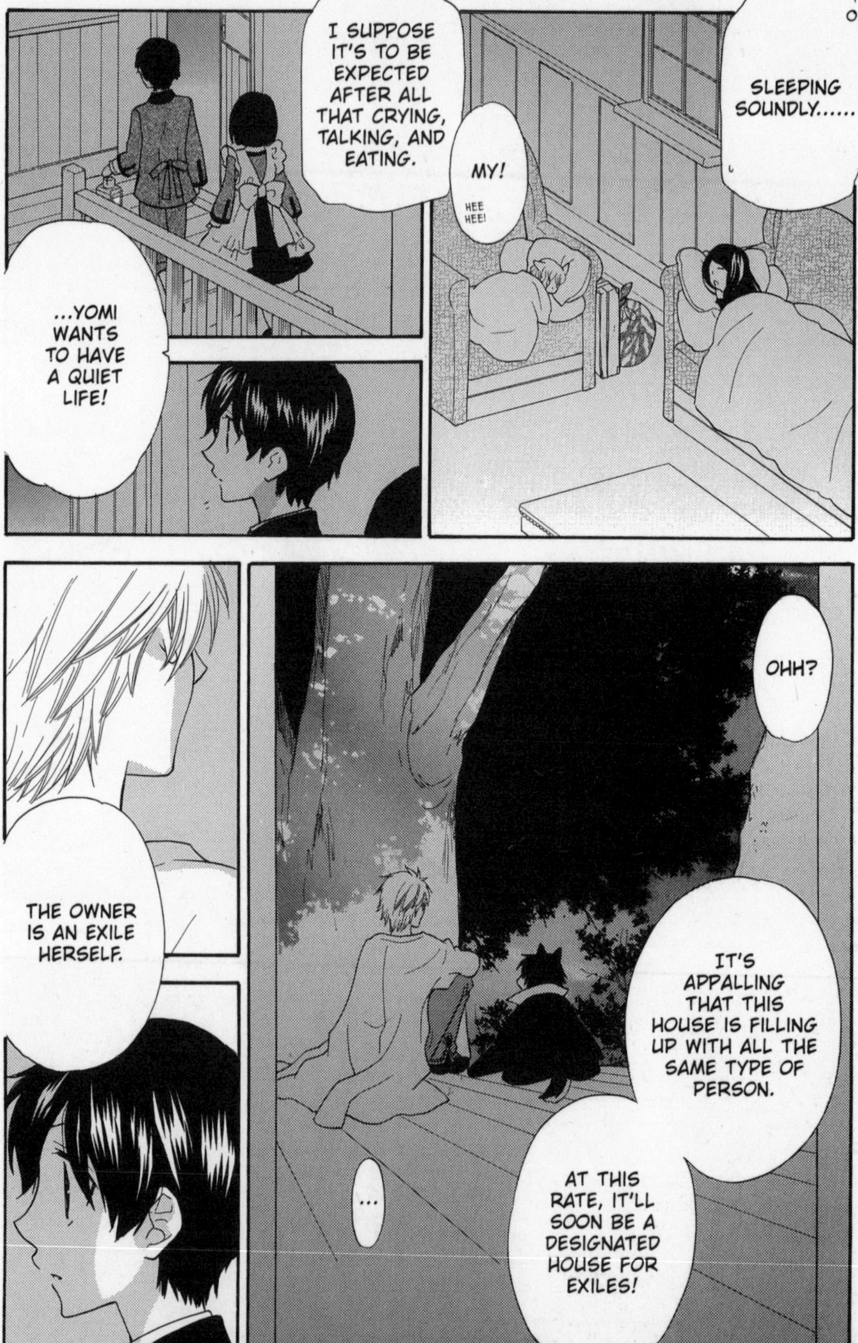
OH...
SLEEPING SOUNDLY......
MY!
HEE HEE!
I SUPPOSE IT'S TO BE EXPECTED AFTER ALL THAT CRYING, TALKING, AND EATING.
...YOMI WANTS TO HAVE A QUIET LIFE!
OHH?
IT'S APPALLING THAT THIS HOUSE IS FILLING UP WITH ALL THE SAME TYPE OF PERSON.
AT THIS RATE, IT'LL SOON BE A DESIGNATED HOUSE FOR EXILES!
...
THE OWNER IS AN EXILE HERSELF.

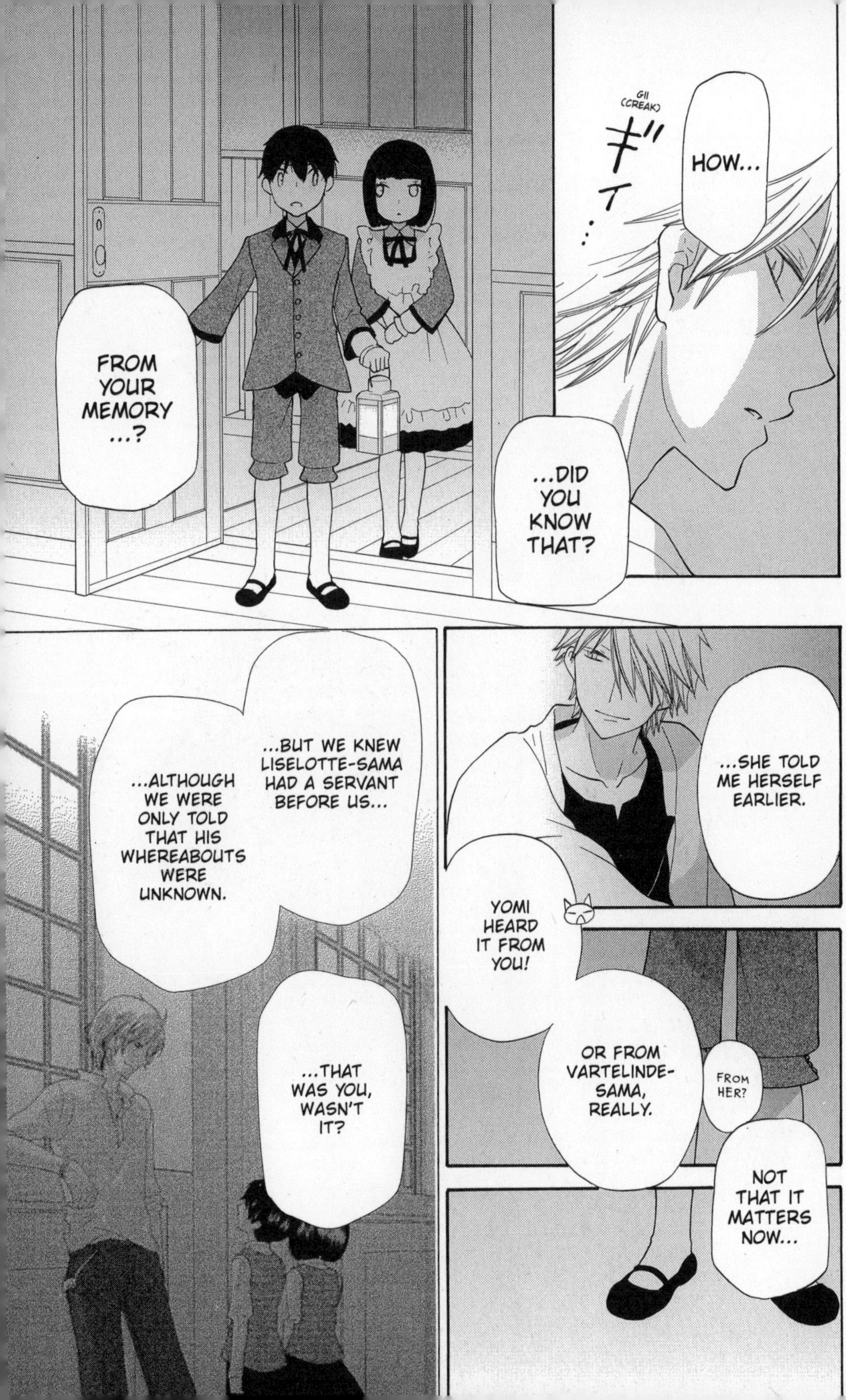
GII (CREAK)
HOW...
...DID YOU KNOW THAT?
FROM YOUR MEMORY ...?
...SHE TOLD ME HERSELF EARLIER.
YOMI HEARD IT FROM YOU!
OR FROM VARTELINDE-SAMA, REALLY.
FROM HER?
NOT THAT IT MATTERS NOW...
...BUT WE KNEW LISELOTTE-SAMA HAD A SERVANT BEFORE US...
...ALTHOUGH WE WERE ONLY TOLD THAT HIS WHEREABOUTS WERE UNKNOWN.
...THAT WAS YOU, WASN'T IT?

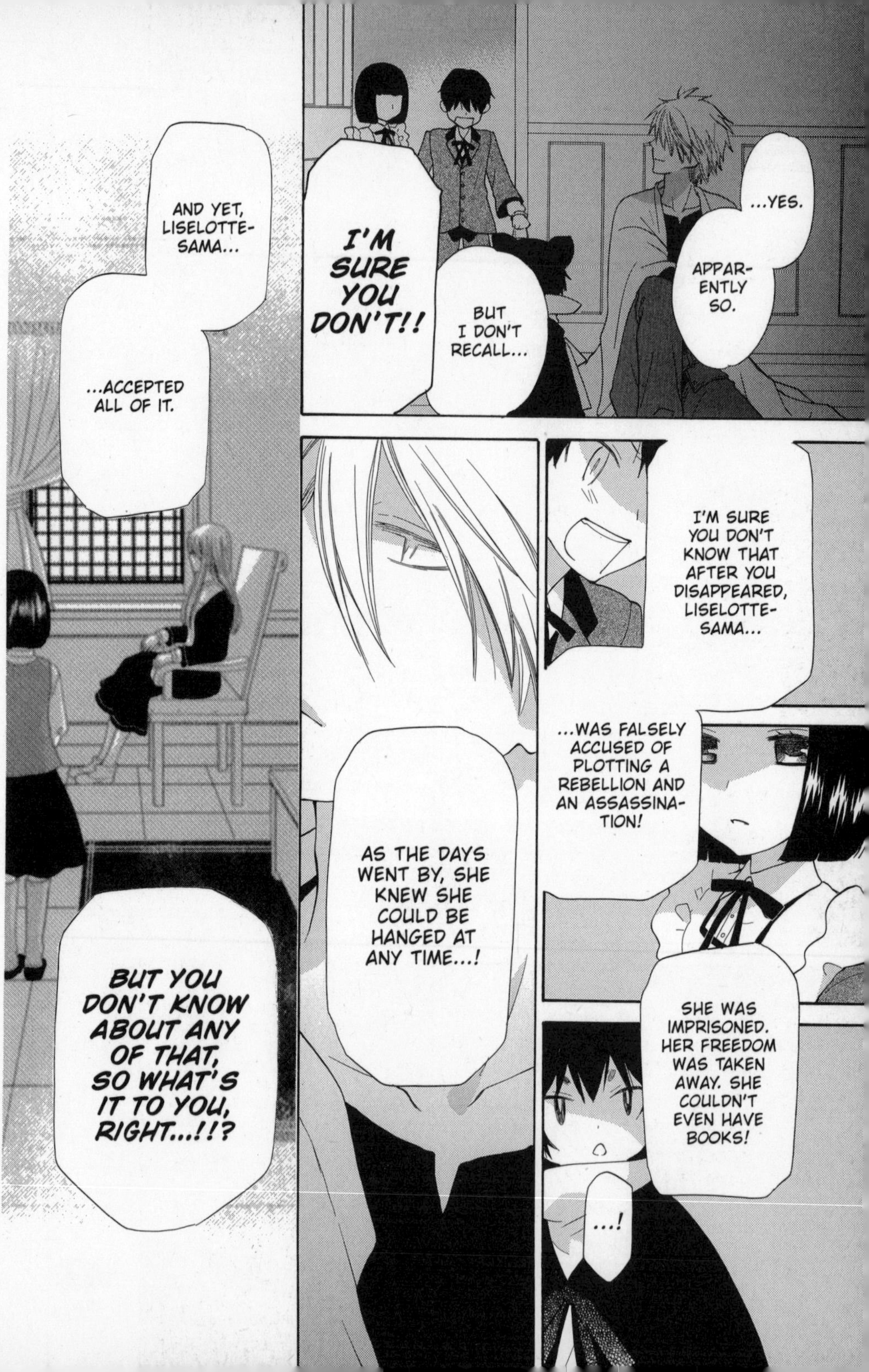

...YES.
APPARENTLY SO.
BUT I DON'T RECALL...
I'M SURE YOU DON'T!!
I'M SURE YOU DON'T KNOW THAT AFTER YOU DISAPPEARED, LISELOTTE-SAMA...
...WAS FALSELY ACCUSED OF PLOTTING A REBELLION AND AN ASSASSINATION!
SHE WAS IMPRISONED. HER FREEDOM WAS TAKEN AWAY. SHE COULDN'T EVEN HAVE BOOKS!
...!
AS THE DAYS WENT BY, SHE KNEW SHE COULD BE HANGED AT ANY TIME...!
AND YET, LISELOTTE-SAMA...
...ACCEPTED ALL OF IT.
BUT YOU DON'T KNOW ABOUT ANY OF THAT, SO WHAT'S IT TO YOU, RIGHT...!!?

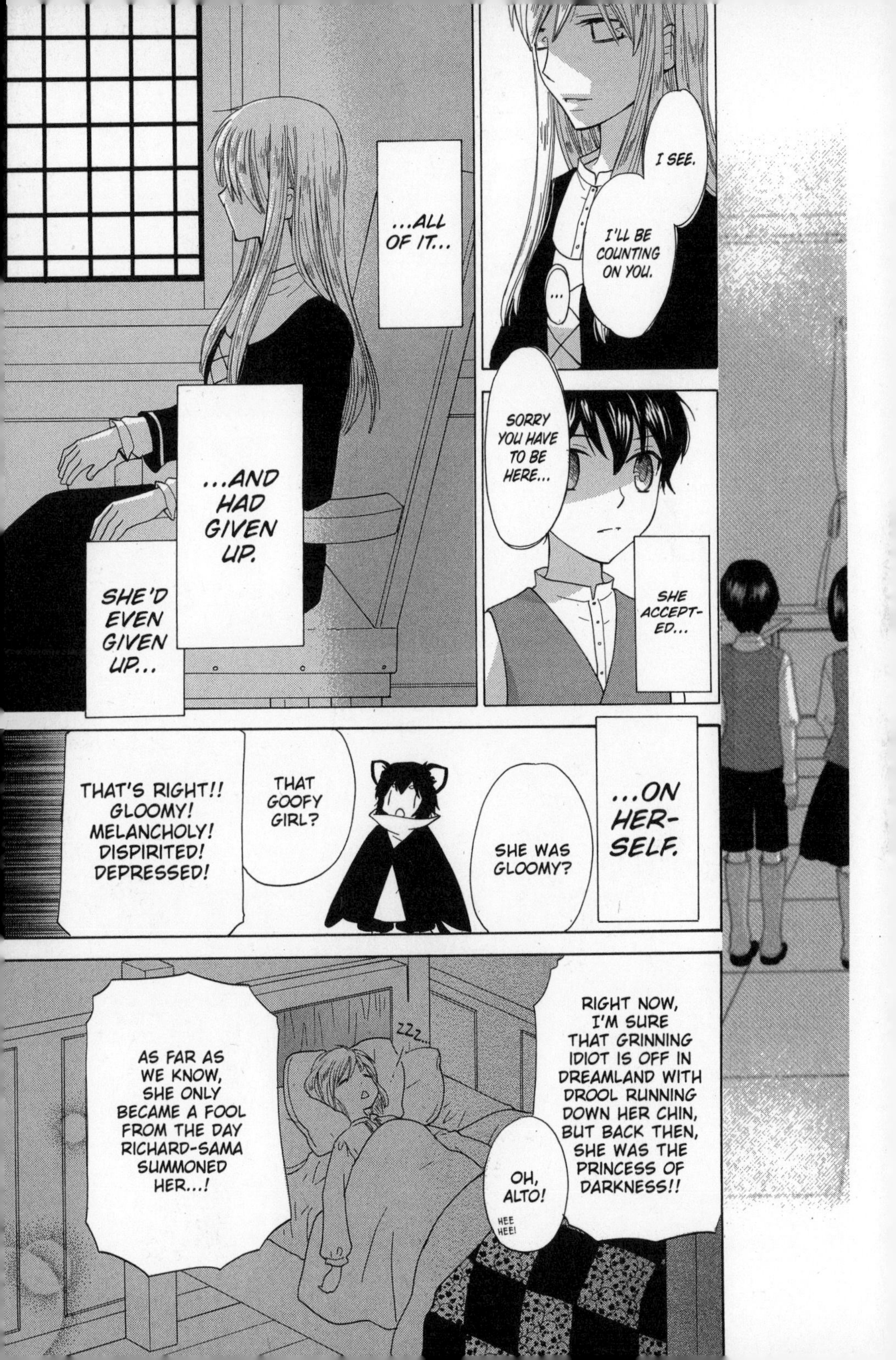
I SEE.
I'LL BE COUNTING ON YOU.
...
SORRY YOU HAVE TO BE HERE...
SHE ACCEPTED...
...ALL OF IT...
...AND HAD GIVEN UP.
SHE'D EVEN GIVEN UP...
...ON HERSELF.
SHE WAS GLOOMY?
THAT GOOFY GIRL?
THAT'S RIGHT!! GLOOMY! MELANCHOLY! DISPIRITED! DEPRESSED!
RIGHT NOW, I'M SURE THAT GRINNING IDIOT IS OFF IN DREAMLAND WITH DROOL RUNNING DOWN HER CHIN, BUT BACK THEN, SHE WAS THE PRINCESS OF DARKNESS!!
OH, ALTO!
HEE HEE!
ZZZ...
AS FAR AS WE KNOW, SHE ONLY BECAME A FOOL FROM THE DAY RICHARD-SAMA SUMMONED HER...!

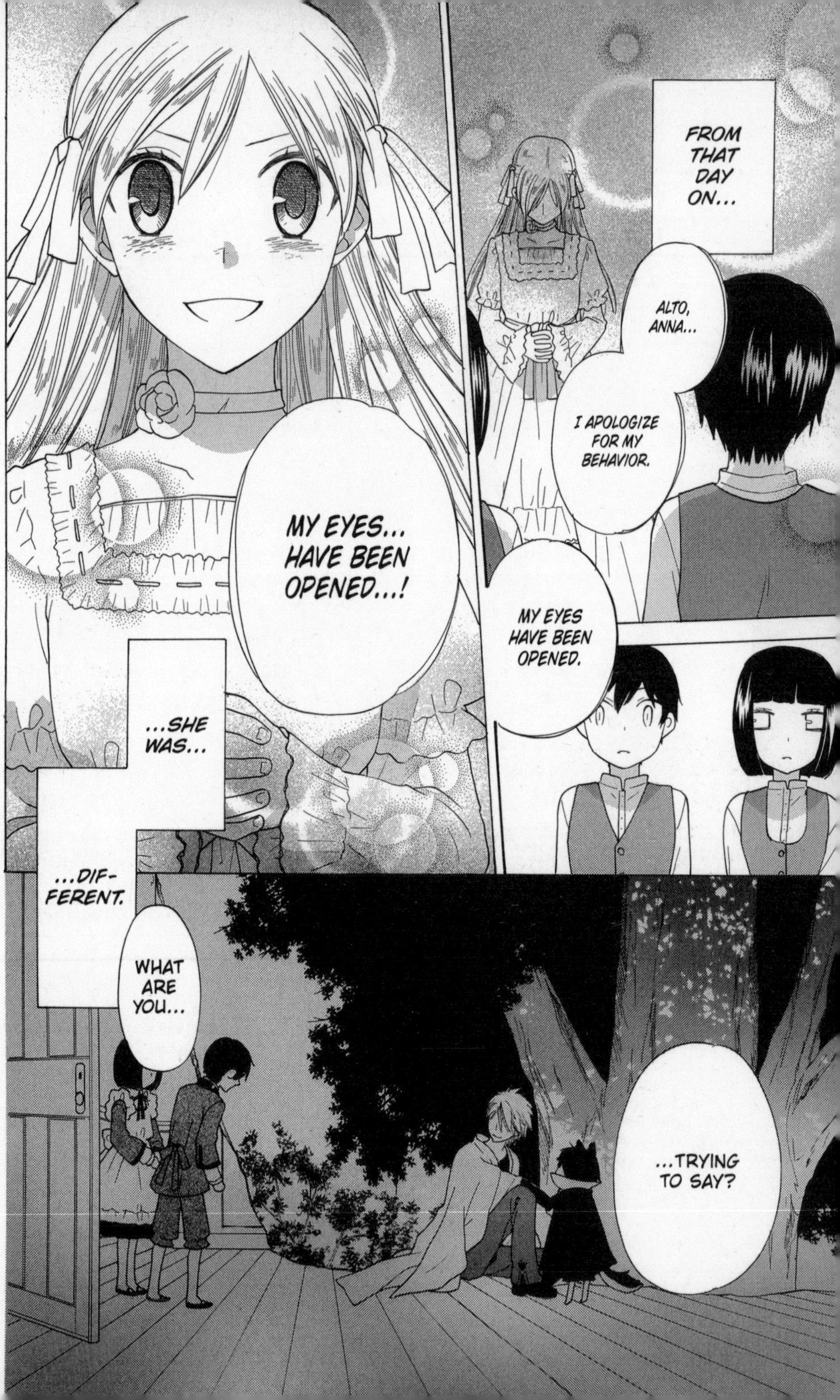
FROM THAT DAY ON...
ALTO, ANNA...
I APOLOGIZE FOR MY BEHAVIOR.
MY EYES HAVE BEEN OPENED.
MY EYES... HAVE BEEN OPENED...!
...SHE WAS...
...DIF-FERENT.
WHAT ARE YOU...
...TRYING TO SAY?

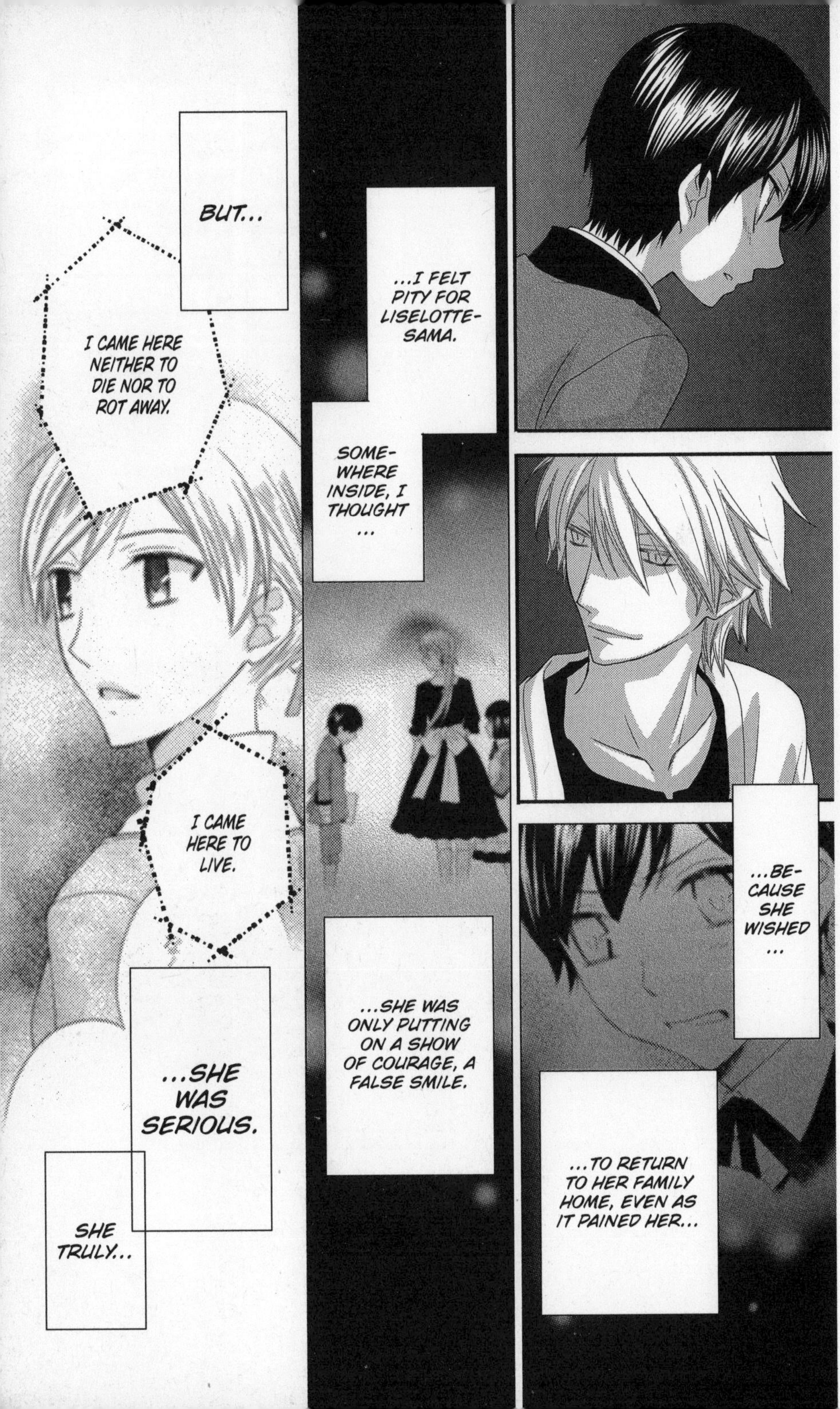
...BE-CAUSE SHE WISHED...
...TO RETURN TO HER FAMILY HOME, EVEN AS IT PAINED HER...
...I FELT PITY FOR LISELOTTE-SAMA.
SOME-WHERE INSIDE, I THOUGHT...
...SHE WAS ONLY PUTTING ON A SHOW OF COURAGE, A FALSE SMILE.
BUT...
I CAME HERE NEITHER TO DIE NOR TO ROT AWAY.
I CAME HERE TO LIVE.
...SHE WAS SERIOUS.
SHE TRULY...

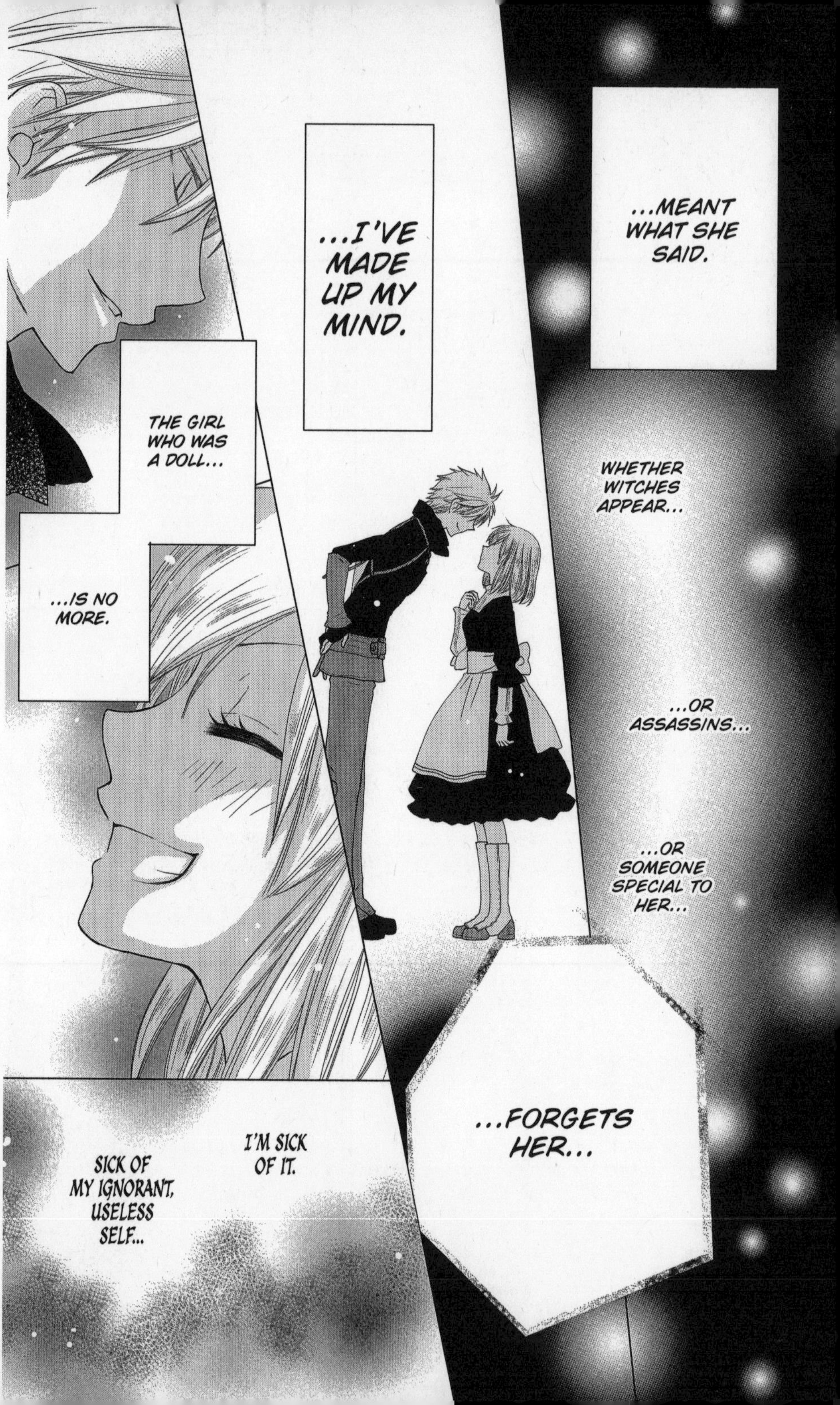
...MEANT WHAT SHE SAID.
WHETHER WITCHES APPEAR...
...OR ASSASSINS...
...OR SOMEONE SPECIAL TO HER...
...FORGETS HER...
...I'VE MADE UP MY MIND.
THE GIRL WHO WAS A DOLL...
...IS NO MORE.
I'M SICK OF IT.
SICK OF MY IGNORANT, USELESS SELF...

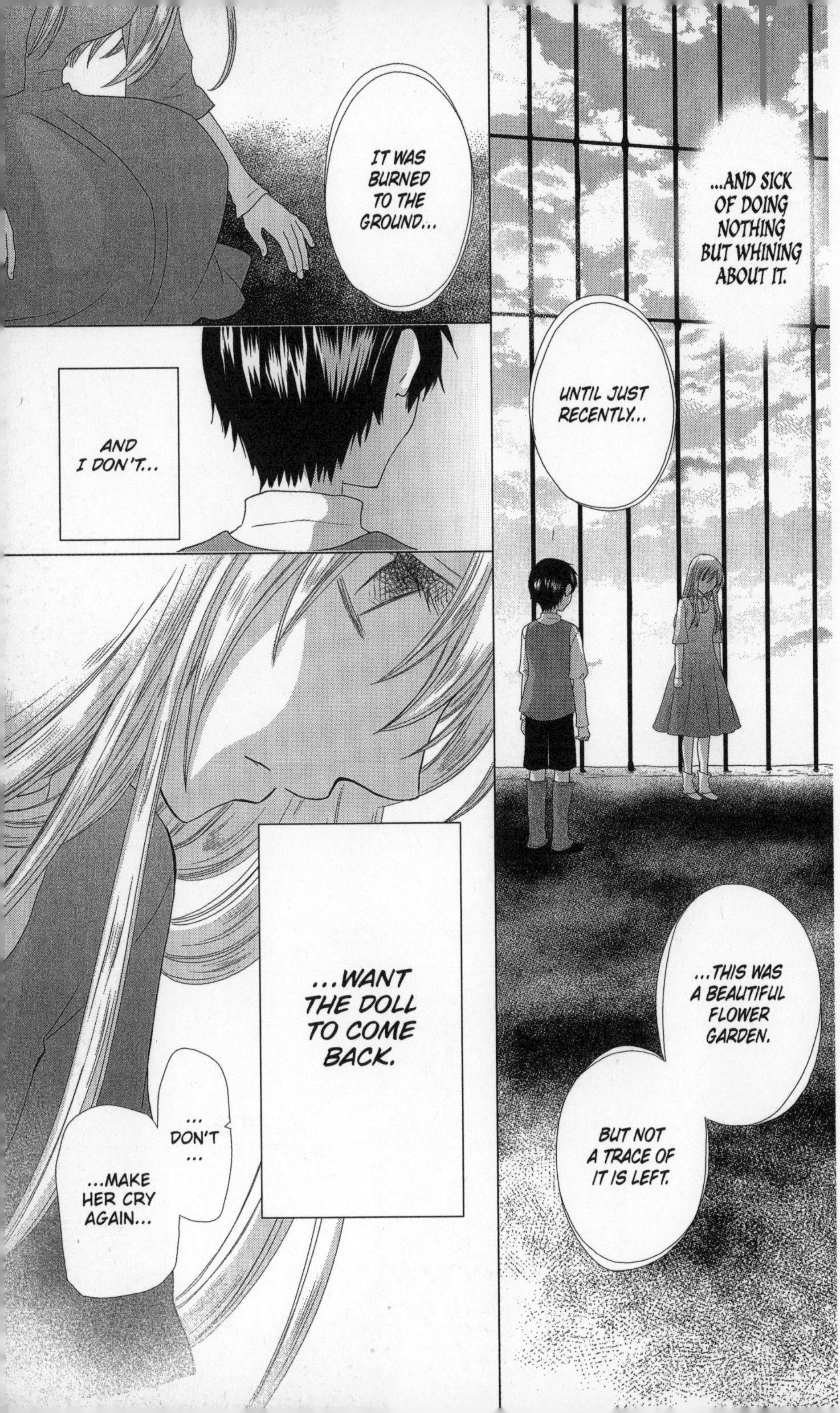
...AND SICK OF DOING NOTHING BUT WHINING ABOUT IT.
UNTIL JUST RECENTLY...
...THIS WAS A BEAUTIFUL FLOWER GARDEN.
BUT NOT A TRACE OF IT IS LEFT.
IT WAS BURNED TO THE GROUND...
AND I DON'T...
...WANT THE DOLL TO COME BACK.
... DON'T ...
...MAKE HER CRY AGAIN...

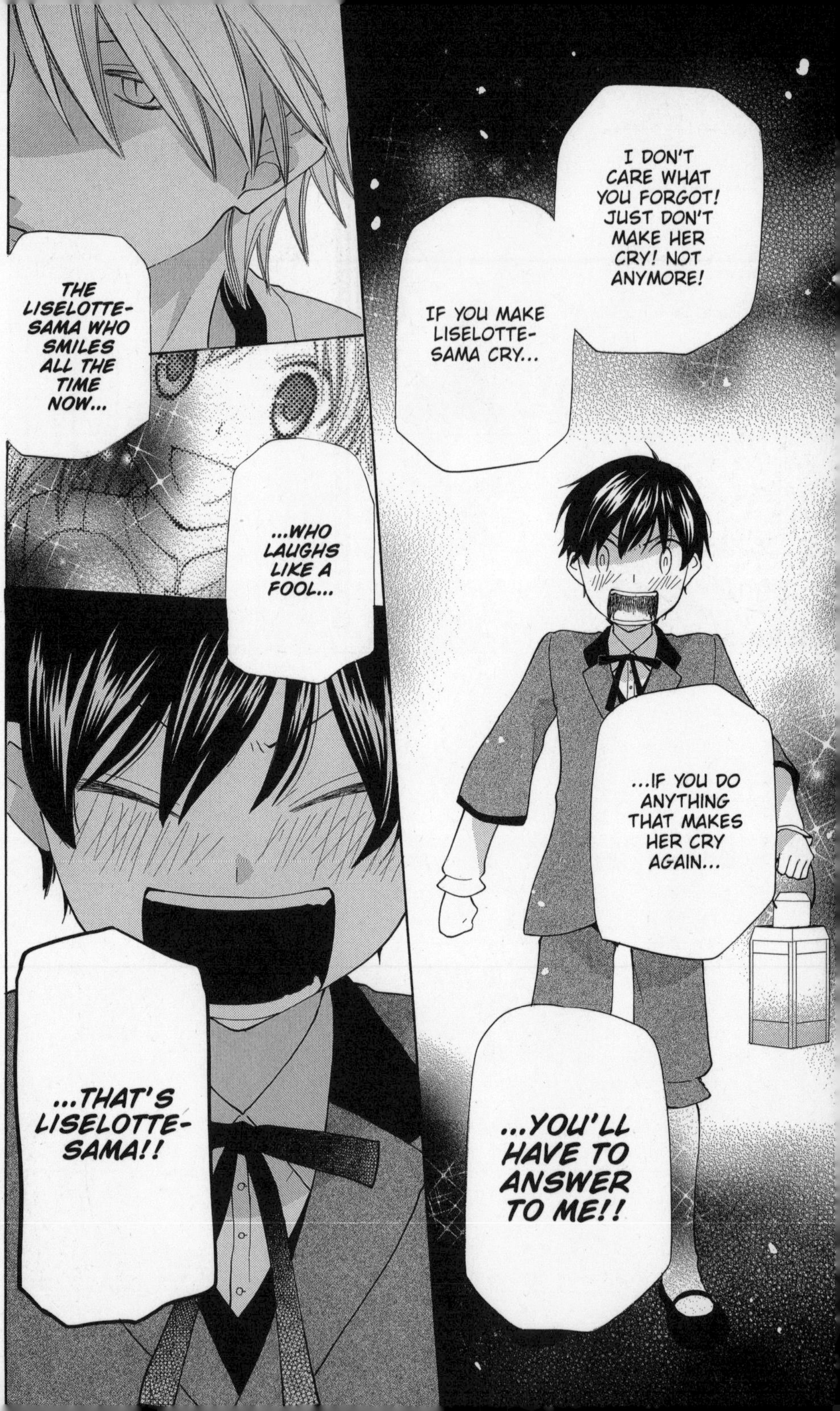
I DON'T CARE WHAT YOU FORGOT! JUST DON'T MAKE HER CRY! NOT ANYMORE!
IF YOU MAKE LISELOTTE-SAMA CRY...
...IF YOU DO ANYTHING THAT MAKES HER CRY AGAIN...
...YOU'LL HAVE TO ANSWER TO ME!!
THE LISELOTTE-SAMA WHO SMILES ALL THE TIME NOW...
...WHO LAUGHS LIKE A FOOL...
...THAT'S LISELOTTE-SAMA!!

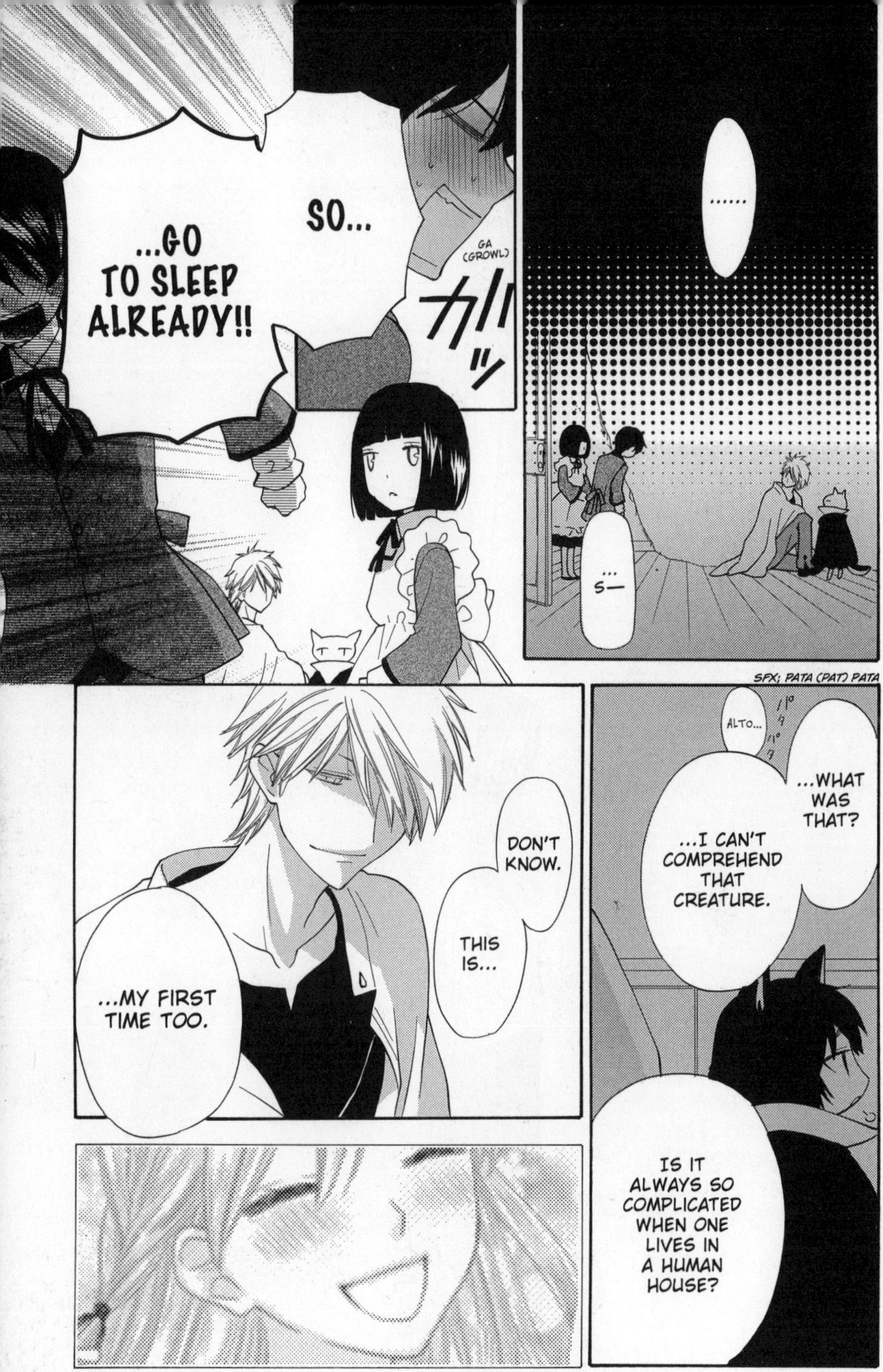
......
... S—
SFX; PATA (PAT) PATA
SO...
...GO TO SLEEP ALREADY!!
GA (GROWL)
ALTO...
...WHAT WAS THAT?
...I CAN'T COMPREHEND THAT CREATURE.
IS IT ALWAYS SO COMPLICATED WHEN ONE LIVES IN A HUMAN HOUSE?
DON'T KNOW.
THIS IS...
...MY FIRST TIME TOO.

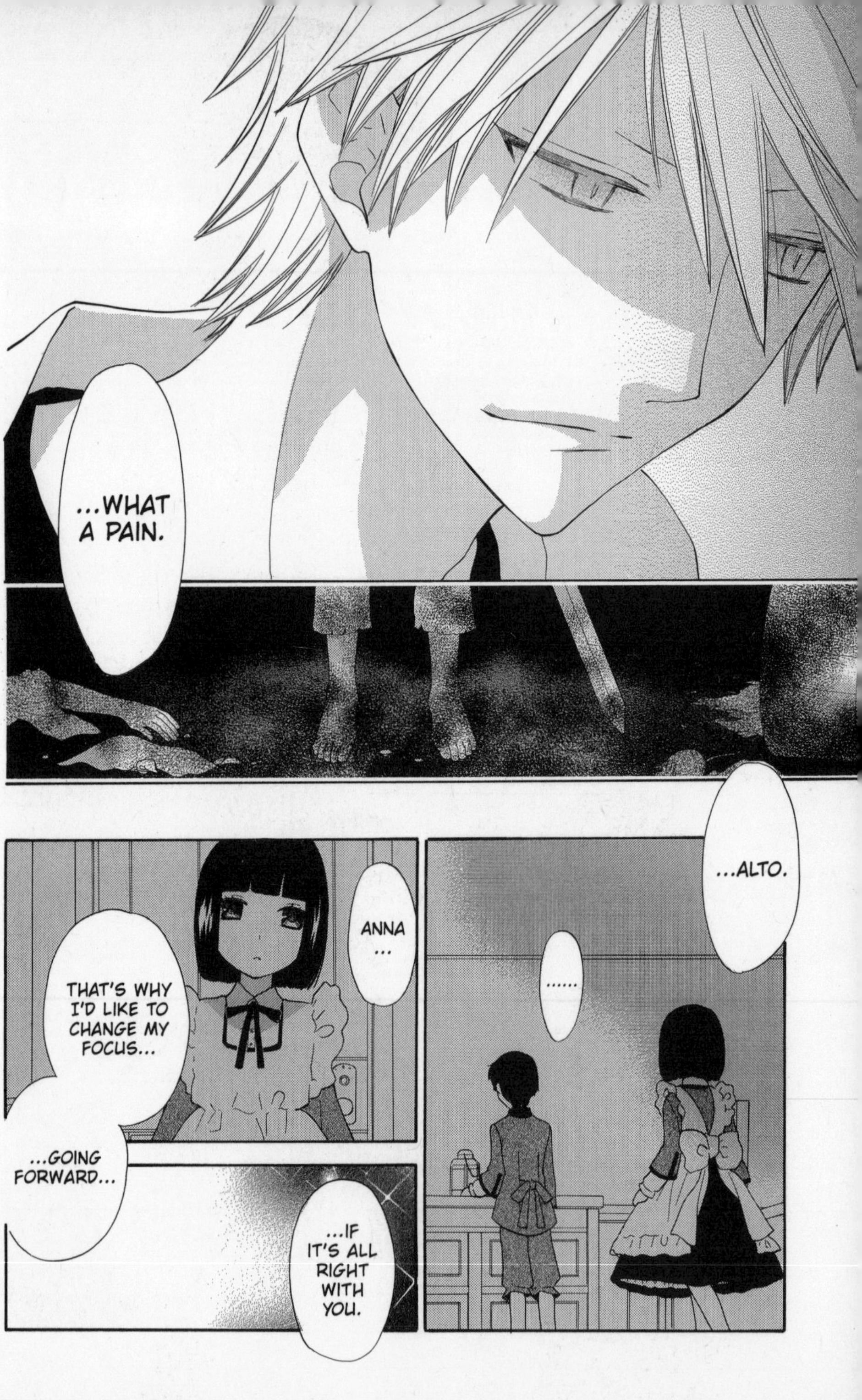
...WHAT A PAIN.
...ALTO.
......
ANNA...
THAT'S WHY I'D LIKE TO CHANGE MY FOCUS...
...GOING FORWARD...
...IF IT'S ALL RIGHT WITH YOU.

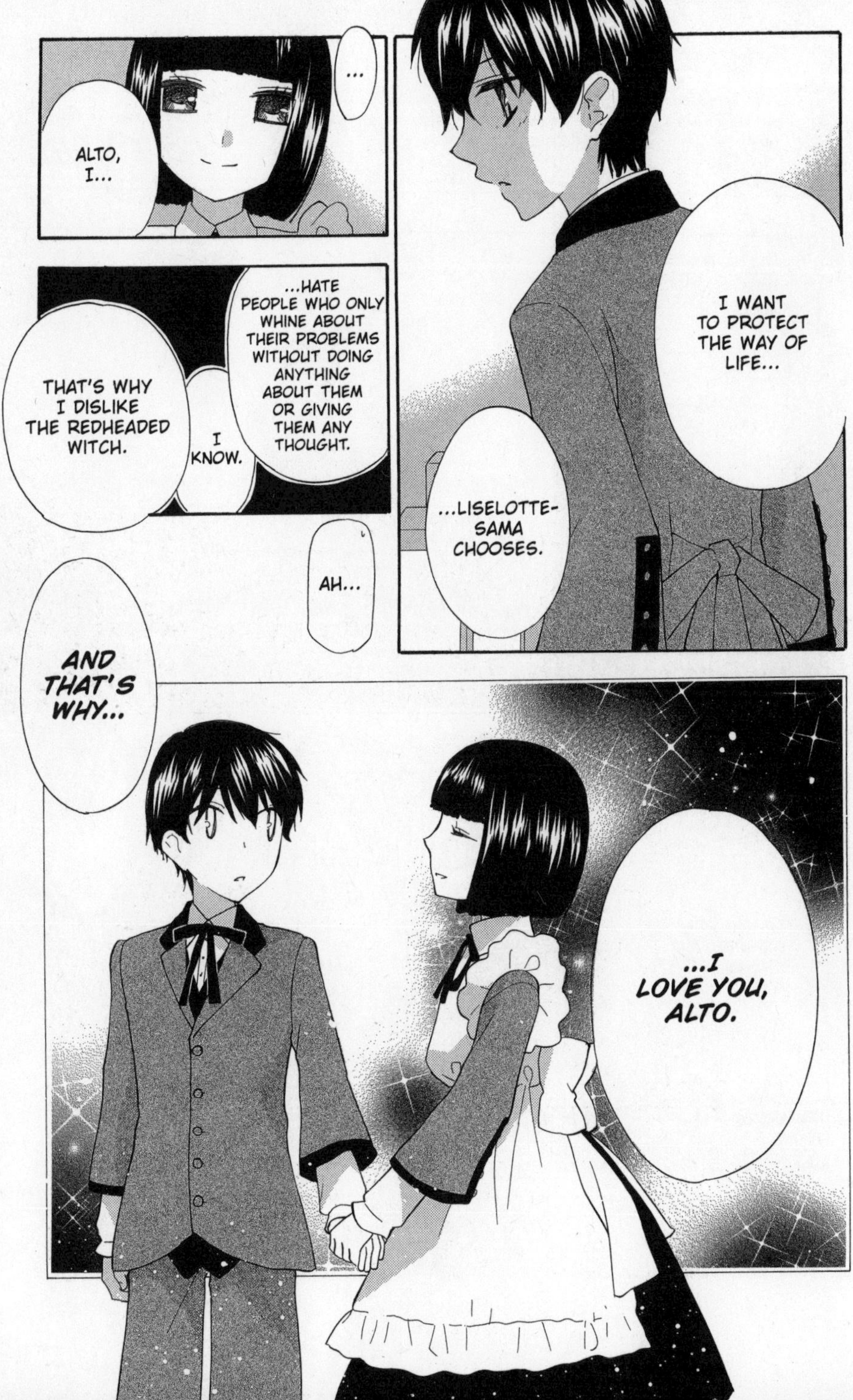

I WANT TO PROTECT THE WAY OF LIFE...
...LISELOTTE-SAMA CHOOSES.
...
ALTO, I...
...HATE PEOPLE WHO ONLY WHINE ABOUT THEIR PROBLEMS WITHOUT DOING ANYTHING ABOUT THEM OR GIVING THEM ANY THOUGHT.
I KNOW.
THAT'S WHY I DISLIKE THE REDHEADED WITCH.
AH...
AND THAT'S WHY...
...I LOVE YOU, ALTO.

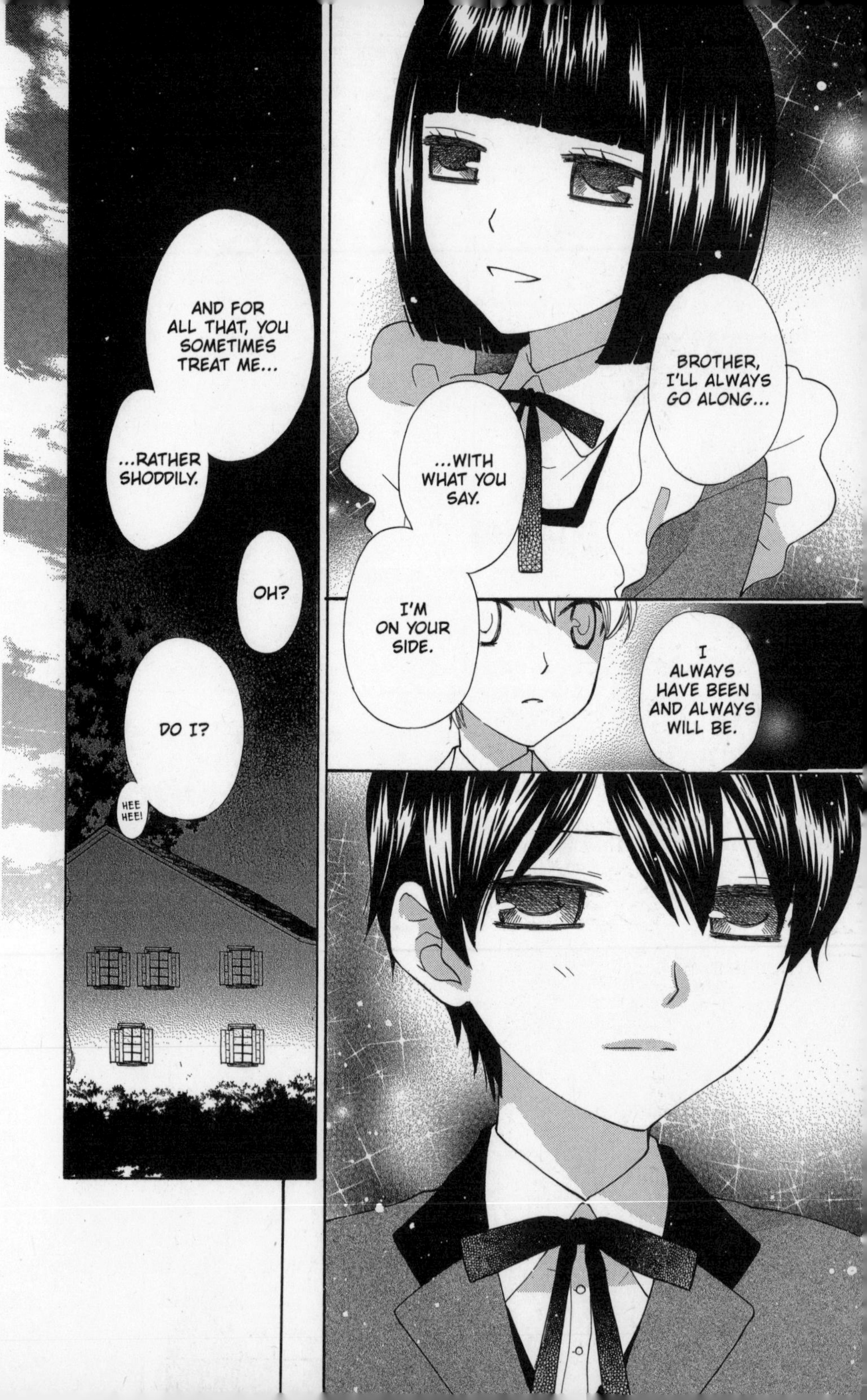
BROTHER, I'LL ALWAYS GO ALONG...
...WITH WHAT YOU SAY.
I'M ON YOUR SIDE.
I ALWAYS HAVE BEEN AND ALWAYS WILL BE.
AND FOR ALL THAT, YOU SOMETIMES TREAT ME...
...RATHER SHODDILY.
OH?
DO I?
HEE HEE!

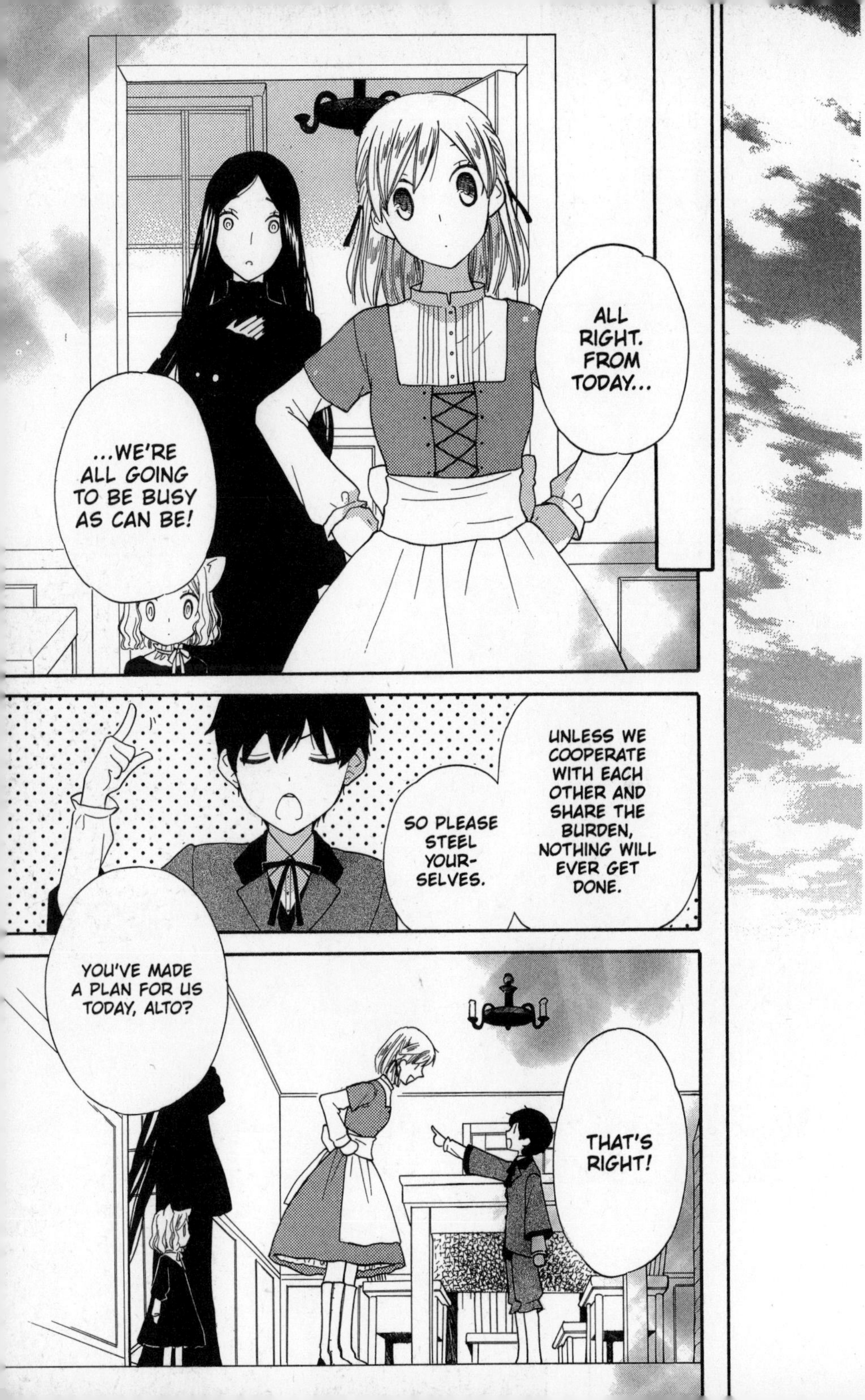
ALL RIGHT. FROM TODAY...
...WE'RE ALL GOING TO BE BUSY AS CAN BE!
UNLESS WE COOPERATE WITH EACH OTHER AND SHARE THE BURDEN, NOTHING WILL EVER GET DONE.
SO PLEASE STEEL YOUR-SELVES.
YOU'VE MADE A PLAN FOR US TODAY, ALTO?
THAT'S RIGHT!

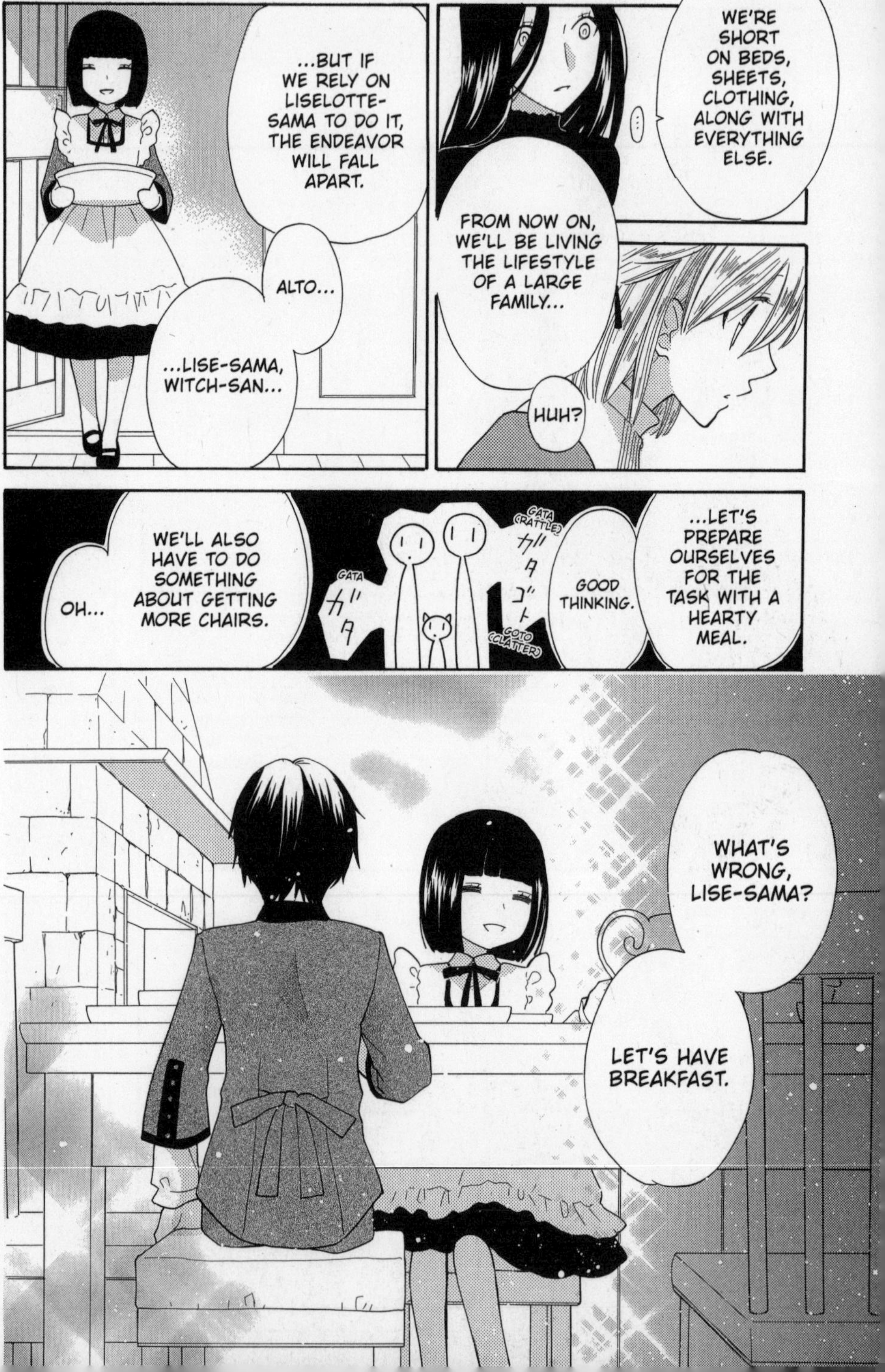
WE'RE SHORT ON BEDS, SHEETS, CLOTHING, ALONG WITH EVERYTHING ELSE.
...
FROM NOW ON, WE'LL BE LIVING THE LIFESTYLE OF A LARGE FAMILY...
HUH?
...BUT IF WE RELY ON LISELOTTE-SAMA TO DO IT, THE ENDEAVOR WILL FALL APART.
ALTO...
...LISE-SAMA, WITCH-SAN...
...LET'S PREPARE OURSELVES FOR THE TASK WITH A HEARTY MEAL.
GOOD THINKING.
GATA (RATTLE)
ガタ
ゴト
GOTO (CLATTER)
GATA
ガタ
WE'LL ALSO HAVE TO DO SOMETHING ABOUT GETTING MORE CHAIRS.
OH...
WHAT'S WRONG, LISE-SAMA?
LET'S HAVE BREAKFAST.

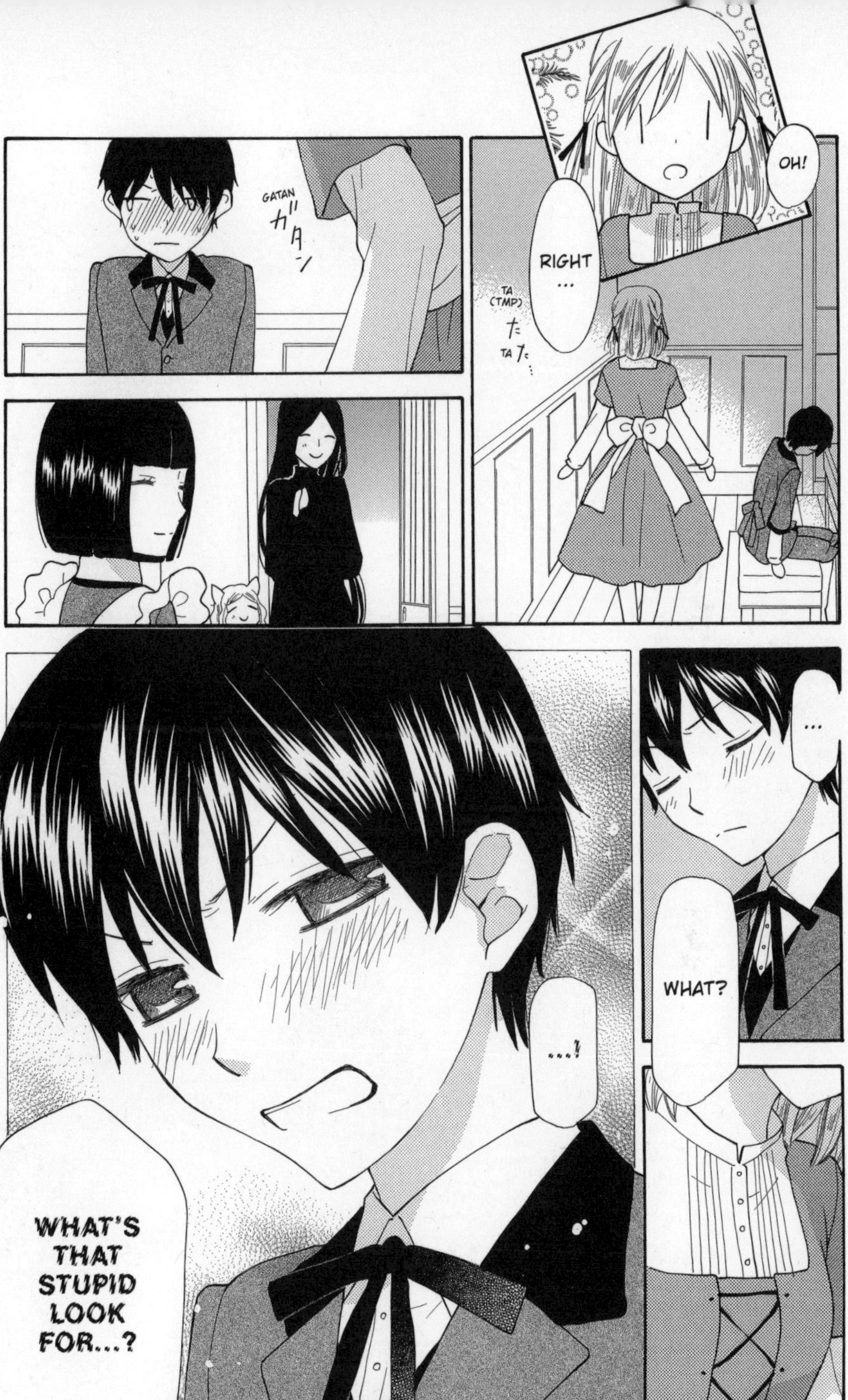
OH!
RIGHT ...
TA (TMP)
た
TA た...
GATAN
ガタン
...
WHAT?
...?
WHAT'S THAT STUPID LOOK FOR...?

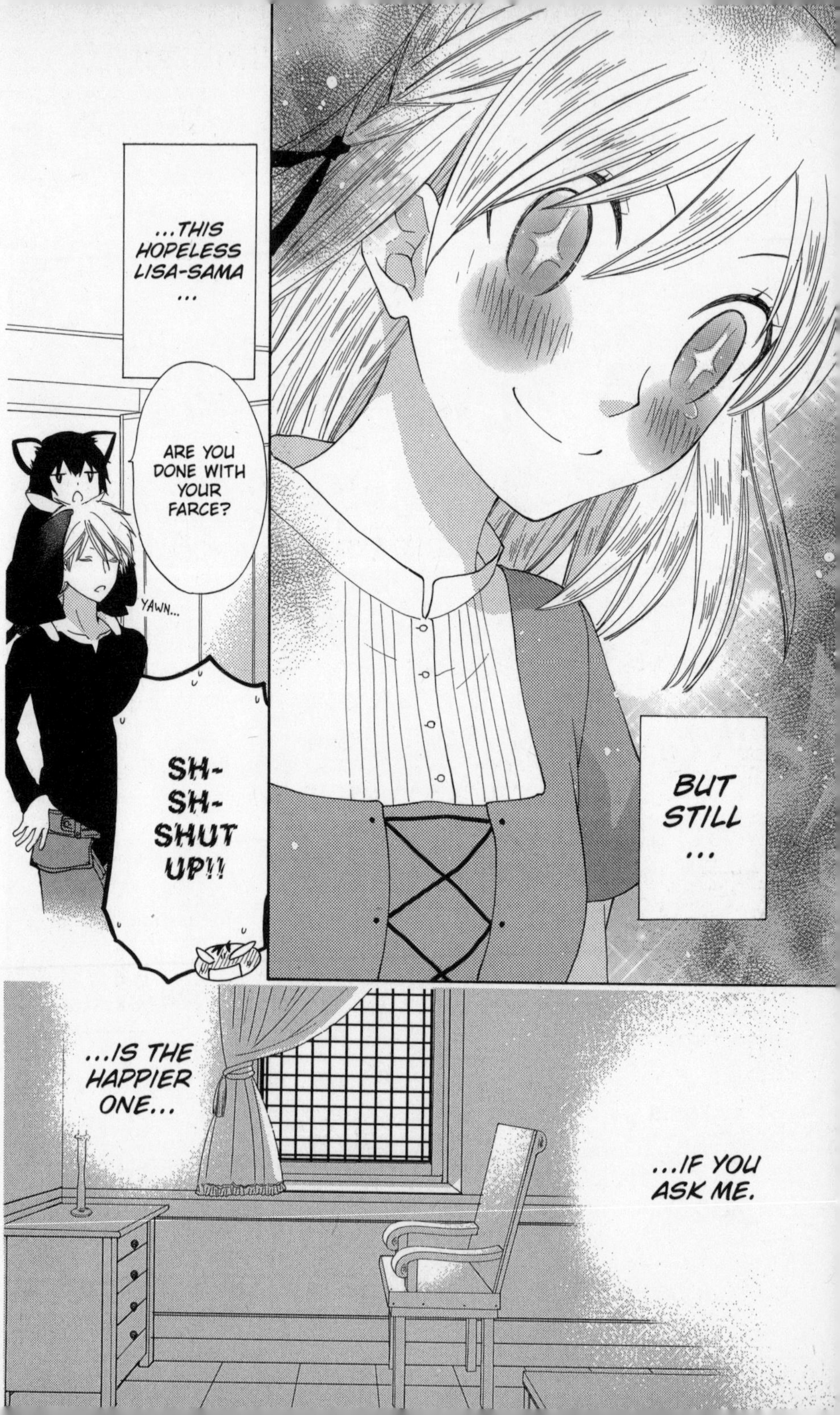
BUT STILL ...
...THIS HOPELESS LISA-SAMA ...
ARE YOU DONE WITH YOUR FARCE?
YAWN...
SH-SH-SHUT UP!!
...IS THE HAPPIER ONE...
...IF YOU ASK ME.

Chapter 17

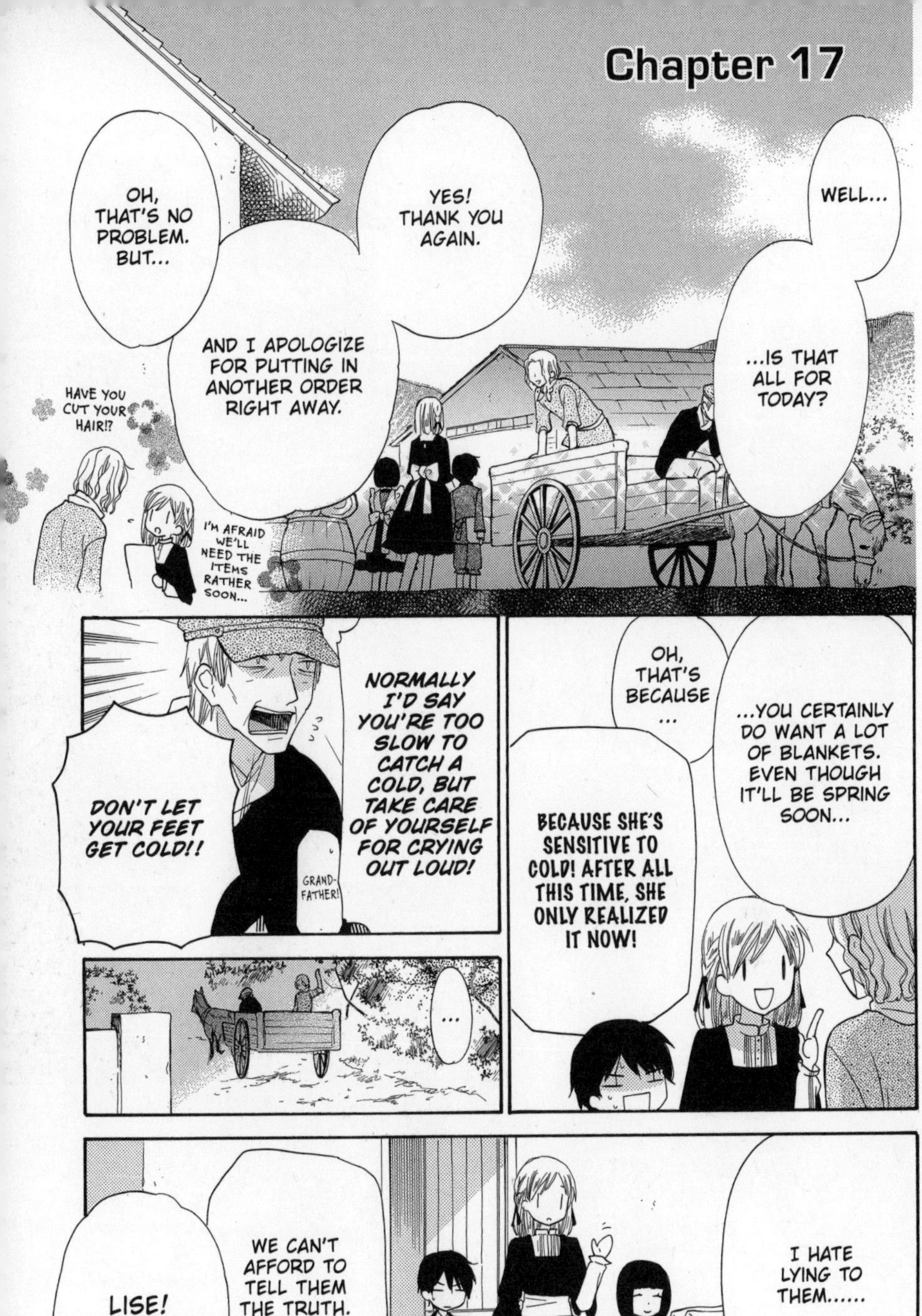
WELL...
...IS THAT ALL FOR TODAY?
YES! THANK YOU AGAIN.
AND I APOLOGIZE FOR PUTTING IN ANOTHER ORDER RIGHT AWAY.
OH, THAT'S NO PROBLEM. BUT...
HAVE YOU CUT YOUR HAIR!?
I'M AFRAID WE'LL NEED THE ITEMS RATHER SOON...
...YOU CERTAINLY DO WANT A LOT OF BLANKETS. EVEN THOUGH IT'LL BE SPRING SOON...
OH, THAT'S BECAUSE ...
BECAUSE SHE'S SENSITIVE TO COLD! AFTER ALL THIS TIME, SHE ONLY REALIZED IT NOW!
NORMALLY I'D SAY YOU'RE TOO SLOW TO CATCH A COLD, BUT TAKE CARE OF YOURSELF FOR CRYING OUT LOUD!
DON'T LET YOUR FEET GET COLD!!
GRAND-FATHER!
...
I HATE LYING TO THEM......
WE CAN'T AFFORD TO TELL THEM THE TRUTH.
LISE! ALTO!

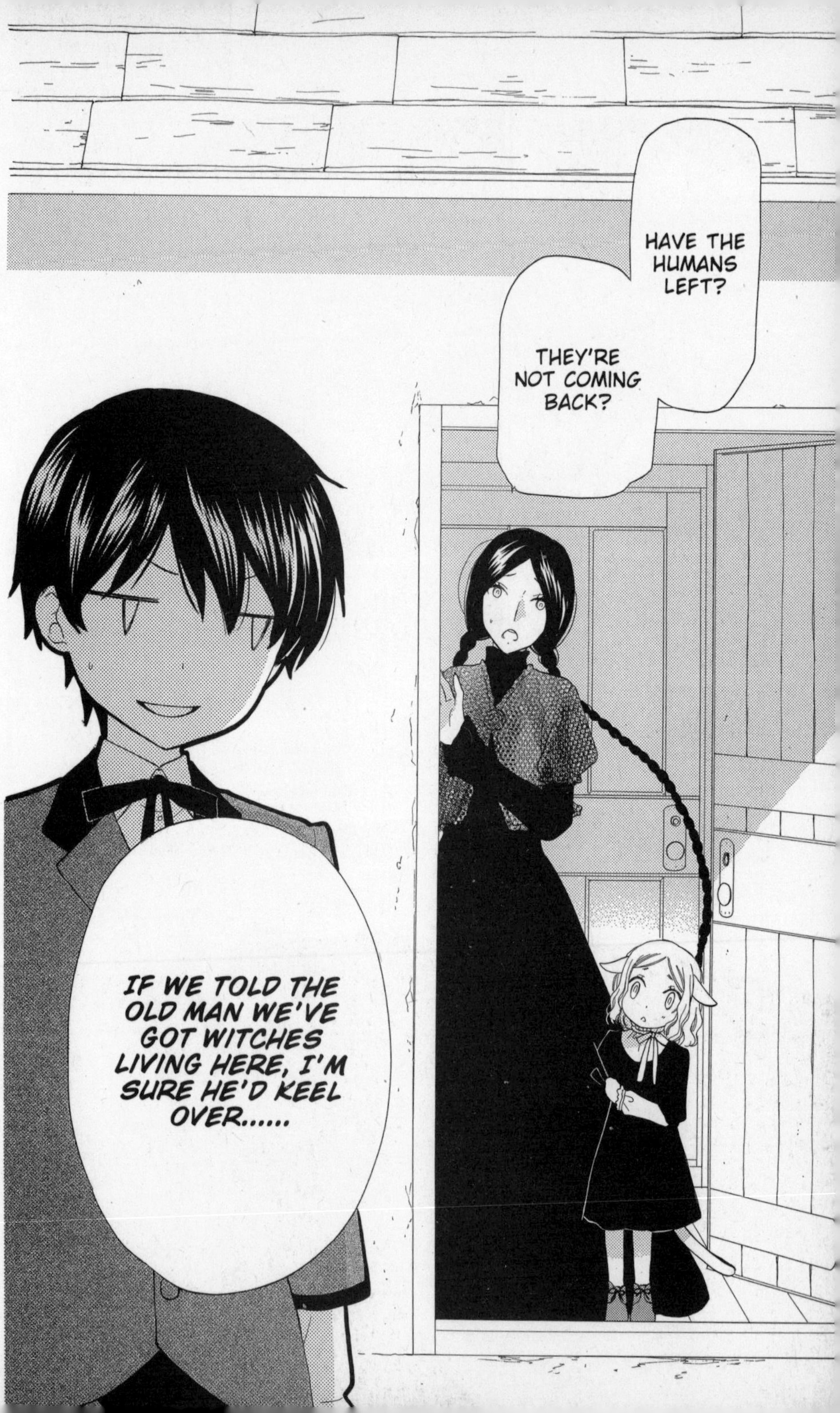
HAVE THE HUMANS LEFT?
THEY'RE NOT COMING BACK?
IF WE TOLD THE OLD MAN WE'VE GOT WITCHES LIVING HERE, I'M SURE HE'D KEEL OVER......

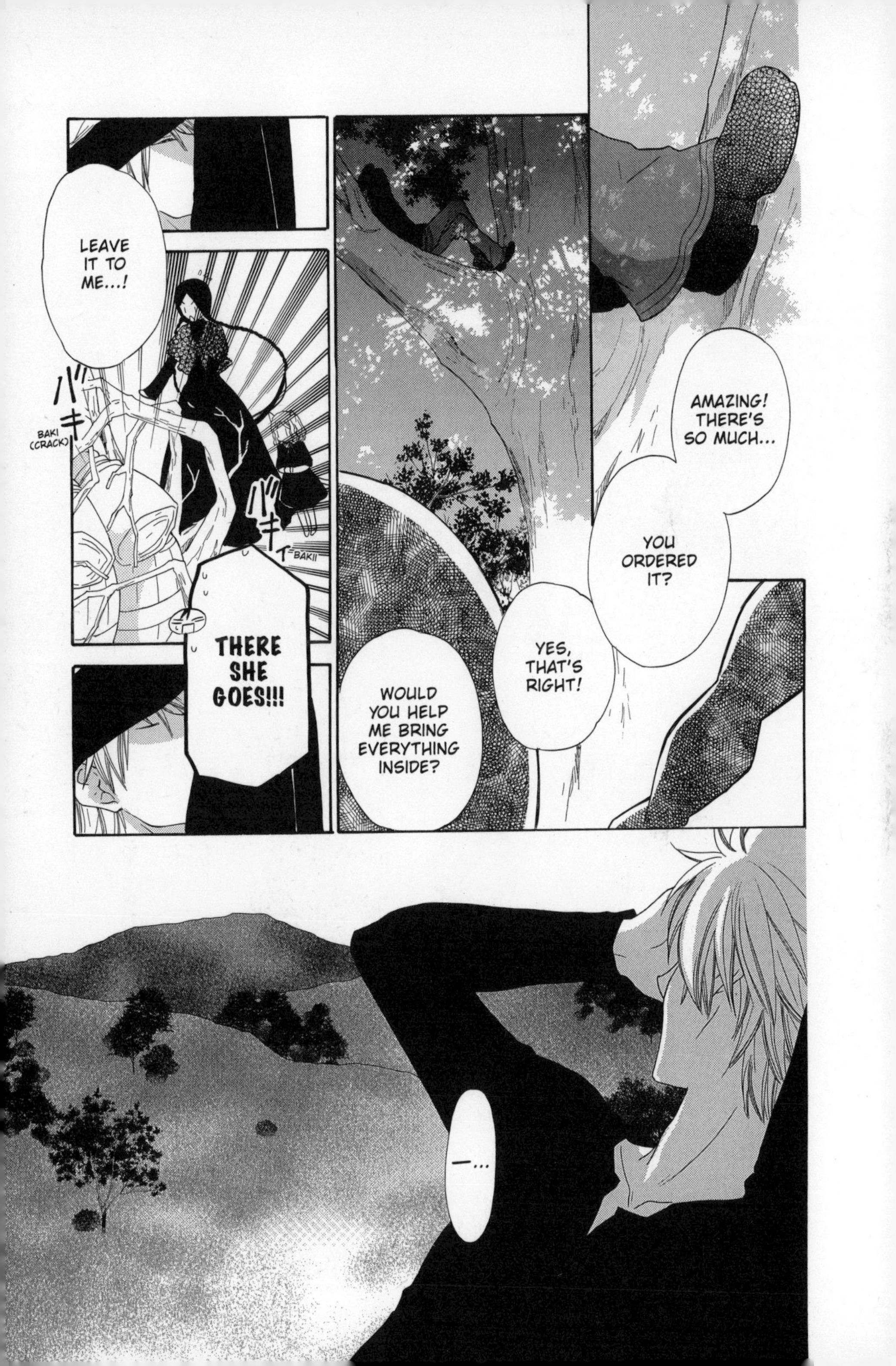
AMAZING! THERE'S SO MUCH...
YOU ORDERED IT?
YES, THAT'S RIGHT!
WOULD YOU HELP ME BRING EVERYTHING INSIDE?
LEAVE IT TO ME...!
バキ
BAKI (CRACK)
バキィ
BAKII
THERE SHE GOES!!!
—...

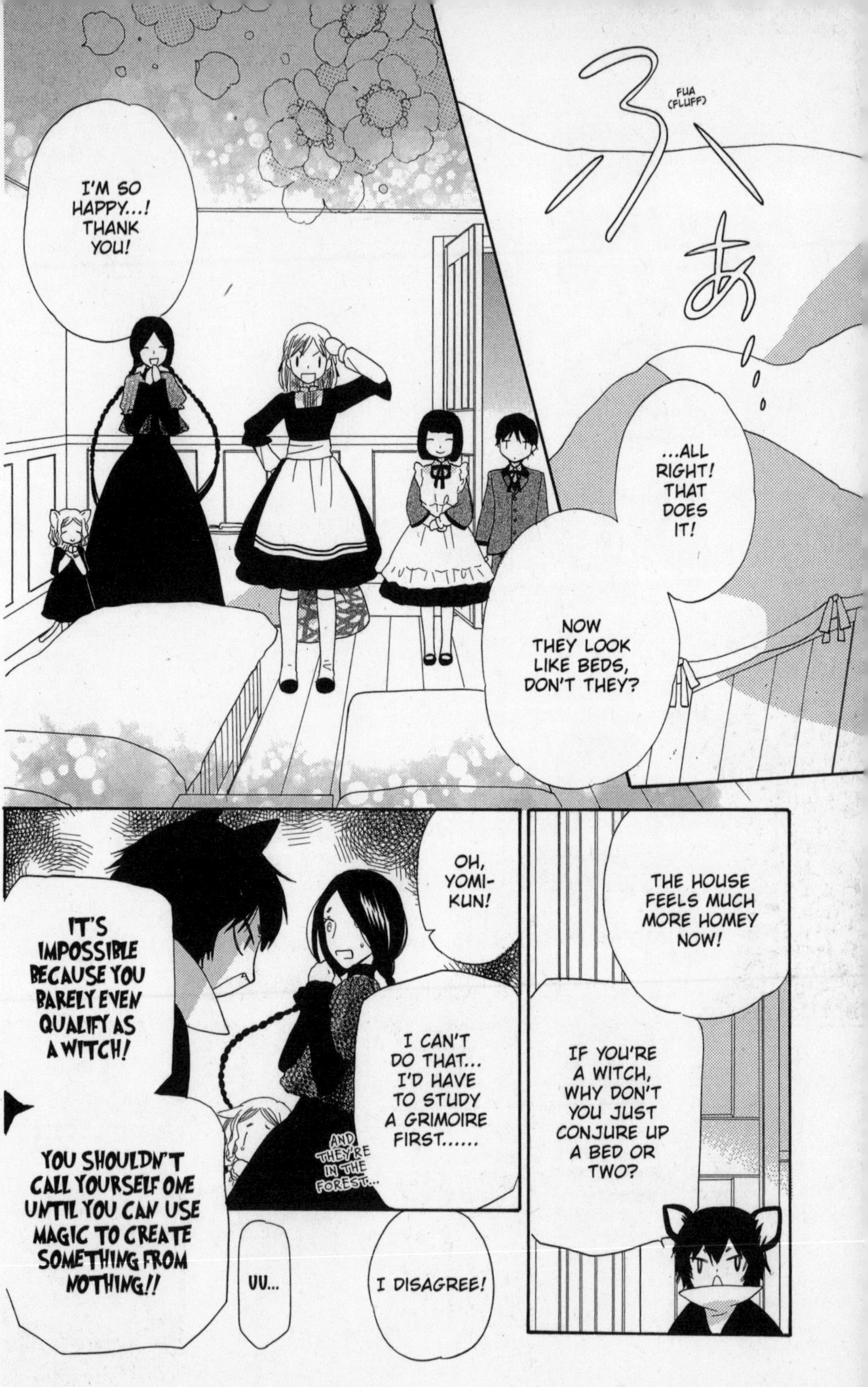
ふあ
FUA (FLUFF)
...ALL RIGHT! THAT DOES IT!
NOW THEY LOOK LIKE BEDS, DON'T THEY?
I'M SO HAPPY...! THANK YOU!
THE HOUSE FEELS MUCH MORE HOMEY NOW!
IF YOU'RE A WITCH, WHY DON'T YOU JUST CONJURE UP A BED OR TWO?
OH, YOMI-KUN!
I CAN'T DO THAT... I'D HAVE TO STUDY A GRIMOIRE FIRST......
AND THEY'RE IN THE FOREST...
IT'S IMPOSSIBLE BECAUSE YOU BARELY EVEN QUALIFY AS A WITCH!
YOU SHOULDN'T CALL YOURSELF ONE UNTIL YOU CAN USE MAGIC TO CREATE SOMETHING FROM NOTHING!!
I DISAGREE!
UU...

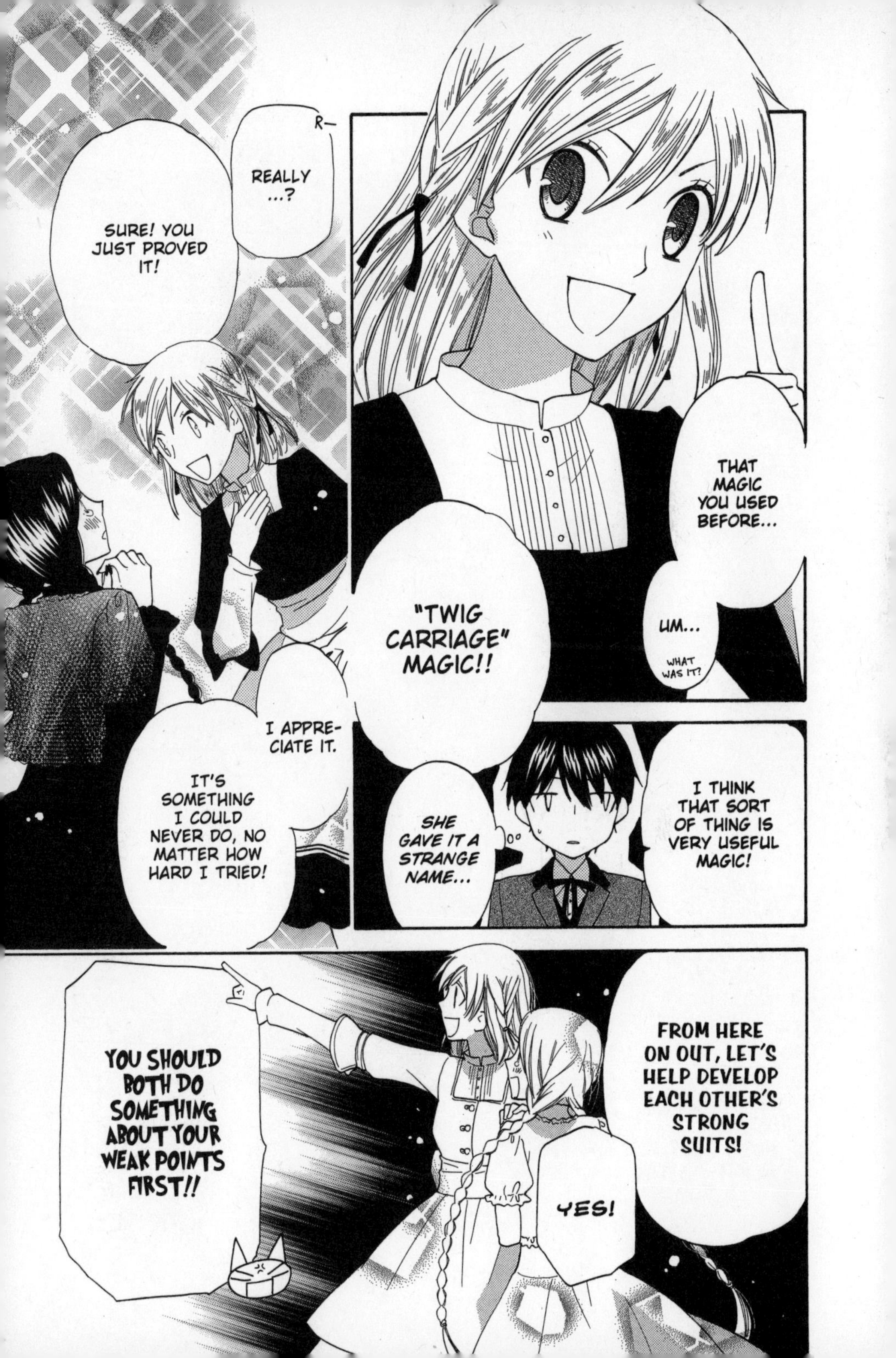

THAT MAGIC YOU USED BEFORE...
UM...
WHAT WAS IT?
"TWIG CARRIAGE" MAGIC!!
I THINK THAT SORT OF THING IS VERY USEFUL MAGIC!
SHE GAVE IT A STRANGE NAME...
R—
REALLY ...?
SURE! YOU JUST PROVED IT!
I APPRECIATE IT.
IT'S SOMETHING I COULD NEVER DO, NO MATTER HOW HARD I TRIED!
FROM HERE ON OUT, LET'S HELP DEVELOP EACH OTHER'S STRONG SUITS!
YES!
YOU SHOULD BOTH DO SOMETHING ABOUT YOUR WEAK POINTS FIRST!!

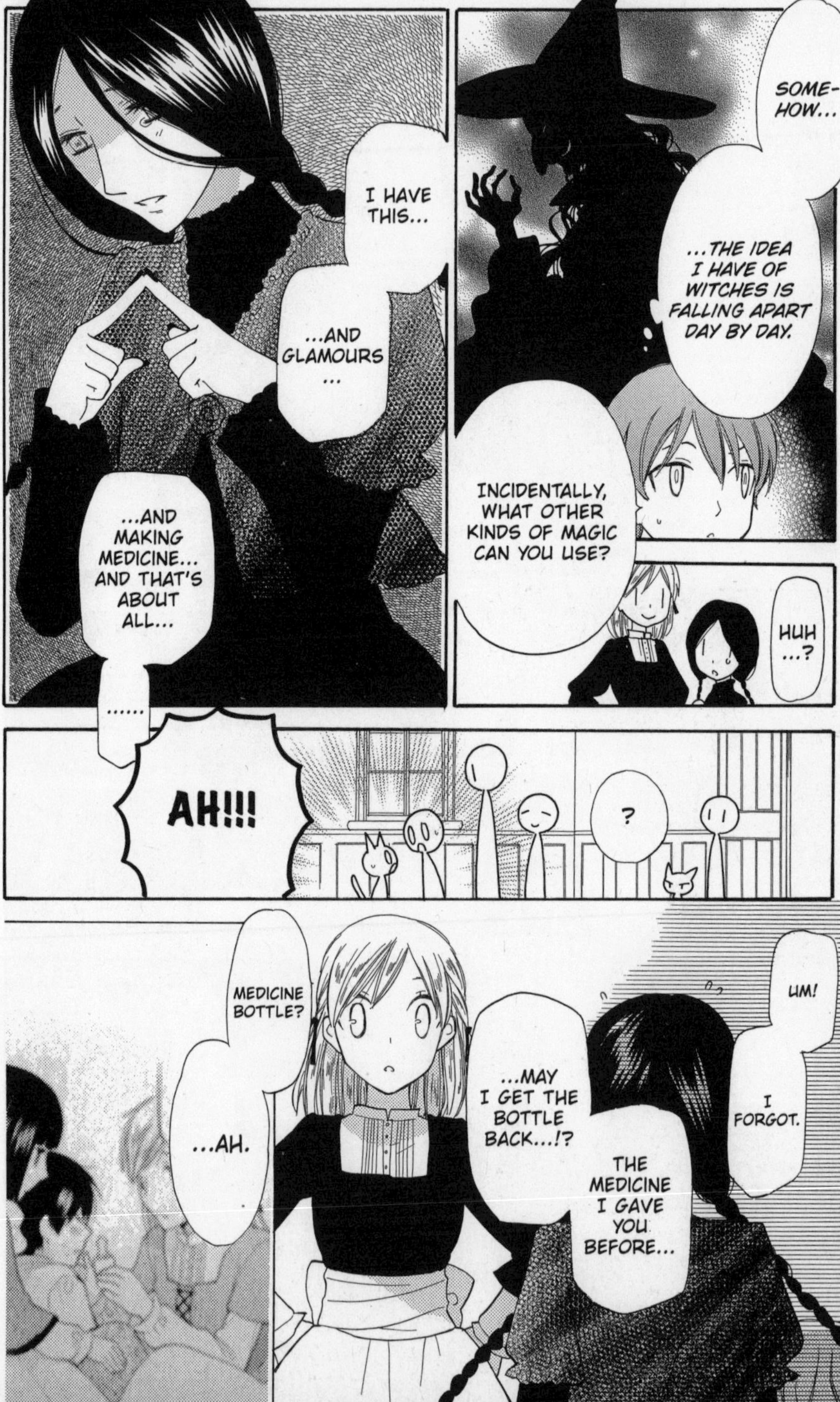
SOME-HOW...
...THE IDEA I HAVE OF WITCHES IS FALLING APART DAY BY DAY.
INCIDENTALLY, WHAT OTHER KINDS OF MAGIC CAN YOU USE?
HUH ...?
I HAVE THIS...
...AND GLAMOURS ...
...AND MAKING MEDICINE... AND THAT'S ABOUT ALL...
......
AH!!!
?
UM!
I FORGOT.
THE MEDICINE I GAVE YOU BEFORE...
...MAY I GET THE BOTTLE BACK...!?
MEDICINE BOTTLE?
...AH.

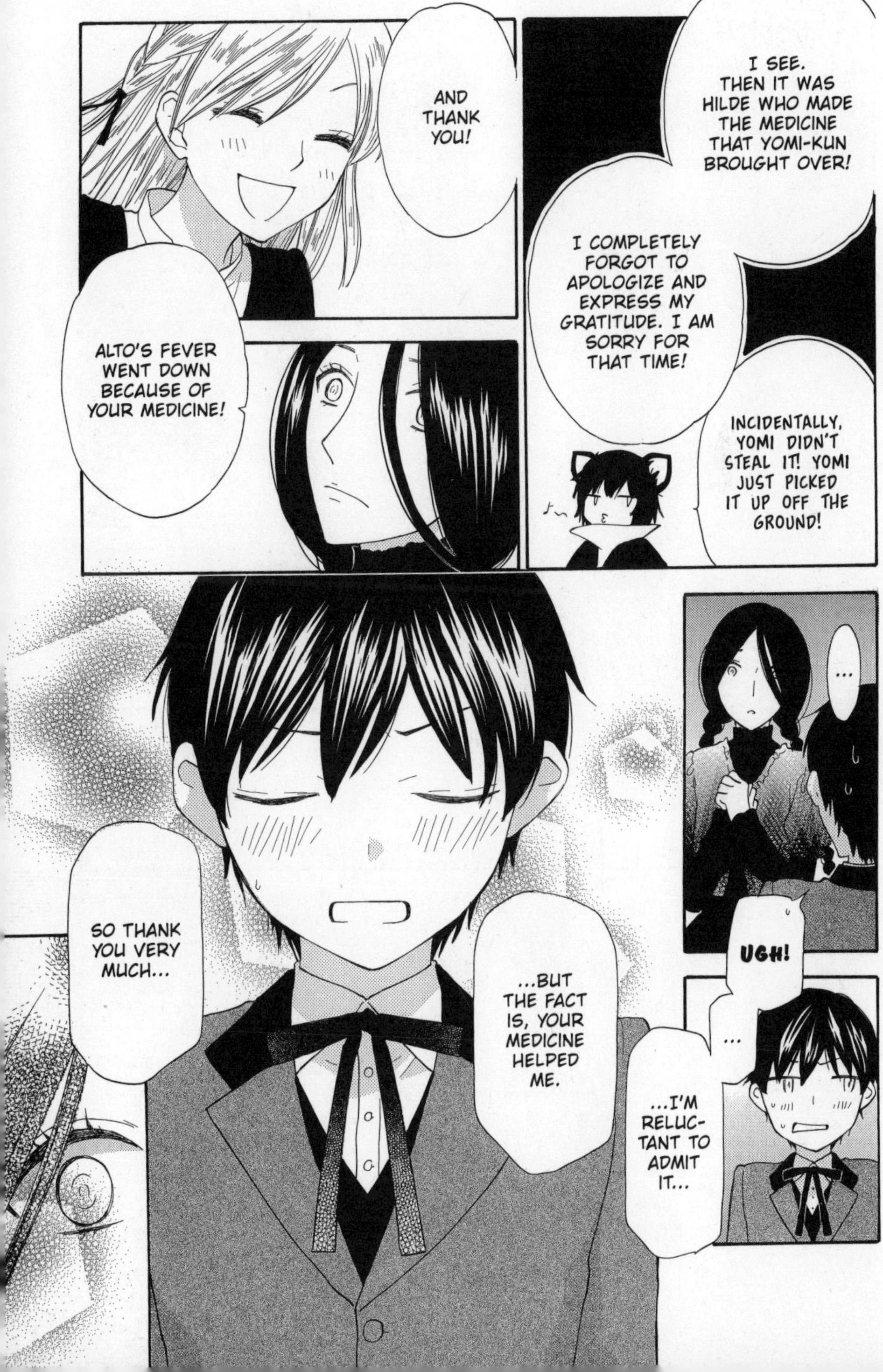
I SEE. THEN IT WAS HILDE WHO MADE THE MEDICINE THAT YOMI-KUN BROUGHT OVER!
I COMPLETELY FORGOT TO APOLOGIZE AND EXPRESS MY GRATITUDE. I AM SORRY FOR THAT TIME!
INCIDENTALLY, YOMI DIDN'T STEAL IT! YOMI JUST PICKED IT UP OFF THE GROUND!
AND THANK YOU!
ALTO'S FEVER WENT DOWN BECAUSE OF YOUR MEDICINE!
...
UGH!
...
...I'M RELUCTANT TO ADMIT IT...
...BUT THE FACT IS, YOUR MEDICINE HELPED ME.
SO THANK YOU VERY MUCH...

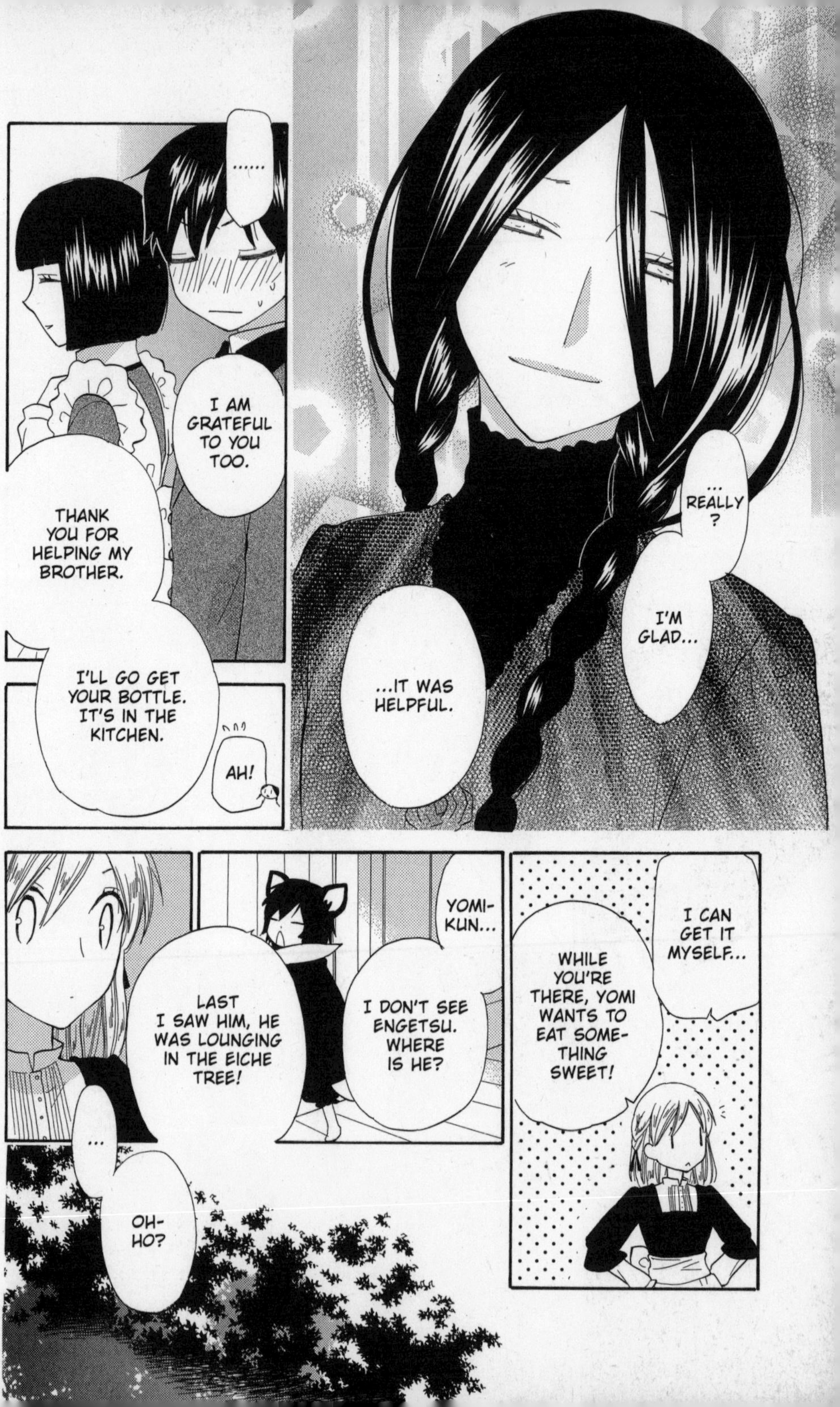

... REALLY?
I'M GLAD...
...IT WAS HELPFUL.
......
I AM GRATEFUL TO YOU TOO.
THANK YOU FOR HELPING MY BROTHER.
I'LL GO GET YOUR BOTTLE. IT'S IN THE KITCHEN.
AH!
I CAN GET IT MYSELF...
WHILE YOU'RE THERE, YOMI WANTS TO EAT SOMETHING SWEET!
YOMI-KUN...
I DON'T SEE ENGETSU. WHERE IS HE?
LAST I SAW HIM, HE WAS LOUNGING IN THE EICHE TREE!
...
OH-HO?

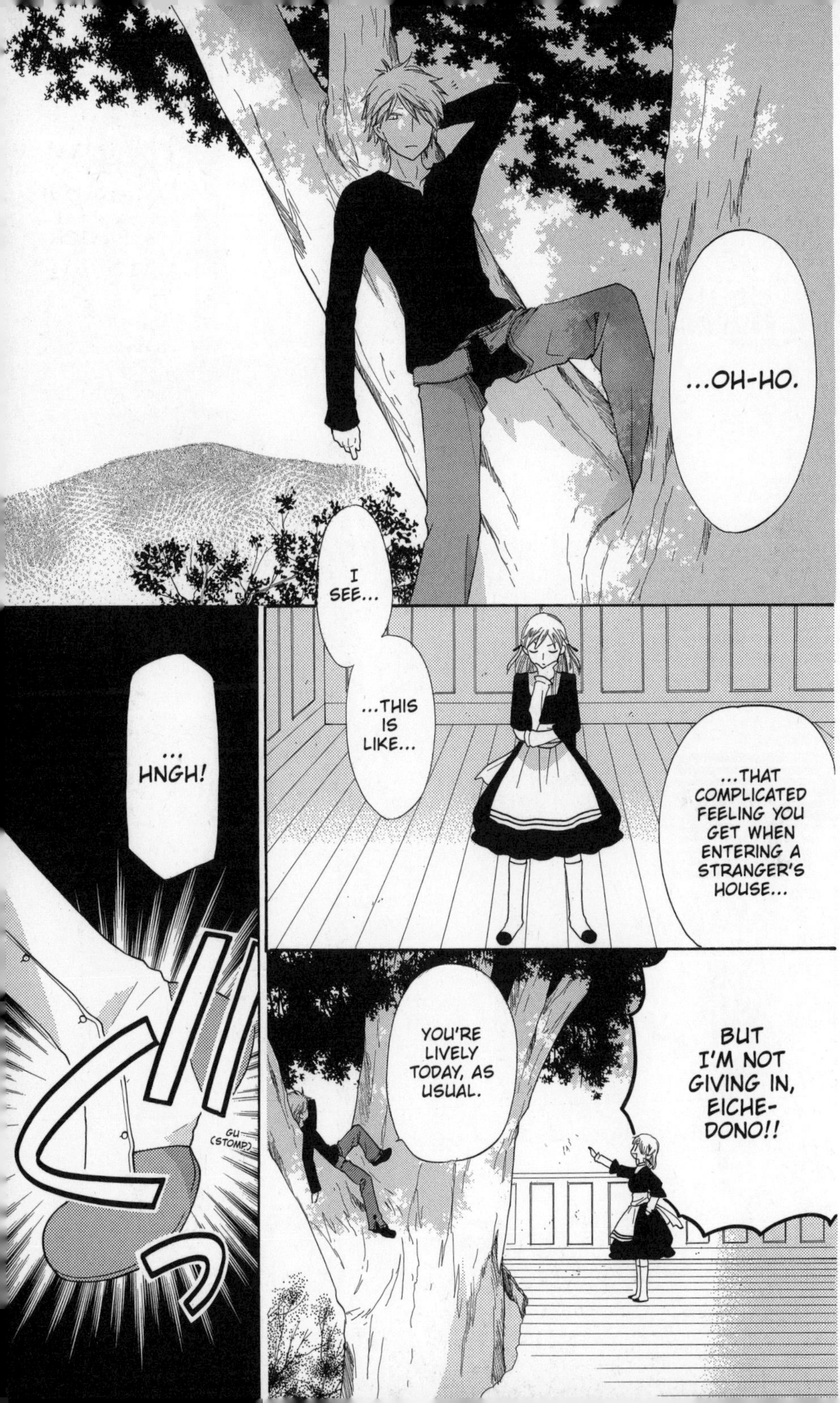
...OH-HO.
I SEE...
...THIS IS LIKE...
...THAT COMPLICATED FEELING YOU GET WHEN ENTERING A STRANGER'S HOUSE...
BUT I'M NOT GIVING IN, EICHE-DONO!!
YOU'RE LIVELY TODAY, AS USUAL.
... HNGH!
GU (STOMP)

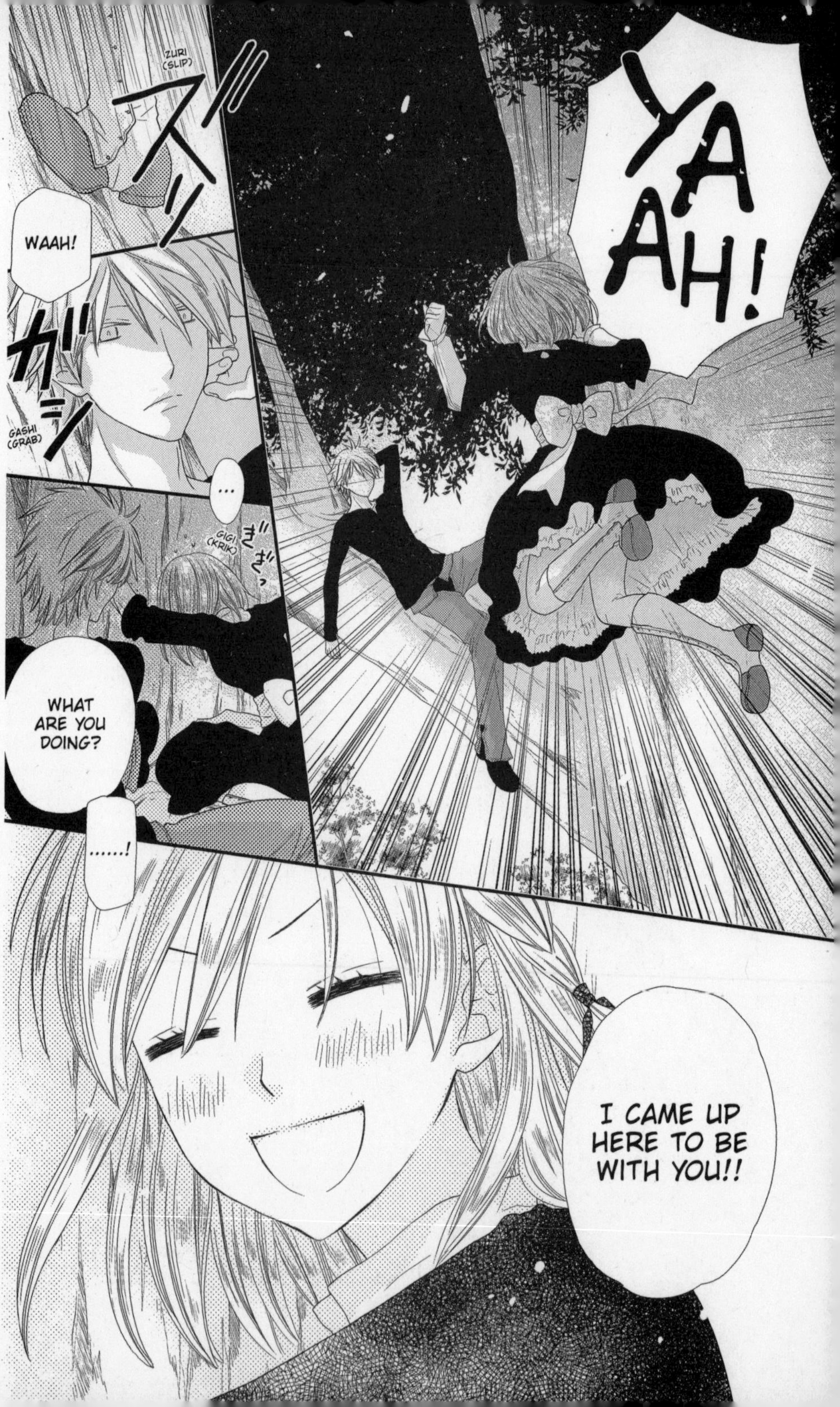
YAAAH!
ZURI (SLIP)
WAAH!
GASHI (GRAB)
...
GIGI (KRIK)
WHAT ARE YOU DOING?
......!
I CAME UP HERE TO BE WITH YOU!!

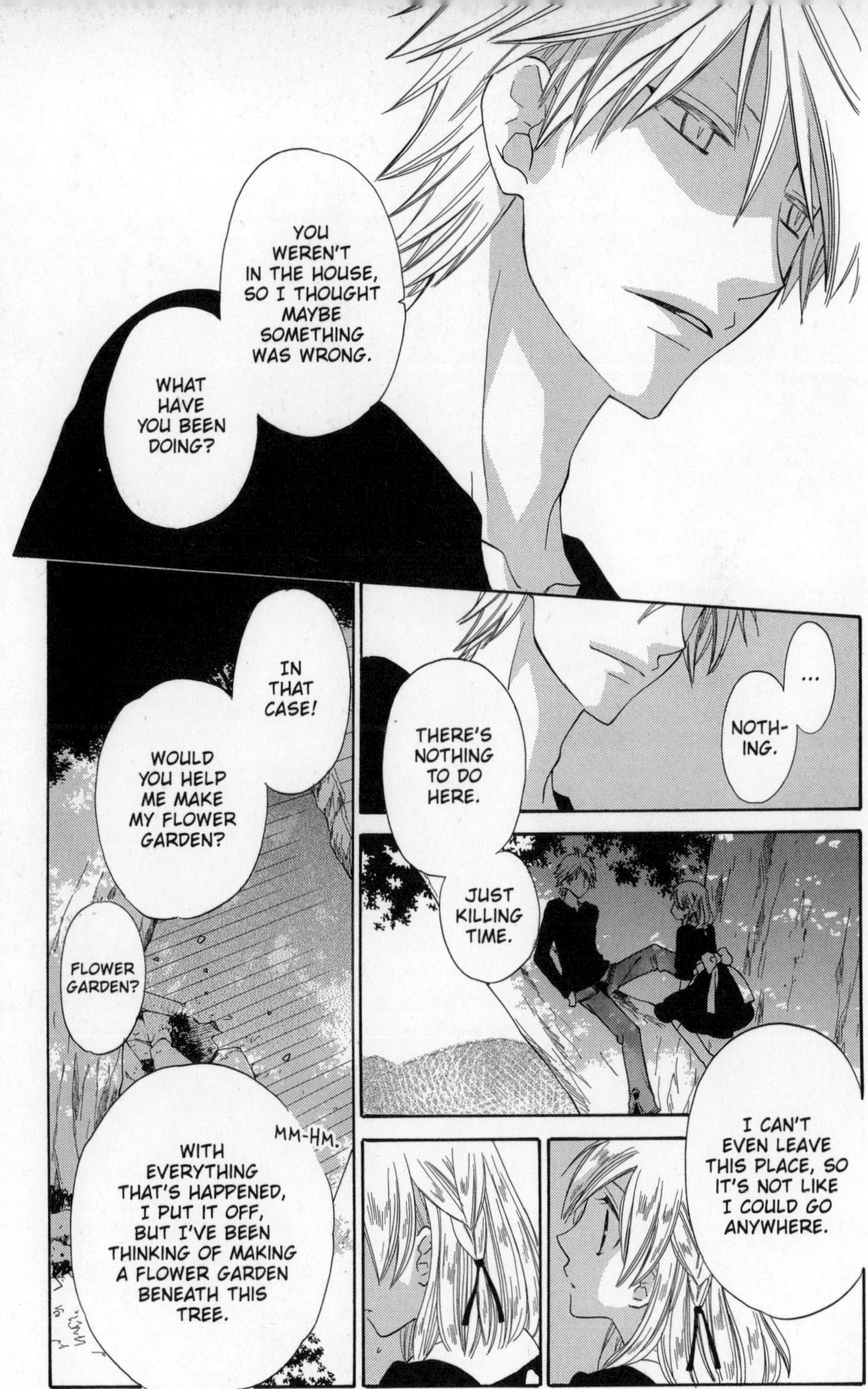
YOU WEREN'T IN THE HOUSE, SO I THOUGHT MAYBE SOMETHING WAS WRONG.
WHAT HAVE YOU BEEN DOING?
...
NOTHING.
THERE'S NOTHING TO DO HERE.
JUST KILLING TIME.
I CAN'T EVEN LEAVE THIS PLACE, SO IT'S NOT LIKE I COULD GO ANYWHERE.
IN THAT CASE!
WOULD YOU HELP ME MAKE MY FLOWER GARDEN?
FLOWER GARDEN?
MM-HM.
WITH EVERYTHING THAT'S HAPPENED, I PUT IT OFF, BUT I'VE BEEN THINKING OF MAKING A FLOWER GARDEN BENEATH THIS TREE.

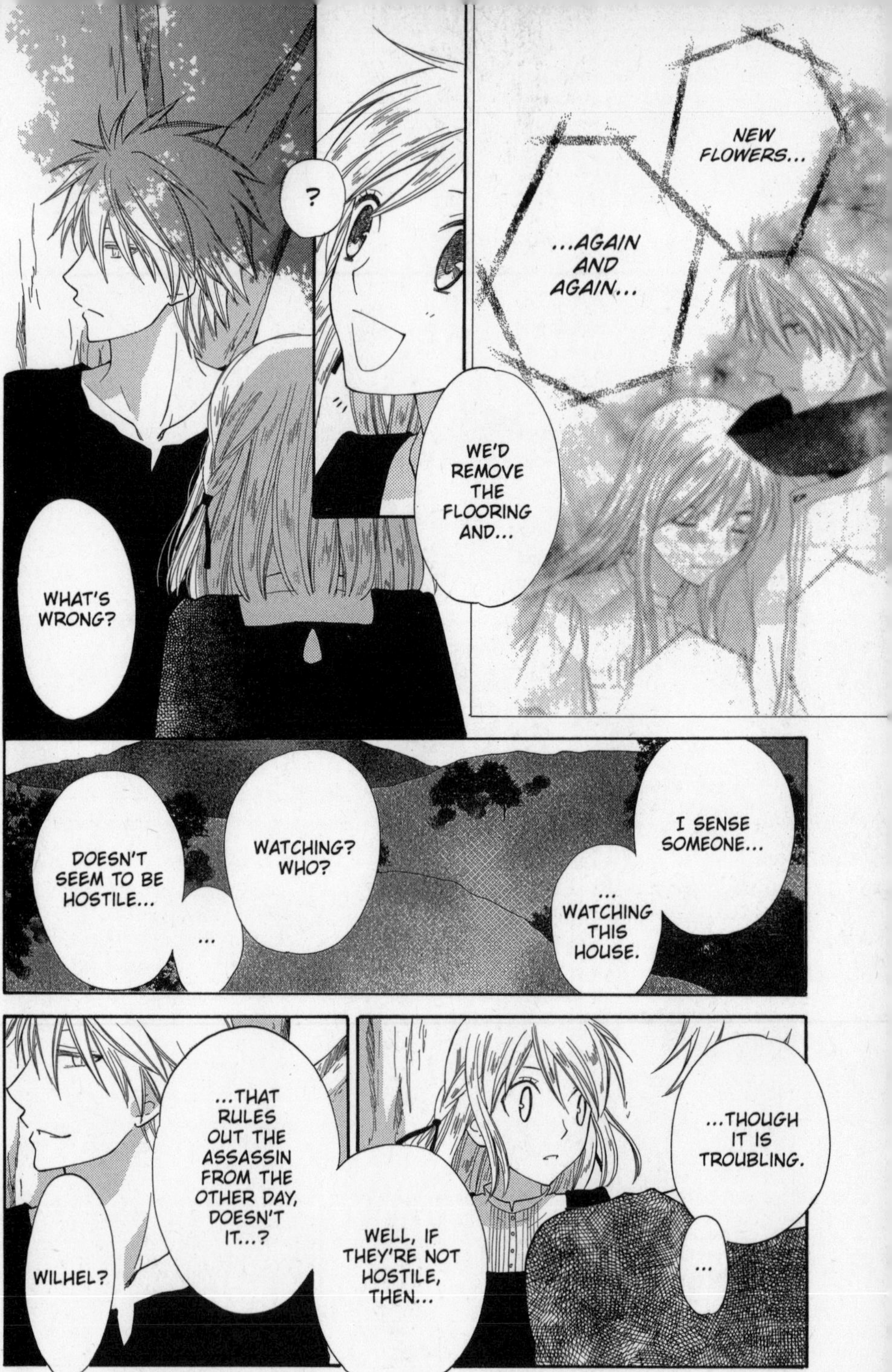
NEW FLOWERS...
...AGAIN AND AGAIN...
WE'D REMOVE THE FLOORING AND...
?
WHAT'S WRONG?
I SENSE SOMEONE...
... WATCHING THIS HOUSE.
WATCHING? WHO?
...
DOESN'T SEEM TO BE HOSTILE...
...THOUGH IT IS TROUBLING.
...
WELL, IF THEY'RE NOT HOSTILE, THEN...
...THAT RULES OUT THE ASSASSIN FROM THE OTHER DAY, DOESN'T IT...?
WILHEL?

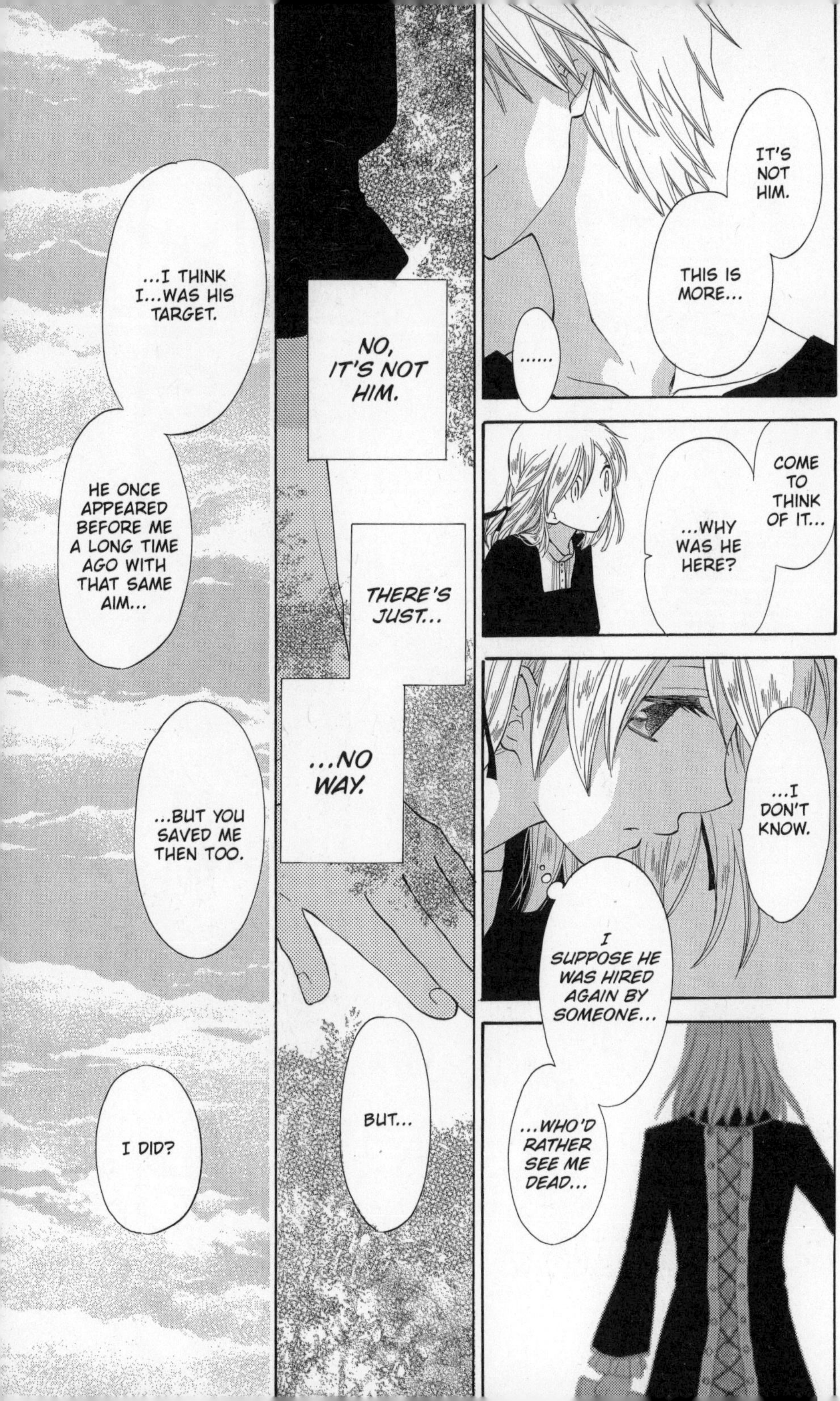
IT'S NOT HIM.
THIS IS MORE...
......
COME TO THINK OF IT...
...WHY WAS HE HERE?
...I DON'T KNOW.
I SUPPOSE HE WAS HIRED AGAIN BY SOMEONE...
...WHO'D RATHER SEE ME DEAD...
NO, IT'S NOT HIM.
THERE'S JUST...
...NO WAY.
BUT...
...I THINK I...WAS HIS TARGET.
HE ONCE APPEARED BEFORE ME A LONG TIME AGO WITH THAT SAME AIM...
...BUT YOU SAVED ME THEN TOO.
I DID?

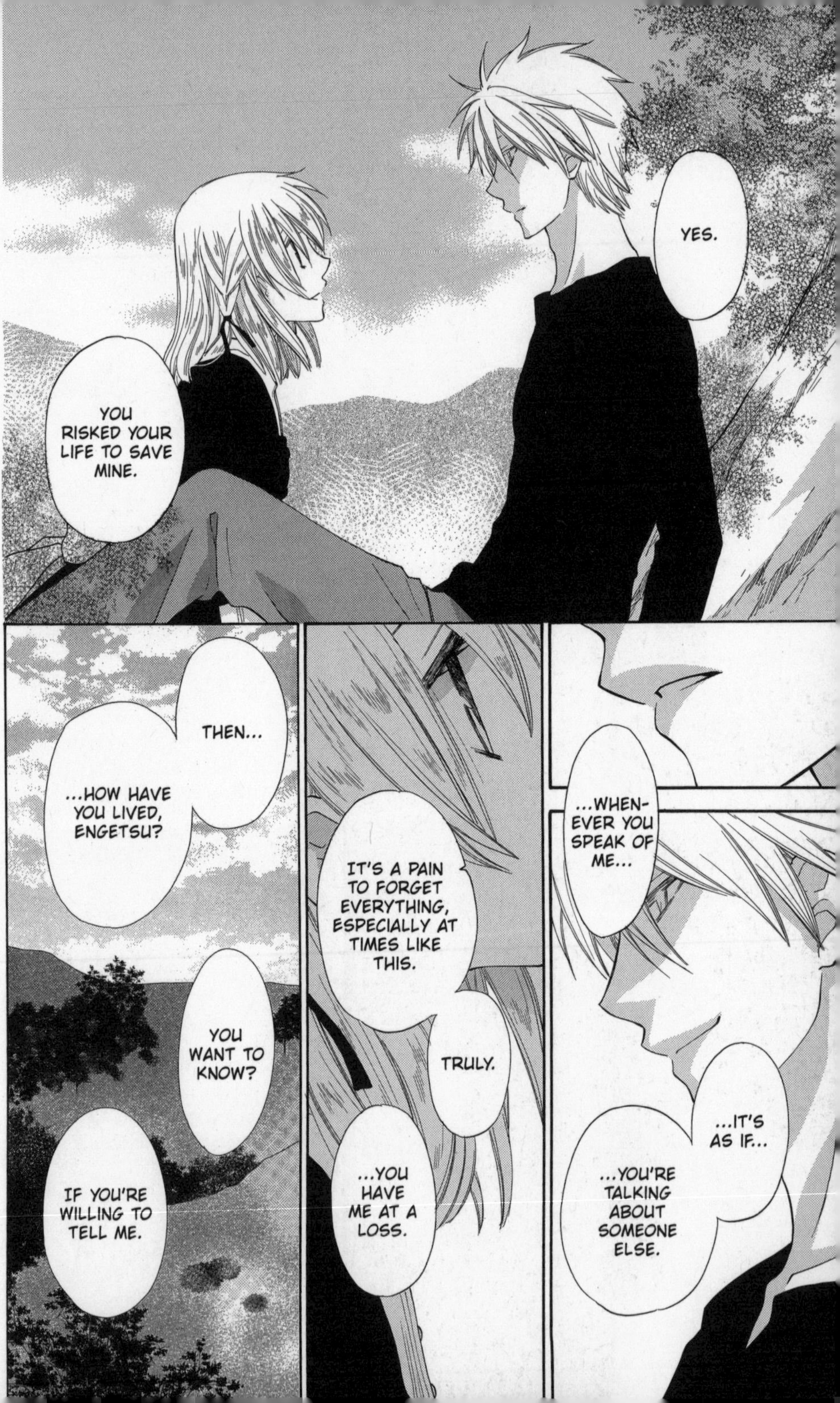
YES.
YOU RISKED YOUR LIFE TO SAVE MINE.
...WHEN-EVER YOU SPEAK OF ME...
...IT'S AS IF...
...YOU'RE TALKING ABOUT SOMEONE ELSE.
IT'S A PAIN TO FORGET EVERYTHING, ESPECIALLY AT TIMES LIKE THIS.
TRULY.
...YOU HAVE ME AT A LOSS.
THEN...
...HOW HAVE YOU LIVED, ENGETSU?
YOU WANT TO KNOW?
IF YOU'RE WILLING TO TELL ME.

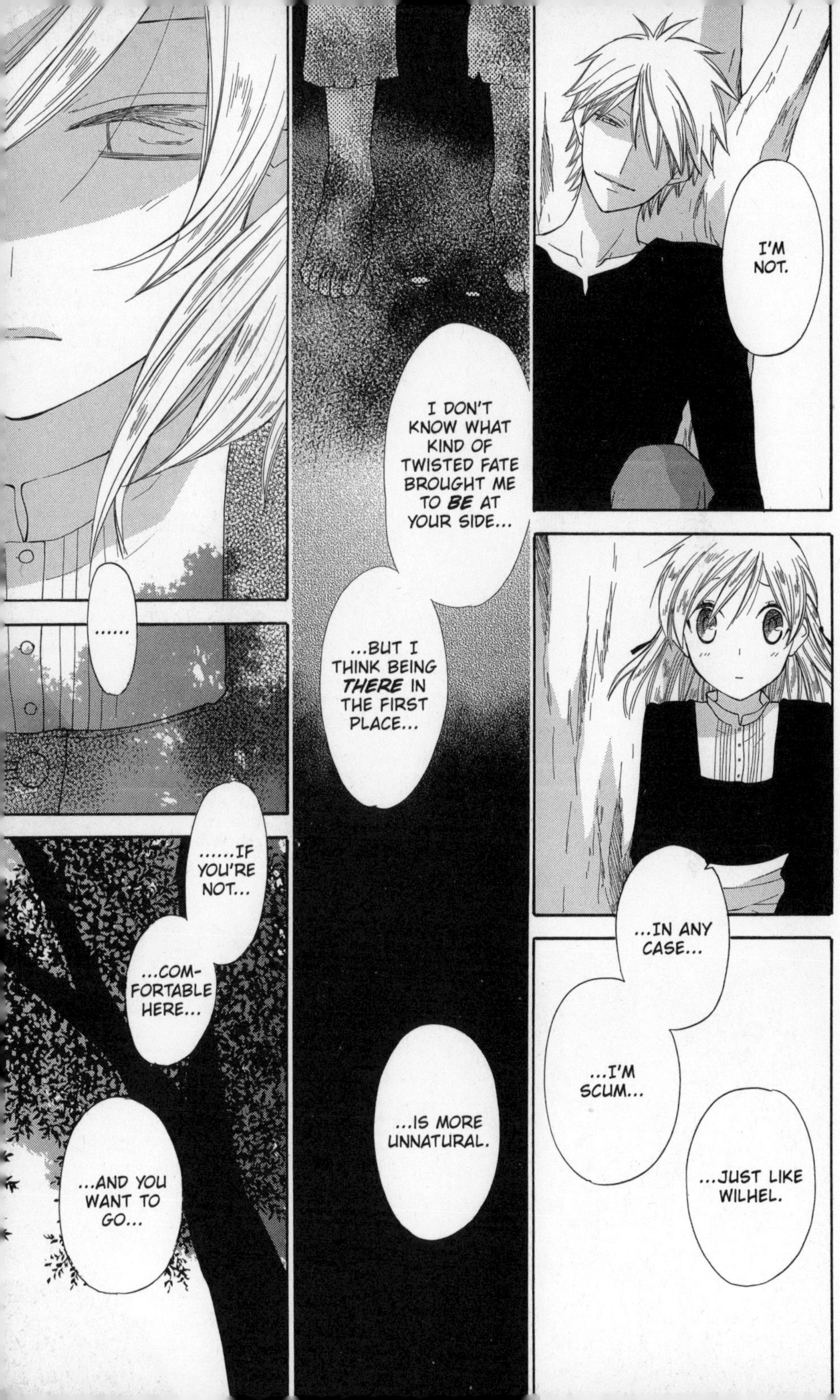
I'M NOT.
...IN ANY CASE...
...I'M SCUM...
...JUST LIKE WILHEL.
I DON'T KNOW WHAT KIND OF TWISTED FATE BROUGHT ME TO *BE* AT YOUR SIDE...
...BUT I THINK BEING *THERE* IN THE FIRST PLACE...
...IS MORE UNNATURAL.
......
......IF YOU'RE NOT...
...COM-FORTABLE HERE...
...AND YOU WANT TO GO...

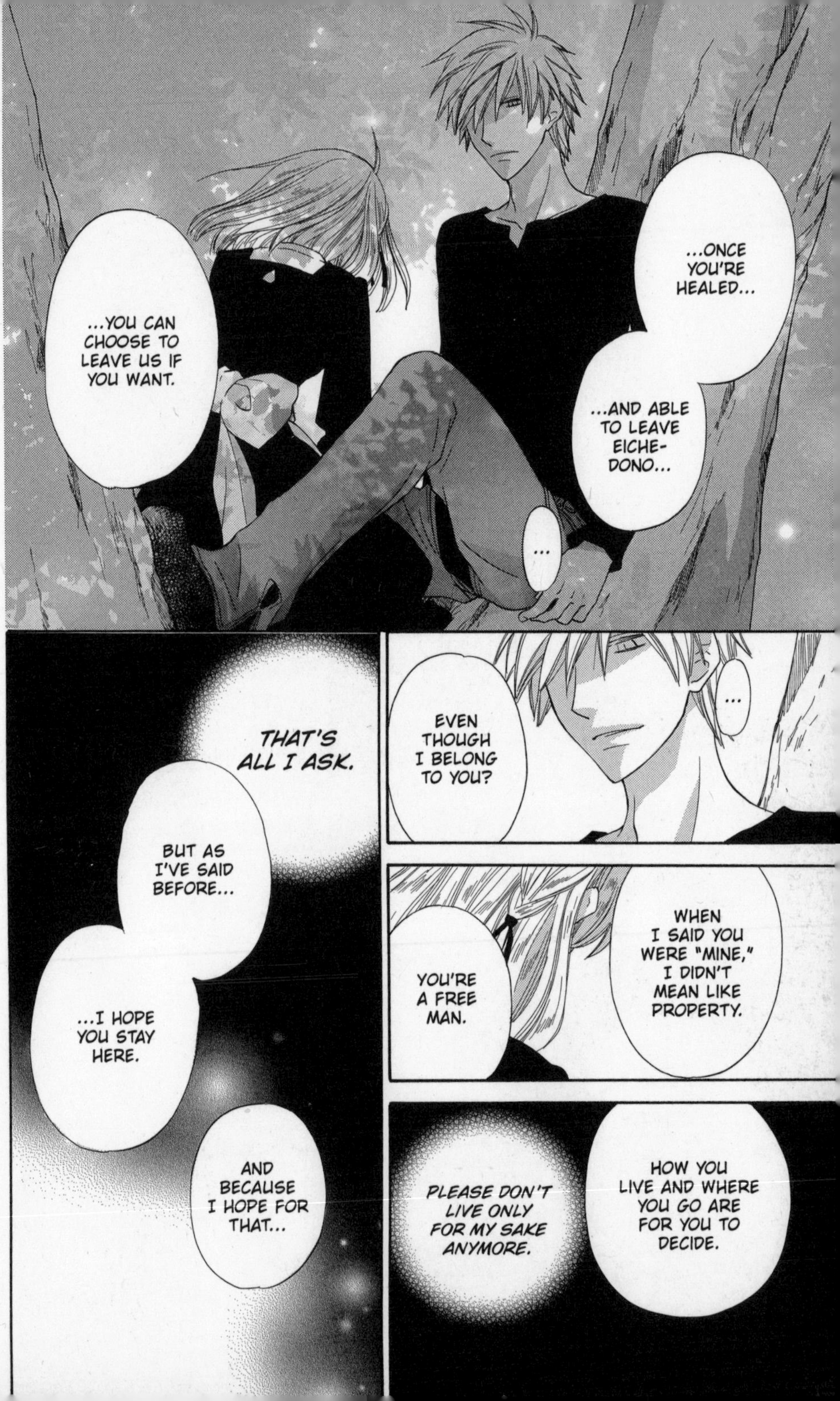
...ONCE YOU'RE HEALED...
...AND ABLE TO LEAVE EICHE-DONO...
...
...YOU CAN CHOOSE TO LEAVE US IF YOU WANT.
...
EVEN THOUGH I BELONG TO YOU?
WHEN I SAID YOU WERE "MINE," I DIDN'T MEAN LIKE PROPERTY.
YOU'RE A FREE MAN.
HOW YOU LIVE AND WHERE YOU GO ARE FOR YOU TO DECIDE.
PLEASE DON'T LIVE ONLY FOR MY SAKE ANYMORE.
THAT'S ALL I ASK.
BUT AS I'VE SAID BEFORE...
...I HOPE YOU STAY HERE.
AND BECAUSE I HOPE FOR THAT...

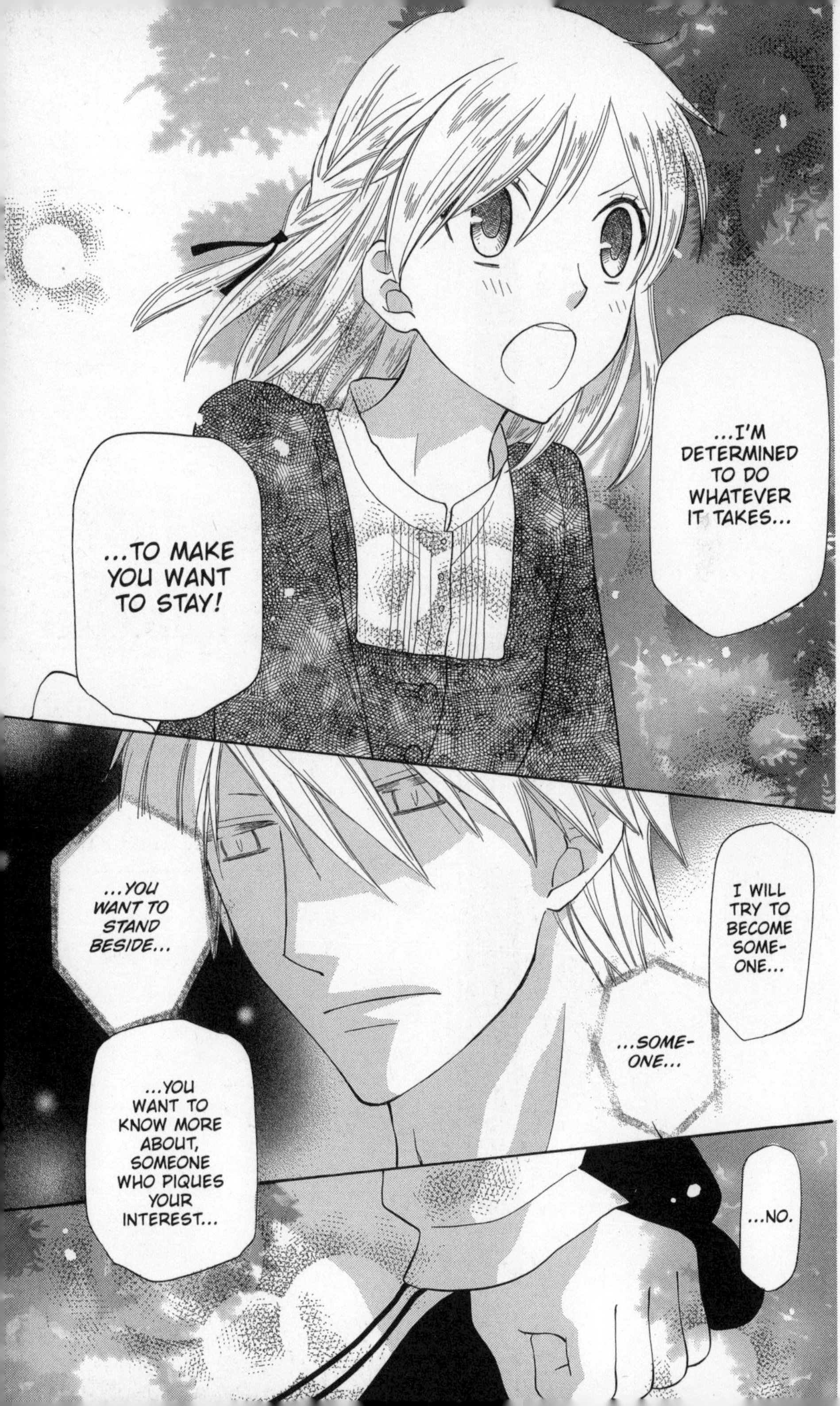
...I'M DETERMINED TO DO WHATEVER IT TAKES...
...TO MAKE YOU WANT TO STAY!
I WILL TRY TO BECOME SOME-ONE...
...SOME-ONE...
...YOU WANT TO STAND BESIDE...
...YOU WANT TO KNOW MORE ABOUT, SOMEONE WHO PIQUES YOUR INTEREST...
...NO.

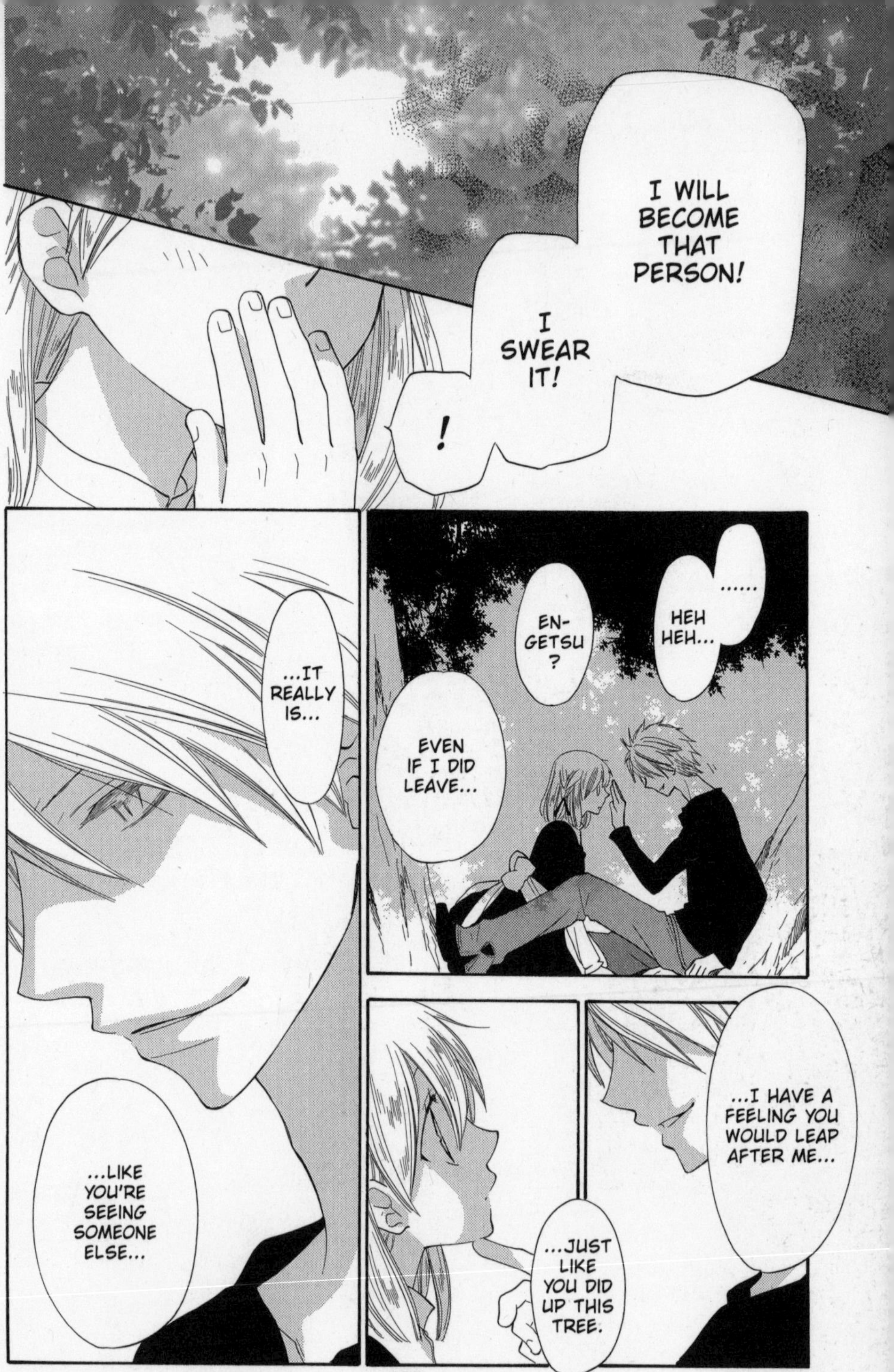
I WILL BECOME THAT PERSON!
I SWEAR IT!
!
......
HEH HEH...
EN-GETSU?
EVEN IF I DID LEAVE...
...I HAVE A FEELING YOU WOULD LEAP AFTER ME...
...JUST LIKE YOU DID UP THIS TREE.
...IT REALLY IS...
...LIKE YOU'RE SEEING SOMEONE ELSE...

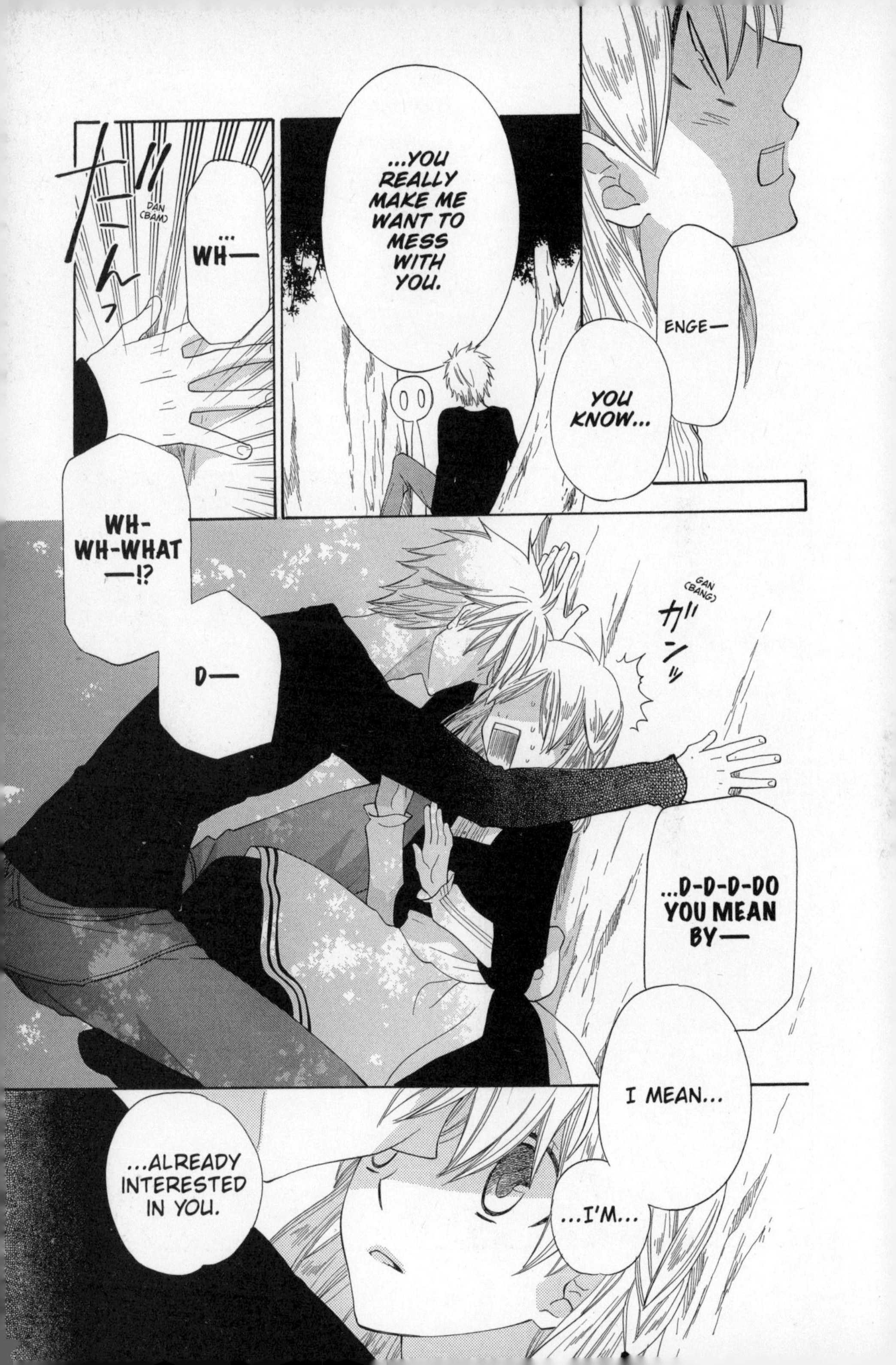
ENGE—
YOU KNOW...
...YOU REALLY MAKE ME WANT TO MESS WITH YOU.
DAN (BAM)
... WH—
WH-WH-WHAT—!?
GAN (BANG)
ガンッ
D—
...D-D-D-DO YOU MEAN BY—
I MEAN...
...I'M...
...ALREADY INTERESTED IN YOU.

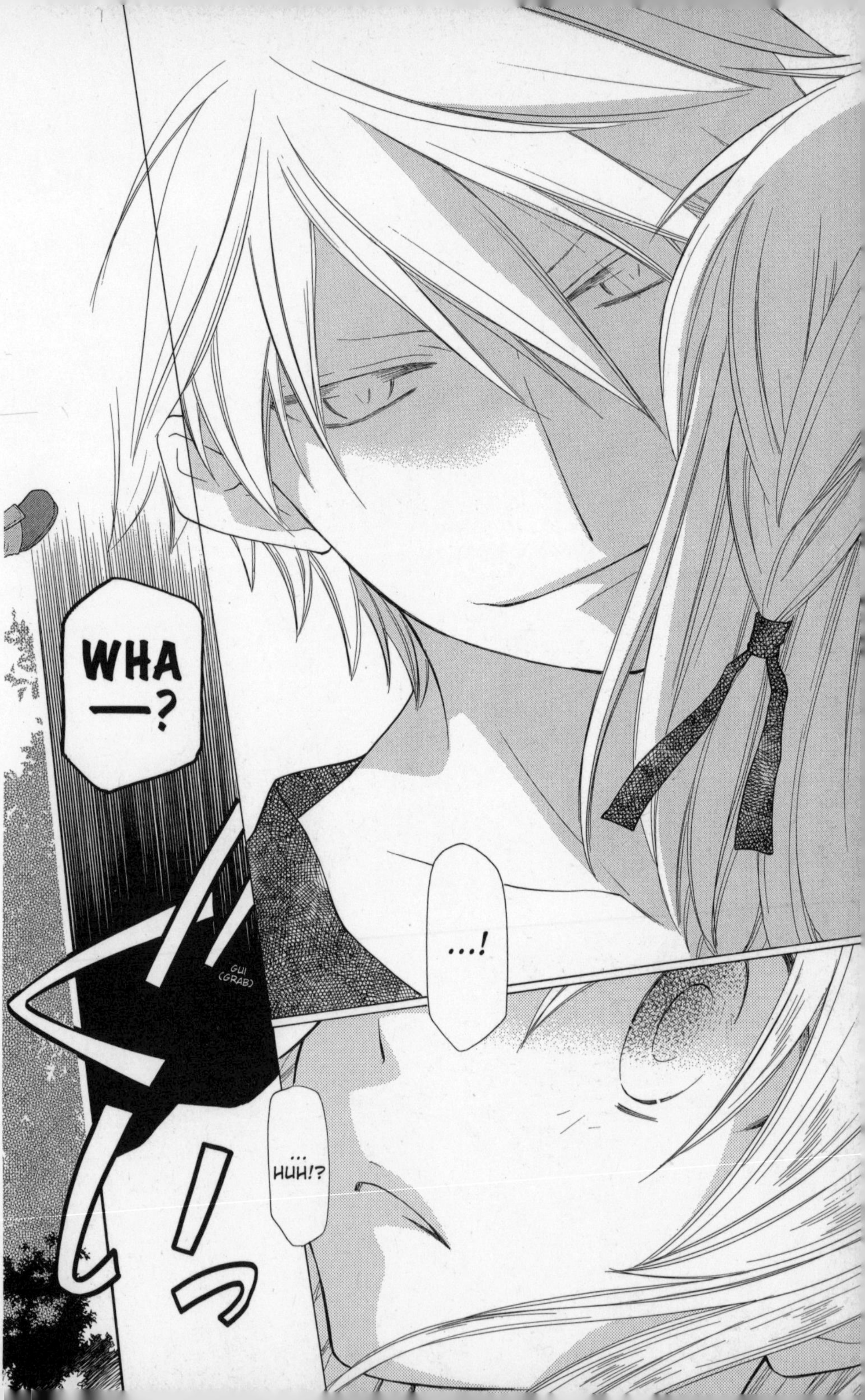
WHA—?
...!
GUI (GRAB)
...HUH!?

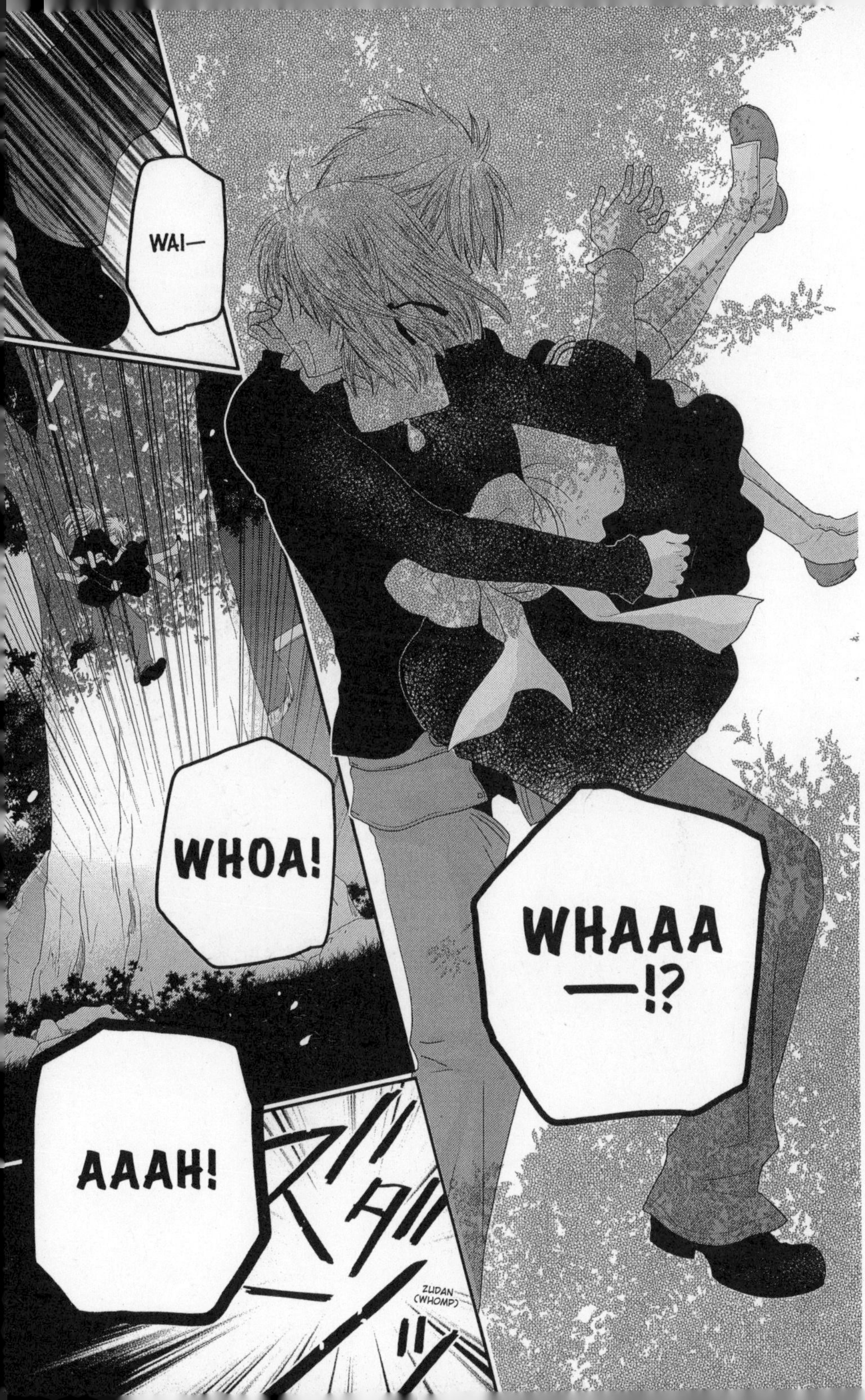
WAI—
WHAAA
—!?
WHOA!
AAAH!
ZUDAN
(WHOMP)

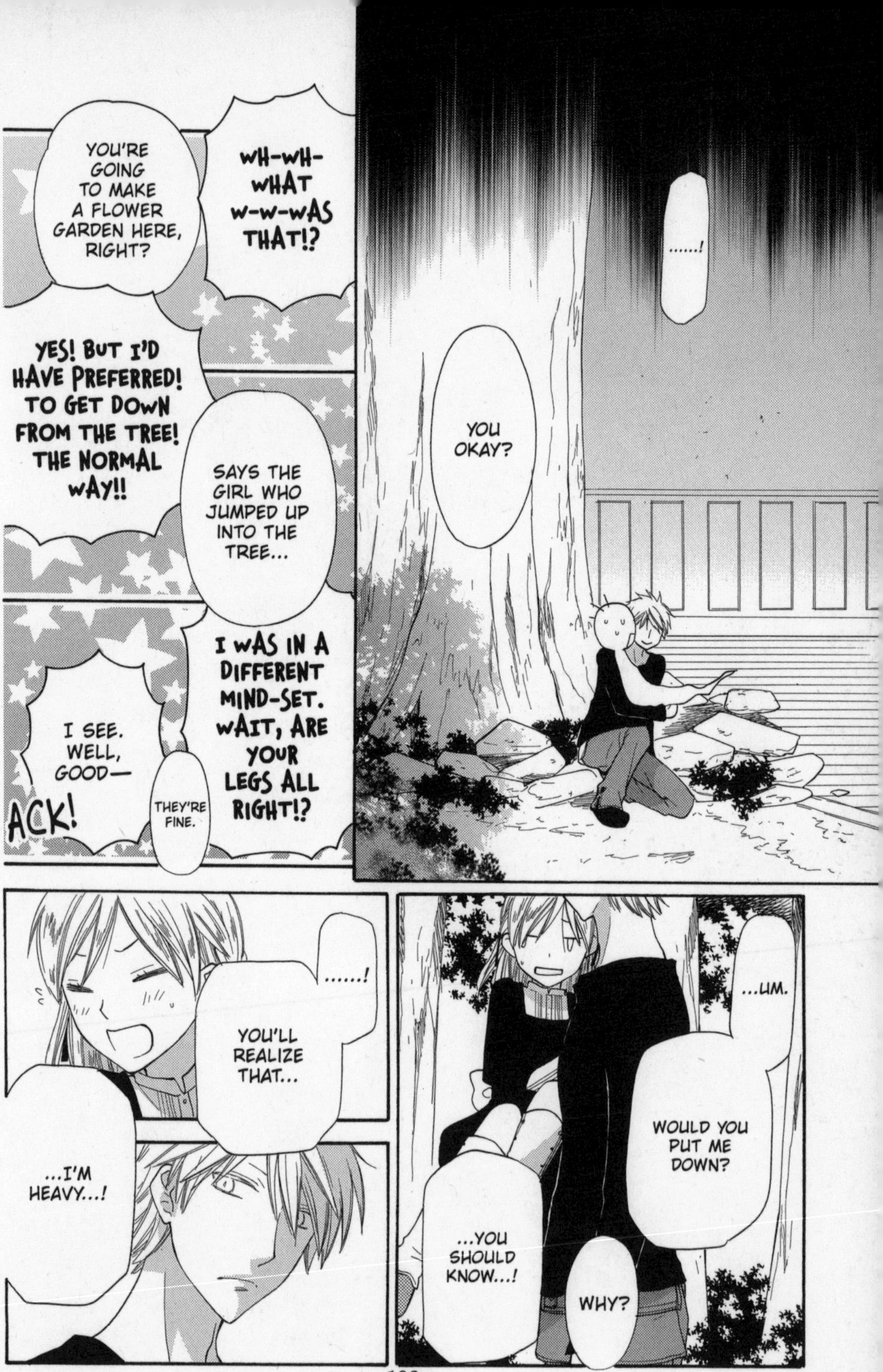
......!
YOU OKAY?
WH-WH-WHAT W-W-WAS THAT!?
YOU'RE GOING TO MAKE A FLOWER GARDEN HERE, RIGHT?
YES! BUT I'D HAVE PREFERRED! TO GET DOWN FROM THE TREE! THE NORMAL WAY!!
SAYS THE GIRL WHO JUMPED UP INTO THE TREE...
I WAS IN A DIFFERENT MIND-SET. WAIT, ARE YOUR LEGS ALL RIGHT!?
THEY'RE FINE.
I SEE. WELL, GOOD—
ACK!
...UM.
WOULD YOU PUT ME DOWN?
WHY?
...YOU SHOULD KNOW...!
......!
YOU'LL REALIZE THAT...
...I'M HEAVY...!

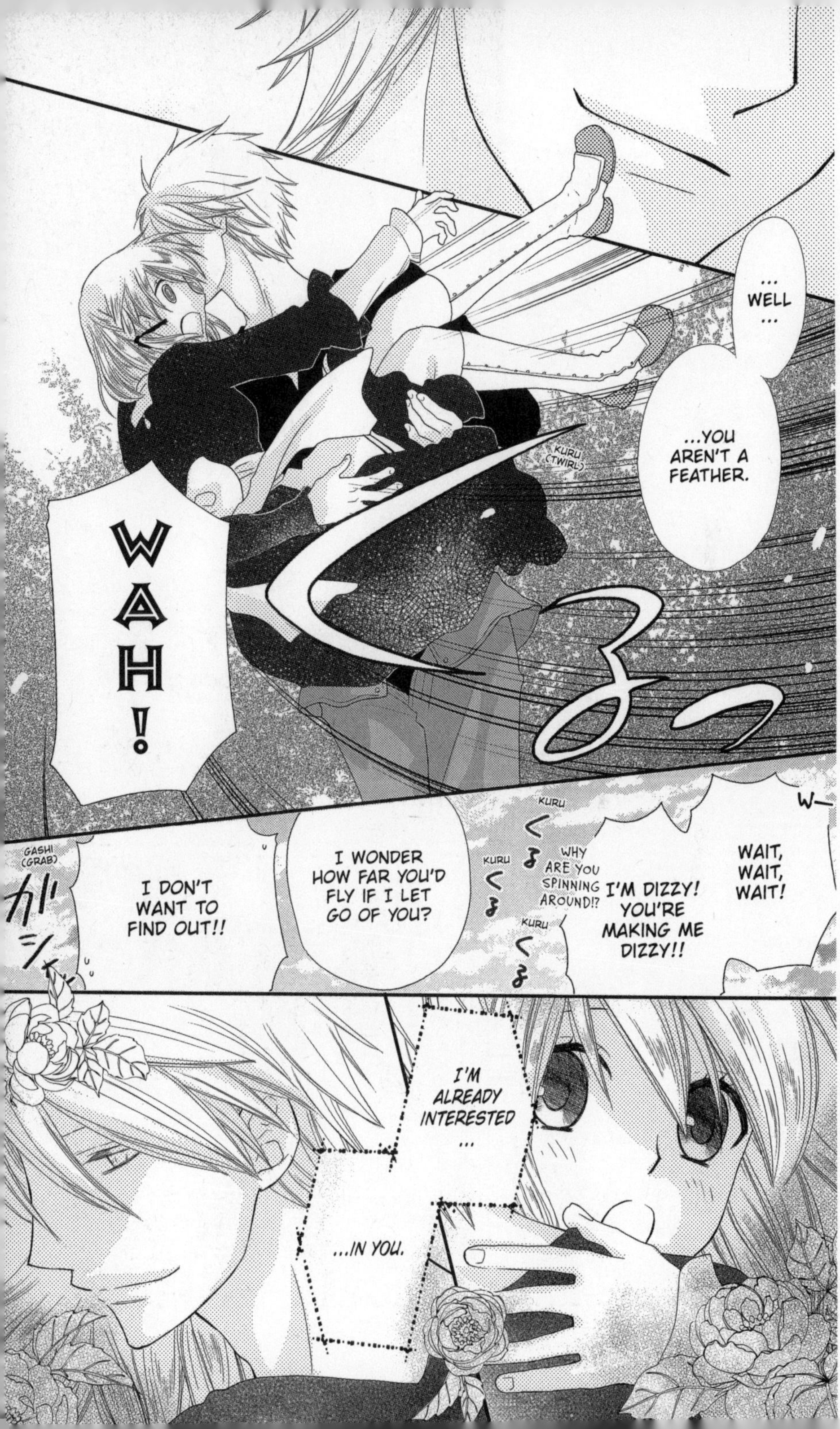
... WELL ...
...YOU AREN'T A FEATHER.
KURU (TWIRL)
くるっ
WAH!
W— WAIT, WAIT, WAIT!
KURU くる
KURU くる
KURU くる
WHY ARE YOU SPINNING AROUND!?
I'M DIZZY! YOU'RE MAKING ME DIZZY!!
I WONDER HOW FAR YOU'D FLY IF I LET GO OF YOU?
I DON'T WANT TO FIND OUT!!
GASHI (GRAB)
ガシッ
I'M ALREADY INTERESTED ...
...IN YOU.

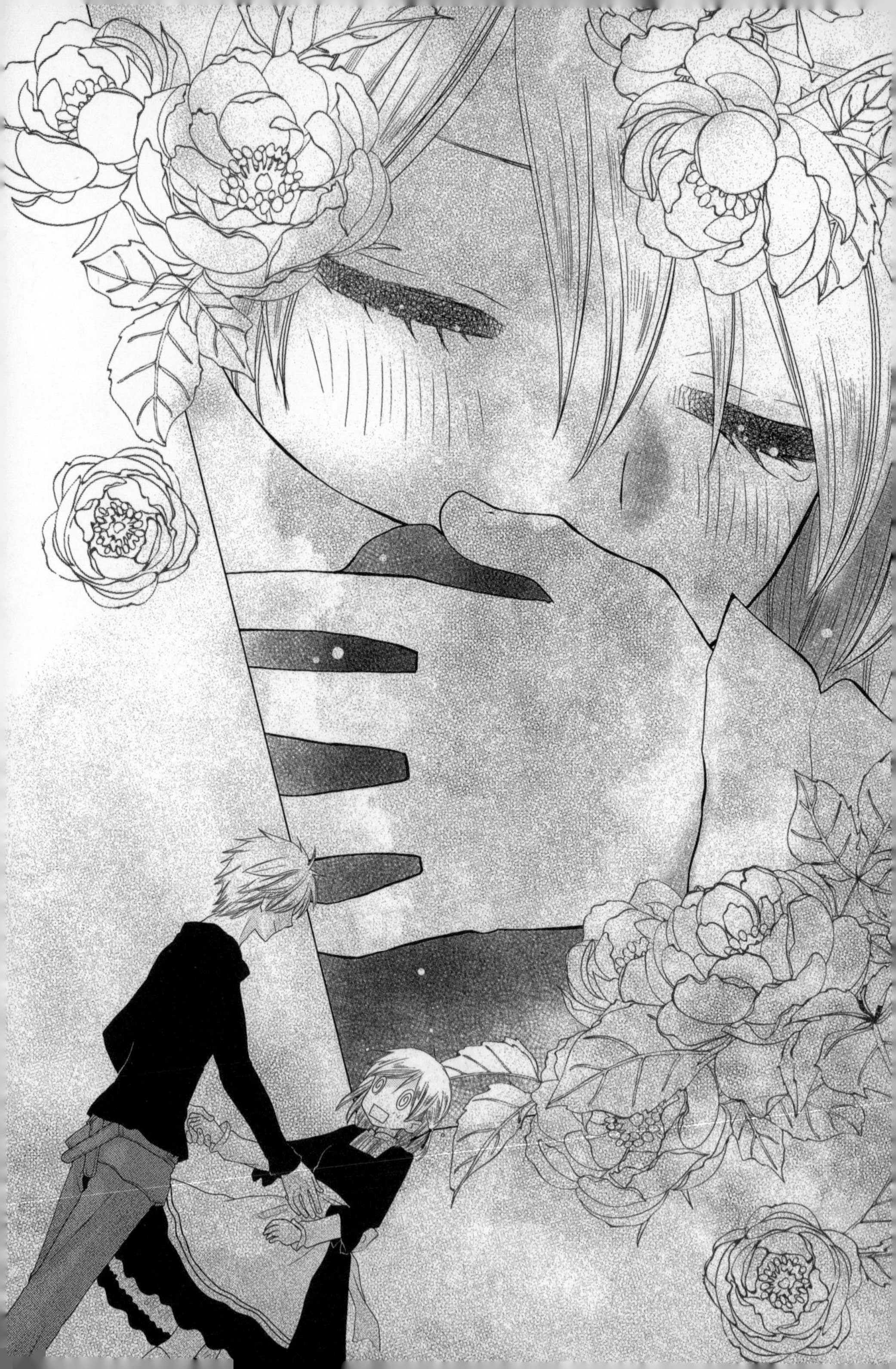

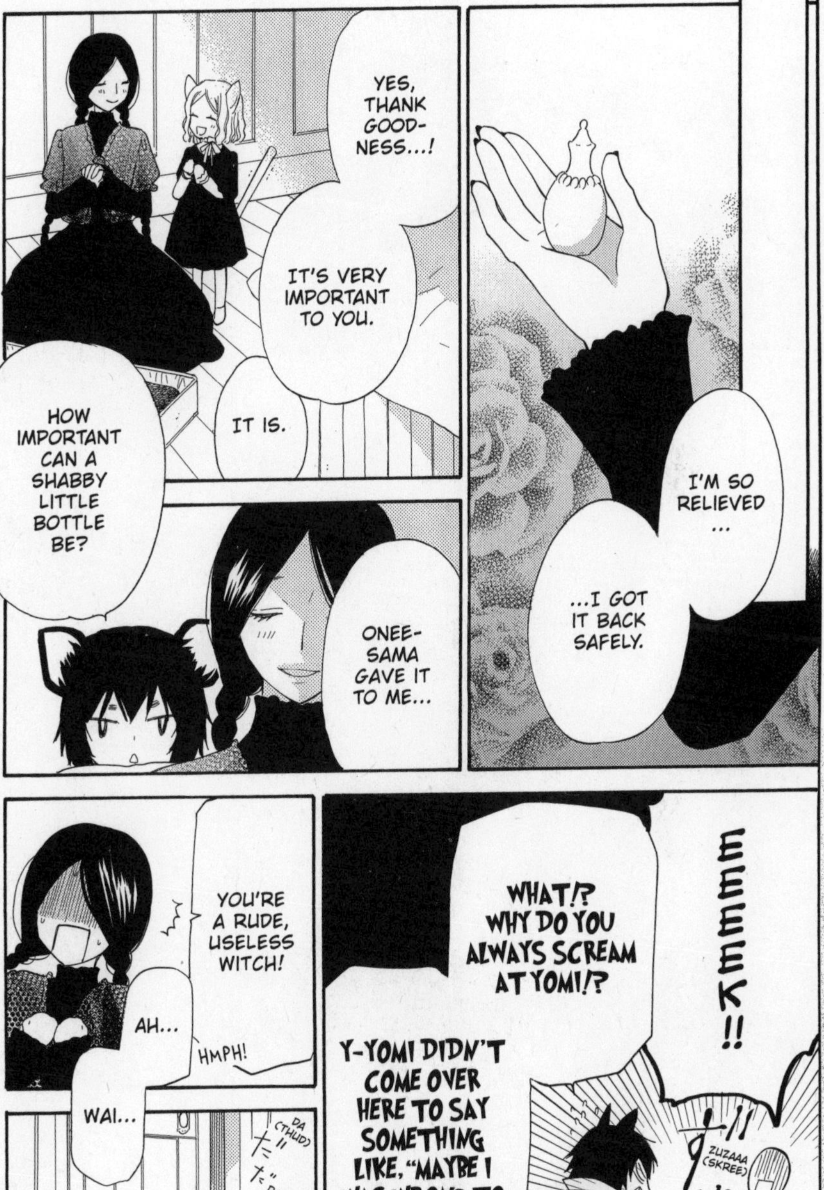
I'M SO RELIEVED...
...I GOT IT BACK SAFELY.
YES, THANK GOODNESS...!
IT'S VERY IMPORTANT TO YOU.
IT IS.
HOW IMPORTANT CAN A SHABBY LITTLE BOTTLE BE?
ONEE-SAMA GAVE IT TO ME...
EEEEK!!
WHAT!? WHY DO YOU ALWAYS SCREAM AT YOMI!?
Y-YOMI DIDN'T COME OVER HERE TO SAY SOMETHING LIKE, "MAYBE I WAS WRONG TO TAKE IT"!!
ZUZAAA (SKREE)
YOU'RE A RUDE, USELESS WITCH!
AH...
HMPH!
WAI...
DA (THUD)
DA
DA
...

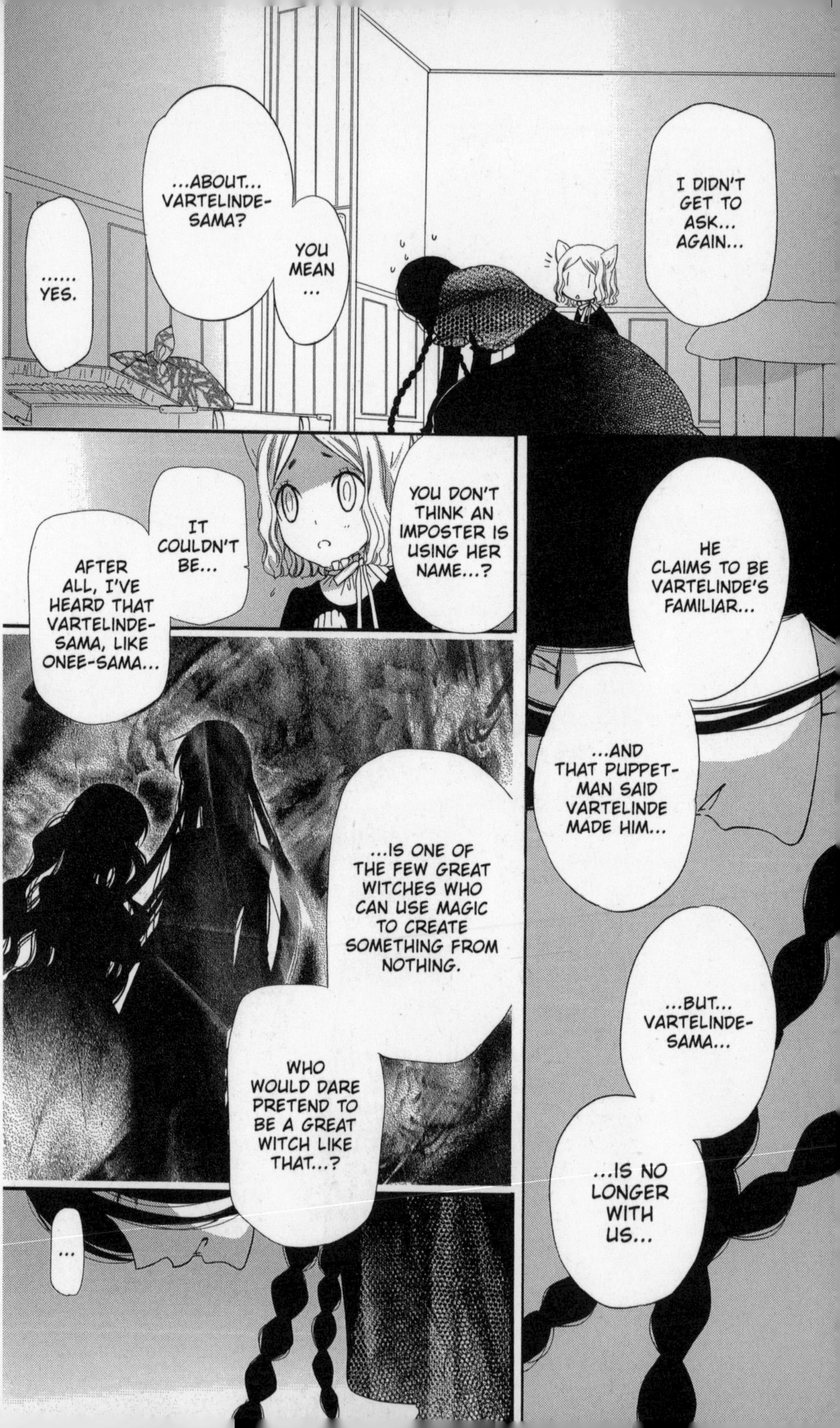
I DIDN'T GET TO ASK... AGAIN...
YOU MEAN ...
...ABOUT... VARTELINDE-SAMA?
...... YES.
HE CLAIMS TO BE VARTELINDE'S FAMILIAR...
...AND THAT PUPPET-MAN SAID VARTELINDE MADE HIM...
...BUT... VARTELINDE-SAMA...
...IS NO LONGER WITH US...
YOU DON'T THINK AN IMPOSTER IS USING HER NAME...?
IT COULDN'T BE...
AFTER ALL, I'VE HEARD THAT VARTELINDE-SAMA, LIKE ONEE-SAMA...
...IS ONE OF THE FEW GREAT WITCHES WHO CAN USE MAGIC TO CREATE SOMETHING FROM NOTHING.
WHO WOULD DARE PRETEND TO BE A GREAT WITCH LIKE THAT...?
...

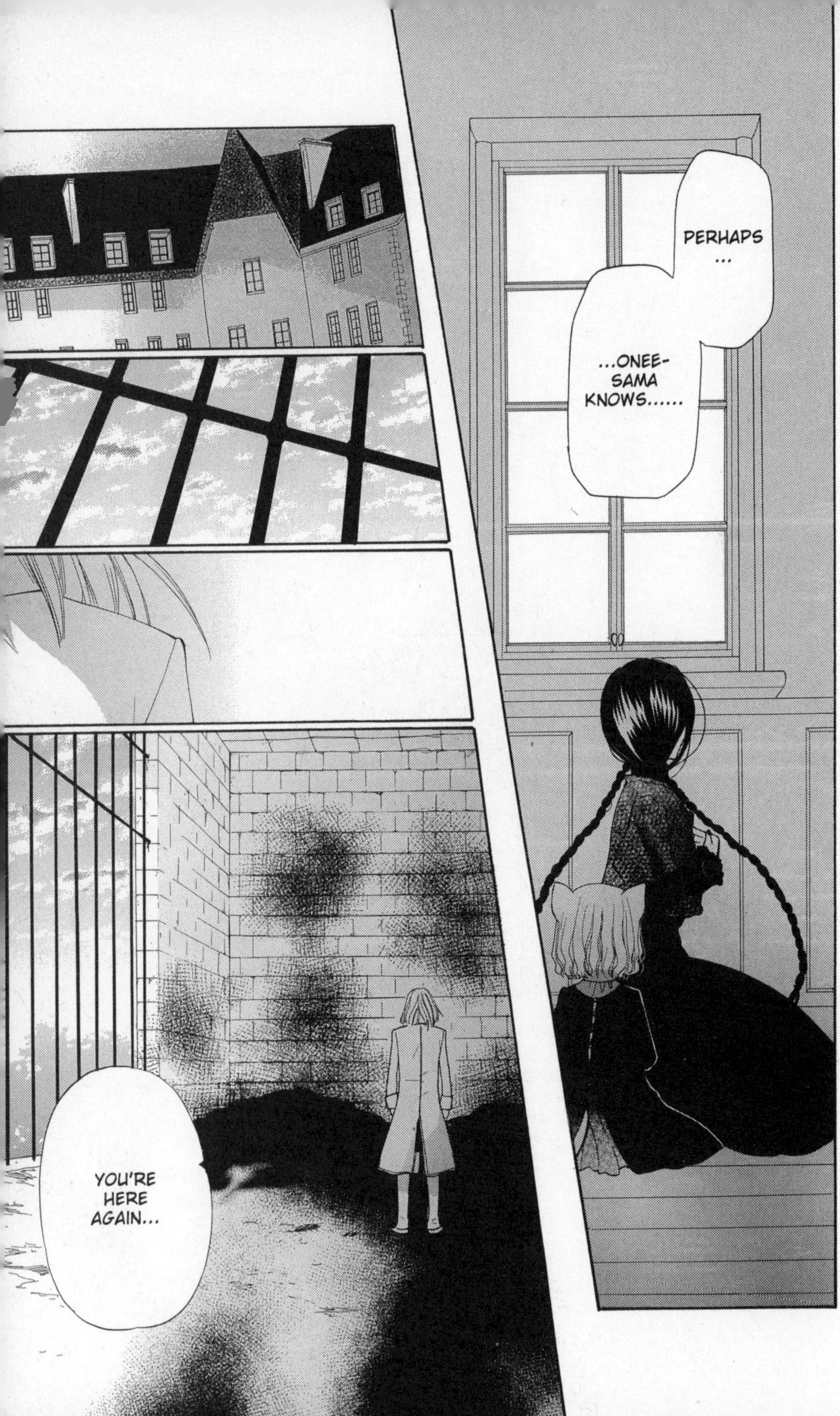
PERHAPS ...
...ONEE-SAMA KNOWS......
YOU'RE HERE AGAIN...

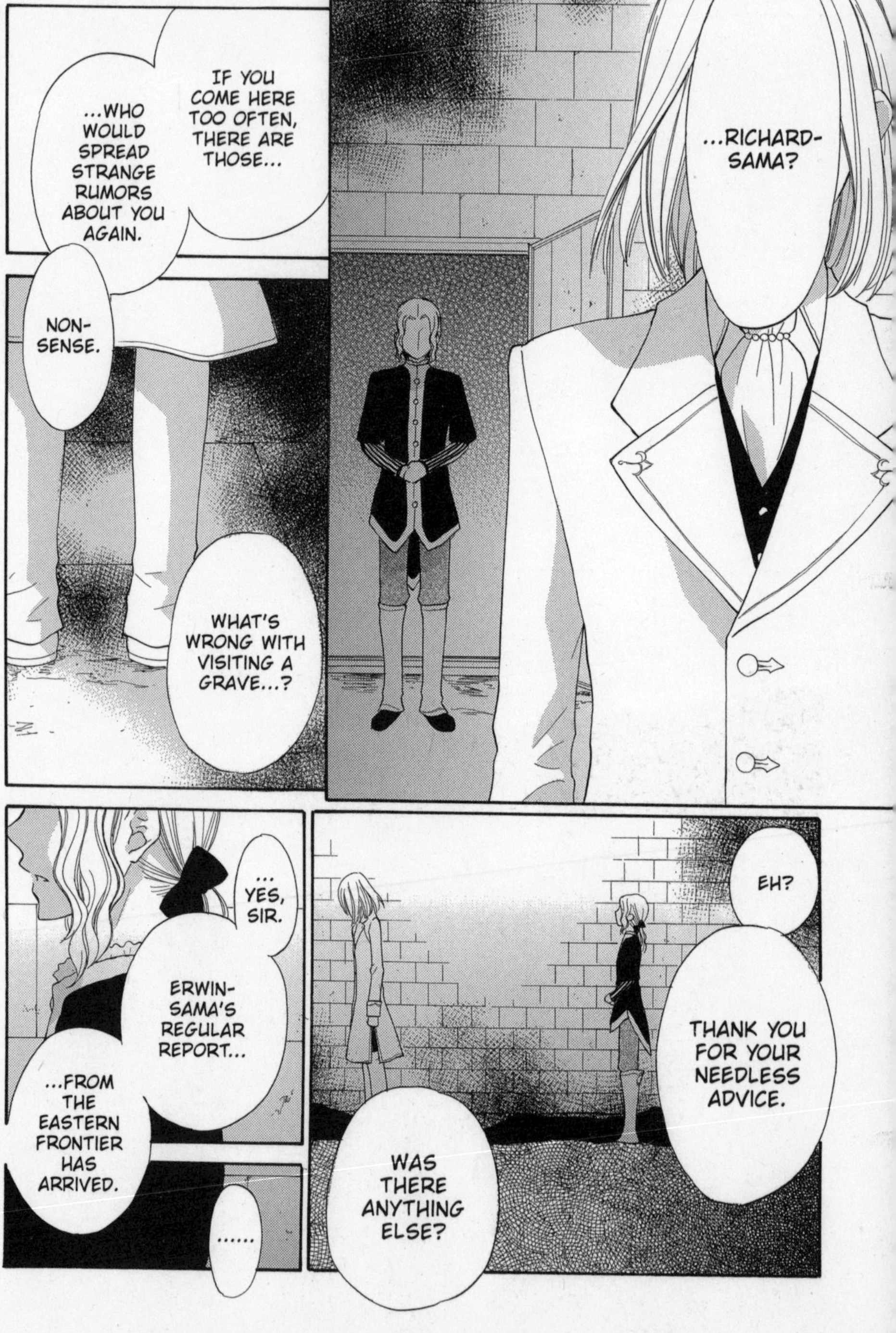

...RICHARD-SAMA?
IF YOU COME HERE TOO OFTEN, THERE ARE THOSE...
...WHO WOULD SPREAD STRANGE RUMORS ABOUT YOU AGAIN.
NON-SENSE.
WHAT'S WRONG WITH VISITING A GRAVE...?
EH?
THANK YOU FOR YOUR NEEDLESS ADVICE.
WAS THERE ANYTHING ELSE?
...YES, SIR.
ERWIN-SAMA'S REGULAR REPORT...
...FROM THE EASTERN FRONTIER HAS ARRIVED.
......

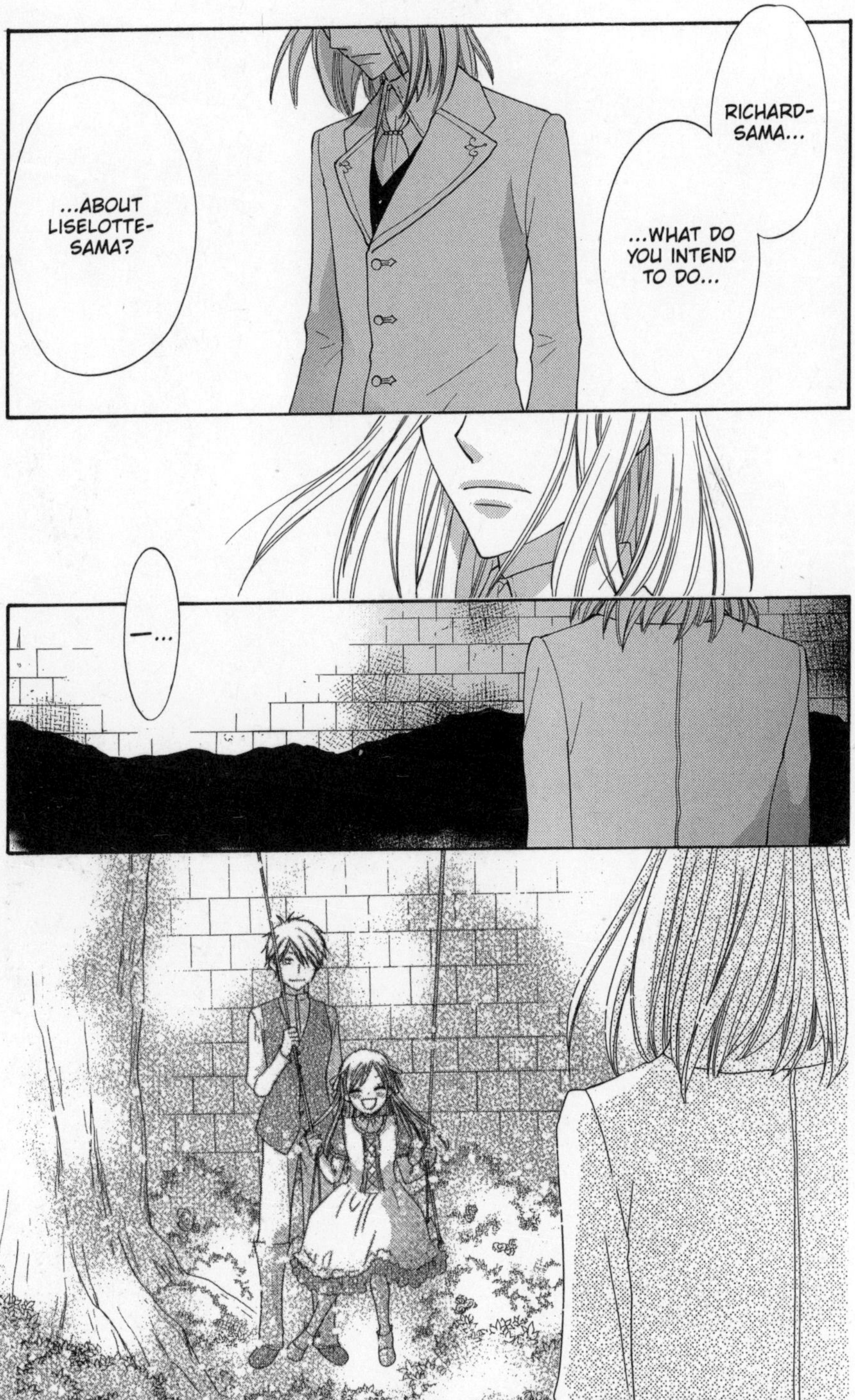
RICHARD-SAMA...
...WHAT DO YOU INTEND TO DO...
...ABOUT LISELOTTE-SAMA?
—...

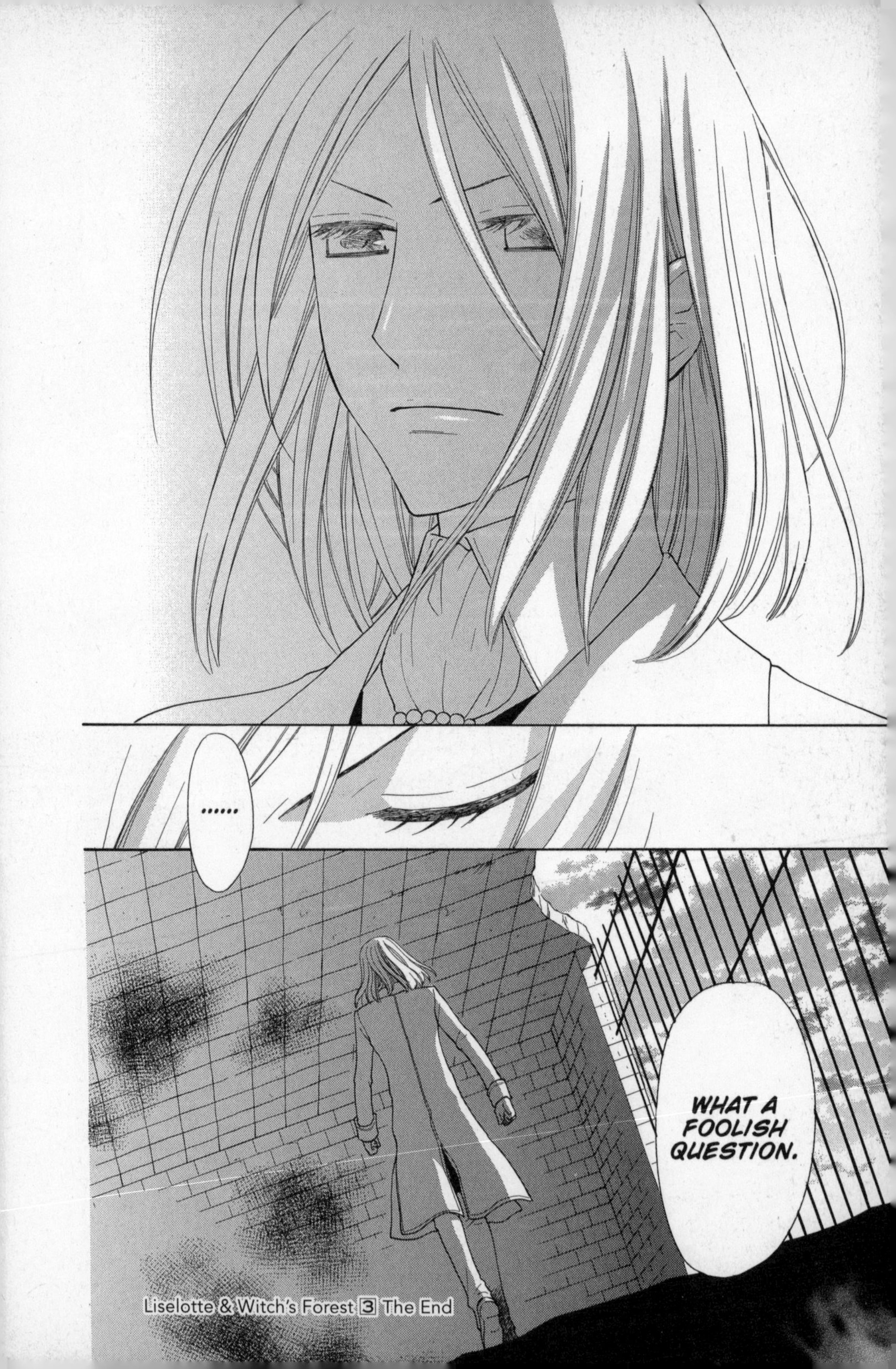
......
WHAT A FOOLISH QUESTION.
Liselotte & Witch's Forest 3 The End

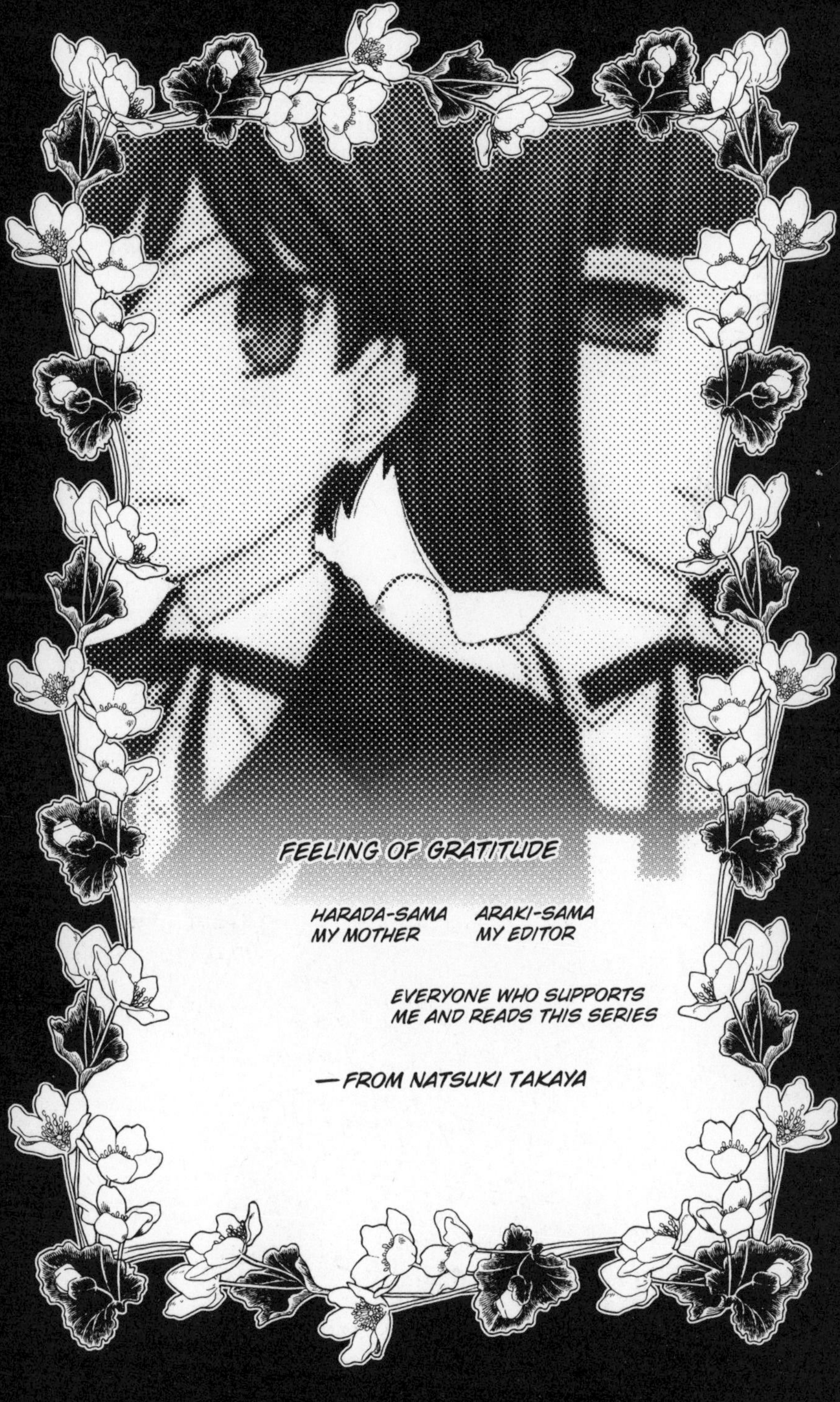
FEELING OF GRATITUDE
HARADA-SAMA
MY MOTHER
ARAKI-SAMA
MY EDITOR
EVERYONE WHO SUPPORTS
ME AND READS THIS SERIES
—FROM NATSUKI TAKAYA

TRANSLATION NOTES

COMMON HONORIFICS

no honorific: Indicates familiarity or closeness; if used without permission or reason, addressing someone in this manner would constitute an insult.

-san: The Japanese equivalent of Mr./Mrs./Miss. If a situation calls for politeness, this is the fail-safe honorific.

-sama: Conveys great respect; may also indicate that the social status of the speaker is lower than that of the addressee.

-kun: Used most often when referring to boys, this indicates affection or familiarity. Occasionally used by older men among their peers, but it may also be used by anyone referring to a person of lower standing.

-chan: An affectionate honorific indicating familiarity used mostly in reference to girls; also used in reference to cute persons or animals of either gender.

-dono: An old-fashioned, uncommon title that conveys more respect than -san. It literally means "My lord" or "My lady."

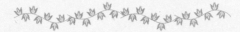

Page 196
Onee-sama: A very polite term for an "elder sister" or an older girl who is not related. In this case, the person to whom Hilde is referring and their relationship are still a mystery.

Liselotte
&
Witch's Forest

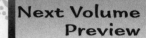

In a certain region...

...of a certain country...

TO FIGHT IN THE GREAT WAR...

...there is a small village on the eastern border.

And not far is a forest that people avoid...

...for it is said that...

...witches dwell there.

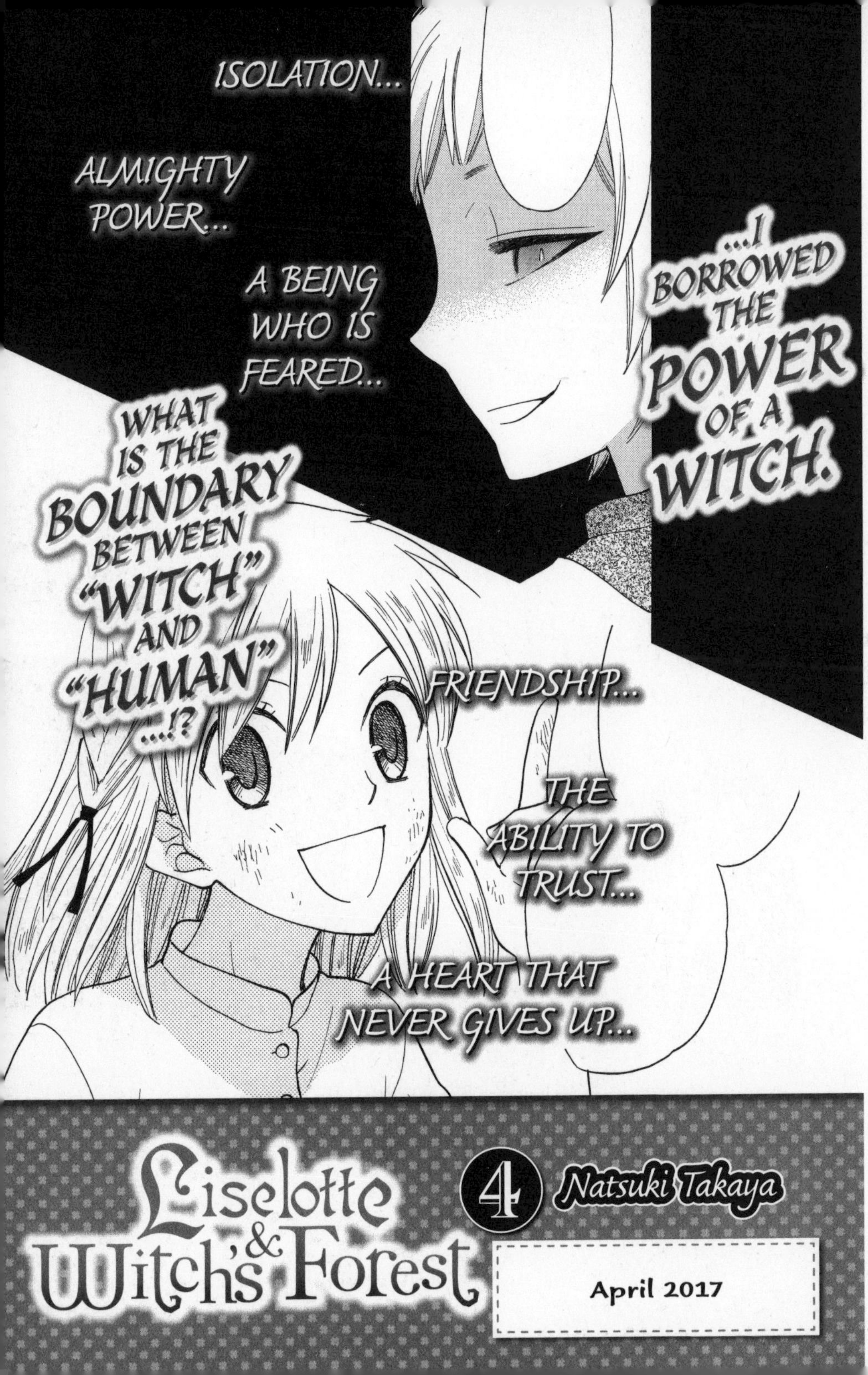
...I BORROWED THE POWER OF A WITCH.
ISOLATION...
ALMIGHTY POWER...
A BEING WHO IS FEARED...
WHAT IS THE BOUNDARY BETWEEN "WITCH" AND "HUMAN" ...!?
FRIENDSHIP...
THE ABILITY TO TRUST...
A HEART THAT NEVER GIVES UP...

Liselotte & Witch's Forest 4

Natsuki Takaya

April 2017

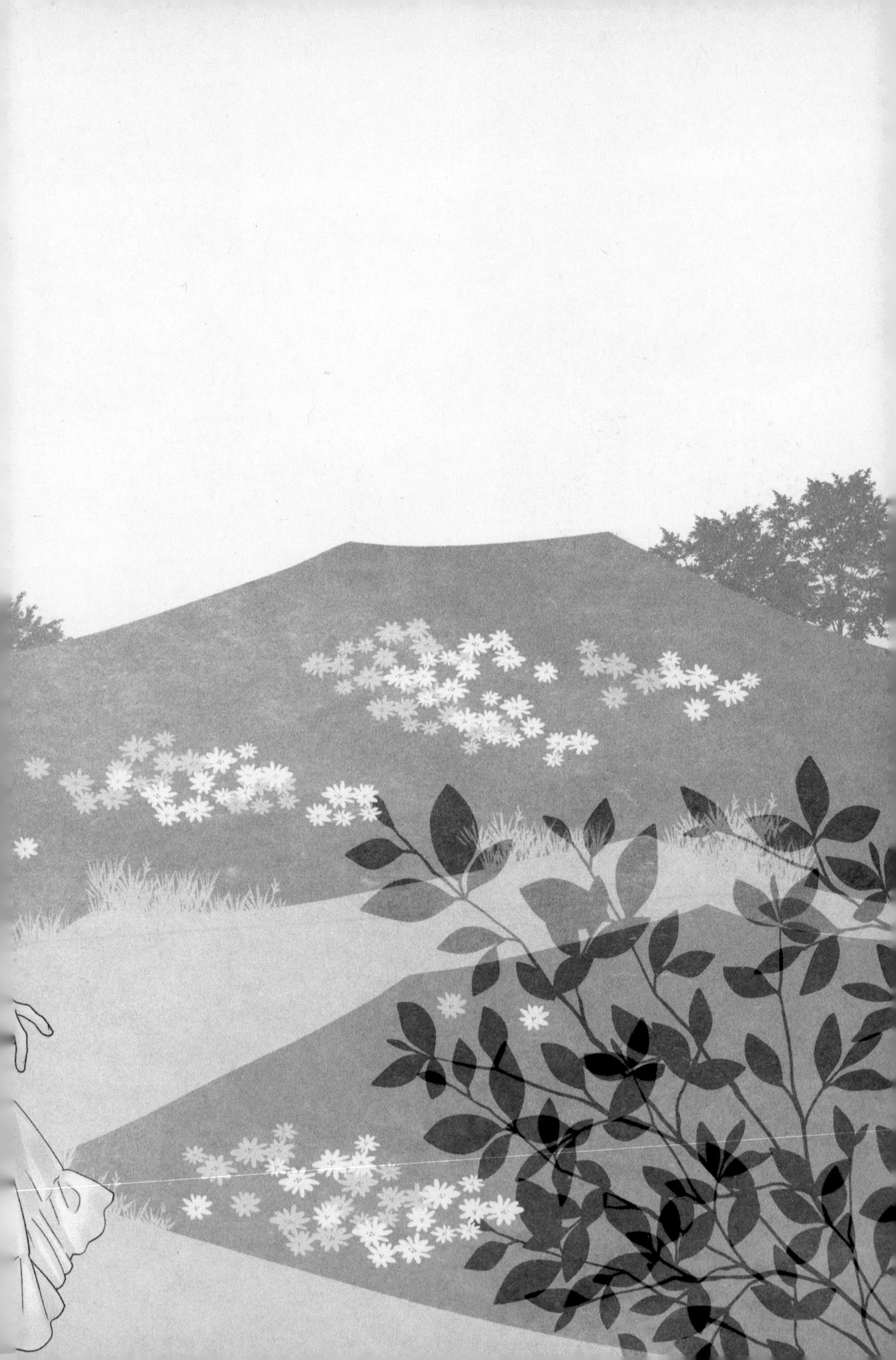

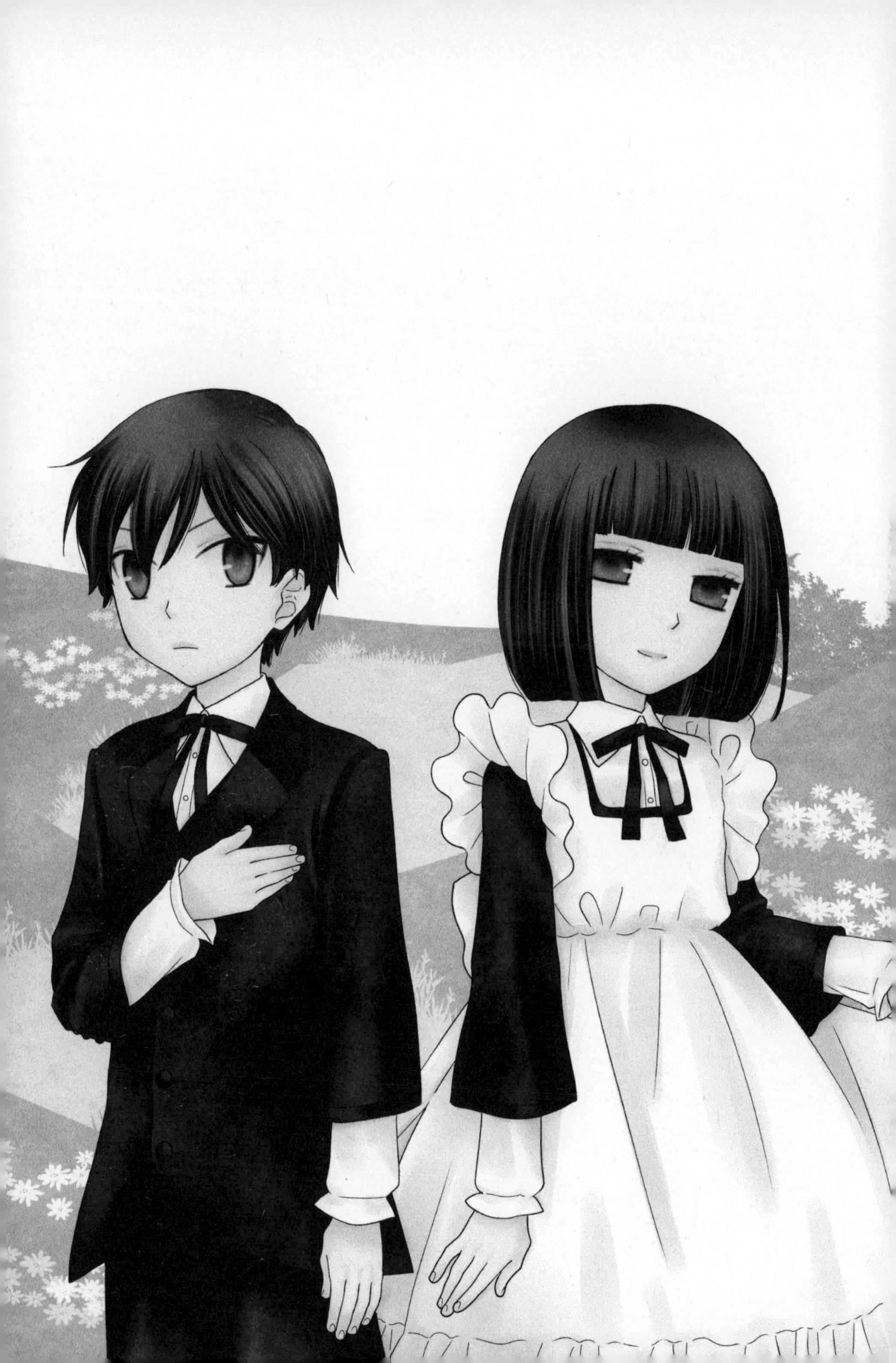

Liselotte & Witch's Forest

Read on for an early look at Volume 4,
coming April 2017!

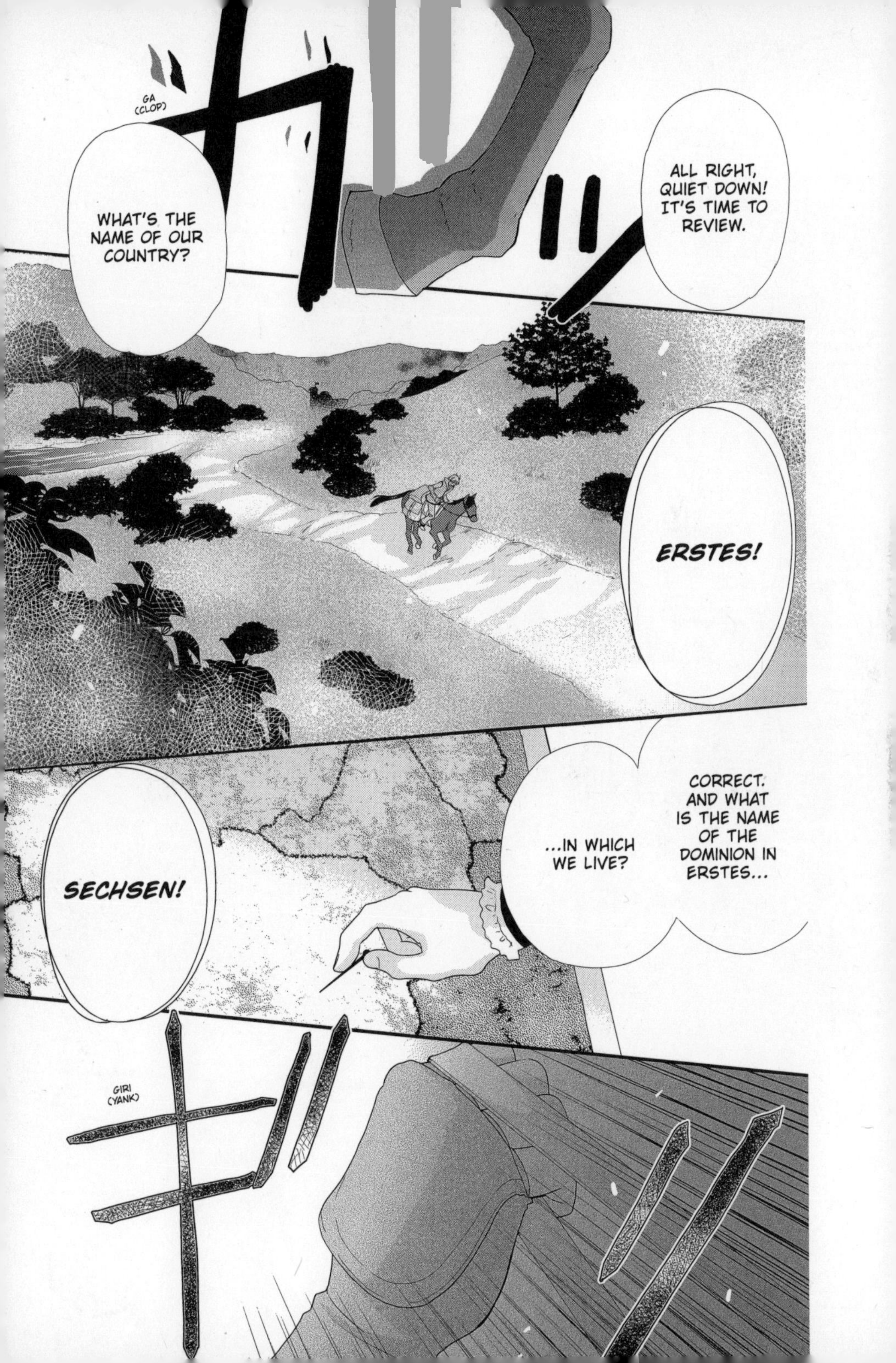
ALL RIGHT, QUIET DOWN! IT'S TIME TO REVIEW.
GA (CLOP)
WHAT'S THE NAME OF OUR COUNTRY?
ERSTES!
CORRECT. AND WHAT IS THE NAME OF THE DOMINION IN ERSTES...
...IN WHICH WE LIVE?
SECHSEN!
GIRI (YANK)

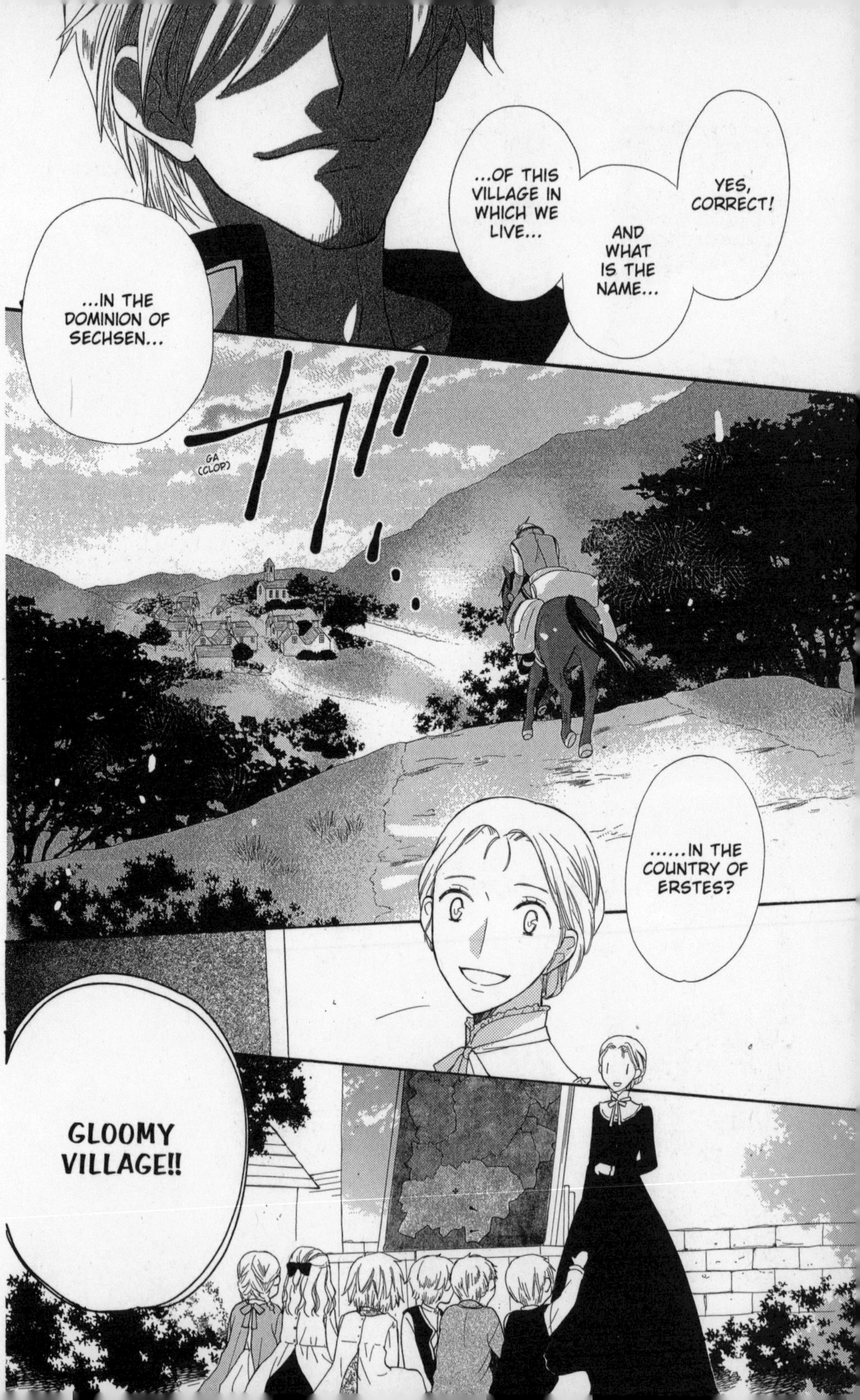
YES, CORRECT!
AND WHAT IS THE NAME...
...OF THIS VILLAGE IN WHICH WE LIVE...
...IN THE DOMINION OF SECHSEN...
GA (CLOP)
......IN THE COUNTRY OF ERSTES?
GLOOMY VILLAGE!!

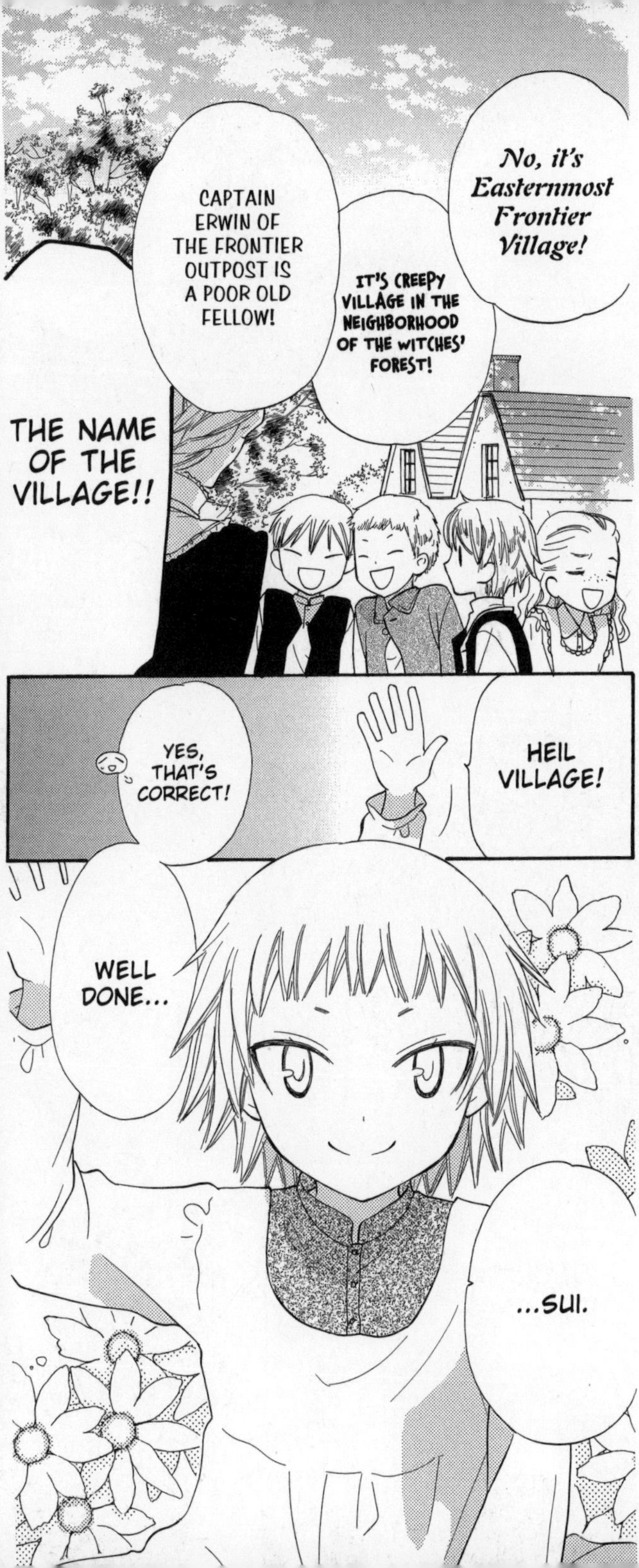
No, it's Easternmost Frontier Village!
IT'S CREEPY VILLAGE IN THE NEIGHBORHOOD OF THE WITCHES' FOREST!
CAPTAIN ERWIN OF THE FRONTIER OUTPOST IS A POOR OLD FELLOW!
THE NAME OF THE VILLAGE!!
HEIL VILLAGE!
YES, THAT'S CORRECT!
...SUI.
WELL DONE...

LISELOTTE & WITCH'S FOREST

NICE TO MEET YOU & HELLO. I'M TAKAYA, AND I BRING YOU VOLUME 4 OF LISE & WITCH.

SOME THINGS HAPPEN, AND SOME DON'T IN VOLUME 4. JUST KIDDING! VARIOUS THINGS HAPPEN (LOL), BUT LISE FACES IT ALL WITH GOOD CHEER.

AND SO VOLUME 4 OF LISE & WITCH BEGINS...

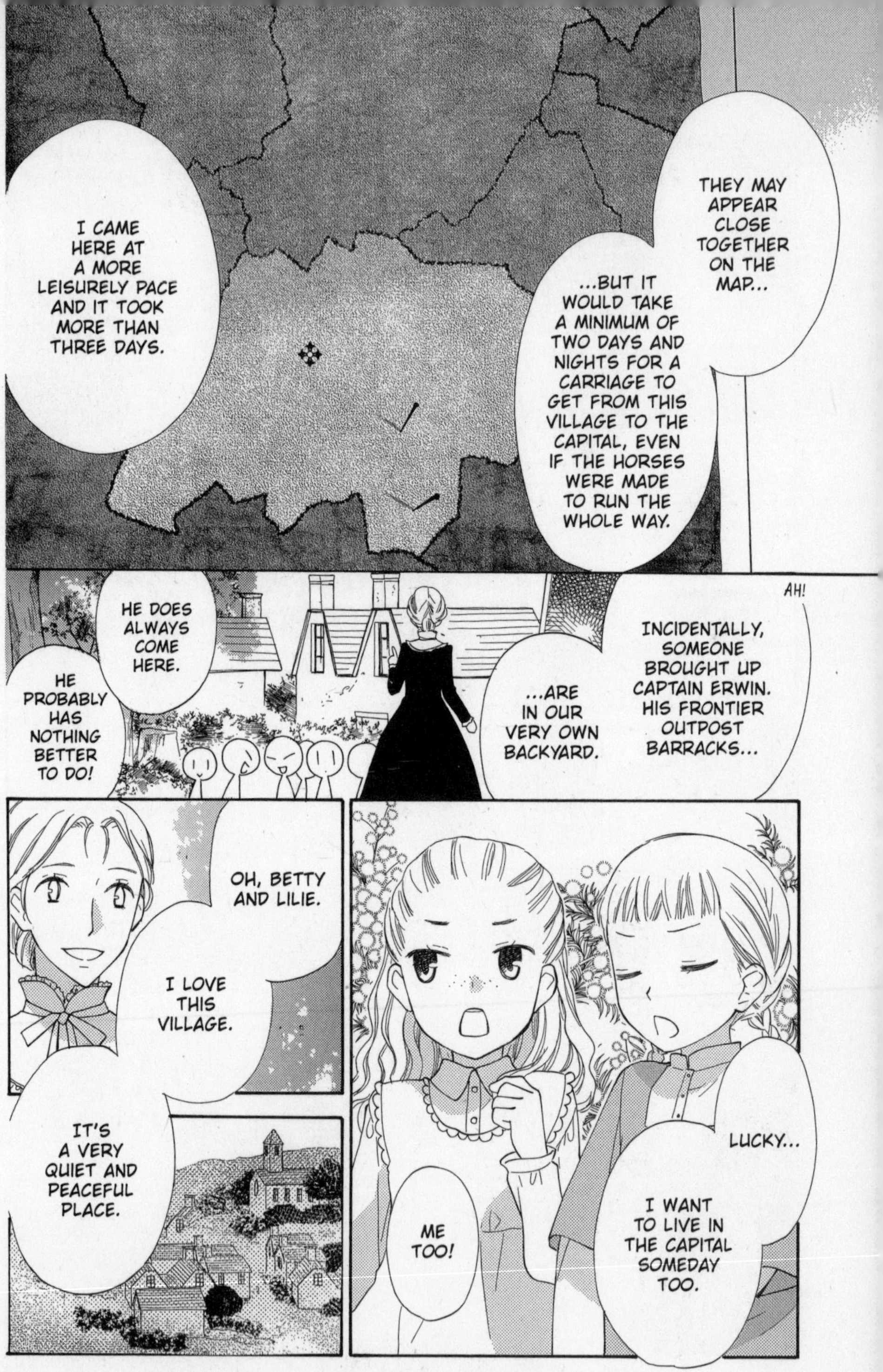
THEY MAY APPEAR CLOSE TOGETHER ON THE MAP...
...BUT IT WOULD TAKE A MINIMUM OF TWO DAYS AND NIGHTS FOR A CARRIAGE TO GET FROM THIS VILLAGE TO THE CAPITAL, EVEN IF THE HORSES WERE MADE TO RUN THE WHOLE WAY.
I CAME HERE AT A MORE LEISURELY PACE AND IT TOOK MORE THAN THREE DAYS.
AH!
INCIDENTALLY, SOMEONE BROUGHT UP CAPTAIN ERWIN. HIS FRONTIER OUTPOST BARRACKS...
...ARE IN OUR VERY OWN BACKYARD.
HE DOES ALWAYS COME HERE.
HE PROBABLY HAS NOTHING BETTER TO DO!
LUCKY...
I WANT TO LIVE IN THE CAPITAL SOMEDAY TOO.
ME TOO!
OH, BETTY AND LILIE.
I LOVE THIS VILLAGE.
IT'S A VERY QUIET AND PEACEFUL PLACE.

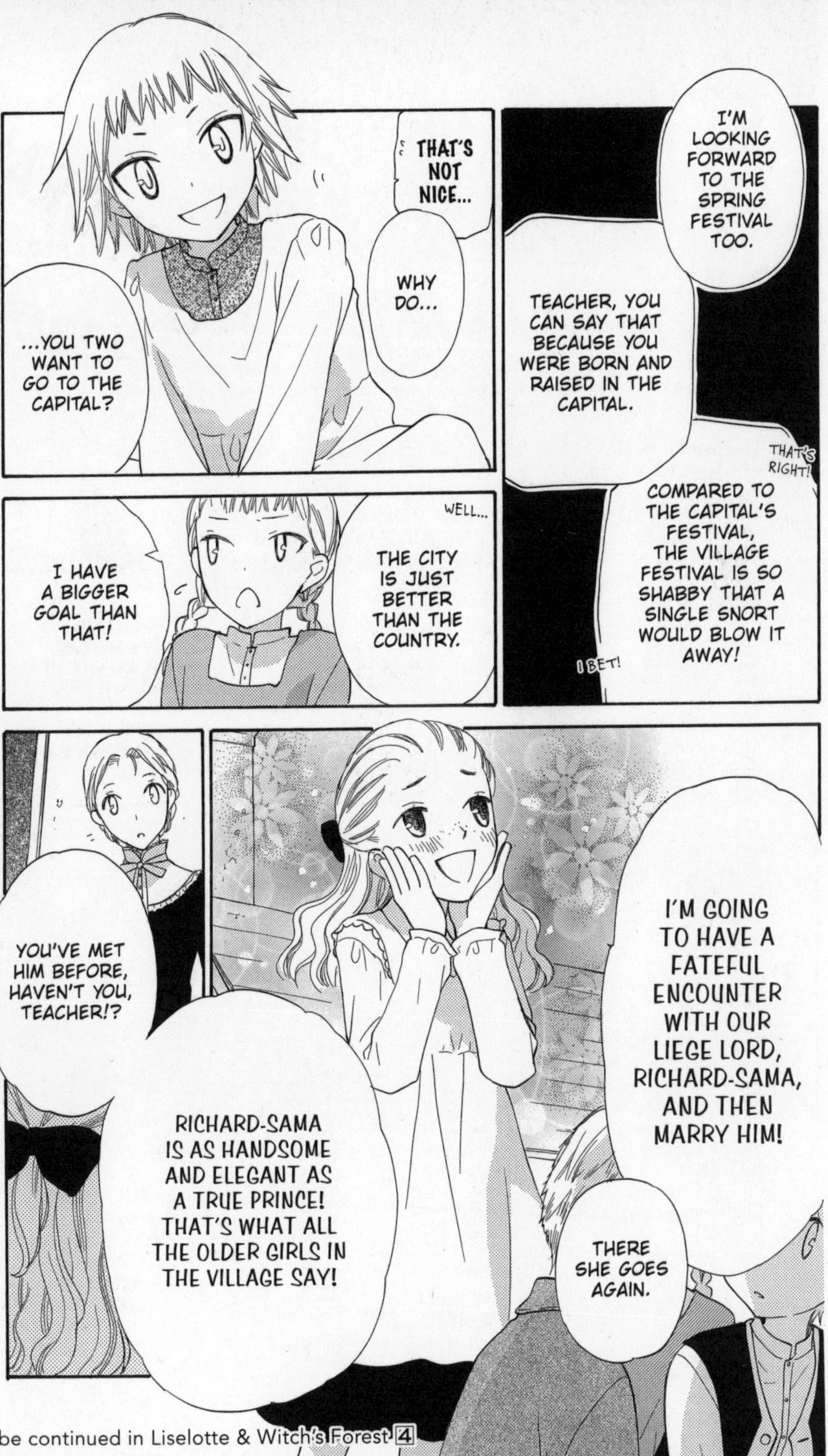
I'M LOOKING FORWARD TO THE SPRING FESTIVAL TOO.
TEACHER, YOU CAN SAY THAT BECAUSE YOU WERE BORN AND RAISED IN THE CAPITAL.
THAT'S RIGHT!
COMPARED TO THE CAPITAL'S FESTIVAL, THE VILLAGE FESTIVAL IS SO SHABBY THAT A SINGLE SNORT WOULD BLOW IT AWAY!
I BET!
THAT'S NOT NICE...
WHY DO...
...YOU TWO WANT TO GO TO THE CAPITAL?
WELL...
THE CITY IS JUST BETTER THAN THE COUNTRY.
I HAVE A BIGGER GOAL THAN THAT!
I'M GOING TO HAVE A FATEFUL ENCOUNTER WITH OUR LIEGE LORD, RICHARD-SAMA, AND THEN MARRY HIM!
THERE SHE GOES AGAIN.
RICHARD-SAMA IS AS HANDSOME AND ELEGANT AS A TRUE PRINCE! THAT'S WHAT ALL THE OLDER GIRLS IN THE VILLAGE SAY!
YOU'VE MET HIM BEFORE, HAVEN'T YOU, TEACHER!?

To be continued in Liselotte & Witch's Forest 4

Liselotte & Witch's Forest 3

Natsuki Takaya

Translation: Sheldon Drzka

Lettering: Lys Blakeslee, Katie Blakeslee

LISELOTTE TO MAJO NO MORI Vol. 3 by Natsuki Takaya
© Natsuki Takaya 2012
All rights reserved.
First published in Japan in 2012 by HAKUSENSHA, INC., Tokyo.
English language translation rights in U.S.A., Canada and U.K. arranged with
HAKUSENSHA, INC., Tokyo through Tuttle-Mori Agency, Inc., Tokyo.

English Translation © 2017 by Yen Press, LLC

Yen Press
1290 Avenue of the Americas
New York, NY 10104

Visit us at yenpress.com
facebook.com/yenpress
twitter.com/yenpress
yenpress.tumblr.com
instagram.com/yenpress

First Yen Press Edition: January 2017

Yen Press is an imprint of Yen Press, LLC.
The Yen Press name and logo are trademarks of Yen Press, LLC.

Library of Congress Control Number: 2016936533

ISBN: 978-0-316-36103-3

10 9 8 7 6 5 4 3 2 1

BVG

Printed in the United States of America